MILTON AND THE RISE OF RUSSIAN SATANISM

VALENTIN BOSS

Milton and the Rise of Russian Satanism

UNIVERSITY OF TORONTO PRESS
Toronto Buffalo London

© University of Toronto Press 1991
Toronto Buffalo London
Printed in Canada

ISBN 0-8020-5795-0

Printed on acid-free paper

Canadian Cataloguing in Publication Data

Boss, Valentin
Milton and the rise of Russian satanism

Includes bibliographical references.
ISBN 0-8020-5795-0

1. Russian poetry – History and criticism.
2. Devil in literature. 3 Milton, John,
1608–1674 – Characters – Devil. 4. Milton,
John, 1608–1674 – Influence. 5. Milton, John,
1608–1674. Paradise lost. I. Title.

PG3065.D4B67 1991   891.7'1'009382   C90-095080-3

This book has been published with the help of a grant from the Canadian Federation for the Humanities, using funds provided by the Social Sciences and Humanities Research Council of Canada.

Dedicated to my mother, Joséphine Boss, née Stapenhorst, whose early childhood prayer may have amused the Prince of Darkness:

'Will Satan mich verschlingen
So lass die Englein singen:
"Dies Kind soll unser Letztes [unverletzet] sein." '

'Should Satan hold me fast
Then let the little angels sing:
"This child must be our last [unharmed]" '

Contents

PREFACE ix

ACKNOWLEDGMENTS xiii

TRANSLITERATION xvii

INTRODUCTION: THE RISE OF RUSSIAN SATANISM xix

PART I The Satan of the Enlightenment 1

1 Satan and the First Translation of *Paradise Lost* 3

2 Introducing Milton's Satan to the Common Reader 14

3 Monks and 'Pocket Poets': Publication 30

4 Masonic Devils and the Light Within 48

5 Satan, Pugachev, and the French Revolution 68

PART II Satan as Romantic and Marxist Idol 79

6 The Demonic Tradition from Zhukovsky to Pushkin 80

7 Milton's Satan and Lermontov 102

viii Contents

8 Banning and Reviving Satan 119

9 1917 and After: The Triumph of Milton's Satan 136

10 Satan as Anti-Imperialist 147

Conclusion: Prince of Darkness, Prince of Light 155

APPENDIXES 165
I Milton's Interest in Russia 167
II An English Oration Concerning Milton's Satan from Lermontov's School 174
III A Chronological Distribution Table 178

ABBREVIATIONS 181

NOTES 183

BIBLIOGRAPHIC NOTE 235

BIBLIOGRAPHY 239

INDEX 255

FIGURES
following 78 and 154

Preface

Modern self-awareness in Russia, like modern Russian literature, stirs into life with Peter the Great, whose window into Europe – St Petersburg – transformed his country. With much else, a European devil climbed through that window. Yet the most arresting symbol of the Petrine transformation was Prometheus, whose likeness the Tsar-Reformer ordered stamped on the coinage of the realm. With that act, loaded with philosophical implications, which Andrei Sakharov and Solzhenitsyn have approached from opposing corners, Russian culture was formally introduced to the idea of progress.

The unpredictable consequences of that encounter are still with us today. The traditional Orthodox view of good and evil, which had the virtue of clarity, gave way to the secular Western one in which Prometheus and the Devil take turns at playing the same role. This confusing ambiguity, itself the offspring of revolution, was captured in much of its modern pathos by *Paradise Lost*, England's first global classic.

Milton's Satan, interpreted in so many ways at various times, is tied historically to Christianity as well as to the new world forged during the Renaissance. Since the nineteenth century he has most often been portrayed as one who expresses both the indomitable revolutionary will of the Puritans and the incorrigible individualism of the capitalist order they helped bring into being.

More recent psychological or structuralist interpretations have not challenged the historical fact that, whatever gloss innovative critics have chosen to give Milton's work, he is by common consent the first in European literature to rid the Devil of the folkloric attributes that, until *Paradise Lost*, marred the intellectual gravity of Satan's posture as the adversary of God and man.

The life of Milton's Satan in Russia proved to be almost as startling as his rise to cultural prominence on home ground. At a certain point, he and Prometheus were pronounced one. In a symbolic sense, to the Europeanized intelligentsia this confusion made revolutions of the Western kind metaphysically justifiable. Indeed, before *Paradise Lost* was translated into Russian, the Devil was hardly visible in eighteenth-century formal literature. Poetry, itself a child of the Petrine era, initially ignored him. At the popular level, he still came in many shapes, being largely derived from Orthodox tradition.

During the Catherinian Enlightenment, when secular Russian literature came of age, the satyr of neoclassical convention helped the Devil survive the loss of faith suffered by Russia's nobility. Much has been written about his subsequent career as reflected, for example, in the writings of Gogol, Dostoevsky, Sologub, or Mikhail Bulgakov – some of whom actually believed in the physical existence of the Devil. But there has been no attempt in any language to trace the influence on Russian poetry and criticism of the titanic creature who prior to Goethe's *Faust* was the most important devil in European literature.

Part I of this book is thus concerned with Milton's Satan as he appears during the Enlightenment, when his image was deeply affected by both the Masonic movement and the ambivalent Russian reaction to Pugachev and the French Revolution. It is this that turned him into a modern political rebel, setting the stage for passionate approval by the Russian Romantics, a phase that is described in Part II. How did this come about? William Blake, Robert Burns, Shelley, and other British radicals who professed to believe that Milton himself was of the Devil's party, were – with the notable exception of Byron and Tom Moore – hardly known by Pushkin's contemporaries. Indeed, it is Pushkin who is conventionally given the credit for bringing the demonic theme to public light with his 'Demon' in 1823. Unlike Lermontov's masterpiece of the same title – begun half a dozen years later – this short poem is not obviously Miltonic, and the motif had been anticipated by others who may have read *Paradise Lost* before Pushkin. This study attempts to show that the demonic tradition in both Russian verse and prose begins several decades earlier and is linked at its very birth to Milton's great epic.

It was Zhukovsky, Pushkin, and Lermontov, assisted by a pleiad of brilliant poets, however, who gave Milton's outcast from Heaven some of his many modern masks. In Pushkin's work there are hints both of the Promethean hero Shelley saw in *Paradise Lost* and also of Goethe's Mephisto. Both Goethe's anti-hero and Lermontov's sensual Demon enriched the satanic tradition in Russian art and letters: but neither of them survived 1917 with quite the same authority or political *savoir-faire*. His connection with the English Revolution gave Milton's Satan an edge his rivals lacked. Marxism, moreover, is rooted in both the Enlightenment and the Romantic era. Milton's Satan, rather surprisingly, flourished in both. Nor were French, Irish, German, or Russian variants on the same literary theme ever as defiant as the dynamic character in *Paradise Lost* whom both Decembrists and Marxists considered its true hero.

Hence the crucial distinction Lunacharsky made between Milton's Satan and Lermontov's *Demon*, which is certainly the best-known Russian example of poetic Satanism but one in which the hero's principal preoccupation is not political rebellion but the seduction of an innocent Orthodox girl. The Puritan strain in Bolshevism enabled Lunacharsky to use the revolutionary ardour of Milton's arch-rebel to steer *Paradise Lost* past left-wing Communists. Like Mayakovsky, they tended, of course, to regard both Milton's epics as Christian propaganda. Should they have known better?

Satan's hatred of the Almighty has often been commented on, and it has even been proposed by the late Sir William Empson that Milton actually shared that dislike. A contemporary of the nihilists, however, seems to have been the first of Milton's Russian admirers to spot Satan's illogical materialist bent. In her translation-adaptation of the epics, Zhadovskaya thus reveals his true proclivities: 'Ia Satana! Ia ateist!' ('I am Satan! I am an atheist!')

The other comparative advantage of Milton's Satan, as this book tries to demonstrate, is more obvious in the sense that no other European devil can claim so long, so continuous, and at times so political a connection with Russian culture. The revival of religion under *glasnost'* and *perestroika* will provide Milton's Satan with fresh ambiguities, some of which are hinted at in the conclusion. But whatever the ultimate fate of Soviet Communism, now in such steep decline, it is well to remember that the extraordinary career Milton enjoyed in Russia after 1917 was due to another revolution – the one in which the poet himself took part. His Satan benefited from this connection because Soviet assessments of *Paradise Lost* were tied to prevailing Marxian analyses of England's 'bourgeois Revolution.' Thanks to this, in the interpretation authorized under Brezhnev, Milton's Satan was finally elevated to official status in the struggle against imperialism. Such heights, it can now be calmly stated, Satan had never achieved before – either in Russia or anywhere else.

If the Satan of *Paradise Lost* thus dwarfs all other Enlightenment heroes – for this is what he became to the secularized intelligentsia – Milton's ties with Russian culture do not end there. A glance at the chronological distribution table at the end of this study will show how often *Paradise Lost* and *Paradise Regained* appeared in Russian. What is particularly interesting about this as a cultural phenomenon is that the prose translations, adapted to the vernacular of the people, came to be disseminated among the *narod* long before the Bible. In the popular mind the prosaic editions were more widely and more intimately associated with Christianity than any other literary work.

This broader theme of how peasants came to read them is traced to its historical roots in the sequel to the present volume, *Russian Popular Culture and John Milton*. This is to be published in a Russian translation, together with the present monograph, by Raduga in Moscow.

Milton's early influence on formal Russian letters and the ups and downs in his own reputation – Fenton's *Life* was the earliest poetic biography to appear in Russian – are discussed in *Poet-Prophet: Milton's Russian Image from the Enlightenment to Pushkin* (forthcoming).

The final book in this series will focus on the poet-revolutionary's idiosyncratic fate under Stalinism. Triumphantly portrayed on the Soviet stage after the October Revolution, for many decades Milton was honoured in name and even stoutly defended against his 'bourgeois falsificators' during the Cold War. At the same time, the ideas Milton had stood for in the eyes of earlier generations were – like the Old Bolsheviks themselves – either muzzled or cleverly distorted in a neo-Marxist light.

Before 1917, what Milton stood for above all to the intelligentsia was freedom of intellectual inquiry. It is pleasant to be able to record that, thanks to *glasnost'*, *Areopagitica*, suppressed since the October Revolution, is scheduled to appear soon in a scholarly Leningrad edition of Milton's work.

Acknowledgments

I am grateful to people in various disciplines whose interest either in Milton or in Russia or in Satan – not necessarily in that order – helped this study to take shape. When I began my Milton project under the auspices of the Canada-USSR academic exchange, I was attached to the Gorky Institute of Literature. In Moscow it was thought bizarre (and by official go-betweens quite unacceptable) that I should demand open access to eighteenth-, nineteenth-, and twentieth-century archives on the mere suspicion that Milton's Satan might have left some traces there. Thanks to *glasnost'* and *perestroika*, however, access to Soviet archives (as I discovered in 1988 and again in 1990) is now very much more civilized, and it is a pleasure to record my appreciation to all those Soviet scholars who took an interest in this book's themes. The late Academician D.D. Blagoi invited me to Peredelkino to discuss them, only to find the invitation countermanded by forces that have since been collectively tagged as 'the administrative-command system.' His essay 'John Bunyan, Pushkin and Lev Tolstoy' reminds us of a side of Pushkin that attracted Dostoevsky and is particularly interesting on Pushkin's last years.

Dr Yu.V. Mann, also of the Gorky Institute, proved stimulating in his comments on Nadezhdin and Russian Romanticism in general. Professor F.E. Kanunova's recovery of Zhukovsky's library in Tomsk came just in time to include this influential mentor of Pushkin's generation among those who attempted to translate *Paradise Lost*. My appreciation is also due to Dr Yu.D. Levin of the Pushkin House in Leningrad. His fastidious and subtle study of nineteenth-century Russia's poetic translators, whose art has since been brought to so high a level, opens a new field. G.P. Makogonenko of Leningrad University had little to add to what we know about the authorship of *True Light*, but his comments on the Masonic movement (still only thinly explored by modern scholarship) were revealing.

xiv Acknowledgments

I am particularly indebted to B.A. Gradova, head of the Manuscript Section of the Saltykov-Shchedrin Library, whose intimate knowledge of eighteenth-century manuscript collections proved so helpful in tracing devils in Leningrad. No less generous was the knowledgeable assistance there of E.F. Tsvetkova in tracking down Milton's published translators and the references to him in Russian periodicals, a task made easier by the access so kindly granted to the legendary Umiken catalogue but sweetened by the unforgettable energy Tsvetkova displayed in finding what Umiken had left out.

I should also thank custodians of other Soviet collections, in particular those of the Manuscript Section, Historical Museum, and Manuscript Section, Lenin Library, in Moscow; and in Leningrad, of the Central State Historical Archives and of the Manuscript Section, Institute of History. Not all of them abided by the curious practice of the Brezhnev era of removing from foreign eyes manuscripts not previously explored by Soviet scholars. This kind of experience was not confined to so-called political literature, as is sometimes thought, nor were manuscript copies of *Paradise Lost* and other Miltoniana immune to it: but I am glad to report that in the end Satan's interest always prevailed.

I also wish to thank George Tillman of the Canada Council, whose persistence made my earlier journey to the USSR possible after both Richard Pipes and Nicholas Riasanovsky commended me to the archival devils. At that point Goethe's Mephisto seemed as worthy of attention as the Satan of *Paradise Lost*, but the notion of serving them both receded in 1987 when my quest in Moscow and Leningrad collections resumed and the extent of Milton's influence became apparent.

To students of my Milton seminars at McGill University I also owe thanks, as well as to the Faculty of Arts for providing financial assistance. Like his decanal predecessor, Robert Vogel, Michael Maxwell has been most helpful. I am also grateful to Jack Gold, a selector until recently at the McLennan Library, without whose services the bibliography would be the poorer. My thanks are due to Margaret Blevins for the quality of the typescript as well as to the late Jack Weldon, an economist who understood Milton. Last but not least I am grateful to my school friend Ian Robinson, who was compelled to read *Paradise Lost* at St Paul's. Unfairly, he was also forced to peruse part of the earliest draft of this volume, making the sorts of suggestions that poets are at liberty to make.

Some of the material in parts I and II is summarized in the *Milton Encyclopedia* (vol 9, 1983), whose chief editor, William B. Hunter, solicited my entry on Milton's influence in Russia – the first in any language.

The 'Satanic' manuscript adaptation of *Paradise Lost* is reproduced by courtesy of the Manuscript Section of the State Historical Museum in Moscow. The portraits of Vasilii Petrov, Mariya Khrapovitskaya, Kheraskov, Derzhavin, and Lermontov were provided by the Pushkin Collection of the Pushkinskii Dom of the USSR Academy of Sciences in Leningrad, which also kindly supplied the photographs of Pushkin's sketch of a *chertik* or *bes*.

The opening page of Chateaubriand-Milton's *Le Paradis perdu* and the frontispiece from Jacques Delille's translation showing Satan 'summoning to revolution' are reproduced by courtesy of the Bibliothèque Nationale in Paris; the painting of Pugachev being observed by the Devil by courtesy of the State Historical Museum in Moscow, which also supplied the reproduction of the *lubki* of Kiukhel'beker inspecting the Devil's tail, of the 'Folk' and of the 'German Devil.' The reproduction of the opening page of the first Russian translation of *Paradise Regained* is reproduced by courtesy of the House of Rare Books of the Lenin Library in Moscow, which also provided illustrations from various editions of *Paradise Lost*, as well of the title pages from Lermontov's *Demon*, Zhadovskaya's translation-adaptation of Milton's epics, and of the anonymous *True Light*. Aleksei Tolstoy's drawing of a devil is taken from *Pictorial Souvenirs of Russian Writers from the 17th to the Early 20th Centuries*, published by Sovetskaya Rossiia in 1988.

Vrubel's paintings are reproduced with the permission of the Tretiakov Gallery in Moscow. I would also like to express my appreciation to the Montreal artist Evgenii Evgenievich Klimov, now eighty-eight years old and probably North America's only living link with Vrubel. Klimov's tribute to the latter is to be found in his collection of essays on Russian painters, published in 1974.

Finally, a word about Gagarin's chromolithographic ancestor, 'Satan in Space.' This is taken from a Sytin edition of *Paradise Lost* in my own library, which is also the source of the two last portrayals of Milton's Satan. Both are taken from a prose edition, also intended for the common people, and published by P.N. Sharapov, a fur trader by origin, whose sympathy for the Old Believers seems to have persuaded him that they would cherish *Paradise Lost* too.

'The folkloric *bes* or Devil as sketched by Alexander Pushkin for his 'Tale about the Priest and His Worker Balda'

Transliteration

In the eighteenth century Russian spelling was often eccentric, especially of Western names, although the transliteration of Milton's (without a soft sign) was closer to the English pronunciation than it is today. There has been no attempt to make it more consistent than contemporary practice allowed, and the same principle has been followed in citing other languages. In the bibliography and index, where a more exact rendition is necessary, the practice is compatible with system two in J. Thomas Shaw, *The Transliteration of Modern Russian for English Language Publications* (Madison: University of Wisconsin Press 1967). In the text, however, proper names are spelled in the form more familiar to English readers, ie, Belinsky rather than Belinskii. Similarly, names such as that of Lermontov's tutor Zinov'ev are rendered in the form of the name (-iev) to which readers will no doubt be more accustomed. In the case of less-familiar names the same transliteration is adopted as in the bibliography, but in the text itself the soft sign at the end of familiar names (Gogol', Vrubel', etc.) has been omitted.

Translations from the Russian are my own, except when otherwise stated, the lines from Pushkin's 'Gabrieliade' being taken from D.M. Thomas's version in *The Bronze Horseman: Selected Poems by Alexander Pushkin* (London: Secker and Warburg 1982). The lines from 'The Prophet' are from the translation by Babette Deutsch, reproduced in the Random House Pushkin anthology.

'You never see it crossing your threshold announcing itself: "Hi, I'm Evil!" That, of course, indicates its secondary nature, but the comfort one may derive from this observation gets dulled by its frequency.'
                Joseph Brodsky 'A Commencement Address' in *Less Than One* (1986)

'That shifting boundary between good and evil ... oscillates continuously in the consciousness of a nation, sometimes very violently, so that judgements, reproaches, self-reproaches and even repentance itself are bound up with a specific time and pass away with it, leaving only vestigial contours behind to remind history of their existence.'
      Alexander Solzhenitsyn 'Repentance and Self-Limitation in the Life of Nations' in
From under the Rubble (1975)

INTRODUCTION

The Rise of Russian Satanism

> 'Ambivalence, I think, is the chief characteristic of my nation ... I merely regret the fact that such an advanced notion of Evil as happens to be in the possession of Russians has been denied entry into consciousness on the grounds of having a convoluted syntax.'
>
> Joseph Brodsky *Less Than One* (1986)

Since evil and ambiguity are the essence of Satanism, the term is hard to pin down. Sometimes it refers to a cult that travestied Christian ceremonies in nineteenth-century France. Or the term can be used to designate (as Southey did) the satanic school of Byron, Shelley, and their imitators, who extolled 'impiety' and delighted in 'lawless passion.' Dictionaries also cite sinister associations with social revolution or the kind of diabolical disposition that reduced Luther to intemperance. But Satan himself, despite his Protestant connections, has ancient lineage, being commonly identified with Lucifer, the chief of the fallen angels, who according to the Talmud was cast out of heaven by Michael. In Christian theology he became the great enemy of man, otherwise known familiarly as the Devil, and as such his travels were worldwide.

In Russia his presence was felt in medieval times in icons and hagiographical writings, replete with fantastic miracles and incredible sufferings. Usually, these were inspired by apocryphal literature, which survived despite ecclesiastical prohibition in Eastern Christendom much as it did in the West. In Kievan Rus' the influence of apocryphal themes was considerable, echoes of it being found even in *The Tale of the Host of Igor*. The legend of Adam's temptation and his signing over his soul that anticipates the Faustian legend probably reached the Eastern Slavs through the Balkans.[1] They were also familiar with the New Testament apocrypha, recounting the events of Christ's childhood, or of his temptation by the Devil, and the story of his descent into Hell before the resurrection. Through these and other sources, Satan in one form or another became a familiar figure in Russia long before the eighteenth century; but in secular literature, as distinct from tales of biblical or apocryphal provenance, he failed to make his mark before the Enlightenment.

How he came to do so is the subject of this book. The culmination of the demonic tradition in pre-revolutionary Russia is, of course, well known. Lermontov's *Demon*, its most famous poetic example, became one of the three masterpieces of classical Russian literature. It inspired not only music and a host of poetic imitators, but also one of the most original painters of the nineteenth century, Mikhail Vrubel. Yet despite its continuing vitality,[2] the origins of the tradition they ennobled have so far been untouched by Soviet scholars. Nor does the Devil's Russian career receive much attention in the most recent Western studies of Satan,[3] whose general prominence in contemporary mass culture has been advanced by the re-emergence of religious fundamentalism.

On the Soviet side this neglect has been partly due to ideology. As Joseph Brodsky suggests, 1917 stripped evil of official status, although previously the subject was either too disturbing in an Orthodox setting, or too unconventional, to attract academic scrutiny. After the revolution it left Soviet intellectuals uninterested or perplexed. Thus, Boris Eikhenbaum, who wrote a fascinating essay on the appeal of Satanism to the Romantic poets of Pushkin's day, was denounced as a formalist.[4] And Lunacharsky, the most erudite Bolshevik, injured national *amour-propre* by turning his back on *Demon*. He did so on much the same ground that Marx's biographer, Franz Mehring, preferred *Paradise Lost* to Klopstock's *Messias*. Milton's Satan, Lunacharsky would argue, is a revolutionary: Lermontov's hero is not. But despite the official endorsement Satan received at the hands of Lenin's commissar for enlightenment, many Bolshevik critics and poets, Mayakovsky included, saw *Paradise Lost* and *Paradise Regained* as Christian propaganda.[5] Even if Satan eventually rose from his unpromising beginnings to become the Promethean arch-rebel of Romantic mythology, the harbinger of human progress venerated by Marx, no one was curious enough to ask how the public's fascination with Adam and Eve and established Christian deities gave way in the nineteenth century to an unwholesome obsession (so the authorities believed) with their evil foe.

One scholar before the revolution did make a half-hearted effort to link Lermontov's *Demon* with the Satan of *Paradise Lost*,[6] but the disappearance of the first Russian translation of 1745 proved an obstacle not only to tracing Milton's influence but also to exploring the sources of the demonic tradition.[7]

My finding of several transcriptions of this early monument to Russian letters encouraged a search for rivals to Milton's Satan in Soviet archives. Indeed, a manuscript of Polish origin, transcribed a few years before Stroganov's translation of *Paradise Lost*, did turn up.[8] It describes the war in Heaven, but its devil is still very close to folklore, being merely a fiend, not a rebel, and his kinship with other apocryphal tales about Satan that are to be found in shorter Russian eighteenth-century manuscripts is easy to see.

Some of these manuscripts, although of ancient origin, may be encountered in many eighteenth-century transcriptions, a fact that proves, presumably, that such devilish tales were popular. 'Genealogies of Adam,' copies of 'the handwriting our First Parent Adam gave the Devil,' which are sometimes to be found next to celestial cycles and copies of the cosmography of Cosmas Indikopleustes, prepared some readers no doubt for the grander themes of *Paradise Lost*.[9] They may even help to account for the astonishing later popularity throughout the Russian Empire of prosaic editions of Milton's epics, in which for some readers Satan may have aroused more interest than the depiction of Christ or Adam. In fiction evil is always more arresting than virtue. But on a popular level literate Muscovites in the seventeenth century were already predisposed to pay particular attention to the Devil's doings owing to the prominence he had acquired in tales of everyday life ('bytovye povesti').

That evil deeds were inspired by the Devil, and good by God, was considered as axiomatic as the Devil's complicity with Eve. The late flowering of something like genuine fiction, despite narrow Orthodox strictures, made it possible to probe the Devil's motives.[10] In the literature of Old Believers, however, he retained his earlier biblical intensity. Hence, in one of the great professions of Christian faith, conceived in the same period as *Paradise Lost*, Satan invades 'our valiant Russia so he might turn her crimson with the blood of martyrs ...'[11]

The psychological traits of this traditional Satan were permanently affected by the Enlightenment. Peter the Great frankly avowed disbelief in his existence. Shown the stain on the wall where Luther had thrown an inkstand at the Devil, the Tsar-reformer expressed astonishment 'that so learned a man' could lend credence to a fiction.[12] Yet even the St Petersburg Academy of Sciences, Peter the Great's tribute to the Age of Reason, was compelled to acknowledge Satan's propinquity. When a decree of 1718 ordered the Tsar-reformer's subjects to hand over to the authorities freaks, monsters, and strange objects, it further explained that such curiosities were not the Devil's work. This the *narod* (folk or people) no doubt declined to accept, but thanks to the nobility's Europeanization and the emergence towards the end of the eighteenth century of a secularized intelligentsia, the Devil lost his rustic accent and the monkish manner imbibed from long dealings with the clergy. The Masonic movement introduced writers of the Catherinian era to a non-theological conception of good and evil that gave Satan entrance to the salon. Schooled in the new secular philosophies and employing surprising social mobility (even in peasant editions of *Paradise Lost* Satan is always portrayed as a gentleman), he quickly rose above his unsophisticated beginnings in popular prose. The poets were particularly in need of him, for the Devil could be presented, as no human character could, as the hypostasis of evil.

In the face of Orthodox custom, the next stage in his development as a literary figure involved the most portentous change of all: his treatment as a sympathetic character. Since *Paradise Lost* was first published in Russia under Masonic auspices, it is likely that for followers of the pantheistic mystic Louis Claude de Saint-Martin (1743–1803) this trend was made respectable by the master's belief that the expulsion of Satan's angelic supporters had been caused by their love of beauty. So intense was this love that the fallen angels desired to possess Heaven for themselves.[13] This aesthetic interpretation of the revolt in Heaven may have been made less attractive by the politics of the Pugachev Rebellion and the French Revolution. Alexander Radishchev's 'Angel of Darkness,' one of the first Miltonic demons in Russian literature, perhaps represents a symbolic response to both these events.

The impression made on the Russian Romantics by the Satan of *Paradise Lost* turned out to be no less marked than his influence on Italian, French, and German verse. In the Russian context his influence may have been even more deeply felt because, until translations of Goethe's *Faust* began to appear in the 1820s, Milton's Satan had no real rivals.[14] As a heroic figure he now overshadowed the native devils, the *besy*, demons, and fallen angels of Russia's Golden Age. What explains this affection of Zhukovsky's and Pushkin's generation for *Paradise Lost*? Native epic poems failed to make the transition into the age of the novel, and the difficulty of Milton's language was a further handicap spared Goethe's Mephistopheles. But there were powerful psychological and political reasons why Milton's Satan survived his rival into the second half of the nineteenth century and, indeed, beyond 1917.

Blake, Shelley, Robert Burns, Byron, Alfred de Vigny, Chateaubriand, Scott, Victor Hugo, and others who appear in these pages were not always captivated by him in the same way; but the Romantics gave the demonic tradition a sensual direction of the kind Vrubel expressed so hauntingly when he devoted the last years of his life to capturing on canvas that combination of evil and the yearning for freedom that poets before him had tried to evoke. This extraordinary Russian artist seems to bring to a conclusion the Romantic obsession with this modern outsider's sensibility, whose all-too-human alienation is first hinted at in Kheraskov's Masonic verse at the time of the French Revolution.

Milton's Satan has two other claims to modernity. The Russian Enlightenment's flying demons, interstellar flights, and cosmic visions can almost all be traced either to *Paradise Lost* or to Voltaire's pioneering piece of science fiction *Micromégas* (which was translated only some four decades later). Voltaire's Swiftian alien from Sirius, however, was too shallow a character to arouse anything but philosophical curiosity. With the fears unleashed by Pugachevshchina and the Jacobin menace abroad, Milton's hero by contrast acquired a political profile: he became the ideologue a new conception of evil required. Readers were reminded of his earlier identification with that 'son of Beelzebub' Oliver Cromwell: and here perhaps lies the key to Satan's emergence as a free-thinker ('vol'nodumets') in the Catherinian era. For Derzhavin, one of the foremost reactionaries of that time, Satan was the prototype of that novel species in Russian society, the intellectual whose questioning brought strife and discord to modern life.

In this post-revolutionary manifestation the prince of darkness repelled but he also fascinated. The decline of revealed religion among the intelligentsia paved the ground for his transition into the nineteenth century. In his distaste for the church, Jean-Jacques Rousseau prepared his Russian readers for an emotional and sentimental religiosity that rejected one of the fundamental aspects of Orthodoxy, its communal nature. For Rousseau evil was social rather than metaphysical in origin: we can be saved by our individual consciences. In the wake of the Decembrist insurrection, with the alienation of the upper levels of society from autocracy, attitudes towards 1789 seem often to parallel attitudes towards the Devil. While in France political reactionaries made common cause against revolution with Catholics, republicans and revolutionaries attacked Christianity and rallied to the support of its opponents – the greatest of whom was Satan. To Alfred de Vigny, Victor Hugo, and others who admired Milton, Satan became a symbol of rebellion against the institutions of the *ancien régime*. In Russia, by contrast, the victory over Napoleon delayed or fudged such blatant symbolism; but to the Russian Romantics, too, the new poetic demon in their midst represented an individualist devil freed of his traditional attachment to the Bible. Thus Satanism took on a sensational literary life of its own, unleashing charges of political insubordination and moral depravity.

For the latter proposition there was support in Judaeo-Christian theology. As tempter and fallen angel, the Romantic Satan consorted with mortals. Such erotic liaisons turned into one of the outstanding themes of nineteenth-century verse. By then German devils, Goethe's following the 'cry-baby' Satan of Klopstock, competed with Milton's and Byron's for the Russian reader's soul; but it was Lermontov's Demon who shocked or titillated Russian feelings most – so much so that the empress requested an unpublished copy. This trend had in some ways been anticipated by Milton. As both Jesuit critics and Voltaire were quick to point out, *Paradise Lost* is extraordinarily explicit about sex. Hence the epic was put on the Index and censored in Eastern Europe. But puritans could explain away the poem's descriptions of our first parents' love-making on the ground that it happens before the fall. It is in this state of innocence that Satan first spies Eve in the Garden. Is there not more than a hint of physical attraction in the renowned soliloquy that her naked beauty evokes? Indeed, Chateaubriand became convinced that it was Satan's jealousy of Adam that prompted mankind's doom.

Yet the seduction of Eve is accomplished by intellectual argument; and Milton, despite his many debts to classical mythology, declined to infringe the taboo his Romantic imitators relished breaking. Milton's angels make love, itself an innovation in Protestant theology, but there is no sexual congress with mortals, a notion Pushkin lampooned with Satan's seduction of the Virgin Mary. But in this respect Nikolaevan censors seem to have made little distinction between Milton's epics and Lermontov's *Demon*. They were all proscribed for undermining civic morality; and, as this book tries to show, anxiety by critics and the public at large about Satan's portrayal in poetry and art persisted into the twentieth century, long after the alleged decline of the notion of original sin. The contemporaries of Mikhail Vrubel were as uneasy about the manner in which his demons flaunted their androgynous sexuality as were Soviet critics after 1917, when the puritanical attitude to sex that had marked the English Revolution was, under Stalin, revived. The Promethean Satan imposed on *Paradise Lost* in Soviet schools was divested of any connection with evil, being portrayed as 'the embodiment of love of freedom ... as well as of the idea of the leadership of the people in a new form.'[15]

If this suggests that Satan survived the Russian revolutions much as he survived 1789 by accommodating himself to the moral and ideological perceptions of the age, a word perhaps is necessary to explain why this book ends with the twentieth century, rather than the Romantic period in which poets felt most in sympathy with the Satan of *Paradise Lost*. Thereafter the demonic theme as it evolved in Russian culture after Zhukovsky owed as much to Goethe's *Faust* as to Milton, a change of key that is anticipated by Pushkin, who admired the intensity of Milton and Bunyan but whose Mephisto shares the scepticism of Goethe's anti-hero. Yet it was possible to be affected by both the English and the German Devil, in part because the latter lacked the qualities Russian poets and artists sought in the former. Pushkin, for example, (as Christopher Hill suggests) was a 'very Miltonic poet,'[16] whose demons and *besy* when they were not drawn from life were affected by both *Faust* and *Paradise Lost*. So were Vrubel and the symbolists, although Bulgakov's *Master and Margarita* (1928–40), one of the most superb creations in all demonic literature, was clearly more influenced by Goethe.

Indeed, there does not even appear to be any proof that Bulgakov read *Paradise Lost*.[17] He may have done so, in much the same way that Dostoevsky, Tolstoy, Chekhov, Gorky, Leonid Andreev, and virtually all the better-known pre-revolutionary writers were familiar with it, because Milton's epic poem had become so much a part of the general culture of the time. My first instinct was to stay within the boundaries of the tradition Milton himself defined, before Goethe and others weakened it by placing it in a non-Christian context. But the chronological scope of this study grew with the realization that Milton's Satan derives his power not only from myth but from his ties with seventeenth-century English politics, whose relevance to the Russian revolutionary movement first began to be noted not by the Romantics but by the next generation.

This is why the final chapters attempt to trace the career of Milton's Satan as perceived by the radical intelligentsia before and after 1917. In the last decade of the century, a Marxist critic transformed him into almost a purely political entity, and after the Bolshevik Revolution the Satan of *Paradise Lost* would eventually take his belligerent place in the struggle against imperialism. His promotion was not unchallenged, recalling the way the poets of Lermontov's day had paved the way for his most recent Soviet incarnation by turning the prince of darkness into a Romantic hero.

Whatever the explanations for the varied Russian fortunes of Milton's Satan, they had little to do with William Blake's perception that Milton was of the Devil's party without knowing it. Blake was unknown to Russia's Romantic writers, and so were Burns and Shelley. Byron, on the other hand, proved immensely influential, but in Russia in his day the demonic tradition unfolded with little prompting from English critics. It owed most to Milton's own genius and to the fecundity and pertinacity of his Russian translators and publishers, as well as to the lingering force of puritanism and to the political legacy of the French Revolution.

But the triumph of the Devil after October, when some justifiably questioned his right to any kind of legitimacy, had powerful historical roots too, above all in Marx's Prometheanism – that potent amalgam with which Soviet culture is imbued to this day. Its Baconian 'faith in men's unlimited powers as self-creator'[18] transformed Milton's Satan after 1917 into a prince of light. By the 1970s he had fully adapted himself to the ambiguous ethos of the Brezhnev era.

Under *glasnost'* he will change again. Evil, which Enlightenment thinkers considered redundant, has survived the age of space flight and Chernobyl. *Paradise Lost*, banned under Stalin and Khrushchev, is again being brought out in editions whose size Western publishers might envy.[19]

PART ONE

The Satan of the Enlightenment

'And where can I more decorously drown the vanities of this world that burden my mortal self than in Milton's Hell?'

Vasilii Petrov

ONE

Satan and the First Translation of *Paradise Lost*

'And moreover I was also moved to that decision [to translate *Paradise Lost*] by the fact that the author, while he was labouring over this work, was wholly blind ...'

Baron A.G. Stroganov

Before the eighteenth-century, devils dominated the Russian imagination much as they did Puritan England, as is demonstrated by the polemics unleashed by the *Raskol*. This, the only major schism in the history of the Orthodox church prior to the Russian Revolution, broke out just as the Restoration in England brought Dissent to yet another turning-point. *Paradise Lost* and *Pilgrim's Progress*, the two world classics brought forth by English Puritanism, express in their different ways the sense of crisis induced by the collapse of the Commonwealth. But for John Bunyan, who unlike Milton did not belong to the class that had taken charge after the Civil War, the Devil is hardly a heroic figure. He represents instead the pervasive meanness and selfishness that is quite close to the character later depicted in Russian literature by Gogol or Sologub. Such an essentially popular perception of evil lacked the philosophical dimension it acquired with the Elizabethans or the uncompromising intensity Satan displays in *Paradise Lost*.

Milton's poem is the earliest major poetic work in Europe to rid the Devil of the fantastic and primitive attributes with which he was identified in folklore. These attributes still marked his portrayal in the poetry of the Renaissance and the baroque period, although none of these literary devils made their way to Russia before *Paradise Lost*. Its novel portrayal of the Devil, so it is often suggested, was perhaps made possible by the fact that Milton was able to invest Satan's character with the authentic ring of revolutionary events the poet himself experienced. Why radicals such as Radishchev and the Decembrists who came after him found Milton's arch-rebel so attractive does not therefore require elaborate explanation. But if the Satan of *Paradise Lost* was so startling a phenomenon that no critic in the West before or after Addison fails to refer to him, why do Russia's earliest modern poets make no mention of him?

The explanation may lie in the fact that in the Russia of Trediakovsky's and Antiokh Kantemir's day, Antichrist, the Devil, and Peter the Great were still too intimately linked, at least in popular lore. For this reason readers of *Paradise Lost* in the first half of the eighteenth century may have thought it best to ignore Satan's prominent presence altogether. Kantemir's 'First Ode' (c 1735), the earliest Russian poem to be written under the influence of *Paradise Lost*, is more concerned with God's creation of the world and with Newtonian cosmology than with Milton's arch-rebel or his seditious politics.[1]

Such natural reticence the progress of the Enlightenment in Russia eventually overcame. Kantemir's translation of Horace, published in 1744, the year of the poet's death, alerted Russian readers to the existence of a major English epic and of a 'glorious' or 'renowned' English poet.[2] But Kantemir's praise, like Trediakovsky's in 1735, would have told a reader unfamiliar with foreign languages nothing of Milton's life or of the background to this epic poem. All this was remedied ten years later by the completion of a manuscript translation of *Paradise Lost*, to which was attached a 'Short Life of John Milton.' Both were translated by an author whose family was well known to Russians in the eighteenth century, although today the Stroganovs seem to be best remembered abroad for the dish named after them. Aleksandr Grigor'evich belonged to a generation of that legendary dynasty, which, after the Petrine era, no longer confined itself to the mercantile interests that had given it titles and great wealth.

Baron Aleksandr Grigor'evich Stroganov did not know English, but as the manuscript notes to his translation of Milton indicate, he had read Homer and Virgil. The French translation of *Paradise Lost* had first been published in 1729, and is usually attributed to Dupré de Saint-Maur, although his relative youth and the fact that he had not published anything before the appearance of *Le Paradis perdu* may have helped sustain the view that he could not have undertaken the translation alone. It is said that Dupré, who was only a little more than thirty when his work was published, made a literal version with the help of his English teacher after his wife, a far more formidable literary figure, had suggested the idea to him. According to this tradition, Dupré then submitted the text to the brilliant Abbé Chélon de Boismorand, a frequent visitor to the Parisian salon of Mme de Saint-Maur, who transformed the verbatim version 'en français véritable.'[3]

The First Translation of *Paradise Lost* 5

STROGANOV'S *PARADISE DESTROYED*

Turning the French translation into veritable Russian would have been no easy task. If the controversy over the attribution of Dupré's translation was really inspired by the reluctance of Voltaire and others to believe that anyone but a superior intellect could successfully solve the problems facing the translator of the English original, then the kind of challenge Stroganov set himself can well be imagined. For not only was French morphologically more expressive than Russian, but it was also free of the specific problems (which Milton had himself earlier confronted) then obscuring the beauty and immense potential of Russian. Thus, when the English poet made his famous resolve 'to fix all the industry and art I could unite to the adorning of my native tongue,' he was stating what virtually became the program of all the major eighteenth-century Russian poets starting with Antiokh Kantemir and Trediakovsky.

With them, however, the rival to the vernacular was not Latin but Church-Slavonic. Sir Jerome Horsey, who expressed admiration for the Russian language in the sixteenth century, probably had the vernacular in mind, but then and still in the Petrine era Church-Slavonic represented the only recognized literary language. In fact, it was the language in which Kantemir began his literary career, and he was far from the last eighteenth-century poet to do so. But this formal idiom did not prove sufficiently flexible to accommodate the secular and technical changes accompanying Peter the Great's reforms. Nor did his civic alphabet, based on the written letters of everyday script, assist its continued survival. Although the new alphabet may have been intended to be limited in its application, more and more books were published employing the new type at the expense of Church-Slavonic, whose dominance was further undermined by neologisms flooding everyday speech.

The effect of this was to widen further the gulf between Church-Slavonic and the vernacular. For virtually all Kantemir's and Trediakovsky's successors, therefore, the question of literary idiom became involved in the larger debate over a national language, and with the practical problem of translation. This was particularly pressing because two-thirds of all books published in the Russian Empire during the eighteenth century belonged to this category. In the still-meagre periodical press the proportion of material of foreign origin was even greater. Stroganov was not, however, like Trediakovsky, an official translator. Nor was literature with him, as with Prince Antiokh Kantemir, his real métier, a vocation that in any case had yet to find official sanction in Russian society. There is thus not the remotest hint that Stroganov's translation of *Paradise Lost* was ordered from above (as was so often the case for those associated with the St Petersburg Academy of Sciences).

Indeed, the reign of Elisabeth produced an especially barren period in publishing. This pious daughter of Peter the Great, who indulged her love of fashion by ordering thousands of dresses from Paris, disdained books. Such disdain was encouraged by an obscurantist clergy, which makes Stroganov's undertaking all the more remarkable. What prompted it? Perhaps he felt the same kind of pride that was communicated by E.G. von Berge, Dupré de Saint-Maur, Paolo Rolli, and others who enjoyed the distinction of translating *Paradise Lost* into their own languages. But the fact that Stroganov did not belong to the slender group of St Petersburg and Moscow literati perhaps militates against so convenient an explanation. Nor did Stroganov attach himself to the court, as his rank entitled him and as some of the Stroganovs under Catherine II and Alexander I were to do with such éclat.

Was it Milton's unorthodox religious convictions or his unconventional portrayals of Christ and Satan that persuaded Stroganov to share *Paradise Lost* with his countrymen? Unlike Berge or Rolli he had no earlier, if incomplete, translations to lean on. Nor was there anyone to whom he could turn for help. Later Catherine the Great would set up a commission, which she subsidized, to advise on the translation of books. But in the years between the death of Peter the Great and her reign such support was rare. In the absence of relevant grammatical manuals, or of rules of literary usage commanding common assent, Aleksandr Grigor'evich Stroganov was left to his own devices. It says much for his taste and ability that he was able to mix the Church-Slavonic and vernacular elements in his Russian version without parodying the sublime style of the original.

That he set out consciously to find an equivalent for this sublimity is indicated by the Foreword, where Stroganov speaks of Milton's 'glorious matter' matched by 'the high style and inventiveness.' These are qualities Stroganov is the first recorded Russian writer to discern in *Paradise Lost*, although he was certainly no more than echoing Addison and Constantin de Magny. But to understand the problems Stroganov faced as translator it is worthwhile considering how Milton achieved the 'sublimity' that so impressed eighteenth-century admirers, thus paving the way for some of the characteristics associated with Romanticism.

According to C.S. Lewis, this sublimity is produced largely by three things: the use of unfamiliar words and constructions, including archaisms; the use of splendid and remote proper names; and the 'continued allusion to all the sources of heightened interest in our sense experience (light, darkness, storm, flowers, jewels, sexual love, and the like), but all over-topped and "managed" with an air of magnanimous austerity.'⁴ This last quality mid-eighteenth-century Russian was simply not sufficiently developed to convey. It is therefore not to Stroganov's discredit that his translation does not evoke the rich quality of experience and the sensual excitement – '*without* surrender or relaxation' – that Lewis perceives in the original. But the Church-Slavonic in the Russian translation, with its majesty and archaic overtones, already apparent in Stroganov's day, was ideally suited to render the other two elements that contribute to Milton's inimitable grandeur. In this sense, Stroganov had an advantage over Dupré.

Because of the status of Church-Slavonic, however, its inclusion also constituted a weakness. Among the poets of the time there was no agreement on its present or future role in the development of a literary language. To what extent Trediakovsky still relied on Church-Slavonic may be seen from his rendition of Fénelon's *Télémaque*, completed some time after *Pogublennyi rai*. Although written in prose, Fénelon's work shared Milton's epic ambitions on two counts: its attempted sublimity and its biblical and classical inspiration. But Trediakovsky's efforts to resurrect archaic Slavisms and to create new Slav equivalents for Fénelon's uneasy mixture was ridiculed by Lomonosov, who proposed to solve the conflicting claims of Church-Slavonic and contemporary speech by regulating linguistic and literary usage. Rather than revive obsolete-sounding Church-Slavonic vocabulary, he proposed to retain only those words that were commonly understood, the proportion in which these were to be mixed with colloquialisms being governed by the literary medium into which they were introduced. The high style would employ Church-Slavonic words not normally used in Russian, but that Russians understood, this being suitable for odes and heroic verse. The intermediate style, more appropriate for satires, elegies, and drama, would use Church-Slavonic vocabulary more familiar to educated Russians, while the low style, especially apt for comic genres, could draw on everyday Russian speech.⁵

This ingenious scheme, which Lomonosov, like Trediakovsky, supported by a historical argument advancing the priority and pre-eminence of Church-Slavonic over Latin – and hence of Russian over other European vernaculars (because the parallel development of Church-Slavonic and Russian did not involve a break with medieval culture) – was doomed to failure. Not least among the reasons for this was the growing intimacy of Russian readers and writers with the languages and literatures of Europe. Stroganov would have been aware of most of these issues (although he could not have read Lomonosov's *Rhetoric*, published three years after the appearance of the first manuscripts of *Pogublennyi rai*). How well Stroganov understood them is implied by the Foreword, where he writes: 'I have used ... many Church-Slavonic phrases ['rechi'], owing to their capacity to render much of the Holy Writ ... to which example I needed to turn ... so that there would be no discord ['raznoglasie'] ...'[6] It is not surprising, therefore, to find him employing the Church-Slavonic for 'Lost' in the title, ie, 'pogublennyi,' with its connotation of 'ruin.' Subsequent translators would abandon this title. For 'paradise destroyed' (the modern equivalent of 'pogublennyi rai') implicitly rules out the notion of 'paradise regained' contained in the sequel.[7]

Does this mean that Stroganov's version was already archaic only thirty to forty years later – when the new published translations began to appear? Ruban, the poet, who published a section of Stroganov's translation in 1780 to set side by side with the parallel passage as rendered by Vasilii Petrov in 1777 and Amvrosii in 1780, apparently did not think so. The notion of a 'high style' in literature was not yet dead. Petrov tried to achieve it by using conventions of the kind noted by Lewis, and his translation was in some ways more 'laboured' than Stroganov's because the author knew English and attempted to follow Milton's phrasing. Here Stroganov's task was simplified by Dupré's decision to disregard this, French punctuation and word order being closer to Russian. Moreover, religious books continued to use the older (and 'higher') style, and to those who read *Paradise Lost* as a biblical work, Milton in everyday speech would have been unthinkable. Indeed, all eighteenth-century Russian translators of his epic poems tried to recapture his 'high' style, which inevitably involved some reliance on the Church-Slavonic lexicon.

To what extent this was considered 'archaic' – not in the literary sense meant by Lewis but in the sense of 'obsolete' – depended on the class of reader. To a merchant family such as the Novosil'tsevs, for example, who lived in the provinces and who seem to have read their copy of *Pogublennyi rai* as primarily a religious and even didactic work, Stroganov's language would probably not have seemed 'obsolete' even in the second half of the nineteenth century.[8] By then, of course, to those accustomed to reading secular literature, the triumph of the vernacular idiom would have made it seem antique, as a reviewer, though full of respect for Stroganov's early achievement, implied in 1838.[9] Yet this reviewer was apparently quite unaware that the translation had actually been published (in an adapted version) only a decade earlier![10] The popular reader for whom this was intended would not have looked askance at its 'antiquated' style – indeed, given his church schooling he would have expected it – but this was not, of course, the attitude of the more sophisticated literate public of St Petersburg and Moscow. By the turn of the century readers in these circles had been persuaded by Karamzin and his friends to believe that written Russian must be like French.

Thus, what is variously called the 'grandeur' or 'elevation' of Milton's style corresponded to a language in Russia for which there was no exact equivalent in England or France. There were, of course, Englishmen who were bewildered by Milton's original, to whom the blank verse was no doubt as confusing as the vocabulary. This accounts for the effort of a 'gentleman of Oxford' who produced a prose version of *Paradise Lost* – 'from the French of the learned Raymond de St. Maur.'[11] Although the common reader in Britain and North America approached Milton in a tradition quite different from that of the universities and the academic critics, however, there did not develop (as in Russia) virtually two dialects in which his epic poems were read – the Church-Slavonic associated with Stroganov's version and (what was initially the less popular) the literary idiom attempted later by Petrov and Amvrosii. This helps to explain the existence of the numerous manuscript copies of *Pogublennyi rai*, which continued to circulate and to be transcribed even after the publication of 'modern' translations.

Dupré and the Abbé Chélon de Boismorand faced problems of a different literary sort. For them the most obvious choice to be made was whether to attempt a poetic translation – of the kind, for instance, that both Theodor Haak and E.G. von Berge had done in German. Some early translators were put off by the blank verse. Others in fact preferred prose as a medium of translation, this being particularly fashionable in eighteenth-century France where Dupré's prose version established a precedent followed by a long and distinguished line of translators of *Paradise Lost*, including Louis Racine (1755) and Chateaubriand (1836). Bodmer made the same choice with his influential translation, also believing that exact verse translation of foreign works was impossible. In his feud over the matter with Gottsched he also anticipated the Romantics by arguing that prose translations were more 'natural.'

In a sense, therefore, Baron Stroganov was following a trend, even if his own reasons for doing so would have been quite different. Since he does not discuss the issue of translation at any length, an increasingly important one for Russian writers, all that can safely be said is that he followed Dupré's version rather more faithfully than the French translation followed the original. Was he aware of the problems publication of *Paradise Lost* encountered in France? There Dupré had felt constrained because of censorship and ecclesiastical criticism to omit parts of the English poem, much as Paolo Rolli had at first considered doing. But in the second edition of the French translation – which Dupré published in Holland only a year later – he inserted the excluded passages, advertising this fact in the new introduction added to the Dutch edition. England had freedom of the press, Dupré observed, but not France.[12] Since the Russian translation does not omit any of the suppressed lines, it may be assumed that Stroganov used either the Hague edition of 1730 or the 'nouvelle édition' of 1740, also published in the Dutch capital.[13]

It was to disarm bigots in his own country that Stroganov seems to have decided on a deliberately misleading introduction to the Russian translation – misleading because it was simply untrue, as Stroganov insists again and again, that *Paradise Lost* is free of 'pagan elements.' Such matter, says Stroganov, is present not only in Homer and Virgil, but 'in their modern imitators – the ones I have had a chance to see.'[14] This was so, despite the fact that those imitations were 'composed by Christian writers.' Milton belonged to a different category, however: *Paradise Lost*, Stroganov assured his compatriots, was the only 'such poem' in which 'true events are described.' By *true* Stroganov means actions not based on fables but 'on those revealed in Holy Writ.'

To sustain this implausible claim, the Russian then cites Milton's own testimony in the opening book of the poem. Does he not say there that 'my song soars above the Aonian mountain [that is, higher than all pagan fables] and encompasses matter no one hath yet attempted in verse, or simple speech'?[15] This assertion by the poet on the sacred provenance of his verse (one that Milton appears at times to have himself believed) was not sustained by any of his French critics. And Constantin de Magny as well as Addison certainly would have been surprised to be told that there were 'no pagan elements' in *Paradise Lost*. Stroganov must have known perfectly well that this claim was untenable, but if his aim was to persuade 'les gens bigots' in the Holy Synod, he had little alternative but to present the English epic as a biblical work. He also appealed to the charity of its potential foes by advancing a more personal motive for the translation: 'And moreover I was also moved to that decision by the fact that its author, while he was labouring over this work, was wholly blind.' In the official family chronicle Stroganov's reasons for translating the epic are presented just as inconsequentially: he did it 'in order to chase away melancholy and pensive reflections.' Evidence of other literary activity rests on the same reticent source. Thus, we are told that Stroganov translated 'many' other works, including a pious tract in French on Christianity, and a work on marriage or divorce (the Russian being so phrased that this could refer to one of Milton's pamphlets on the subject).[16]

None of Baron Stroganov's wives had literary pretensions of the kind that set Princess Mariia Dmitrievna Kantemir apart from the noblewomen of her day. She, incidentally, knew the Stroganovs, as did her brother Antiokh; but while Aleksandr Grigor'evich could have heard of *Paradise Lost* through either of them, there is no published evidence to confirm it. Another possibility is that Stroganov was introduced to the epic through Pyotr Buslaev, a syllabic poet highly thought of by Trediakovsky, but this connection too is only a surmise. The fact remains, however, that in 1734 the St Petersburg Academy published an ambitious poem (the only one by which Buslaev is remembered) commemorating the passing of Aleksandr Grigor'evich's mother. And Buslaev supposedly wrote his *Spiritual Speculations* under the influence of *Paradise Lost* and *Paradise Regained*.[17] By then *Paradise Lost* had already appeared in German, Dutch, Italian, and French editions, but it had not been translated anywhere in Eastern Europe. Nor are there references to Milton in Russian sources between the time Kantemir's edition of Horace appeared and the 1760s. The exception is an allusion by the dramatist A.P. Sumarokov to that 'renowned English poet.'[18] Sumarokov, who is generally considered to have been the first Russian 'gentleman' to earn a living as a writer, had no knowledge of English. What makes Sumarokov's Miltonian allusion interesting is the fact that it occurs in the same poetic line as his reference to Shakespeare: 'Mil'ton i Shekespir, khotia neprosveshchennyi ...' ('Milton and Shakespeare, although unenlightened'). The latter epithet applies only to Shakespeare, being probably derived from a German lexicon of 1733.[19] The view it conveys echoes Milton's own of 'sweetest Shakespeare, Fancy's child / Warb[ling] his native woodnotes wild.'[20] In the absence of other published references to *Paradise Lost* in the middle of the century, Stroganov's manuscript became the sole source of information about the author.

SAMIZDAT

These were bleak years in Russian letters. Yet this silence is suspect. For it is precisely at this time that on the Continent so many editions and translations of Milton appear. Dupré's *Paradis perdu*, for example, came out several times in mid-century, and Louis Racine's version of 1755 was especially well received.[21] German poets also outdid themselves by adding new translations of *Paradise Lost* in this period, as well as of *Paradise Regained* and *Samson Agonistes*.[22] In England, too, Tonson's, Thomas Newton's, and John Baskerville's many editions of Milton at this time give some indication of public demand, while the controversy emanating from the charges of plagiarism fraudulently raised by William Lauder (and at first supported by Dr Johnson) was closely followed abroad.

None of this was echoed in Russia. Could the explanation for this be political or religious – as in the nineteenth century, when censorship was secretly imposed on prose translations of *Paradise Lost*?[23] If so, any stigma attached to Milton's name in the reign of Elisabeth (1741–62) would have been ineffective in preventing *Pogublennyi rai* from being read in manuscript. Indeed, if Stroganov's translation was rejected by someone in authority, there was no other recourse. It would become possible to turn to a private printer under Catherine II, as Vasilii Petrov did in 1777 with his translation, but in Stroganov's time publishing was still exclusively under government control. He therefore had only two alternatives: he could wait for more auspicious times, a prospect a man approaching fifty is unlikely to have favoured, or he could engage in a premature form of *samizdat* by having his translation transcribed and distributed privately. Given his wealth, Baron Stroganov would perhaps have found this an attractive way to enable his literary *chef d'oeuvre* to acquire at least some recognition.

This possibility did not occur to the anonymous author who declared in 1838 that the work had indeed been suppressed on religious grounds.[24] Nor was this obvious notion entertained by A.N. Pypin, the well-known literary historian, who half a century later published a few passages from the translation to commemorate a noble monument to early Russian letters.[25]

Professor Pypin and his predecessor are not to blame for this oversight. Stroganov's original manuscript had disappeared. In compiling his extracts for publication from a version in the Rumiantsev Collection Pypin believed that he had got hold of a rare copy of the translation. That it had been published in modernized form as late as 1820 he did not realize, nor did he make any effort – as far as is known – to locate further copies of the Stroganov manuscript. This is a pity because many would have perished during the world wars and the intervening period. Today the manuscripts in Soviet archives can hardly represent more than a fraction of the number circulating in the eighteenth and nineteenth centuries, and we shall suggest later why some of these are particularly difficult to trace.

In mid-eighteenth-century Russia, manuscripts rather than books were still widely read. This is a tradition that has yet to be systematically examined, but it is not a practice Stroganov would have had to inaugurate. It was common in his time for proscribed or interdictable literature, such as some of Kantemir's satires (many of which could not be published until Pypin's day), to be disseminated in manuscript.[26] The only peculiarity of *Pogublennyi rai* in this context would have been its length.

Other secular works to which Stroganov's translation may be compared either in genre, length, or origin (such as Trediakovsky's *Tilemakhida*, his proscribed *Theoptiia*, Pope's *Essay on Man*, or Klopstock's *Messias*) may also be found in Russian manuscript collections, but never in quantity. What makes the manuscript translations of Milton unique is their number and, given the embryonic literary conventions of the period, the fastidious care with which the early manuscripts were copied. Does this mean that Baron Stroganov used his ample means to have them transcribed and put into circulation? Or is this early evidence of the public demand that, in the nineteenth century, would produce frequent and massive editions of Milton's two epics? Such questions are difficult to answer because literary journals had not sprung to life in Stroganov's lifetime, and the art of reviewing had yet to be born. But a recently discovered manuscript adaptation suggests that already Satan interested some readers more than any of Milton's other characters.

TWO

Introducing Milton's Satan to the Common Reader

> 'Satan said he would never bend knee[s] before God and with humiliation beg mercy ...'
>
> Barsov-Stroganov-Amvrosii manuscript

The attempt to adapt *Paradise Lost* has been made hundreds of times – beginning with Dryden's dramatization – the latest today being that of a Polish composer-librettist who has been criticized for focusing his opera on Adam and Eve. Their love, however approached, is devoid of action. Except for a little gardening, there is not much they actually do until Satan's menacing appearance in Eden (Book IV). By then the outline of the principal plot, involving the momentous conflict of good and evil, the account of which is resumed by Raphael's narration in Book V, has been established. The temptation and the transgression (Book IX) may constitute the poem's moral climax, but it can also be read as only an incident in the struggle announced in the opening lines. If so, Satan becomes the poem's main character. His appearance is crucial to the narrative of the first six books, as well as to the ninth, since the plot's resolution is contingent on his temptation of Eve. But it is possible to avoid making the Devil into the hero of the story by concentrating on the celestial cycle in Book VII, and the scenes in the Garden of Eden, an alternative to be found in some pre-Romantic adaptations of *Paradise Lost*. God then becomes the unchallenged protagonist of the narrative, Adam the hero, and the creation can take the place of the epic battle between the forces of light and darkness as the dramatic focal point of the action. Thus, Kantemir was attracted by Milton's cosmology, and many Russian poets at the end of the eighteenth century were drawn to Raphael's account of the creation in Book VII; but this is omitted in the Barsov manuscript as well as all of Book VI with its description of the epic battle in Heaven. Nor is there any mention of celestial motion as explained by Raphael in Book VIII.

THE BARSOV TRANSLATION-ADAPTATION

Thus in the Russian version Raphael, whose sojourn in paradise serves Milton's purpose in retelling the battle and in relating how God made the universe and how it works, loses his *raison d'être*. In other words, the Devil rather than God moves to the centre of the Barsov adaptation of *Paradise Lost*. This is noteworthy because it suggests an inspiration secular rather than devout or biblical, a supposition confirmed by the words at the head of the quarto-sized manuscript: 'Copied out of curiosity for knowledge's sake.'[1] (See Figure 1.)

What the reader would have learnt from the opening paragraph (and there is no prefatory material of any kind) is that Satan after his defeat and ouster from Heaven, 'swam for ten days amid the fiery waves with his entire accursed armed crew.'[2] Of Milton's invocation to the Heavenly Muse there is no trace, or of his digressions throughout the poem. The story is presented as an early Russian *povest'* might have been, told from the point of view of an unidentified narrator, but with this difference: some of the information furnished by Stroganov in the footnotes of his translation has found its way into the text.

Thus, where Stroganov explains Beelzebub's presence next to Satan by reference to 'a Philistine tribe,' whose idol he was, in the Barsov manuscript this becomes part of the story: 'according to the Philistines of yore, Beelzebub was [Satan's] companion.'[3] Similarly, more complex figures of speech are simplified or changed. For example, where Milton evokes the horror of Satan's condition as he

> Lay vanquished, rolling in the fiery gulf
> Confounded though immortal (I. ll 52–3)

and describes the duration ('nine times the space that measures day and night' [l 56]), in the Russian this is transformed into a ten-day swim.[4]

It might be tempting to ascribe these and other 'errors' to a particularly obtuse copyist, but in all the extant Stroganov manuscripts (with the exception of the Titov-Davydova copy) the distinction between text and commentary is so clear that it is difficult to conceive how any one scribe could commit them. How, then, did they arise?

The answer to this is suggested by a comparison of the text with the Stroganov translation. From this it transpires that the Barsov manuscript is not to be traced wholly to that source. Book IX and what follows is in fact almost a verbatim transcription of the corresponding passages in the new translation Amvrosii published in 1780.⁵ How is this contrast to be accounted for?

Perhaps the most obvious conjecture is, in this instance, also likely to be the true one. Since the Barsov manuscript is composed of excerpts derived from the Stroganov text and the recent Amvrosii translation, is it not natural that errors crept into the earlier parts? The Barsov manuscript is written by a single hand. The copyist can surely be assumed to have shown the same fidelity in his transcription of the rest of the text as he demonstrates in copying the Amvrosii translation.

This being the case, why would the passages from the new translation have been added? The old copy may have been too corrupt, and the language of the fresh translation appealing. All the writer had to do, presumably, was to throw out the old and bring in the new. But if that was so easy, why did he retain so much of the Stroganov-derived translation?

Between the 1740s and the date of Amvrosii's *Paradise Lost*, literary Russian had changed so much that any copyist swayed by considerations of language would have known what to reject. But this assumes that the Barsov compilation was consciously arrived at by an author who had seen the fresh translation. If so, the retention of Stroganov's Church-Slavonic lexicon can only be explained by one individual's conservatism, which, it turns out, was so erratic or eclectic that the author could mingle the language of the two widely spaced translations without any qualms.

The key to this puzzle is perhaps to be found in the Titov-Davydova text, which begins – the opening page having been damaged – with a transcription from the Amvrosii translation. This would prove, if proof were needed, that the published translation of 1780 did not make the Stroganov Milton redundant. For the common reader the older and the more recent translation continued to retain their meaning, and it is probable that extracts or transcriptions from both continued to be made into the nineteenth century, when both manuscripts and books were still being copied in Russia's provincial depths.

The Barsov manuscript must represent an example of the merger of these two traditions, the transcription of the manuscript and of the published book being found side by side. But if the Stroganov-based portions were derived from an earlier retelling of *Paradise Lost*, it is not to be ruled out that the same process of 'novelization' occurred with the published translation. If so, the peculiar marriage of the Stroganov-Amvrosii passages in the Barsov

Milton's Satan and the Common Reader 17

manuscript may be explained. The copyist, whose script suggests a provincial origin, either had two popular *povesti* before him, one derived from Stroganov, the other from Amvrosii, which he then neatly condensed into a forty-one-page narrative. Or, it can also be surmised, this had already been done for him. All he had to do was copy what has come down to us as the Barsov manuscript.

THE MANUSCRIPT TRADITION

A more sophisticated writer would have abandoned the older translation-adaptation with its corruptions and chosen to base his entire narrative on Amvrosii's text. That he did not do so suggests that the author was a mere copyist and that the Barsov manuscript is perhaps only one of a series of 'povesti' derived from *Paradise Lost*. Were the earlier versions on which it is based to be recovered, its origin might be represented schematically in the following way:

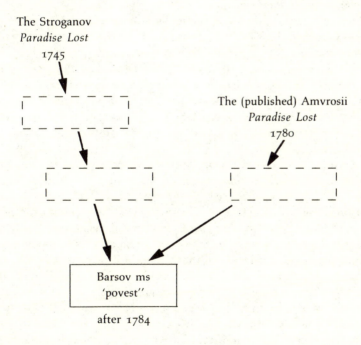

It would be interesting to discover when the precursors of the Barsov manuscript came into being, because with their transcription Satan takes his first formal steps as a Russian literary character. To those familiar with Dante, Marlowe, Tasso, Vondel, or Marino, to name but a few, this claim may seem surprising, but none of the poets who brought the Devil into secular literature in the West were translated into Russian before Milton. The Stroganov *Paradise Lost* represents the earliest literary work to introduce Russian readers to Satan.

They had of course met him before 1745, but this was in another shape and context. In medieval times he made his presence felt in hagiographical writings, replete with fabulous episodes, fantastic miracles, or incredible sufferings. These were most often inspired by apocryphal literature, which thrived in both Western and Eastern Christendom despite ecclesiastical prohibition. In Kievan Rus' the influence of apocryphal themes was considerable, echoes of it being found even in *The Tale of the Host of Igor* (in which the phrase 'Not of their own free will have the trees shed their leaves' recalls the apocryphal 'Confession of Eve'). Some of the Old Testament apocrypha reached the Eastern Slavs through the Bogomils, who made the Devil into a co-creator and contaminator of the world.[6]

The legend of Adam's temptation and his signing over his soul to the Devil also probably reached the Eastern Slavs through the Balkans, and they were familiar too with the New Testament apocrypha, recounting the events of Christ's childhood, or of his temptation by the Devil, and the story of his descent into Hell before his resurrection (which does not necessarily contradict Christian dogma). Through these and other sources, Satan would have been known to readers of Stroganov's translation of Milton; but in secular literature, as distinct from tales of biblical or apocryphal provenance, he had yet to make his mark.

Indeed, prior to Stroganov's translation there appears to be only one eighteenth-century work of any length devoted wholly to Satan. It is a manuscript dealing (as is disclosed by the title, 'The Book about Satan's Ejection from Heaven' ['Kniga a sverzhenii s neba satany']) with the same theme as the beginning of *Paradise Lost*. In the second chapter it also touches on the transgression, although the emphasis is on Satan's seduction of Adam rather than Eve.[7] In the third chapter 'the demons bring a charge of complaint against the Lord God and take counsel.'[8] In the seventeenth, they gather together in a 'duma' reminiscent of Pandemonium;[9] and in the thirteenth, under Satan's leadership, they launch and lose a battle against the forces of Christ.[10] Such parallels with Milton's work may suggest that the author of 'The Book about Satan's Ejection from Heaven' was familiar with *Paradise Lost*.

Indeed, this is not impossible, although all that is known about this singular composition is that it was translated from the Polish in 1740 and made enough of an impression for Dmitrii-Rostovtsev to express astonishment at Satan's contumely. But the rest of the Polish manuscript – if the Polish text was itself not a translation from another language – is far from Miltonic. For a major portion of the Russian version appears to be based on apocryphal legends of the kind described above and on popular lore about demons. Thus, chapter eighteen is devoted to their bestial shenanigans and the tricks they devise to entrap upstanding Christians;[11] the nineteenth depicts their magical powers;[12] the twentieth reveals how they can be spotted;[13] the twenty-first tells of sorcerers, magicians, and their sundry allies;[14] the twenty-second of some of their other attributes and proclivities, such as their love of conundrums and riddles.[15]

To balance all this, there is some account of celestial matters: particularly, of Christ's antipathy to demons and of the efficacy of prayer against them. Yet enough has perhaps been said to indicate where (from a demonological point of view) the chief difference between the Polish work and *Paradise Lost* lies. In the former, the Devil, while armed with many of the appurtenances that his alter ego enjoys in the English epic, is not developed as a character. The closest the author of the Polish work comes to a psychological analysis, and it is not very close, is in the profile of Belial (in a chapter assigned to him), but neither this nor the description of the Devil is related to the narrative as a whole. He is merely a fiend, not a rebel, and his kinship with other apocryphal tales about the Devil that are to be found in shorter Russian eighteenth-century manuscripts is easy to see.[16]

Although of ancient origin, the fact that they are encountered in so many eighteenth-century transcriptions proves that these tales were still popular. Indeed, 'genealogies of Adam' and copies of 'the handwriting our First Parent Adam gave the Devil' are to be found next to celestial cycles, books from the Bible, and copies of the sixth-century cosmography of Cosmas Indikopleustes.[17] This type of matter may have prepared readers for some of the grand themes of *Paradise Lost*, and may even explain its popularity. It may explain, for instance, how it came into the possession of Old Believers, who normally avoided secular literature of any kind.[18] Indeed, their beautiful representations of Adam and Eve, the Tree of Knowledge, and other motifs to be found in *Paradise Lost*, which are so touching in their naïvety, suggest how well translations of Milton's work may have fitted into an accepted world view.

What is novel about the Barsov manuscript, however, is that in it the Devil emerges as a literary character in his own right. This is achieved simply enough. Milton's Satan is divorced from much of the biblical matter that makes his victory over Adam and Eve a hollow one in *Paradise Lost*. In the shortened tale he emerges as the hero. In this sense the demonic tradition in Russian literature begins with the Barsov manuscript. To be more precise, its date of birth will be determined once the original copies on which the Barsov manuscript is based are recovered and traced to their ultimate source. But the emergence of this tradition in its secular form, although relegated until now by literary historians to the nineteenth century, can be dated fairly accurately.

The first Russian imitation of *Paradise Lost,* in which Satan plays the central role, was published in 1780.[19] Three years earlier Petrov had brought out his translation of the first three books, and between 1777 and 1780 there was one attempted translation of either *Paradise Lost* or *Paradise Regained* every year.[20] In a sense, therefore, the emphasis on Satan of the Barsov 'novelization' (which, it may be recalled, was transcribed after 1780) is less surprising than it may seem. As a literary phenomenon it represents something new, but the connection in Russia with *Paradise Lost* is not.

Milton's work had no native devils to contend with in the 1770s and 1780s, and only three foreign ones. Thus, Torquato Tasso's *Gerusalemme Liberata* appeared as early as 1772 in a prose translation from the French;[21] and in 1779 Ya.B. Kniazhnin brought out Giambattista Marino's *La Strage degl' Innocenti.*[22] Both epic poems were known to Milton, one of the more familiar parts of *Jerusalem Delivered* being the cantos in which the sorceress Armida seduces Rinaldo on her enchanted island, and it is to this that *Paradise Regained* may refer (II: ll 340–47). Yet in *Paradise Lost* Milton rejected the 'tinsel trappings' of that kind of epic.[23] *Jerusalem Delivered* does portray a demonic council that anticipates Pandemonium in *Paradise Lost;* but the prototype for both lies in the councls of the gods in the *Iliad.*

Tasso's poem is concerned with the first crusade, Godfrey of Bouillon being its hero. Marino's *Strage,* by contrast, retells the incident of the Slaughter of the Innocents. Milton read Marino, whom he praised when he was in Italy,[24] and in the Russian translation there appears an undeniable similarity between the Italian Devil and the Satan of *Paradise Lost.*[25] But Kniazhnin-Marino's work, which (like Amvrosii-Milton's *Paradise Lost* in 1780) was published by Novikov, appeared in a small edition. Most of the published copies were confiscated in 1787, so that it remained relatively unknown.[26]

This certainly is not true of Klopstock's Devil. Despite the fact that he is derived from Milton's, Klopstock's Satan never threatens to become the hero of the German poem; nor does he share the political characteristics of Milton's Satan.[27] Of these Russian readers became aware, as will be shown below, in the immediate aftermath of the French Revolution.

The Barsov Devil has not yet been politicized, and it might be appropriate at this point to ask how the Russian mutation compares with the original.

Sergei Eisenstein, who turned the cosmic battle in Book VI into a shooting script, remarked that for the film-maker Milton's visual images make it easy to adapt *Paradise Lost* to the screen.[28] If true, this might explain why adaptation is so much harder when the medium is prose. There is about *Paradise Lost*, as with perhaps all great poetry before the twentieth century, a 'seamless' quality that makes it difficult to reduce into a faithful précis. Milton was called upon to do so by Simmons the printer who thought that a synopsis of the plot would help the public understand the blank verse. The poet obliged with the second edition, but anyone who sees the 'argument' prefixed to each book *after* reading the poem must surely be struck by a contrary emotion. The matter of *Paradise Lost* is so grandiose, its scale so vast, and the tension between the physical bravura and its moral resolution so acute that any bare summary of the subject must seem anti-climactic.

This juxtaposition is felt keenly for another reason. Verse, whatever eighteenth-century authorities said on the subject, cannot be reduced to prose without invoking a different kind of reaction. The attempt of Dupré to 'explain' the poetry by voluminous notes to the prose translation transforms the medium of perception still more. Stroganov took one step further along this road by putting the 'arguments' together before the text, thus producing the kind of effect that might be duplicated today by anticipating the viewing of a film by showing its trailer. The exercise might help to identify certain scenes or sequences in the main feature, but the element of surprise is lost.

Yet this type of duplication would have made it easier for Stroganov's contemporaries to recognize Milton's plot and to separate his poem into its component strands. The Barsov adaptation constitutes a remarkably vivid retelling of Satan's part of the story. The plot is so well reconstrued that it ceases to be surprising why copies were produced that must, to a modern reader, seem a travesty not only of the original, but of the two translations on which the Barsov manuscript is based.

The scene opens, as we have seen, with Satan completing a ten-day swim in the company of Beelzebub, a fact attested by 'the Pharisees of yore.' Then, the narration plunges into the action: 'Satan rose from the lake ... left the awful valley surrounded by flames, spread his wings, rose to the top over the dark air, and then alighted on the ground. And said, this is the country, this the land and climate, this is the habitation that has been determined for us, and if the doleful darkness is meant to replace the celestial light for us, then so be it. Farewell happy fields, where joy reigns ...'[29] And with this adieu to his past abode, comes Satan's refusal

> To bow and sue for grace
> With suppliant knee, and deify his power. (I. ll 112–13)

which the Russian renders in the third person: 'Satan said he would never bend his knee[s] before God and with humiliation beg mercy.'[30] The remainder of his speech is drastically shortened from Stroganov-Dupré's version. Satan merely proclaims himself 'the new monarch' and then matter-of-factly enumerates his seventeen 'commanders,' which is more than are to be found in Milton or Stroganov.

How is this accomplished? In *Paradise Lost* the roster of Satan's allies begins with Moloch, the 'horrid king besmeared with blood,' whom 'the Ammonite / Worshipped in Rabba and the watery plain' (1. ll 392, 396–7). The meaning of the biblical reference is explained by Dupré and Stroganov, but in the Barsov text 'Ammonit' becomes another of Satan's generals. Even more curious is the fate of Moloch's

> grove
> The pleasant valley of Hinnom, Tophet thence
> And black Gehenna called (1. ll 403–5)

which in the Russian becomes 'Otogotophet,' another general. Adonis is elevated to the same rank through a similar confusion.[31]

But these and other misunderstandings do not affect the development of the plot. Indeed, it may even be argued that the list of names, just as alien-sounding and exotic in the Russian as in the original, serves rather the same effect in the corrupted text as in the poem by bolstering 'their great commander' (1. l 358). More interesting than the many errors in the Barsov manuscript are the omissions. Since the narrative is so intricate, these have to be made with some care, and they are.

Thus, in *Paradise Lost* the long description of Satan's accomplices is followed by another speech, in which (according to the Argument) he 'comforts them with hope yet of regaining Heaven, but tells them lastly of a new world and new kind of creature to be created, according to an ancient prophecy or report in Heaven; for that angels were long before this visible creation, was the opinion of many ancient Fathers.' But none of this is to be found in the reduced Russian text. Nor, since Satan's intentions are soon revealed anyway by his actions, is it essential for the plot to include them. Indeed, in this sense, the debates in Pandemonium, the palace in which Satan and 'the infernal peers ... sit in council,' are also unnecessary. Accordingly, they are also omitted in the Barsov manuscript, although it does refer to 'a large and full meeting of Cherubim and Seraphim' and 'a thousand spirits seated on golden thrones.'[32] The first book then ends with the same lines as *Paradise Lost*:

> After short silence then
> And summons read, the great consult began. (I: ll 797–8)

ie, '[T]hen, after a short silence and the reading of the summons, the council began.'³³

Book II is somewhat longer, the stage being set for Satan's next move. In the original his proud speech opening the debate –

> I give not Heaven for lost ...
> ... we now return
> To claim our just inheritance of old (II. ll 14, 37–8)

– is omitted. The Russian narrative turns instead to the replies of Moloch, Belial, and Mammon. The first, whom Milton describes as a 'sceptered king,' stands up:

> the strongest and the fiercest spirit
> That fought in Heaven, now fiercer by despair.
> His trust was with the Eternal to be deemed
> Equal in strength. (II. ll 44–7)

Moloch counsels 'for open war.' Here the French translation is not very accurate. In the original Moloch does not have 'le sceptre en main': nor is Dupré's description of him as 'violent & le plus furieux des esprits qui combattirent dans les plaines de l'Empirée' quite what Milton says, although the last two lines are faithful: 'le désespoir augmentoit encore la férocité naturelle. Il avait l'audace de se soutenir égal au Tout-Puissant.'³⁴ Yet by the time all this has filtered down into the Barsov manuscript, it is surprising how close the Russian equivalent is to the Stroganov translation, which is in fact closer to the French than the French is to the English. The description of Moloch, although reduced in length, catches his essential characteristics, adding to his 'violence and natural malice' ('zlobo,' which is Stroganov's rendering of 'férocité') one of its own: Moloch is a flatterer ('l'stets').³⁵

The descriptions of Belial and Mammon also echo Stroganov and, though much reduced, are recognizably Miltonic. The former, 'in act more graceful and humane' (II. l 109) ('v priatneishem vide') utters 'slanders polite, agreeable to the ears; I am inclined for war, and yield to none in hate.' But he concludes: 'we cannot hope to win.'³⁶ Mammon also counsels against war 'to overturn the Divine monarch ... He might relent and declare a general pardon for all [of us].'³⁷ His speech is followed by Beelzebub's, who suggests a compromise. The vote, and Satan's speech ending the debate, are omitted in the Russian. In Milton's words, Satan then decides to set off in search of 'another world, and another kind of creature ... about this time to be created.'[38] In the Russian he says simply: 'I shall go myself through the dark fastnesses.'[39]

The plot of the Barsov version then follows that of *Paradise Lost*. Satan is shown setting off in quest of another world to suborn:

> Puts on swift wings, and toward the gates of Hell
> Explores his solitary flight; sometimes
> He scours the right-hand coast, sometimes the left (II. ll 631–3)

In the Russian he unfolds 'his swift wings, and flies to the Hellish gates, venturing sometimes to the right, sometimes to the left.'[40] This brings Satan to his encounter with Sin and Death, who guard the gates, an encounter that is described at somewhat greater length in the Barsov manuscript than any of the previous scenes, the scribe being clearly impressed by the magnificent if horrid setting. The 'terrible' gates with their nine locks, 'three bronze, three iron, and three of adamantine rock, enveloped always by flame, impenetrable to any force' are depicted with the same relish as 'the most hideous two monsters' barring Satan's way. 'One, half its body like a beautiful woman's, below a serpent' has 'hellish hounds around her waist ceaselessly coming in and out' of her womb:[41]

> About her middle round
> A cry of Hell-hounds never ceasing barked
> With wide Cerberean mouths full loud, and rung
> A hideous peal; yet, when they list, would creep,
> If aught disturbed their noise, into her womb,
> And kennel there, yet there still barked and howled,
> Within unseen ...(II. ll 653–66)

Next to Sin, Satan sees 'a second shape like a blackened shadow darker than night, fierce like ten furies,'[42] but his fight with Death, the issue of his union with Sin, is averted through her intervention. Hence, Satan 'immediately decided what had to be done.' He acquiesces with 'gentle voice' to her entreaty 'since you take me for your father.'[43] With their reconciliation she 'took the infernal key off from her waist,' opened 'the great portcullis which without her the powers of Hell could not have opened, and the iron fell off with the first movement of her Hand':[44]

> Which but herself not all the Stygian powers
> Could once have moved; then the key-hole turns
> The intricate wards, and every bolt and bar
> Of massy iron or solid rock with ease
> Unfastens ... (II. ll 875–9)

With the grating 'jarring sound' comes 'Harsh thunder, that the lowest bottom shook of Erebus' (ll 882–3) – a Miltonic phrase whose effect is not completely missed in the Russian: 'the tempest roaring like thunder shook the very depths of Erebus.'[45]

Satan thus leaves Hell behind him and is next seen winging his way through 'abysses, suddenly espying Chaos.' In the Barsov manuscript, as in the original, Chaos is represented allegorically enthroned next to her consort, Night, and 'Hellish Orcus and most dreadful Demogorgon.'[46] But in *Paradise Lost*, as in Stroganov's translation, the confrontation with Chaos is followed by Satan's appeal to that 'Anarch old' to help Satan find his way out of Chaos's 'gloomy bounds.' Chaos concurs after Satan promises to reduce the new region (ie, the world) 'to her original darkness,' making his response in a speech in which he reveals

> 'I know thee, stranger, who thou art,
> That mighty leading angel, who of late
> Made head against Heaven's King, though overthrown.' (II. ll 990–2)

But although this speech is echoed in the Russian version, by an interesting reduction – or confusion? – it is given by Uriel, the angel sent by God to guard the sun, rather than by Chaos. In *Paradise Lost*, Uriel's meeting with Satan occurs only in Book III, where Uriel becomes the unwitting agent of Satan's discovery of the world. But in the poem this is preceded by a long section taking up about half the book, in which Satan's flight is interrupted by the development of what technically constitutes the main plot. To cite Milton's own synopsis:

God, sitting on his throne, sees Satan flying towards this World, then newly created; shows him to the Son, who sat at his right hand; foretells the success of Satan in perverting mankind; clears his own justice and wisdom from all imputation, having created man free and able enough to have withstood his tempter; yet declares his purpose of grace towards him, in regard he fell not of his own malice, as did Satan, but by him seduced. The Son of God renders praises to his Father for the manifestation of his gracious purpose extended towards man without the satisfaction of divine justice: man hath offended the majesty of God by aspiring to Godhead, and therefore with all his progeny devoted to death must die, unless someone can be found sufficient to answer for his offence, and undergo his punishment. The Son of God freely offers himself a ransom for man; the Father accepts him, ordains his incarnation, pronounces his exaltation above all names in Heaven and Earth; commands all the angels to adore him: they obey, and hymning to their harps in full choir, celebrate the Father and Son.[47]

All this is omitted from the Barsov manuscript, where Book II ends with Sin and Death constructing a bridge over the abyss leading out of Hell; and Satan 'contin[uing] the madness of his revenge obsessing him,' he 'in accursed minutes, with passion continues on his way':[48]

> Thither full fraught with mischievous revenge,
> Accurst, and in a cursed hour, he hies. (II. ll 1055–6)

Thus, Book III in the Russian adaptation opens with Satan's flight through the firmament until he reaches the Sun, 'that place from where the huge luminary spreads out afar the light of his days.'[49] Here, rather inconsistently, the encounter with Uriel is renewed, after which there is some attempt to follow Stroganov-Milton's description of the cosmos, and of the perspective that greets Satan as he

> Looks down with wonder at the sudden view
> Of all this World at once ...(III. ll 542–3)

Even more interesting is the Russian reference to a 'starcounter,' ie, Galileo, to whom Milton alludes in *Paradise Lost*. But the English poet's meaning is changed to correspond to the Devil of popular fantasy. In the original, Satan's unforgettable flight through space concludes with his descent:

> There lands the Fiend, a spot like which perhaps
> Astronomer in the sun's lucent orb
> Through his glazed optic tube yet never saw. (III. ll 587–90)

In the Russian the meaning of the last three lines is transformed to say that by landing on the sun 'the Prince of Darkness ... perpetrated a spot such as was never perhaps seen by a single starcounter through his looking tube.'[50]

The rest of Book III, however, is more or less faithful to Milton's intention. Uriel is shown fooled by the guile of Satan, whose professed desire to see

Paradise and the creatures God has created is presented as a token of reverence to the Almighty. The Russian ends with:

> Satan bowing low,
> As to superior spirits is wont in Heaven,
> Where honor due and reverence none neglects,
> Took leave ...(III. ll 736–9)

ie, 'Satan bowed low before the great Archangel according to the custom ordained between the spirits of Heaven.'[51]

With Books IV and V Satan's goal is half attained. He has found the Garden of Eden, and although he encounters trouble entering it, once inside, armed with the knowledge he has overheard concerning the forbidden fruit, he seems assured of success. All that remains for the Russian variant to reach its climax is the seduction of Eve and her punishment. In this, of course, it duplicates the structure of the original, but, with the omission of Books VI, VII, and most of Book VIII, that climax is reached sooner. For in the Russian Satan still retains his central place in the narrative after he alights on the Tree of Knowledge, whereas in *Paradise Lost* his shadow becomes less threatening with Raphael's long account of the battle in the heavens, the creation, and the explanation of the workings of the universe.

Book IX is the longest in the Barsov manuscript (as it is in the original). Satan returns by night to Paradise, enters into the serpent, and, with Eve separating herself from Adam, all is set for the wreaking of Satan's vengeance: Eve's seduction and Adam's connivance at the outcome. This part of the Russian text, as already noted, is free of the misunderstandings and errors of the earlier Stroganov-derived sections; but it would be implausible to assume that all the copyist had to do was to transcribe Book IX from the Amvrosii version of 1780 to make a coherent narrative. For in Stroganov's translation, as in Dupré's, Satan's re-entry into the Garden of Eden is preceded by a digression (close to fifty lines in the original poem) in which Milton appeals yet again to his Heavenly Muse.

The intent of this important digression will be discussed in the next chapter. The point that needs to be stressed here is that in Book IX and the following section (all of which are taken either from the published edition of *Paradise Lost* or from a copy thereof) what is omitted corresponds to the same principles of selection as in the earlier parts of the Barsov manuscript. Within the extracts chosen for inclusion in the manuscript, however, there are emendations and minor changes of a kind that make it impossible to ascertain whether it was the printed source that the copyist had before him or another manuscript.

What is certain is that the Russian narrative as resumed in Book IX is wholly consistent with the previous story extracted from the Stroganov translation. Satan returns to Paradise, 'in meditated fraud and malice, bent / On man's destruction ...' (IX. ll 56–7), and the Barsov manuscript then skips to his famous plaint as he beholds the idyll he is about to destroy:

> O Earth, how like to Heaven, if not preferred
> More justly, seat worthier of gods, as built
> With second thoughts, reforming what was old! (IX. ll 99–101)

O zemlia! koliko ty podobna nebesam, est'li tokmo eshche nepredpochtenneishee prebyvanie ... zrelishche bogov! Desnitsa sozdatelia bezsomneniia [*sic*] obogatila tebia bolshe [*sic*] prepokhodneishikh del svoikh ...[52]

What follows is a skilful précis of Eve's and Adam's exchanges before she goes off by herself:

> O much deceived, and failing, hapless Eve
> Of thy presumed return! event perverse! (IX. ll 404–5)[53]

And the Russian narrative then describes Satan's unwitting admiration of Eve before delivering the speech that spells her doom:[54] Her reply and the scene before the fatal tree are also given in the Russian; and the serpent is then seen slithering off into 'the thick woods' while Eve decides to share the fruit with Adam. Their mutual reprimands, although much reduced in length in the Russian, are also included, but Book IX in the Barsov manuscript ends on a less tragic note than the original. There, it may be recalled, Eve defends herself against Adam's rancour:

> What words have passed thy lips, Adam severe!
> Imput'st thou that to my default, or will
> Or wandering, as thou call'st it, which who knows
> But might as ill have happened thou being by,
> Or to thyself perhaps? (IX. ll 1144–8)

To which Adam replies, incensed, with the lines beginning:

> Is this the love, is this the recompense

> Of mine to thee, ingrateful Eve, expressed
> Immutable when thou wert lost, not I,
> Who might have lived and joyed immortal bliss,
> Yet willingly chose rather death with thee?
> And am I now upbraided, as the cause
> Of thy transgressing? (IX. ll 1163–9)

This entire speech is left out, presumably because the exchange to which it refers is also omitted. Instead, the Russian ends rather more positively with Adam reluctant to share Eve's thoughts of death: 'his elevated soul comforted him with better hopes.'[55]

These sanguine words, the only ones invented by the copyist or his predecessor(s), are not matched by the conclusion of the final book in the Barsov manuscript, which ends like the original: 'and holding each other by the hand they went their way with quiet and unsure steps through the solitary fields of Eden.'[56] But enough has been said about the similarity between Book IX of the Barsov manuscript and Amvrosii's text to indicate that their aim is the same as the one underlying the reduction of the earlier parts of the 'povest': ie, to tell a good story, which Satan dominates until the appearance of Adam and Eve in Book IX.

After that there was apparently little in *Paradise Lost* that interested the Russian authors of the Barsov manuscript, since the substance of Books XI and XII (Christ's intercession on Adam and Eve's behalf before God and Michael's revelation of the future in store for them) are reduced to a mere five and a half pages. But that the Russian narrative, as it stands, manages to be both poignant and moving cannot be denied. And if the view here advanced concerning the origins of the Barsov manuscript is confirmed by the recovery of intermediate copies, it may be possible to see in what stages this Russian 'novelization' of *Paradise Lost* took shape.

The light that this would shed on the Russian narrative tradition (the strength of which in the eighteenth century should not be measured by the relative immaturity of the formal literature) might be less important than what it tells us about the relationship of the epic and the novel. In England the novel succeeds the epic. *Paradise Lost* paves the way for the transition. In the Russian context, the epic and the novel are born in the same period, and *Paradise Lost* seems to cut across both lines of development.

THREE

Monks and 'Pocket Poets': Publication

> 'It is true [Milton] includes in some places excesses and mistakes; but they, in comparison with the perfections, would be pardonable and endurable, for they are not noticeable at all; if he had not greater and more evident blunders.'
> Amvrosii, archbishop of Ekaterinoslav (from the preface to the 1780 edition of *Paradise Lost*)

Vasilii Petrov (1736–99) was not necessarily more widely read in Russia than Ivan Vladykin, whose prolific compositions were bought by common people, but he was better known in the circles that counted, and he wrote in the refined style St Petersburg literati valued. His social connections and superior talent provided Petrov with the patronage that Vladykin's fulsome odes to Catherine the Great and her heir-apparent had failed to obtain. And it was Petrov who reaped the honour of being the first Russian poet to publish a translation – albeit an incomplete one – of *Paradise Lost*.[1]

Before Vasilii Petrov turned to Milton, he too had already dispensed more than his due of poetic eulogies to the Empress and some of her most eminent favourites, including Prince Potemkin and Grigorii Grigor'evich Orlov, one of the formidable brothers whose criminal boldness had put her on the throne. Dmitriev, the same authority who had mistaken Vladykin's *Paradise Lost and Regained* for Milton's original, would suggest in retrospect that Petrov's odes were 'worthy of being placed between those of Lomonosov and Derzhavin,' which is high praise indeed.[2] He is less kind about Petrov's translation of the *Aeneid*, although Maikov discerned in it proof of the power of the Russian language.[3]

But on the poet's own admission he abandoned it in favour of *Paradise Lost*: 'Bored by the rhymes in Virgil, I am resting with the prose in Milton.

And where can I more decorously drown the vanities of this world that burden my mortal self than in Milton's Hell? It is more agreeable to wander with this Bard in nether regions than with others in Elysium.'[4] How exactly he discovered Milton Petrov does not say. His predecessor Luka Sichkarev, who also knew English, had come across Adam's eulogy in an essay in the *Tatler* on dreams.[5] Petrov seems to have discovered *Paradise Lost* in the course of the three years he spent in England, but while the circumstances are not recorded, the chain of happy accidents that led to his sojourn there are known.

The first of these concerned a 'carousel' erected in the Russian capital on the fourth anniversary of Catherine's accession. The two Orlov brothers who had enabled her to seize power – Grigorii, her favourite, and Aleksei, one of the murderers of her husband – both prided themselves on their skill as horsemen. To please them the Empress built an equestran ring in the palace grounds in St Petersburg. At the behest of Prince Petr Ivanovich Repnin – to whom Petrov would dedicate his translation of *Paradise Lost* in gratitude for the gesture that sparked his literary career – the poet was asked to compose an ode on this, the Empress's carousel.[6]

Catherine was so delighted by the result that other commissions soon followed, and Petrov became – as he called himself – 'the Empress's bard,' her pocket poet. His swift celebrity and imperial favour irked N.I. Novikov, who wrote that before being compared to Lomonosov Petrov would have to come up with 'some major work, and only after that would it be appropriate to say whether he will be a second Lomonosov or remain only Petrov.'[7] The odes that Vasilii Petrov found himself writing – on Catherine's Legislative Commission, on the victories of her armies over the Turks and Swedes, on the 'unification' of Poland with Russia, and so on – are not in fact very different in form from those of some of his illustrious predecessors, whom at first he imitated. One outcome of Catherine's bounty was Petrov's appointment in 1768 as translator to her privy cabinet, a duty he shared with a more occasional obligation as reader royal.

Petrov's family background – clerical and poor – had not prepared the poet for such heights, but he had shone as a student at the Moscow Theological Academy, which provided him with mastery of Greek, Latin, Hebrew, and 'modern languages.' English was probably not among these, for according to Jason – as Petrov called his son – once settled in London his father 'soon learnt English ... and acquired the friendship of learned Britons, who had him sit for a portrait' (see Figure 2).[8]

Petrov's impressions of Georgian England, where he arrived in 1772, are reflected in the poems he wrote for his friends in Moscow and St Petersburg.[9] They are not as informative as N.M. Karamzin's letters in prose, which, although written somewhat later, convey more vividly what it meant to a literate Russian to go abroad before the guillotine transformed national and political stereotypes. In England, it seemed to Karamzin, more people had died as a result of rebellion and civil disturbances of all kinds than in any other country in the world: 'Here Catholics killed reformers, reformers – Catholics, royalists – republicans, republicans – royalists; here there was more than just one French revolution. How many benevolent patriots, ministers, and royal favourites were beheaded! What frenzy of the heart! What turmoil of the mind! ... Who can love the English after reading their history? What parliaments! The Roman senate at the time of Caligula was no worse than theirs.'[10] Karamzin thought that after Shakespeare, Milton, Gay, and Pope, the Muses had temporarily abandoned the banks of the Thames. Both Gay and Pope had long been dead when Petrov arrived in London, but it has been suggested that much of the verse he wrote thereafter was influenced by the latter.[11] According to his son, Petrov did his translation of *Paradise Lost* while in England. Indeed, there had been so many editions of Milton since the middle of the eighteenth century that it is difficult to see how anyone interested in English literature could avoid being aware of him.[12] The stature of his fame is reflected in the diary of Nikita Aleksandrovich Demidov, who arrived in London in the same year as Petrov. After visiting Westminster Abbey, he noted that Milton shared with Isaac Newton the glory of being England's greatest 'adornment.'[13] Thomas Warton, the first volume of whose *History of English Poetry* came out in 1774, would have agreed: Dr Johnson, then compiling his *Lives of the Poets*, would not.

That year Petrov received an order from the Empress to come home. After a tour of France, Italy, and Germany with the bigamous Duchess of Kingston,[14] the poet returned to England and then set off for Russia to immerse himself further 'in the Hell' of Milton's epic. Why did he conclude his translation with the third book? There is a suggestion that Petrov felt he needed to be cautious – as the fate of Stroganov's old translation indicated – in dealing with Milton's faith and politics. These are dismissed with an unconvincing shrug on the ground that 'it was unnecessary to elaborate upon this writer in any detail.'[15] Since no biography of Milton had yet been published in Russian, such reasoning in the introduction to the first printed translation of his work is obviously suspect.

Only three years after the publication of Petrov's translation in 1777[16] a new version appeared in St Petersburg that indicates what objections Petrov had to fear:

It is true [Milton] includes in some places excesses and mistakes; but they, in comparison with the perfections, would be pardonable and endurable, for they are not noticeable to all; if he had not greater and more evident blunders. To warn the reader, I shall mention them here briefly, and especially those pertaining to the law, and (1) he nowhere says that the world was made from nothing; but he always assumes some substance, which was before creation; (2) in Book Four he introduces marriage into Paradise; but this is asserted by only a few, and those Jewish rabbis; but the Church teaches the opposite on the basis of Genesis iv, 1. The fact that he approves this action with such fervour and censures those who reject it as something unlawful is not surprising, for he was thrice married, yet he blames only heretics of that kind which Paul predicts in I Timothy, iv; (3) in Book Five, where Adam excuses himself to the Angel for the poorness of the cooking and the latter accepts, to show that he can eat this food too, and turn it into his own being, etc., in this book, I say, the writer places in the mouth of the Angel the language of the materialist. And these are his most important defects, to which I shall add the last – although not so evident, yet perhaps the greatest – and that is, that he maintained the Arian heresy ...[17]

These comments by Amvrosii, prefect of the Moscow Academy and later archbishop of Ekaterinoslav, may indeed explain why Petrov left his translation unfinished. The first two books of *Paradise Lost*, which deal with Satan's rebellion, his fall into Hell, and the plot to seek revenge against God, do raise some theological problems. In the third book, in which man's transgression is foretold, Milton with his discussion of free will skates over far more dubious ice; but although the tone of Satan's earlier speeches may seem blasphemous and the attacks against the 'embryos and idiots' of the church in Book III sacrilegious, there are no places in it that Orthodoxy held demonstrably heretical. Petrov could therefore bury any qualms he had by concluding his translation with Satan's escape from Hell and his stunningly completed flight through the firmament 'to behold the new creation' from the top of Mount Niphates.

In stopping there the Russian poet could also claim a certain artistic unity for his translation without risking censure by dipping into the troubled waters of sex in Paradise in Book IV. But Petrov's unfinished effort probably prompted another translation, one that has remained virtually unheeded to this day.

Its author, Mariya Vasil'evna Khrapovitskaya, belonged to a talented literary family, and she herself represented a new phenomenon that appeared on Russian soil only in the Catherinian era – the literary polyglot bred under the inspiring tutelage of the Empress and the formidable Dashkova. If these two energetic representatives of their sex captured or bought the applause of celebrated correspondents abroad, the labours of half a dozen other literary women (Sumarokova-Kniazhnina, Kamenskaya-Rzhevskaya, Veliasheva-

Volyntseva, Rumskaya-Korsakova-Zubova, E.A. Dolgorukova, and Kheraskova) were admired at home for following the Empress's and Dashkova's literary example by diligent effort. Khrapovitskaya belonged to this Pleiad of female writers and translators as a linguist, being perhaps the most accomplished of them all. For she was fluent in French – and translated some of Kheraskov's verse into that language – as well as Italian and German, while the quality of her translation of Milton proves that she mastered English too.

The sole surviving likeness (see Figure 6) shows a sensitive face. Mariya was born in 1752, her father being Vasilii Ivanovich Khrapovitsky, a minor denizen of the court of Empress Elisabeth Petrovna, who ennobled him in 1746.[18] Her older brother, Aleksandr Vasil'evich, the well-known dramatist and author of a famous 'Diary,'[19] was state-secretary to Catherine from 1783 to 1793. Before his political career began he devoted much time to the tutoring of his sister, whose main difficulty – we are told – lay in mastering the rules of Russian grammar, to which she was introduced only after her baptism in foreign tongues.[20] In Russian she had the same teacher as Radishchev, and she is credited with turning Petrarch's sonnets into Russian verse as well as with writing several of the stanzas for one of Aleksandr Vasil'evich's tragedies. Together with him she participated in Sumarokov's *This and That* (*I to i sio*), as well as some of the oppositional journals associated with Novikov. Her younger brother, Mikhail Vasil'evich, also became a poet, and so did her nephew (N.V. Sushkov). She translated part of Young's *Night Thoughts* as early as 1772, possibly her first translation of English poetry, but her earliest ambitious translations (from the French) appeared in 1777 and 1778, some time after her marriage to the governor of Simbirsk.[21] It is perhaps shortly thereafter that she began her translation of *Paradise Lost*.

The one known manuscript copy, which is not in the author's hand, is of later vintage.[22] It breaks off with the beginning of Book II, but in the absence of any other evidence, this may be construed as a clue to the date of the translation's original composition. For if Khrapovitskaya set out with the intention of doing a complete translation of *Paradise Lost* after the publication of Petrov's edition in 1777, then the appearance of Amvrosii's new version in 1780 would have made her effort seem superfluous.

If this conjecture is correct, the timing of Amvrosii's translation was unfortunate, because Khrapovitskaya's version – so far as it goes – is not only the most accurate but also the most readable of all Russian translations of *Paradise Lost*, published or unpublished, that were attempted in the eighteenth century. Using Thomas Newton's edition of Milton's work,[23] with its annotations and scholarly remarks, her translation is meticulously faithful to the original, without Petrov's error of trying to imitate in prose the phrasing that gave Milton's blank verse its peculiar character. She retained the Church-Slavonic diction he had used in order to match Milton's sublimity, but her vocabulary is less artificial and she discarded the long periods and laboured paragraphs Petrov used to render the effect of Miltonic punctuation.[24]

Whether Mariya Khrapovitskaya's translation was prompted by other considerations than her perception of Petrov's shortcomings it is impossible to say. Her exceptional literary talents attracted the attention of the Empress after Catherine's favourite, Count Kirill Grigor'evich Razumovsky, told her how Mariya had begun 'to sing in rhyme,' and 'this sufficed to bring Khrapovitskaya an invitation to Court, to encourage her even more in her passion for writing verse, to make her translate and publish in the journals of the time.'[25] If this was indeed so, the date of her début in St Petersburg literary circles remains to be established, as well as the identity of some of her literary friends. It would be interesting to learn, for instance, when she discovered – if she did – that Amvrosii was engaged on the same poetic enterprise.

As it is, most of the credit for translating Milton's major epic into Russian is customarily given to Amvrosii Serebrennikov. In pre-revolutionary and post-revolutionary encyclopaedias, literary manuals, and histories of the period, Stroganov's priority is rarely mentioned and Mariya Khrapovitskaya's never.[26] Amvrosii does indeed deserve some plaudit for seeing a 'complete' translation into print, but he knew no English; and what he achieved – for there was no other translation in the eighteenth century from 'modern' poetry into Russian of comparable stature – was really made possible by his predecessors. Although Amvrosii never reveals the source of his translation – he says simply that it was taken 'from the French' – it is clear from the text itself that he used both Petrov's and Stroganov's as a crib. That he was also familiar with Dupré's version is equally certain. The final result, however, represents more an improvement on the labour of others rather than the ground-breaking work with which Amvrosii is usually credited.

What is intriguing about Amvrosii's translation, apart from its style, is the author's ecclesiastical position and the fact that he should have undertaken it at all despite the heresies (as we have seen) that he perceived in Milton's poem. This is to be explained perhaps by the character of the man and of his ties with the Catherinian court. Amvrosii's literary reputation was not based entirely on *Paradise Lost*. He gained renown for the eloquence of his sermons and orations, especially for the eulogy he composed on the death of Prince Potemkin in 1791, which came to be regarded as a model of its kind.[27] Amvrosii, which is the name he adopted on becoming a monk, was born in 1745 of a deacon's family, and like Petrov he owed his education to the

Moscow Theological Academy. There his ability was soon recognized, and he began a quick ascent through the hierarchy of the church after forming a lasting friendship with Platon, archimandrite of the Holy Trinity – St George monastery, at whose seminary Amvrosii taught. It is to him that Amvrosii dedicated later editions of *Poteriannyi rai*. Since Platon was a member of the Holy Synod, which often had the final word on what was published, the dedication was not necessarily wholly disinterested.

In 1778, probably before he began the translation, Amvrosii was appointed prefect of the Theological Academy. Offered a bishopric in 1784, he became archbishop of Ekaterinoslav two years later. He had long enjoyed the benevolent disposition of the Empress, whose interest in Amvrosii was awakened by a sermon he had delivered several years earlier on her name-day. He also acquired the protection of Prince Potemkin, whose mysticism and philosophical interests brought the two men together. It is Potemkin who allegedly introduced Amvrosii to court at the very moment when the prince himself professed to harbour monastic ambitions. He enjoyed conversing with Amvrosii, and the latter, in his capacity as exarch of Moldavia-Wallachia, accompanied Potemkin on the campaigns that brought victorious imperial armies into the Tauride. Amvrosii survived his noble patron by only a year, but in his short life he also left a notable mark on the history of Russian literary usage.

The debate over language and the extent to which Church-Slavonic and the vernacular should be employed in poetry and prose, which as we have seen had been opened by Trediakovsky and Lomonosov, had not abated.[28] Amvrosii, whose election to Dashkova's Russian Academy compelled him to face the problem in discussion with its members, decided to bring Lomonosov's *Rhetoric* up to date by compiling his own 'short guide' on the subject.[29] Here he tended to follow the lead of Lomonosov, whom he admired; but Amvrosii did introduce new examples of his own to illustrate rhetoric as practised by Cicero, Lucian, Erasmus, Sumarokov, and so on. He was also forced to consider the relevance of Trediakovsky's distillation of classical wisdom on the subject, more especially that of Cicero's disciple Quintilian, whose *Institutio Oratoria* was designed to stem the current of popular taste that found its expression in what came to be called silver Latin.

French neoclassical theoreticians took over Quintilian's anti-populist sentiments, the most influential of these being probably the Baron Vaugelas (1585–1650), because of the esteem in which he was held by Boileau. Their relevance to Russian usage was derived from the parallel that Amvrosii and his contemporaries discerned between the superior parlance of Versailles ('la partie la plus saine de la Cour') and the illegitimate jargon of the masses. The best style as Amvrosii defined it, consisted of both Russian and Church-Slavonic vocabulary, the essential purity of which could be maintained only by imitating the language 'used in the important works of our best writers ... and the spoken idiom and expressions approved by all ... *in the capital cities in general converse by the best kind of people.*'[30]

Amorphous as this solution to the insistent problem facing eighteenth-century writers may seem, Amvrosii's contribution was considered a significant step forward, particularly in the practical directions his manual offered. He rejected the contemporary equivalent of modern slang, as well as rustic expressions (of the kind that jar the elevated tone of Church-Slavonic in Stroganov's manuscript translation of *Paradise Lost*). The other grave error to avoid, it seemed to him, was excessive use of neologisms and grammatical constructions alien to the Russian language: 'There is nothing more awful than reading some of the translations ... in which, owing to the ignorance of the translators, Russian is invested with expressions from foreign languages quite contrary to the rules of grammar. Incomprehensible expressions are introduced, which are either most ancient, new fangled ["novomyshleny"], used in quite a different sense from the original or are wholly borrowed from foreign languages.'[31]

All this Amvrosii tried to avoid in his translation of Milton, to whom he was drawn for reasons still of interest today because they represent the earliest published appreciation by a Russian writer of the English poet:

It is enough to say in his praise that having commenced this poem at that age when the imagination, enriched by long experience, acts with the greatest fervour, he used all his knowledge even to excess and all his art in its adornment. Zealous reading of the Holy Scriptures, and especially Isaiah, the Prophet, gave him the highest thoughts. For this cause, it is filled with inimitable beauties, which seem not so much poetical as stamped out of the Word of God. Besides this, he loved of the Greek writers Homer especially and of the Latin the Metamorphoses of Ovid. All this, being united with a poetic spirit about which he spoke in the beginning of the Seventh Book, when he mentions some deity (for he actually believed in its inspiration), all this, I say, being united, poured out that splendour, power and attractiveness in all parts of his poem, which are rarely visible in other works of this kind. His Judgments are deep, his thoughts keen, his similes great, his passions blazing, his descriptions living. For if he takes us to heaven, we seem to see the holy mountain, lighted with glory; we see the Throne of the Eternal and His Son sitting on His right hand; we hear their consultations, we see the gathering of all the angelic powers, their evening joy; we see the rebellious spirits, gliding away quietly at dawn to the north; we see the war, the terrible battle, then the coming of the Messiah, His thousands of lightnings flying from all sides on his enemies; we see the opened heavens, the terrible abyss and the falling headlong of the demoniac hosts. If we go down to Hell, he describes the deeds of the outcasts, their councils, their schemes and different seats; we seem, as it were, ourselves, fearing to move among them. If he shows us the flying Satan, if he depicts the site of Paradise, the appearance and condition of our ancestors, their conversations, their prayers, conversations with the Angels, their crimes and condemnation, all this is so touching and living that, as we read, we think that we are there. Finally an Angel comes to cast them out. That is a sad spectacle, from which the reader, touched with pity, would without doubt turn away his eyes, if Milton had not known how to soften the cruelty of this evil fate. He presents the Angel talking as a friend to our Forefather and then without any sternness taking them both by the hand out of Paradise, but consoled and walking through the fields of Eden, so that it seems as if we are following them further with our gaze. In a word, everywhere we see beauty, grandeur and splendour.

How much of this comes across in Amvrosii's translation? French was not taught at Russian theological seminaries at the time that Amvrosii was educated, and it is said that he picked up the language himself rather late in life, his translation 'from the French' of *Paradise Lost* sometimes being cited as evidence of this.[32] One of the excellent qualities of his version is that it does not read like a translation – hence, perhaps, its popularity and longevity despite later rivals. In Amvrosii's text much of Stroganov's Church-Slavonic lexicon has been polished or brought up to date.[33] Yet contemporaries were probably aware that his was not an independent translation in the true sense.

Indeed, it is quite possible that this is what the reviewer meant to convey when he placed extracts from Stroganov's, Petrov's, and Amvrosii's translations side by side in the *St. Petersburg Messenger* in 1780.[34] Not that this necessarily means that Vasilii Grigor'evich Ruban, the poet and historian who wrote the review, intended to charge Amvrosii with plagiarism. Such a charge could not in any case be lightly levelled against a man with Amvrosii's connections. Besides, at that stage in the evolution of Russian letters such matters were not regarded with the gravity ascribed to them in the nineteenth century.[35]

On the whole Amvrosii was more at ease (as Stroganov had been) with the more lyrical sections of *Paradise Lost* than, for instance, with the abstract terminology Raphael uses in describing Milton's cosmology, for which the appropriate Russian vocabulary was still volatile. Amvrosii's contemporaries, it would seem, were often taken aback by Milton's physical descriptions of the love between Adam and Eve:

> nor turned, I ween
> Adam from his fair spouse, nor Eve the rites

Mysterious of connubial Love refused;
Whatever Hypocrites austerely talk
Of purity and place and innocence,
Defaming as impure what God declares
Pure, and commands to some, leaves free to all. (IV. ll 741–7)

This, as has often been pointed out, is still the Milton of the divorce pamphlets: and Amvrosii's ironical reference to the poet's three wives in the introduction suggests what kind of impression passages such as these made on the Russian monk. Indeed, the historian of the Russian Academy congratulates Amvrosii for not removing them from his translation: 'he dealt with [this matter] with the greatest respect, without any intolerance or fanaticism, even retaining much that was contrary to commonly held beliefs. Thus he conveys the poetic picture of conjugal love, not destroying those lines which are aimed directly against celibacy and monasticism.'[36]

Congratulations were perhaps in order. In Poland, where the first translation of *Paradise Lost* appeared in 1791, the description of Adam and Eve's naked beauty was relegated, we are told, to the library Ossilineum at Lwow. There it was consigned to 'the most indecent collection of the eighteenth-century obscenities copied by a Polish amateur.'[37]

Amvrosii was also more conscientious in another respect. Father Jacek Przybylski (1756–1819), who was responsible for the rhymed *Paradise Lost* of 1791, 'embellished' his translation with numerous additions of his own: and at least one eminent Polish critic is sorry it was ever made.[38] Amvrosii resisted such temptations, and although in referring to Milton's Arian heresy in his introduction he hinted darkly that 'such expressions and some other passages have been changed,' in actual fact the emendations are few. Thus, the eating habits of the angels in Book V are altered to accommodate materialist hunters, but there are no other notable departures from Stroganov and Dupré, not even in Book XI where the 'outward rites and specious forms' of popery are excoriated.

As an Orthodox monk Amvrosii may, of course, have found such vituperative condemnations of Rome to his taste; in Poland translators of Milton, whose vogue there did not really begin until the beginning of the nineteenth century, were differently placed. Amvrosii's task in steering *Paradise Lost* past censors was not necessarily easier, however. As the prefect of the Moscow Theological Academy well knew, the Holy Synod had prevented several works from being published in Cyrillic whose theological and other shortcomings were perceived to be less grave than Milton's. Thus, Amvrosii's namesake in the Holy Synod at the end of Empress Elisabeth's reign had mutilated a translation of the *Essay on Man* on the ground of its 'naturalism.' Even if the charge were true, the grounds on which *Paradise Lost* could be proscribed, as its publishing history on the continent demonstrated, were far more visible than Pope's innocent poetization of Bolingbroke-Newton.[39] And of these the most difficult to conceal were the facts of Milton's political engagement.

Amvrosii, whose manual on rhetoric shows that he was liberal enough to suggest to his readers that the arguments for and against republicanism should be carefully weighed, obviously understood this. He therefore followed Petrov's tactic of saying virtually nothing about Milton's biography. His introduction to *Poteriannyi rai* is almost as cryptic on the matter as Petrov's: 'I do not intend to describe [Milton's] life in detail; for that would take time and be of little use.'[40] Indeed, was there 'any use' in describing the English poet's conduct in the Civil War at a time when Russian society had just witnessed an even larger social upheaval with the Pugachev Rebellion? Amvrosii cleverly side-stepped the issue, and it would be left to later writers to come to terms with the embarrassing legacy of the Good Old Cause – increasingly embarrassing in the climate of growing political reaction after Pugachev's insurrection.

Ruban, himself a translator and an able linguist who knew Turkish as well as Latin and who served for a while as Potemkin's secretary, probably realized all this. In his review of 1780 he may have wished to draw attention to such a glaring omission in Vasilii Petrov's and Amvrosii's editions of *Paradise Lost* by subtly recalling the existence of an earlier translation by 'Count Aleksandr Sergeevich [sic] Stroganov.'[41] Thus, Ruban got hold of a manuscript belonging to Prince P.N. Trubetskoi, and published the Stroganov translation of Elijah Fenton's *Life* of Milton in the *St. Petersburg Messenger*.[42]

In this circuitous fashion the less palatable facts of Milton's biography found their way into Russia for the first time in cold print. Thus Vasilii Petrov's and Amvrosii's qualms were overcome. Ruban's ploy in publishing the *Zhizn'* of Milton did not affect the fate of Amvrosii's translation, although one of the versions from which the Archbishop had cribbed remained, for all its archaisms, superior in another respect. Stroganov's notes supplied the reader with the background any close reading of Milton's work requires.

Amvrosii retained very few of these notes. Could this partly explain why copies of the manuscript translation continued to be made even after the appearance in print of *Poteriannyi rai*?[43] Another reason is that the book trade was still feebly developed in the Russian provinces, and to some places – such as Archangel[44] – to which late copies of the Stroganov-Milton may be traced, news of the publication of *Paradise Lost* would have been slow in coming.

The linguistic and social differentiation of the reading public at the end of the eighteenth century must also be taken into account. In the popular Barsov 'novelization' of *Paradise Lost*, as we have seen, publication of the Amvrosii edition did not prevent the transcription of passages and their 'splicing' with extracts from the more archaic language of the Stroganov-Milton.[45] But the Archbishop did not apparently have to confront any of the problems that had probably prevented the earlier version from being printed. Camouflaged by the protection its author received from court and church, the first 'complete' edition of *Paradise Lost* went out into the world with the best possible prospects.

It was published by N.I. Novikov, the most active representative of the Russian Enlightenment, whose increasing preoccupation with religious themes did not shield him from harassment and persecution by Catherine.[46] Yet this had no apparent effect on *Poteriannyi rai*, which came out with a different publisher in 1785, 1795, 1803, and then again as late as 1860, by which time it had seen seven editions.[47] By then more 'modern' translations gave it the same period flavour that the appearance of Amvrosii's translation had bestowed on the manuscript versions.

The most interesting of the subsequent editions, however, turned out to be that of 1803, for this was published together with the Russian translation of *Paradise Regained*. It thus initiated a tradition imitated by dozens and dozens of publishers up to the Russian Revolution. Consequently, *Paradise Regained*, although never as highly appreciated by Russian critics as *Paradise Lost*, became almost equally famous. Indeed, it first appeared in Russian translation before the Amvrosii-Milton – in 1778.

PARADISE REGAINED AND OTHER POEMS

Ivan Greshishchev, the author of Russia's first translation of *Paradise Regained*, which was published by the press of Moscow University (see Figure 4), enjoys no other title to fame except the erroneous attribution to him by Professor W.R. Parker of the first Russian translation of *Paradise Lost*.[48] This Greshishchev would probably not have dared to attempt, for he had neither the protection Vasilii Petrov and Amvrosii enjoyed nor their literary experience. Greshishchev knew no English. For his translation, as is stated on the title page, he turned to a French version. There is no other indication of its provenance, but comparison of the Russian text with the Abbé Mareuil's *Paradis reconquis* makes it clear that this is its source.

Mareuil, a Jesuit and a contemporary of Dupré de Saint-Maur, had been very critical of *Paradise Lost* when the latter's translation appeared: 'Depuis longtemps les scrupules n'ont guère lieu en Angleterre, surtout en fait de Religion. Ainsi je conçois que les sectaires du pays sont charmés de voir l'Archange Raphaël travesti en Prédicant débiter à Adam la doctrine de Calvin sur la justice imputative et la Foi justifiante, insinuer adroitement les calomnies des Puritains contre l'Eglise romaine.'[49] Another grave fault was the materialism Mareuil discerned in Milton's poem, especially in Book v where Raphael explains the eating habits of the angels (ll 482–7): 'Ainsi l'âme de l'homme n'est qu'un composé lumineux des esprits volatiles qu'exhalent les fleurs et les fruits de la terre.'[50] And the lines in which Raphael reassures Adam that

> Time may come when men
> With angels may participate, and find
> No inconvenient diet, nor too light fare;
> And from these corporal nutriments perhaps
> Your bodies may at last turn all to spirit,
> Improved by tract of time, and winged ascend
> Ethereal, as we, or may at choice
> Here or in heavenly paradises dwell; (v. ll 493–9)

are seen by Mareuil as tacit support of Lucretius, whose atomism had been made popular by a contemporary of Milton, Father Gassendi: 'Ce que nous appelons esprit n'est donc qu'une portion de matière subtilisée et raffinée jusqu'à certains degrés. Le Chaos immense et sans bornes, qui se recule à mesure que le monde se forme, où l'Auteur semble admettre une matière éternelle d'où l'univers est tiré comme par éducation ne peut déplaire aux Lucrèces modernes.'[51] Such criticisms were echoed – as we have seen – in the introduction to the full Russian translation of *Paradise Lost*. Indeed, Amvrosii may well have learnt of them from the French Jesuit, because Mareuil's critique was inserted into the preface of his *Paradis reconquis*. In fact, the French preface – expanded in subsequent editions to six 'lettres critiques' – anticipates the Russian introduction to *Paradise Lost* in 1780: Milton's errors are boldly stated with the intent of disarming potential critics. At the same time Mareuil's strategy was more consistent than the Russian monk's because he chose to draw a sharp but convenient distinction between the Milton of *Paradise Lost* and the author of *Paradise Regained*. Citing Elijah Fenton's testimony that Milton preferred the latter to his great epic, Mareuil further justifies his own translation by interpreting the reasons for Milton's preference:

Peut être goûtait-il moins alors cette espèce de merveilleux outré que la belle nature et le bon sens désavouent, et qui bien loin de surprendre agréablement la raison, la jette dans un étonnement d'autant plus révoltant pour elle n'y voit nulle vraisemblance. Ce merveilleux grotesque peut divertir dans les peintures d'un Callot, dans le *Gargantua* d'un Rabelais, mais dans une épopée il trouve peu d'admirateurs. Peut-être l'Homère anglais avait-il reconnu ... qu'il ne convenait pas à un poète chrétien de présenter des Anges ou des idées païennes dans une poésie sainte ...[52]

Above all, it seemed to Mareuil that in *Paradise Regained* 'religion was better served than in Paradise Lost.'

All this may account for the fact that *Paradise Regained* was published in Russia prior to the 'complete' version of *Paradise Lost*. Which edition of Mareuil's *Paradis reconquis* Greshishchev used we cannot be certain: the translation was well received in France and there were several printings before 1778. The 'lettres critiques' appended by Mareuil to the text of his version would have made it evident to Ivan Greshishchev that he faced no risk of censure by making a Russian translation of *Paradise Regained*. But there is no introduction of any kind to the Russian text, or even a dedication. Perhaps Greshishchev reasoned that the charges commonly levelled at Milton were best left to Amvrosii to sort out.

Greshishchev's only addition to the body of the French text are summaries of the argument to each of the four books of *Paradise Regained*. Milton had not found it necessary to add these, although he did make this concession to readers on his publisher's suggestion after the first edition of *Paradise Lost*. This means that Greshishchev had almost certainly seen French translations of this poem, in which the same practice was adopted, as it was by Stroganov in *Pogublennyi Rai* (which Greshishchev would probably have read too).

Unfortunately, little has come down to us about Greshishchev and still less about the circumstances that may have prompted him to undertake his translation. Novikov, writing in the following year, describes him as a student of philosophy 'who wrote poems, of which one was published in Moscow in 1771.'[53] By the time he translated *Paradise Regained,* the student had become a teacher of divinity at his old seminary of the Trinity–St George monastery. This is where Amvrosii had also taught before moving to Moscow as prefect of the Theological Academy. That the two men knew each other can then be assumed; and if so, there may have been some connection between Greshishchev's enterprise and the translation of *Paradise Lost* Amvrosii presumably began not long after.

During the eighteenth century *Paradise Regained* did not generally run into the theological and political objections aimed against its predecessor. Even in Russia, where both works were proscribed during the Nikolaevan era, criticism of *Paradise Regained* was less acute, although a common charge was that in it Milton so humanized the figure of Jesus Christ that little remained of his divinity.[54] The subject of the poem was supposedly suggested to the blind poet by the Quaker Thomas Ellwood, who had asked Milton in the autumn of 1665: 'Thou has said much here of *Paradise Lost*, but what hast thou to say of Paradise Found?'[55] According to Ellwood, Milton took up the challenge, and he had personal reasons for doing so. Ellwood, whose Christianity had not been corroded by the deism that invests most eighteenth-century Miltonic imitations, had thought of the heavenly paradise opened to mankind by the sacrifice of the crucifixion, and Milton took this into consideration. But he chose the temptation in the wilderness as the central theme of his poem rather than the passion, the descent into hell, or the resurrection. Here Christ rejected the avenues proposed by Satan, after which only one way remained open – the one that led to Calvary.

Dostoevsky would choose this interpretation of the Gospel text for the best known chapter in *The Brothers Karamazov*. Milton saw it in the same light as Dostoevsky, for the Grand Inquisitor's long speech is anticipated by this question of Satan:

> 'Since neither wealth, nor honor, arms nor arts
> Kingdom nor Empire pleases thee, nor aught
> By me proposed in life contemplative,
> Or active, tended on by glory, or fame,
> What dost thou in this World? ...' (PR IV. ll 368–72)

Christ's response constitutes the moral climax of *Paradise Regained*, but it has none of the action associated in the eighteenth century with heroic verse, and more than one eminent authority refuses to consider the poem a true epic.[56] 'The Messiah,' says Rex Warner, 'goes through the temptations with an effortless confidence which, however admirable, is scarcely dramatic.'[57]

Coleridge did not think this a defect, and if critics today do not on the whole share his verdict that *Paradise Regained* is 'in its kind ... the most perfect poem extant,' it continues to inspire a diversity of judgments.[58] Chateaubriand, whose admiration of *Paradise Lost* knew no bounds, described its sequel as 'une oeuvre de lassitude, quoique calme et belle.'[59] But the erstwhile master of Balliol warns us not to think of some of its lines 'too passively,' and compares the Milton of *Paradise Regained* to Lenin after 1905.[60] Greshishchev is consistently faithful to Mareuil's text. Therefore, any criticism of the Russian translation must also take into account the character of its French source.

Mareuil's translation was considered superior to the earlier one by Chélon de Boismorand, although it begs the kind of question raised by Silhouette then and by Nabokov in our own day. Can any prose version, however accurate, correspond to Milton's blank verse? The narrative line in *Paradise Regained* is a good deal simpler than in its predecessor, but it would seem that the translator's task is especially daunting where Milton's effect depends not on dramatic structure and plot but on the overwhelming beauty and metrical harmony of the words.

Here, for example, is the sequel to the first temptation; during the following night Jesus' hunger engenders a dream that God was feeding him miraculously. Satan appears on the next day and offers a feast. The aridity and desolation of the desert are transformed by a scene that in its opulence and colour has been compared to the most splendid canvas of Poussin[61] – at its shaded centre a table magnificently prepared with meat, game, fish, and laden with rare wines served by 'tall stripling youths':

> distant more
> Under the trees now tripped, now solemn stood
> Nymphs of Diana's train, and Naiades
> With fruits and flowers from Amalthea's horn,
> And ladies of the Hesperides, that seemed
> Fairer than feigned of old, or fabled since
> Of fairy damsels met in forest wide
> By knights of Logres, or of Lyonnesse,
> Lancelot or Pelleas, or Pellenore;
> And all the while harmonious airs were heard
> Of chiming strings or charming pipes, and winds
> Of gentlest gale Arabian odors fanned
> From their soft wings, and Flora's earliest smells. (PR II. ll 353–65)

How much of the magic of these lines comes across in either the French or the Russian translation? Greshishchev punctiliously translates Mareuil's footnotes to the proper names, in which the third book of *Paradise Regained* is especially rich, but needless to say this does nothing to augment the poetry of the original. Nor are the most ornate or exotic verses necessarily the ones that suffer the greatest distortion. Sometimes quite straightforward passages are refracted in French translation and then unwittingly restored in the Russian text to reflect the English more faithfully. Take, for instance, the passage where Jesus is baptized by John the Baptist:

> Now had the great Proclaimer, with a voice
> More awful than the sound of trumpet, cried
> Repentance, and Heaven's kingdom nigh at hand

To all baptized. To his great baptism flocked
With awe the regions round ...(PR I. ll 17–21)

In *Le Paradis reconquis* this becomes: 'Le Précurseur du Messie, d'une voix plus perçante que le son de la trompette, crioit en invitant au Baptême: repentez-vous, *le Royaume de Dieu s'approche*. On accouroit de toutes parts; on l'écoutoit avec respect ...'[62] 'Respect' is not Milton's 'awe': nor, of course, does 'the precursor of the Messiah' correspond to 'the great Proclaimer.' Greshishchev inevitably gets this wrong too, but he comes up with a better equivalent for awe; and, his translation of 'regions' as 'narod' (people or folk) – although it is not the same as Mareuil-Milton's 'parts' – gives the scene a tone that is less formal than the French, and therefore perhaps a shade closer to the mood conveyed by Milton's actual lines: 'Predtecha Messii glasom pronzitel'neishim zvuka trubnago vopiial prizyvaia ko kreshcheniiu: *pokaitesia, priblizhivoisia tsarstvie nebesnoe*. Narod stekalsia otvsiudu, vnimal Emu so blagogoveniem ...' (my emphasis).[63] One advantage Greshishchev enjoyed over the French text was being able to draw on the dignity and majesty of Church-Slavonic: 'priblizhivoisia tsarstvie nebesnoe' rings almost the same note of Miltonic sublimity invoked by the 'great Proclaimer.' Is this not closer to the tone of the original than 'le Royaume de Dieu s'approche?'

Such distinctions do not, however, affect the moral significance of *Paradise Regained*, which both Russian and French readers no doubt found easier to understand than *Paradise Lost* because of its proximity to the New Testament. Yet there were not at any time as many separate editions of *Vozvrashchennyi rai* as of Milton's longer epic. Greshishchev's translation was republished in 1785, 1787, and again in 1803, when it appeared together with Amvrosii's translation of *Paradise Lost* as well as in 1820 and 1828.

By then changes in the literary language, which was moving ever closer to the vernacular, and the continuing decline of Church-Slavonic should have made it seem progressively more archaic to Russian readers. But this apparently was not the case, since Greshishchev's version was still being read in the third decade of the nineteenth century. Proof of this is the publication in 1820 of a new translation of *Paradise Regained* from a 'foreign tongue' that was considered far inferior to Greshishchev's.[64] So unworthy of Milton's genius – 'nezabvennyi Milton' – did this new version seem, that one of Pushkin's teachers, Efim Liutsenko, promptly set about a new translation for which Greshishchev's *Vozvrashchennyi rai* clearly served as the basis.[65]

Its literary life of half a century was therefore impressive, although three decades shorter than that of Amvrosii's *Paradise Lost*. Like the latter, it received almost immediate attention in the form of imitation; but before turning to this aspect of the Miltonian awakening in Russia in the second half of the 1770s, we must consider one other translation of the period.

Between 1777 and 1780 (as we have seen) there was one attempted translation of *Paradise Lost* or *Paradise Regained* every year, and these were soon joined by 'Il Penseroso,' one of the best-known poems in the English language. The translation appeared in the pages of the *St. Petersburg Messenger* in the same year as the publication of Amvrosii's version of *Paradise Lost*, which might suggest that Milton's non-epic verse was beginning to be known to Russian readers too; but of all the prose translations it represents the least successful. Platon Beketov, its author, published it without a commentary, his source being obviously the French version of the Jesuit Pierre de Mareuil, whose objections to Milton's materialism we have already noted.[66]

Mareuil's translation of 'Il Penseroso' was first published together with his translation of *Paradise Regained* in 1730, and both were subsequently included in editions of Dupré's *Le Paradis perdu*.[67] Beketov may thus have learnt of its existence through either Ivan Greshishchev or Amvrosii, although a new French translation of 'Il Pensieroso' – a spelling Ribouville preferred in deference to Lombard usage – came out in 1766.[68] It omits the same lines in the original that Pierre de Mareuil – and Platon Beketov – leave out in their translations, although Ribouville's version is in verse.[69]

Beketov added notes to his prose translation to explain the mythological figures in 'Il Penseroso' but there is no biographical background of any kind on Milton. The Russian translation suffers inevitably from the same defects as Pierre de Mareuil's. Thus, the penultimate couplet –

> Till old experience do attain
> To something like prophetic strain (ll 173–4)

– becomes 'jusqu'à ce qu'une expérience consomée m'ait donné un de Prophète'; while the Russian – 'do tekh por, kak uzhe sozreloe ispytanie pridast mne vid proroka'[70] – is no less pedestrian. There is no Cambridge mist emanating from either the French or the Russian translations; and without the latter's title – 'Il Penseroso or Miltonic Thoughts' ('Mysli Mil'tonovy') – its true source could easily be overlooked.

Not long after Beketov's truncated translation appeared, Luka Sichkarev's earlier extract in verse from *Paradise Lost* was republished,[71] further testifying to the rising interest in Milton's poetry. Nor did the awkwardness of most of these translations inhibit the emergence of Miltonic imitations, which in the Catherinian era were connected – it will be shown – with the Masonic movement.

FOUR

Masonic Devils and the Light Within

'And we shall be not slaves, but Gods and Tsars.'
Satan in Kheraskov's *Universe* (1790)

It is not at all obvious why rationalists of the Enlightenment were so drawn by Milton's passion and intensity. Certainly, there was here none of the perceived mutual affinity of the kind seen in the Victorian deification of the Puritan poet. In the Age of Reason it may rather have been the reverse: the attraction of opposites. This, as has often been pointed out, is what drew the Augustans with their polished ways and elegant infidelities to Milton's soaring imagination and faith. But this cannot account entirely for his appeal to poets in Russia, where natural philosophy and what Peter Gay describes as the pagan side of the Enlightenment had not struck deep roots. The awakening of interest in Milton in the 1770s and 1780s did not necessarily reflect the progress of Enlightenment thought; rather it indicated a reaction against its rationalism by the aristocracy of St Petersburg and Moscow. This may explain why Milton's influence was felt in the second half of the Catherinian era by Freemasons, who brought into their arguments with the once fashionable rationalists or '(Voltaireans' 'Vol'teriantsy)' an unfamiliar conception of good and evil. To them goes the distinction of being the first to introduce Milton's Satan into Russian poetry.

The earliest connection between *Paradise Lost* and a Masonic text of Russian origin seems to be a copy of Stroganov's translation transcribed between 1761 and 1763.[1] Book x of the manuscript is followed by a 'Theological Moral Instruction [.] A Discussion Concerning Adam's Fall.' Now the transgression, it may be recalled, occurs in Book IX; and in its sequel Christ is sent to pass judgment on Adam and Eve. The subject of the 'Moral Instruction' was therefore not arbitrarily chosen. What conclusions did the anonymous moralist draw? The most surprising fact about his sermonizing gloss to *Paradise Lost* is its attitude to Eve. The blame for the fall is laid squarely on Adam. He was unreasonable, and being unreasonable he knew not God. For to know God one must know truth (istina): but truth can only be attained through reason. For faith is born of reason and knowledge. Without them, man cannot be worthy of God's love.[2] And the author then goes on to disclose what 'steps' in the ascending spiral of reason and knowledge must be negotiated before 'entering The Temple of the Lord.'[3] First, man must know himself: and this he cannot achieve until he understands matter and 'all the things in this world that are visible.'[4] Only after this rather challenging assignment, can man stride upward in anticipation of his 'total union by Love with God.'[5]

All this is not, of course, the stuff of which conventional Orthodox preaching was made. The writer's message is clearly inspired by a Masonic source, of which the 'Moral Instruction' may be a tedious echo; but its connection, however slender, with Adam's unsuccessful striving for self-knowledge is obvious too. Nor is the association here between Freemasonry and Milton's poem fortuitous. For, as this chapter will try to show, some of the earliest Russian imitations of it were in fact written by Freemasons. Yet the Masonic movement as it developed in St Petersburg and Moscow was not at first considered incompatible with Orthodoxy, although it did appeal to those disgusted by the Russian clergy's parochialism. Lodges had first been introduced by James Keith, a Jacobite who served as military governor of the Ukraine before leaving the country in 1747.

It was not long before 'the Masonic sect' came under police surveillance, but Peter III appears to have joined it, and in St Petersburg the movement flourished under the aegis of I.P. Elagin, who is, quite incorrectly, sometimes viewed as 'the founder of a special Masonic system, close in its traditions to the original English Freemasonry in its purest form.'[6] In Russia it appealed no doubt to the same pious enthusiasts who on the Continent studied Boehme's *Path to Christ* or Arndt's *On True Christianity*; but is there not an affinity between the millenarianism of Milton's day and the hopes and ecstasy aroused by this type of literature in eighteenth-century Russia? Despite its comforting admixture of deism, as a philosophical and religious movement Freemasonry began to be proscribed even before the French Revolution, when Catherine II's suspicions of secret societies forced the closure of the lodges. Whether it was the mysticism of the Masons and their dabbling in occultism that displeased her or the movement's ties with radical social aspirations is a moot point. Some of its members were political reactionaries, but the movement's lofty goals and philanthropic activities also attracted liberals like Novikov and radicals like Radishchev.

Like N.I. Novikov, Elagin came under the influence of the Encyclopaedists, and his initial dalliance with Freemasonry did nothing to undermine his facile rationalism. As early as the middle of the century, this was in vogue with the fops of the capital who conformed to the stereotype already satirized by Antiokh Kantemir. His modish and superficial Medor had undergone only minor changes at the beginning of Catherine's reign, scepticism and a trendy materialism derived from the *Philosophes* being now added to native crudeness and ignorance. Elagin's change of heart came after meeting 'a certain traveller,' an Englishman who revealed to him that Freemasonry was 'a science [nauka]; that it is a mystery preserved in London, in a special, ancient, lodge.'[7] By the middle of the seventies Elagin's own lodges had more than two hundred members, the most influential convert being Novikov.[8] Novikov refused to submit to the customary initiation rules, however, and in breaking away to found another lodge in Moscow, began a new phase in Russian Freemasonry whose dominant source was Berlin and Stockholm rather than England. The casual ties of the earlier movement were replaced by a more intricate hierarchy, mutual obligations, catechisms, and vows of various kinds.

Some of the values of this 'higher order' Masonry are reflected in Novikov's *Morning Light* (*Utrennii svet*), a philosophical journal of the late seventies aimed against 'Voltaireanism' (which in its Russian manifestation stood for a particularly virulent scepticism and agnosticism). Two other talented men played a decisive role in the new movement: Johann Georg Schwarz and Mikhailo Matveevich Kheraskov, who collaborated on *Morning Light* and was the most celebrated poet and dramatist of the time. Schwarz, a Transylvanian enthusiast of occultism, had been brought by Prince Gagarin to Russia, where he became the inseparable companion of Novikov.[9] Their partnership, which opened a fresh chapter in the history of the Russian Enlightenment,[10] was made fruitful by Kheraskov who, as curator of Moscow University, invited Novikov to run its dormant press.

In the same year (1779) Kheraskov also provided a chair of German for Schwarz, whose lectures on philology, transcendental philosophy, and the philosophy of history attracted the attention of numerous admirers, including Joseph II of Austria and Prince Frederick William of Prussia, both of whom came to hear him in 1780. In the following year Schwarz and Novikov persuaded Kheraskov and others to organize 'the gathering of University foster children,' the first secret student society in Russian history. It was Masonic in origin and espoused the ideals that each of the three founders pursued in a common attempt to reform society. Schwarz, who became inspector of a new 'pedagogical seminary,' tried to integrate Russian higher education with higher Masonry. He was supported at Moscow University by Kheraskov, while Novikov organized a suitable program of publication.

These activities soon awakened the interest and support of prominent patrons who joined Schwarz and Novikov in a new 'clandestine scientific [skientificheskaia] lodge of Harmony' in 1780. Its aim was to revive pristine Christian values, and to infuse the quest for knowledge with a sense of Christian purpose. Not long afterwards, while on a trip abroad, Schwarz was initiated into Prussian Rosicrucianism, and this influenced the final form of 'higher order' Masonry, which the Moscow brethren adopted before Schwarz died in 1784. In the brief but ardent period of his activity in Russia Schwarz anticipated the more salient features of Russian romanticism with its antipathy to reason and the belief in the inner harmony of nature. This and the emphasis of Schwarz, Novikov, and Kheraskov on self-improvement and purification, on moral regeneration and good works, was especially compatible with the message of *Paradise Regained*, as well as that of *Paradise Lost*. Indeed, perhaps the most intriguing evidence on how Novikov's friends read Milton is the imitation he published with Moscow University Press in 1780.

TRUTH VERSUS EVIL: *TRUE LIGHT*

As its title implies, *Istinnyi svet* or *True Light* (which consists of nine books) is Masonic in character – goodness, purity, truthfulness, and love being advocated in its concluding lines as essential stages in the continuing struggle for inner perfection and knowledge of God. In the finale, as the allegorical curtain is thrown open to the initiated reader in a scene reminiscent of the *Magic Flute*, 'the celestial throne' is shown in all its glory – illumined by love 'burning like a flame' and guarded by archangels whose 'brightness ... in the silence and mystery ... remained undarkened by the sun.'[11]

But all this is not intrinsic to the poem's structure, the beginning of which is clearly suggested by *Paradise Regained*. The narrative of *True Light* opens with the same setting – St John's baptism of Jesus – but the appearance of Satan is delayed until Book III, the rest of books I and II following the New Testament rather more closely than Milton. Christ is shown gathering his disciples, preaching against the Pharisees, performing miracles, and revealing himself to Peter; but to this biblical story are then added various episodes brought in from *Paradise Lost*. Thus, there is the same conflict between God and the angels loyal to Satan; and – as in the English poem – Archangel Michael appears with similar consequences. Indeed, many of the Russian passages, such as the description of the humiliation of the fallen angels, the assembly in Hell and Satan's manipulation of it, the battle in the heavens, and the construction of the bridge out of Hell, are almost literally lifted out of *Paradise Lost*. There are also some changes. Sin and Death, for example, in their Cyrillic manifestation appear as Satan's generals; but the opening of the gates of Hell and Satan's flight through space are almost a paraphrase of Milton's original, as are the lines on the beauty of God's creation.

The imitation of *Paradise Lost* begins with the third book of the Russian poem and its description of Hell and Pandemonium (although it is not called that). Satan and his commanders ('nachal'niki') are shown not in their abject state lying in the burning lake after their defeat, but in the magnificent palatial splendour described by Milton at the end of Book I, 'Vissonom oblechen porfiroiu odetyi' / 'Covered in mink and decked in porphyry' (III. l 141). Satan's speech to his legions dwells at greater length on the celestial battle than does Milton at the beginning of *Paradise Lost* (since this is related later by Archangel Michael in Book VI), but his intention is the same: to prepare his 'comrades in misery' / 'tovarishchi neschast'ia' (III. l 30) for the next round in the struggle with the Almighty. Similarly, Satan – who is depicted seated like a tsar on his throne – gives his one-sided account of his relationship with God: 'I was first in [His affection]' / 'la pervyi byl pri nëm' (III. l 54) – a status undermined by the appearance of his son.

The expulsion from Heaven is also described in some well-articulated detail in Book III (ll 74–153), including the encounter with Michael (1 127) and the victorious entry of Christ's chariot (III. ll 125ff), but at this point the plot of the Russian poem retrieves its earlier connection with *Paradise Regained*. Satan, having built the bridge out of Hell – singlehanded, it would seem (ll 176–9) – then reveals his encounter with Jesus in the desert while flying over Judaea. Jesus resists the temptations Satan offers in his disguise as an old man (1 203), but this setback and his complaints about Christ's miracles and growing number of disciples have no visible effect on the morale of Satan's auditors in Hell. Death, who addresses him as 'my kind father' / 'liubeznyi moi otets' (l 249) suggests opening the gates of Hell to seek immediate revenge against God: 'let us quench our pleasure in blood' by destroying mankind.[12] His sister, Sin, heartily agrees, and an autobiographical digression on her part discloses (like her namesake in *Paradise Lost*) the circumstances of her birth – out of the brooding brow of Satan in Heaven (ll 273–5).

But Satan rejects the counsel of Death and Sin. Having confessed his failure to tempt Jesus – 'He is above all passions, the Divine Spirit is in Him' (l 437) – Satan embarks on a strategy that also marks the point where the Russian poem departs from *Paradise Lost*. Instead of seeking vengeance by striking out at the new world created by God, as in Milton's poem, Satan in *True Light* announces his success in having found Judas,

Masonic Devils and the Light Within 53

Predast on nam Togo, ia zlatom obol'shchu,
Ne mozhet ustoiat', kak strely izpushchu. (ll 483-4)

(He will betray That One, I shall enrich him with gold,
He shall not be able to resist when I release my darts.)

Judas, who is first mentioned at the beginning of the poem, then becomes Satan's agent in the further resolution of the plot. He succumbs to Satan's temptations and betrays the Saviour. In Book v, Christ is condemned to death, and in Book vi this is followed by a description of the crucifixion. The poem ends with the resurrection, Satan's recognition of his defeat (Book viii) and the triumph of Christ's teaching (ix), which is then given the appropriate Masonic gloss.

The moral of *True Light* is in fact similar to that of *Paradise Regained*:

> For therein stands the office of a king,
> His honour, virtue, merit, and chief praise,
> That for the public all this weight he bears.
> Yet he who reigns within himself, and rules
> Passions, desires, and fears, is more a king.
> Which every wise and virtuous man attains[.] (ii. ll 463-8)

Is it conceivable that this message was thought to be provocative by the authorities who confiscated the Russian poem from Novikov? Few copies of the sole edition of 1780 have survived.[13] This may explain why scholars have so far totally neglected it.

Who was the author? That he had ties with Novikov or Kheraskov and Moscow University is likely, and there may be some other undetermined link with the 1780 edition of Amvrosii's *Paradise Lost*. For both this and *True Light* were published under Novikov's auspices by the university press, and the Masonic eye appears above Book i in each of them. Possibly the author was a member of the secret student society Schwarz and Novikov organized at the university[14] and may have seen Amvrosii's translation as it was going to press. Or he may have read Milton in the original or one of the French editions, in which *Paradise Lost* sometimes appeared together with the imitation. This happened with Dupré's *Paradis perdu*, which was published together with *La Chute de l'homme* by David Durand. In this instance the precarious practice rather diminished Durand's poetic reputation. Were the pains the author of *True Light* took to remain anonymous an insurance against a similar fate?

Whatever the identity of the author, his Masonic mysticism no doubt helped to inspire a portrayal of Jesus that is a far cry from Milton's. *Paradise Regained*, so often criticized at the time for humanizing Christ, did not have the same effect on the Russian poet. As in Klopstock's *Messiade*, his miracles are depicted with evident relish; and in dealing with the Devil and his crew 'krovavyi' or 'bloody' is the author's favourite epithet to qualify their somewhat histrionic activities. At times, the tone is closer to Grand Guignol than to *Paradise Lost*.

This may partly be explained by the emphasis in *True Light* on battle and gore rather than on the lyrical parts of Milton's epic. By contrast, in *La Chute de l'homme*, David Durand – like many writers after him – focuses on Adam and Eve and the transgression. As we shall see, this is the part of *Paradise Lost* to which many Russian poets would be drawn in the Romantic period. They would also be fascinated by Milton's Satan. Indeed, if (as in *Paradise Lost* and *True Light*), the temptation of Christ is made into the axis of the poem's action, then the transgression cannot be included without making the Devil appear the chief protagonist of the narrative. The author of the Russian work took the theme of the temptation from *Paradise Regained* and followed the New Testament in greater detail than Milton by building the narrative around Christ's life. Yet there were certain passages in *Paradise Lost* that so impressed him that he evidently felt the need to introduce them into the body of the Russian poem. These are in fact irrelevant to the life of Jesus, its central theme. Thus, the flashback to Hell and that 'gloomy consistory' (I. l 42) that occurs at the beginning of *Paradise Regained* (which is all a reader requires to be reminded of the earlier contest of Satan with God and His Son) is extended by the Russian poet into a whole book (III. ll 1–592).

FLYING THROUGH SPACE

This section ends with Satan's paraphrase in the first person to his 'fallen comrades' of what many imitators of Milton tried to emulate – the unforgettable flight through space in Book III of *Paradise Lost*. There Satan

> Down right into the World's first region throws
> His flight precipitant, and winds with ease
> Through the pure marble air his oblique way
> Amongst innumerable stars, that shone
> Stars distant, but nigh hand seemed other worlds:
> Or other worlds they seemed, or happy isles,
> Like those Hesperian Gardens famed of old,
> Fortunate fields, and groves and flowery vales,

Masonic Devils and the Light Within

> Thrice happy isles, but who dwelt happy there
> He stayed not to inquire. Above them all
> The golden sun in splendor likest Heaven
> Allured his eye. Thither his course he bends
> Through the calm firmament (but up or down,
> By center, or eccentric, hard to tell,
> Or longitude) where the great luminary
> Aloof the vulgar constellations thick,
> That from his lordly eye keep distance due,
> Dispenses light from far; they as they move
> Their starry dance in numbers that compute
> Days, months, and years, towards his all-cheering lamp
> Turn swift their various motions, or are turned
> By his magnetic beam, that gently warms
> The universe, and to each inward part
> With gentle penetration, though unseen,
> Shoots invisible virtue even to the deep:
> So wondrously was set his motion bright. (III. ll 562-87)

Here Milton's visual imagery and the cosmology made such an impression on the Russian poet, that both elements are introduced into *True Light*:

> Vznosilsia vyshe ia! ... i verkh ee protiav,
> Granitzy ia svetil tam snezhnykh obozrevshi,
> Pokoiasia otdykhal, i vzor na vsiu prostrevshi.
> Razlichiem krasot poriadok sotvoren,
> O kol' Pravitel' sei, o kol' On umudren!
> Tam mnozhestvo luchei, blestiashchiia svetila,
> I sotriaseniia v razlichneishikh tam sila,
> V efire tonkost' est', on bleshchet krasotoi,
> Priemlet meru luch ot sotriasen'ev moi,
> Chto svetlost'iu svoei zemnoi shar pokryvaet,
> I sviazi chudno vsei sotvetstvo prinimaet.
> Tam sila vse vlechet, i pritiazhenie est',
> Vsemu tam est' predel i polozhenna mest',
> Granitsy prevsoiti tam tiazhest'iu svoeiu,
> Planeta ni odna uzhe ne mozhet eiu,
> Svoi krug peremenit' nikudy uklonias',
> No klonitsia vsegda ko tsentru ta stremias'.
> Zemnyi ne mozhet um ni nash' kogda postignut',

Gde kroetsia sei punkt, soboi shto mozhet dvignut',
Razrushit' estestvo, i sferu vsiu potriast'. [*sic*]
Rastorgnuv krasotu, vo smes' obratno spast'.
. . . .
Sie pereletev i vyshel kak na svet,
O kol' prekrasen zlak! O kol' priiaten svet!
Polia priiatnyiia, doliny s krutiznami,
I roshchi, s zelenymi luchami. (III. ll 552–72, 579–82)[15]

The analogue for the 'Fortunate fields, and groves and flowery vales' comes at the conclusion of Satan's flight (ll 581–2), and a major change is introduced by the Russian poet into Milton's cosmology. If Milton really did intuitively anticipate universal attraction, as the Continent's first popularizer of Newton's doctrines averred,[16] the author of *True Light* makes the suggestion explicit. Indeed, Milton's reference to the 'vulgar constellations' being 'turned by [the sun's] magnetic beam' can be understood in the same sense as Kepler's 'anima motrix' – the magnetic power the German astronomer ascribed to the sun in his premature attempt to establish the validity of the Copernican view.[17]

But Milton, as was pointed out by Dupré (and by Baron Stroganov in his translation), did not necessarily abandon the Ptolemaic system – hence the alternative course proposed for the 'vulgar constellations.'[18] For if the planets 'turn swift their various motions' in accordance with the epicycles still defended by Aristotelians, then Milton's lines could be taken to mean that he supported Ptolemy too.[19]

The Russian poet, therefore, did the sensible thing, and brought Milton's cosmology up to date. 'The magnetic beam' (l 583) is transformed into attraction ('pritiazhenie,' l 563), and the ambiguity of Milton's lines is altered in the next four lines (ll 564–8) to accommodate those certainties of the Enlightenment – universal gravitation and the great chain of being. But faith in this equilibrium and the stability of the Newtonian system had yet to be secured, as the next quatrain suggests.[20]

A similar doubt is expressed in the *Essay on Man*, which the author of *True Light* is likely to have read.[21] He may also have been familiar with Voltaire's *Micromégas* (translated into Russian in the same period), in which Satan's flight through space is repeated by an immense inhabitant of Sirius, whose precise knowledge of Newton's laws gives him an edge over the cosmonaut of *Paradise Lost*. This *conte philosophique*, with which modern science fiction is commonly supposed to begin,[22] was probably influenced more by *Gulliver's Travels* than by Milton. It too was proscribed when published in Moscow. *True Light*, however, is the earliest work by a Russian writer to indulge in this scientific fantasy (as it then seemed). The poem can claim distinction in another respect: next to Vladykin's *Paradise Lost and Regained*, it is the earliest poem in the Russian language in which Milton's Satan makes his auspicious appearance.

SATAN À LA RUSSE

No devil in literature has attracted more attention or has elicited as much controversy as Satan in *Paradise Lost*. The Romantics, who saw him as the hero of the epic, based this view almost exclusively on books I and II of the poem, for Satan's later degradation diminishes the persuasiveness of this interpretation. But since the first translation published in Russian omitted the last nine books, in which sympathy with Satan is destroyed step by step until finally the fallen angels are turned into snakes, it might be thought that Vasilii Petrov also favoured the Romantic view.

Unfortunately there is no record of what he thought about an issue that would assume such importance for the next generation of poets. All that can be said is that Petrov's translation was often preferred to Amvrosii's by men of letters. This preference was no doubt natural because of both Petrov's literary reputation and the simple fact that his translation was so much closer to the original. But, since only four hundred copies or so were published – there were no new editions after 1777[23] – it is difficult to judge to what extent Russian readers would have been affected by the one-sided perception of Satan that the first three books Petrov chose to translate inevitably convey.

What seems to have mattered in the evolution of the Devil as a literary figure in the second half of the eighteenth century is that the Byzantine demonic tradition connected with early Russian literature had finally died, except among Old Believers and the uneducated populace at large.[24] Western demonic literature had begun its incursion with the growing secularization of Russian life in the previous century, but the great baroque devils (as conceived, for example, by Hugo Grotius or Calderon) simply never made their appearance in Cyrillic.[25]

Milton's Satan had his first influential rival in 1785–7, when Aleksei Kutuzov translated Klopstock's lyrical epic *Der Messias* into Russian, a monumental work inspired by *Paradise Lost* and the Bible.[26] Catherine the Great thought the translation unreadable; and Coleridge's description of Klopstock as 'a very German Milton'[27] was enough to condemn him in the eyes of English readers, although Russian writers at the end of the eighteenth century took very seriously the vast reputation the *Messiade* had acquired, thanks in part to Bodmer and the literary foes of Gottsched. Whether the author of *True Light* had already heard of the German poem can only be surmised. Since Kutuzov was a fellow Mason, the Russian poet could have heard either through him or some other source – such as Schwarz – of Klopstock's celebrated opus before the Russian translation appeared.

Der Messias, which took twenty-five years to complete, is far more ambitious in scope than *True Light*, and its cast of characters is larger. The one striking parallel between the Russian and the German epics is that both take the redemption as their main theme. But if their use of the Gospel story is in some ways similar, the Russian work suffers from the same flaws as the German. The Gospel story is too meagre for heroic verse, and even Milton's treatment of the temptation in the desert in *Paradise Regained* seems static when compared with the action and physical violence of *Paradise Lost*. This impression is overcome in the English poem by the acuity of the intellectual and moral duel between Christ and Satan. That is almost entirely absent in Klopstock. Nor is it present in *True Light*, although the Russian poet may have realized by the time he reached the end of Book II that Christ could not be treated as a heroic individual in the classic tradition. Hence the imitation of *Paradise Lost* in Book III, where Satan is portrayed far more vividly than Jesus.

In reading the Russian work one might therefore expect to see some hint of the mettle demonstrated by Milton's Satan: 'Better to reign in Hell than serve in Heaven.' But this expectation is not fulfilled, and one is reminded of Franz Mehring's verdict on Klopstock. Marx's biographer saw in the German Satan a lack of revolutionary spirit, symbolizing – in Mehring's view – the stark contrast between the political maturity of the English middle class of Milton's day and the lack of such maturity among the German bourgeoisie of the eighteenth century.[28]

The Russian Satan, as reflected in *True Light*, is no less feeble when likened to his original. He lacks any of Milton's depth. The conscious imitation of Milton is perhaps closest in Book IV, where the Russian Satan describes the tantalizing glory of the ancient empires, their dominion being offered not to Jesus (as in *Paradise Regained*) but to Judas.[29] The effect of this transposition only weakens Satan's stature. Instead of being treated as the intellectual equal of Christ, as in Milton's subtle treatment, the Satan of *True Light* turns out to be no more than a bloody-minded and vindictive trickster. Judas is, if anything, even more shallow. His motives are never explored. Against the Devil, Judas Iscariot never has even a remote chance. And his moral level, as portrayed by the Russian poet, only further reduces Satan.

Nor is the Devil endowed with much political consciousness, an attribute shared by Klopstock's Satan.[30] This does not mean that the author of *True*

Light imitated *Der Messias* – the parallels could be biblical too – but it is hardly necessary to adopt Mehring's class analysis to see that the pietism professed in the Catherinian era by Russian Freemasons and Rosicrucians was closer in spirit to Klopstock's than to Milton's. This is true despite the fact that Novikov and his friends were familiar with Boehme and other mystics who are said to have influenced Milton, the most notable of these being John Pordage.[31] Nonetheless, the Russian Masons as a group shared the optimism Klopstock derived from Leibniz and Christian Wolff via Bodmer and Breitinger. To them revelation was the manifestation of God's reason, and faith in God the expression of human reason. Evil in Milton's terms was absent, the inaccessibility of God being usually explained as a failure of self-awareness.

Self-awareness, however, was invariably affected by political events, a path well mapped by Tolstoy in Pierre Bezukhov's 'pélerinage de l'âme' in *War and Peace*. Thus, however intangible and abstract the figures in the *Messiade* may seem when compared with their concrete representation in *Paradise Lost*, Klopstock himself welcomed the French Revolution, although he was Blake's senior by more than twenty years. Most of the Russian Freemasons and Rosicrucians did not. But Catherine's persecution of them – Novikov was arrested in 1792 – was not in fact due to the same considerations that made her turn against Radishchev and others who merely continued to believe in the principles she herself had once shared. Rather, it seems, she was deeply hostile to the kind of obscurity and obscurantism she discerned in the Freemasons and the literature they read, as well as in the secretiveness with which they organized their affairs. This does not mean that government officials could interpret her intentions in such matters with any finesse. For it is odd that among the books confiscated from Novikov in 1787 they should have included *True Light*, the *Messiade*, and Bunyan's *Pilgrim's Progress*.

Christian piety is what these dissimilar works have in common. Did they also seem at the time to offer a comparable antagonism to secular power and authority? Certainly, none of them present political ambiguities more blatantly than those in *Paradise Lost*. And the French Revolution made these ambiguities explicit by giving a new and sharp focus to the way good and evil were henceforward to be represented in literature. This is seen most characteristically in Kheraskov's *Vselennaia* (*Universe*, 1790), an epic poem separated from *True Light* by only a decade.

THE DEVIL IN KHERASKOV'S *UNIVERSE*

But much had happened in those ten years to heighten the political consciousness of Russian writers, the fear induced by Pugachev's insurrection being revived by the events in France and, on a different plane, the harassment of Catherine's censors and police. In the pages of *Universe* Satan seems to appear for the first time in Russian poetry as a politically conscious figure. His kinship with Milton's original is unmistakable. Indeed, Kheraskov acknowledges his debt to Milton (and to Klopstock) at the very beginning of his poem, while dissociating himself most emphatically later on from the English poet's politics.[32]

Kheraskov is often represented as an aristocratic liberal, spokesman of the independent gentry that looked down on the court nobility, the government bureaucrats, and the mercantile interest; but Gukovsky evades discussion of the poet's Masonic views. These defy class analysis.[33] Like Novikov or Radishchev, Kheraskov believed in a golden age before the fall, a notion powerfully expressed in *Paradise Lost*. As Novikov put it in the opening number of his new journal (the *Twilight Glow*) in 1782, however, despite the transgression 'the light of Adam is, nonetheless, still within us, only hidden.' How to retrieve it was an issue about which there were many views among the Freemasons and Rosicrucians, but it is surely not surprising that the light they sought could be confused with the 'light within' of which Milton speaks in *Paradise Lost*.

Schwarz called on his friends to abandon rationalism for the teachings of Holy Writ, which superficially (it might be argued) moved them one step closer to the kind of program promulgated by leading Puritans in Milton's time. Following Boehme, Schwarz insisted that it was impossible to comprehend revelation without first developing the mind and the spiritual powers that were the key to an understanding of the Bible. To regain those spiritual powers, man must return to God and seek restitution for Adam's transgression. This is only possible by following Christ's example.[34]

But Christ's example did not necessarily have to be understood in a passive way, and it is precisely on this point that readers of *Paradise Regained* have historically differed.[35] On this crucial issue the authority of Jakob Boehme or Arndt or Louis Claude de Saint-Martin is often cited by Russian Freemasons; that of Milton rarely. Few of them, Radishchev being one who did, advocated political reform. Kheraskov was no exception.[36] Yet he did criticize court life and the abuses of officialdom. Unlike some of his acquaintances, with whose reaction against the rationalism of the Enlightenment he sympathized, he also continued to believe in human perfectibility. At the same time, he lost his earlier faith in science as the means of attaining it, and agreed with Rousseau's position on the subject, which is also compatible, of course, with Milton's distrust of natural philosophy (see PL VII. ll 111–30).[37]

In *Pilgrims, or the Seekers after Happiness* (*Piligrimy, ili iskateli shchas-*

tiia), which was published five years after *Universe* when the poet was over sixty, Vel'mir undergoes many adventures reminiscent of Ariosto's *Orlando Furioso* and Tasso's *Gerusalemme Liberate*, but neither passion nor knowledge bring him contentment. 'My Pansoph ... disliked Locke, was scornful of Newton, cursed Tasso, Young, and Milton, and Kant and Wieland seemed unintelligent to him.'[38] But even this degree of superficial sophistication is not enough to bring the epic hero peace of mind. The moral of Kheraskov's allegory is that happiness cannot be found by those who look for it consciously; he advises Prince Vel'mir, rather as Raphael tells Adam, 'Ne liubopytstvui kniaz'!' / 'Prince, don't force your curiosity upon the world!'[39] Kheraskov was an advocate of the golden mean in life, and it was thought that he practised what he preached. D.S. Mirsky is surely right in describing him as 'one of the most enlightened and universally respected men of the century.'[40]

Born not long after Antiokh Kantemir left for England, Kheraskov was also of Danubian origin. His father, who served as an officer in the Imperial Army, died when Kheraskov was still an infant, and his mother (*née* Princess Drutskaia-Sokolinskaia) married a second time. Thus the noted magnate (and Kantemir's literary patron) Prince N.I. Trubetskoi became the boy's stepfather, endowing him with an excellent library, which introduced Kheraskov to literature. He began to write poetry at an early age while receiving his formal education at the Corps des Pages. Much of his life thereafter (from 1755 to 1802) was connected with the fortunes of Moscow University, the country's first institution of that nature, of which he became director in 1763. Since Kheraskov died only in 1807, his career spans Catherine's reign and the beginning of the Alexandrian era. A folk tale he set to verse in 1803 was used by Pushkin in 'Ruslan and Liudmilla.' Of the eighteenth-century poets he was one of the most prolific and versatile, and in a sense the most successful. His *Rossiade* (1779) ended the quest of his countrymen for a national epic. It earned him the title of Russia's Homer, and he followed the same historical formula in 1785 with a vast narrative poem dealing with the introduction of Christianity to Rus' by St Vladimir.[41] Its pietism and Kheraskov's Masonic mysticism, in no way different from that of *True Light*, reflected the shift in taste that occurred as the twelve books of the *Rossiade* were being written.

By the late 1770s neoclassical works were no longer admired to the exclusion of other literary forms. Perhaps this made *Paradise Lost* doubly appealing. Some hint of this is contained in Kheraskov's 'View of Epic Verse,' inserted between the 'Historical Introduction' and the poem itself in the third edition of his *Rossiade*, which carries the following description of the English work: 'In *Paradise Lost* worthy and important [vazhnyi] Milton describes the fall of the first man, the eating of the forbidden fruit, the triumph of the Devil, the expulsion of Adam and Eve from Paradise for their disobedience, and the reason for the ill-fated genesis of the entire human race.'[42] This summary could serve almost as well for scenes in Kheraskov's own *Universe*, although its formal structure is different. The Russian poem consists of three books: the World of Spirit ('Mir Dukhovnyi'), Chaos, and the World of the Sun. It opens, following Milton and Klopstock, with an invocation to the Muse; and in acknowledging his debt to the two poets (and the Bible), Kheraskov states that 'I follow them – but at a distance, shyly [robko] and indirectly. They are immortal, and my song [pesnoslovie] is ephemeral and insignificant, but the writing of it gave me pleasure – and I hope that some among my readers may feel a sudden pleasure in reading *Universe*.'[43]

The Russian poet's humility was not perceived as a pose and is one of the qualities that made Kheraskov so beloved a figure at Moscow University. It crops up again in the question put at the beginning of *Universe*: 'Is it appropriate to inquire into the Creation of the Creator?' / 'Udobno l' postigat' tvoreniiu Tvortsa?' The answer to this appears only at the end of the poem as a variation on Raphael's response to Adam in Book VIII of *Paradise Lost*: 'Be lowly wise: / Think on what concerns thee and thy being.' (ll 173–4). Milton, as Marjorie Nicolson points out, did not side with the poets of the seventeenth century to whom the universe revealed by the new science opened up vistas of infinite inspiration: but nor was he content with limitation.[44] Milton chose a middle ground, as did Kheraskov, whose ethical restraint dampens the occasional 'scientific' optimism that nonetheless surfaces from time to time in *Universe*.

Its author's moral emphasis is one Milton would have approved: 'Ne tainy nuzhny nam, no dobryia dela' / 'It is not mysteries we need, but good deeds.'[45] But this is not necessarily Miltonic in inspiration, since the issue of good works had been debated by the Freemasons and the Rosicrucians. Kheraskov may also have been thinking of Christ's response to Satan in *Paradise Regained*. Yet the narrative of *Universe* opens with a scene reminiscent of Book III of *Paradise Lost* where God in Heaven 'commands all the angels to adore him.' 'Nebesnyi khor glasil: privet! privet!' / 'The celestial choir pealed forth: Hail Lord! Hail!' (*Universe* p 34). Not even the seraphs can read the Almighty's intentions, which are revealed in the Russian poem as soon as God consults his book:

> Sviashchenny tainstva Prevechnyi v nei chital,
> I kratkii vzor Ego nezapno grozen stal ... (*Universe* p 37)

Masonic Devils and the Light Within 63

(Holy mysteries the Eternal One read in it,
And His austere aspect suddenly became awesome ...)

To absolve man's transgression Christ – as in the English poem – then pleads on his behalf:

> Ia smert' vkushu, i zhizn' Vselenni vozvrashu.
> Ia ves' tvoia liubov', zhivu, dyshu liubov'iu;
> To mne ne iskushit' Tvoikh tvorenii krov'iu? (*Universe* p 39)

(I shall taste death, and return life to the universe.
I am all your love, I live and breathe by love;
Then am I not to absolve Your creatures with [my] blood?)

When Kheraskov brings in Satan, he does so not in the desert to tempt Jesus, but in Heaven in a setting reminiscent this time of *Paradise Lost* where Satan ruminates on his rebellion against God:

> O! kto ia esm', kto ia? On sam v sebe veshchal;
> Nepostizhimy mne moi razum, ni nachalo,
> No bytie moe otkuda vozsiialo? (*Universe* p 43)

(Oh! Who am I, who? He said to himself:
My reason and my beginning are both unfathomable to me,
From where did my being arise?)

The Russian Satan then uses the materialist argument to undermine God's *raison d'être*:

> Net! ia ne sotvoren ni Bogom, ni Sud'boiu;
> I, mozhet byt', iznik iz sveta sam soboiu,
> Daby svetilsia ia, i tsarstvoval i zhil,
> Ni Boga ia o tom, ni tvarei ni molil. (*Universe* p 43)

This is very close to the argument Satan invokes in *Paradise Lost* when Abdiel reminds him of his duties towards the Creator:

> We know no time when we were not as now;
> Know none before us, self-begot, self-raised
> By our own quickening power, when fatal course

Had circled his full orb, the birth mature
Of this our native Heaven, ethereal sons. (v. ll 859–63)[46]

Kheraskov's Satan makes a similar admission, but the Russian characterization wholly lacks the Faustian dimension Milton gives to his Satan in a passage that comes soon after the lines above, in which he thinks of himself as too deeply sunk ever to win grace again:

> For never can true reconcilement grow
> Where wounds of deadly hate pierced so deep;
> Which would but lead me to a worse relapse,
> And heavier fall ... (IV. ll 98–101)

He then comes to the fatal decision:

> Evil be thou my good: by thee at least
> Divided empire with Heaven's King I hold,
> By thee, and more than half perhaps will reign [.] (IV. ll 110–12)

In the Russian poem the battle between good and evil described by Raphael in the seventh book of *Paradise Lost* is fought at the conclusion of Book I. It is certainly more strident in a superficial sense than the original, since it is not fought by proxy. Satan with 'hatred in his soul aflame' / 'v dushe vosplamenilas' zloba' (*Universe* p 53) jousts not with Christ but with God himself. The lines describing the war in Heaven are very much poorer in their imagery, however, even if they do catch some of the cadences of Milton's original:

> Iz bezdny v bezdnu on kak molniia letel,
> V poriadok smutnyi mir ustroit' vozkhotel,
> Kak vetrami korabl' shumit v volnakh nesomyi,
> Tak vozdukh vozshumel, ot kril [*sic*] ego sekomyi;
> Prestan' svirepstvovat'! ogniu on govorit;
> No ogn' ne slushaet, sverkaet i gorit;
> Miatezhnaia voda maitezhniku ne vnemlet;
> Kak goru shumnyi val u nog ego podemlet,
> Naprasno buri on stremitsia obuzdat':
> Oni revut krugom i ne khotiat prestat'. (*Universe* pp 53–4)

(From abyss to abyss he flew like lightning,
He wanted to impose [his] order on the troubled world,

> Like a turbulent ship driven by winds groaning in the waves,
> So the air winced sliced by his wings;
> Cease your roaring! He tells the fire;
> But the fire obeys not, sparkles and burns;
> The rebellious water hearkens not the rebel,
> In vain he tries to calm the storms.
> They rage around [him] and refuse to desist.)

As God's angelic hosts take the upper hand, the Almighty turns the universe to darkness, and Satan and his fiery supporters are thrown headlong into abysses of chaos and hell. Kheraskov draws the following moral, which comes as something of an anticlimax:

> Pal Angel za grekhi, my takzhe mozhem past',
> Za prestuplenie priemlem ravnu chast'.
> Byl prezhde chelovek bezplotnykh k Bogu blizhe,
> No nizko, nizko pal, a mozhet past' i nizhe. (*Universe* p 70)

> (The Angel fell for [his] sins, we too can fall like that,
> Our lot will be the same if we transgress.
> Before man was closer to God than the aethereal ones.
> But low he fell, so low, and can fall lower still.)

The Russian poet's third and final book describes the creation of the world and of Adam and Eve, and the transgression in Paradise, all of which is preceded by a discussion of free will echoing Milton's view on the subject. Adam *chose* his own ruin through his love of Eve, and Kheraskov's depiction of her charms and Adam's passion for her – 'liubov' sil'na, slepa, volshebna' / 'love is strong, blind, and magical' – represents the most lyrical part of the poem. It is also the least sophisticated, owing to Kheraskov's Masonic propensity for moralizing. This he indulges in with an utter lack of restraint in *Pilgrims*, in which Prince Vel'mir is seduced by the enchantress Felina.

In describing his amorous encounters with this 'pupil of Hell' / 'vospitannitsa ada' (p 52), the Russian poet often turns to the reader to condemn their conduct. Pope uses this device too in *The Rape of the Lock* (which is cited in *Pilgrims*) but his tone is mock-censorious: Kheraskov's is prim-naïve. This is one reason why the Russian poet's imitation of Milton in rendering Adam's love for Eve does not come off. Adam's passionate avowals are convincing enough – 'tebe vse otdal zhizn'' / 'I gave you all my life' (p 82) – but the play of sunlight in her eyes, the tenderness he feels in approaching her and listening to her (p 83) are cut short by tedious didactic admonitions.

Thus, the vivid evocation of Adam's feelings for Eve (which in *Paradise Lost* he confesses to Raphael) is interrupted by the reflection that love is destructive – 'kogda predel preidet' / 'when it transcends the bounds' (p 84):

> No ta, kotoraia Adama oslepila
> Ta strastnaia liubov' mir tselyi pogubila.
> Adam v liubvi svoei i slab i ne umeren,
> Stal Evve preden ves', i Bogu stal ne veren. (*Pilgrims* p 84)

> (But the passionate love that blinded Adam
> Ruined the whole world ...
> Adam in his love is weak and immoderate;
> He became wholly dedicated to Eve, and untrue to God.)

Yet if these lines do recall Milton's, the Russian poet's conclusion reads more like a pastiche. For, unlike Milton in *Paradise Lost*, he is coy about physical passion: 'v slepoi liubvi vsegda sut' nemoshchny serdtsa' / 'in blind love hearts are always powerless' (p 84). But at the same time Kheraskov counsels his readers rather inconsistently that, should they wish to stay happy in matrimony, then like Adam they must 'love [their] wives.'[47] Thus, the conclusion of *Universe* is as pedestrian as the moral maxims in *Pilgrims*.

While Kheraskov's attachment to Masonic teaching may have been responsible for this didactic vein in his verse, *Universe* does deserve to be remembered for its representation of Satan. The poet was not (as we have seen) the first to portray Milton's Devil in Russian verse, but he was the first to present Satan as a romantic character more or less cut loose from his biblical moorings. In this sense, Kheraskov's Miltonic Satan, appropriately russified, initiates the demonic tradition in Russian poetry that reaches its maturity in the nineteenth century with Lermontov.[48]

Indeed, the passage in *Universe* evoking the flight of Satan 'from abyss to abyss' like a 'turbulent ship' reminds one not only of Milton but of Lermontov's famous lines in *The Sail* (*Parus*) on another romantic rebel with a similar literary lineage: 'A on miatezhnyi ishchet buri / Kak budto v buri est' pokoi' / 'And a storm the rebel seeks, / As if in storm[s] there is calm and peace.' The descriptions of nature in *Universe* also bear the stamp of Milton's imagery. In painting nature as wild and uncontrolled Kheraskov introduced *das Wunderbare* into Russian verse as Klopstock had done into German poetry after Bodmer had chosen this aspect of *Paradise Lost* for particular praise. The Russian poet also injected a new element into his poem, for which the French Revolution was directly responsible. Yet unlike William Blake, Shelley, Byron, Pushkin, Lermontov, and other Romantic poets who were influenced by Milton, Kheraskov gives no hint of approval for Satan 'the rebel.'

Instead Kheraskov echoed the domestic reaction of most of the Russian nobility to the events in France. Although *Universe* was written only in 1790, it becomes – as we shall see – both a commentary on the French Revolution and a gloss on *Paradise Lost*, as reinterpreted by a pious upholder of law and order fearful of the world's collapse. Not all Russian artists and intellectuals, still so insecure in their social status, would respond to 1789 in this way. But for all the confusing reactions it provoked, the French Revolution did have the effect of turning Satan into a political figure, a rebel whose respectability largely depended on one's attitude to that event. In Russia, almost as important in that context was the peasant insurrection led by Emel'ian Pugachev. How both these cataclysms affected literary and ideological perceptions of Milton is the subject of the next chapter.

FIVE

Satan, Pugachev, and the French Revolution

'Miatezhnik pervyi byl na svete vol'nodumets!' (Earth's first rebel was a freethinker!)

Kheraskov

The eighteenth century transformed the Devil in its symbolism to the degree that Christian theology gave way to the certainties of Newtonian science.[1] As belief in the transcendent waned elsewhere in Western Europe, among Russian writers and poets there was a reaction against the rationalism of the Enlightenment that often seems to have been paralleled by attitudes towards Milton's Satan. The traditional feudal Devil had been condemned as a rebel against God, much as a runaway serf would be condemned for escaping from his *barin*. Pugachev, the leader of Russia's largest peasant uprising, would be seen in this light; but in the one and a half decades between that massive rebellion and the French Revolution, Satan acquired an individualist profile. Unmoored from the Scriptures, the Devil as perceived by the foremost intellectuals of the period reflects the unconscious fears and hopes of a cultivated élite fascinated and perturbed by the events in France.

SATAN'S POLITICS AND DERZHAVIN

The real contrast after 1790 between the voice of conservatives and erstwhile liberals such as Kheraskov and Derzhavin on the one side, and radicals such as Radishchev on the other, was their attitude to serfdom. The latter wished to see it abolished. But all three, who were indeed the best-known writers at the end of the Catherinian era, had lived through the formative political experience of their generation – the nightmare (as it was for the gentry) of 'Pugachevshchina.' Does this have any bearing on the literary preoccupation of these three poets with Satan?

Satan, Pugachev, and the French Revolution 69

To the anonymous author of *True Light*, Satan, as we have seen, is cast in a Masonic mystical framework. The Satan who haunted the imagination of Kheraskov, Derzhavin, and Radishchev after 1789 may have been unconsciously suggested as much by political reality as by their reading of Milton and Klopstock. But it is noteworthy that for all the differences in the nature and degree of their commitment to the Enlightenment – which in Derzhavin's case are particularly questionable – their public reaction to the French Revolution as it progressed was essentially alike.[2] Where they differed as poets was in their treatment of Satan, whose connections with the events of the time is as blatant (at least in Kheraskov's and Radishchev's case) as their debt to *Paradise Lost*. Portrayal of the Devil becomes almost a touchstone of political and religious orthodoxy. Thus, if Radishchev's 'Angel of Darkness' is the first Miltonic devil in Russian literature in the sense that its author seems to anticipate the sympathy the Romantics felt for the hero of *Paradise Lost*, for Derzhavin he is still a fiend and foe.

Derzhavin was directly involved in suppressing the Pugachev Rebellion, which may explain his early conservative attitudes of mind, while the author of *Universe* became an instant reactionary only in 1790.

Thus, while eighteenth-century critics were all too aware of the connection between Cromwell's republicanism and the arguments deployed by Milton's Satan, Kheraskov took this analogy one step further by making his Satan the protagonist of Jacobinism. He did this not with the understanding shown for the Good Old Cause in *Paradise Lost*, but by reversing Milton's stand. Satan's angelic supporters in the Russian poem are 'coarse' and 'black.' They are identified explicitly with the French revolutionaries.

> V miatezhnoi Galii my vidim v nashi dni,
> Kol' strashnye goriat razdorov tam ogni;
> Pered sviashchennymi razboi Altariami –
> Bezumnye raby alkaiut byt' Tsariami![3]

> (In rebellious Gaul we see in our days
> What terrible fires of discord burn there;
> Crazed slaves presume to be Tsars
> [While] battling before holy Altars.)

And since the French Revolution was caused – according to Kheraskov – by freethinkers, Satan is transformed by the poet into the first of the species:

> Miatezhnik pervyi byl na svete vol'nodumets!

Izmenu vsplamenil, otpal ot Bozhestva,
I v buistve vozmutil zakony estestva.⁴

(The first rebel on earth was a freethinker!
He fanned the flames of treason, fell away
From Godhood, and in [his] insurrection
Upset the laws of Nature.)

Reviving an argument used by Salmasius against the English regicides, he sees popular sovereignty as intrinsically evil. Once the people 'tear up the bonds of obedience ... law is corrupted and so are the people [themselves].' The tyranny Milton ascribed to Charles I is in fact wielded by the people, ie, the mob:

Narod est' liutyi zver', ne pravimyi zakonom;
Komu podobiatsia tol' buinye serdtsa?⁵

(The people are a cruel beast, ungovernable by law;
Who needs such rebellious hearts?)

And God's cause is identified with that of monarchy and legitimacy: 'narodu buinomu vo zlobe net prepon' / 'there are no limits to the malice of a rebellious people.'⁶

Tak tsarstva rushatsia; gde vlast' utratit tsar';
Tak rushitsia prestol i Bozhii tam altar'.

(So kingdoms collapse, where the tsar loses power;
There the throne will perish and God's altar.)

Even before the flight of Louis XVI in 1791, Derzhavin reacted to the French Revolution in the same forthright fashion. He is not likely to have read Milton as early as his friend Kheraskov, whom he first visited at his Grebenev estate in 1775.⁷ But what is interesting about his response to the 'perfidy [kovarstvo] of the French turmoil' is that like Kheraskov, Derzhavin uses images inspired by *Paradise Lost* to make Satan responsible for the events in France.

Gavrilo Romanovich Derzhavin is generally considered the most powerful Russian poet of the eighteenth century, the heir of Kheraskov. He is more inventive than the latter, but he had little of the older man's education and refinement. In the school he attended in Kazan', Derzhavin learnt enough German to acquaint himself with Klopstock in the original, although it is difficult to believe that he could have studied him closely.[8] Derzhavin knew neither Latin nor French nor English, and it is likely that he read Milton only in Russian translation.

Novikov, whom Derzhavin came to know in the same period as he became acquainted with Kheraskov, supplied him with the books he published at the press of Moscow University. To these Derzhavin is known to have paid particular attention owing to his ignorance of foreign languages.[9] His literary career began rather late in life. Although his family belonged to the gentry, it had no influential connections, and Derzhavin's promotion in the Imperial Army (in which he enrolled as a private) was unspectacular until the Pugachev Rebellion in 1773. At that time, finding himself on leave in Kazan', he composed a loyal address to the Empress Catherine on behalf of the fearful nobility of the province. This furnished him with an entrée to the staff of General Bibikov, who had been ordered to suppress the revolt. As the general's ADC, Derzhavin tried 'to ensnare the villain,' but Pugachev long evaded 'the net' spread out to capture him, although Derzhavin was privy to the gruesome punishment meted out to the peasant leader's supporters.[10] As a reward the poet was given lands in Belorussia, after which Derzhavin began to devote his leisure to literature.

He returned to St Petersburg in the same year that Vasilii Petrov published his unfinished translation of *Paradise Lost*. The friendship of Kheraskov and Novikov helped Derzhavin to gain recognition among the capital's littérateurs, and by 1780 he already enjoyed poetic recognition. Derzhavin's reputation then took wing with the appearance of 'Felitsa,' a semi-humorous ode to the Empress. His celebrated 'Ode to God,' once elevated to the status of a classic and thought to be Miltonic,[11] added to his fame.

In 'Felitsa' Derzhavin sang the virtues of Catherine and satirized the vices of her courtiers, but his own subsequent service as governor (as well as in other positions close to the Empress) was accompanied by quarrels with superiors and subordinates, so that he found virtually every new post he was given intolerable. Alexander I appointed Derzhavin minister of justice, but he was too outspoken a reactionary to fit in with the liberal optimism of the young Emperor's administration. Indeed, Derzhavin's political sentiments were not softened by anything that happened after the French Revolution, so that the ode he wrote in 1789 to stigmatize it reflects – like Kheraskov's *Universe* – his mature views.

Yet interestingly enough, 'On the Perfidy of the French Turmoil' was written initially under the impression of the unpleasantness Derzhavin had suffered as governor of Tambov. In 1790, on hearing of the upheavals in France, he decided to rewrite his poem, moved by the passions the French Revolution apparently inspired in him. Like Kheraskov he believed in a golden age, a golden age destroyed by satanical wickedness:

> Kto vozvrashchat['] vozmozhet veki
> I zrit deian'ia drevnikh let,
> Tot znaet, skol'ko cheloveki
> Toboiu preterpeli bed![12]

> (He who would return the centuries
> And see the acts of ancient years,
> Knows how many sufferings men
> Have endured because of you!)

Hardly had our first parents appeared in Eden, when they were seduced into transgression by Satan. Adam was no match for him –

> Lish' praotets v Edem iavilsia,
> Tvoim pronyrstvom iskusilsia, –
> Izchez ego blazhenstva sad;
> Sokrylos' zlatoe vremia
> S tekh por, kak zemnorodnykh plemia
> Vkusilo tvoi tletvornyi iad.[13]

> (Hardly had our forefather appeared in Eden,
> Than he was tempted by your cunning, –
> The garden of his felicity disappeared,
> The golden age ended
> When the earthborn tribe
> Bit into your putrefying poison.)

And the poet sees mankind's political trials, culminating in the French Revolution, as a chain of wickedness perpetrated by the Devil:

> Lezhat poverzhennyia tsarstva
> Miatezhnoiu tvoei rukoi,
> Chuzhie trony i nachal'stva
> Ne raz pokhishchenny toboi.[14]

> (Kingdoms lie overturned

By your rebellious hand; many a time
Have alien thrones and governments
Been abducted by you.)

Derzhavin then attacks the professed ideals of the French revolutionaries – 'a return to innocence, equality, freedom'[15] – as nothing but bait diabolically contrived to conceal their own selfish interests. 'Equality and freedom,' he says in reference to Catherine's *Nakaz* or *Instruction*, 'exists nowhere but only in that kingdom where laws are obeyed: the first – in justice for all; the second – in desiring what is not against the laws.'[16]

RADISHCHEV'S 'ANGEL OF DARKNESS'

Radishchev would counter such arguments by drawing on a rich legacy of Enlightenment thought, to which he added Milton's authority. But it is noteworthy that this philosophical radical's reaction to the French Revolution does not differ essentially from Derzhavin's. In his poem 'The Eighteenth Century' ('Osmnadzatoe stoletie'), Radishchev describes his disappointment at the failure of 1789 to realize the ideals of his youth; and in his 'Historical Ode' ('Pesn' istoricheskaia') he compares the Jacobin dictatorship with one of the darkest periods in Roman annals. All this makes it the more remarkable that when Radishchev began to write an epic at the end of his life, its hero is a satanical figure who has none of the shallow attributes imposed on Milton's complex characterization by Kheraskov and Derzhavin. In other words, Radishchev's literary Satan, who is chronologically also the last to be conceived, has already acquired some of the positive characteristics associated with Milton's Satan in the verse of the Romantic poets.

Many of them, of course, sympathized with the French Revolution, and their literary Satan is indistinguishable at times from Prometheus. In Radishchev's attempted epic, this transition in the 'Angel of Darkness' with 'his baneful eyes' and 'obdurate pride and steadfast hate,' is only hinted at.[17] But Radishchev's sketch is undoubtedly more Miltonic than any of the Russian portrayals of Satan so far discussed.

The surviving section of the piece, composed in Siberia, describes the flight of Satan to 'the top of the Ural range,' a realistic substitute (we may assume) for Mount Niphates. Apart from this detail, Radishchev's 'father of rebellion' ('otets miatezha') resembles Milton's 'apostate Angel,' and there are close parallels (as Z.V. Zapadov has pointed out) between the Russian text and books I and IV of *Paradise Lost*.[18]

The cosmic flight of the 'Angel of Darkness,' the sublime vistas, the grandiose images, the struggle of the elements, the vivid evocation of chaos, and the passionate characterization of Satan himself – all are reminiscent of Milton's original. In Radishchev's figure there are the same romantic overtones as in Kheraskov's ideological Devil, but Radishchev's evocation is more authentically demonic and therefore more poetic (despite the fact that the epic is in prose). To suggest that Russia's 'first radical' – as Radishchev is often called[19] – consciously sympathized with Satan's politics is to say more than the extant evidence warrants. But it is surely significant that the epic may have been conceived as a vehicle for telling the heroic story of Ermak's conquest of Siberia.

As far as is known Radishchev never completed the 'Angel of Darkness,' and the rest of the manuscript is lost. From what remains, however, it is clear that the biblical restraints inhibiting the imaginative exploration of the Devil's character in Masonic imitations of Milton – Radishchev himself was for a while a Mason – had no influence on him. Christ, humanized in *Paradise Regained*, could not so easily be adapted to the demands of a secular literature. Presumably, Orthodox traditions were too strong to tolerate this.

Satan overcame comparable taboos. If we exclude the earlier 'novelization' of *Paradise Lost* as represented in the Barsov manuscript, Radishchev's evocation of Milton's Satan is the first such attempt in Russian prose. Is it a mere coincidence that in non-religious Russian art Satan also makes his appearance in the same decade as the French Revolution and the publication of Russian editions of Milton's epics? The Fiend manifests himself, appropriately, in a painting of Pugachev (see figures 9 and 10 and n20).[20] In it Russia's great Cossack leader shares the same canvas as the Devil, whose political affiliations centuries of Byzantine religious convention had concealed. The French Revolution revealed them.

'TEARS IN RIVERS FROM OUR EYES'

Satan's subsequent secularization was most marked, as we shall see, in the Romantic period. Its beginning, although delayed in Russia, was heralded by sentimentalism. Radishchev was certainly one of the more vivid literary exponents of this movement, as his tears over the plight of the peasants in the *Journey from St. Petersburg to Moscow* (1790) bear witness. But the movement's most influential poet was a younger writer whose early sympathy for the French Revolution yielded to a patriotic endorsement of autocracy.

Karamzin may have come across Milton thanks to Novikov, whose edition of Amvrosii's translation of *Paradise Lost* was wholly compatible with the 'selected Library of Christian Readings' Novikov had begun to publish when the two met. Yet Karamzin's interest in English literature was arrived at

Satan, Pugachev, and the French Revolution 75

independently of Novikov's circle. Indeed, his earliest published literary effort was a translation of Shakespeare's *Julius Caesar*, which appeared in 1787.[21]

In that same year he wrote his ode 'Poeziia' ('To Poetry') in which Milton is characterized as a 'lofty spirit.'[22] The poem is reminiscent in aim of Trediakovsky's and Sumarokov's odes on the same theme,[23] with two qualifications. None of the 'chorus of Frenchmen' placed on Parnassus by the earlier Russian poets are even mentioned by Karamzin. Among the moderns their place is taken by Shakespeare, who 'had found the key to all the great secrets of Fate': by John Milton, Young, Thomson, James Macpherson, Gessner, and Friedrich Gottlieb Klopstock. The latter was favoured as a 'chosen singer' because he had been 'initiated into the divine mysteries.' The other striking difference when compared with its forebears is that the imagery of 'To Poetry' is no longer largely classical.

Instead it is Christian. The poem begins in the manner of Milton and Klopstock with the creation of the world, when 'man appeared ... who, feeling the benevolence, wisdom and greatness of the Creator, his heart poured into a gentle hymn ...' The hymn 'soared to the Father,' and thus poetry was born.[24] Karamzin goes on to describe the prelapsarian state of man in Paradise, and the decline of poetry after his transgression. Orpheus makes his bow in the seventh stanza, and not long after – Milton:

> Mil'ton, vysokii dukh, v gremiashchikh strannykh pesniakh
> Opisyvaet nam bunt, kogda poet Adama,
> Zhivushchego v raiu, no golos nispustiv,
> Vdrug slezy iz ochei ruch'iami izvlekaet,
> Kogda poët ego, podpadshego grekhu.[25]

> (Milton, a sublime spirit [who] in strange thundering verses
> Describes the revolt when he sings for us
> Of Adam living in Paradise;
> But lowering his voice when singing of him
> Who transgressed, he suddenly draws tears
> In rivers from our eyes.)

For Karamzin, as the tone of these lines perhaps implies, poetry was the highest manifestation of the human spirit. No Russian poet is mentioned in the poem, but the author prophesies that 'even now in Aurora's light / In * * * * is gleaming, and soon all nations of the world / Will northward flow in pilgrimage to light their lamp.'[26] It may have been Karamzin's intention to fill the space marked by the asterisks with his own name, or (as some think) by that of Kheraskov or Derzhavin.[27]

In 1789 Karamzin went abroad for one and a half years. The *Letters of a Russian Traveller* were one outcome of that journey, the book being received by the Russian public as something of a revelation. Not only did Karamzin displace Prévost d'Exile as an authority on England, but his enlightened and cosmopolitan sensibility struck a new note. One of his most moving experiences was hearing a performance of Handel's *Messiah* in Westminster Abbey performed by six hundred musicians and a choir of three hundred voices: there tears came to his eyes again on hearing 'I know that my Redeemer lives,' and the duet: 'O Death, where is thy sting, o grave, where is thy victory?'[28]

The recollection of this moment may have inspired Karamzin after his return from Russia to turn his talents to one of the best-known as well as the most frequently performed versions of *Paradise Lost*. Haydn's oratorio *Die Schoepfung* was first performed in 1800 in Vienna. The libretto of *The Creation* was prepared by a Mr Lidley (or Lindley or Liddell) and revised by Baron van Swieten; and it was this that Karamzin brought out in a Russian translation in 1801.[29] Other Russian translations followed.[30]

Radishchev was inspired by the same theme to write a *pesnoslovie* to which he gave an identical title – *Tvorenie* (*The Creation*). It used to be held that this work was written under the influence of Haydn's work of that name, but the obvious parallels between Book VII of *Paradise Lost* and Radishchev's 'oratorio' (as N.D. Kochetkova points out) make this hypothesis unnecessary.[31] It should be added that the creation theme was generally fashionable among Russian poets of the 1780s. One of the first poems by S.S. Bobrov, a young contemporary of Radishchev, also deals with this subject.

Radishchev's social conscience was probably awakened by the same *Philosophes* Catherine herself had worshipped before the 'French madness.' He became acquainted with their writings at the University of Leipzig, where he attended classes with Goethe. In reading Voltaire and listening to the lectures of Professor Christian Fürchgott Gellert, then at the height of his fame as a literary pundit, young Radishchev may have learnt of Milton's significance as a poet. Few of Goethe's generation were ignorant of it.

The five years Radishchev spent in Saxony were not all happy ones. The treatment he and other Russian students received at the hands of Hofmeister Bochum, their supervisor, was such that they contemplated running away through England to North America.[32] As it was, Radishchev returned to Russia in 1771. There he entered the civil service, publishing his earliest work two years later. It was a translation of Mably's *Observations sur l'histoire de la Grèce*, which was remarkable for the notes added by the young author.

His connection with the St Petersburg élite began when he entered the Corps des Pages as a boy – the same aristocratic establishment that some decades later would give the anarchist Prince Kropotkin his lasting hatred for tsarism. Radishchev may have been thinking about the political implications of serfdom in 1775 on a trip from the Russian capital to the distant estate of his parents in the country. There he was told how his father's peasants had helped his family in the woods while Pugachev's rebels were wreaking terror nearby.

He also heard what happened to less enlightened and less popular landowners. His reaction to all this was the opposite of Derzhavin's. Later, in his *Journey from St. Petersburg to Moscow*, which established Radishchev's notoriety and fame, he would warn his peers that failure to free the serfs would bring a revolution far more terrible than the Pugachev Rebellion.

Until the *Journey*, Radishchev's most radical piece was 'Vol'nost' ' an ode to liberty. It was written in 1781–3 under the impression of the American War of Independence, its lines on regicide being perhaps inspired (as V.P. Semennikov points out) by Milton.[33] The execution of Charles I is also mentioned in a later writing of Radishchev ('The Life of F.V. Ushakov'), but 'Liberty' had ominous consequences for the author. Although the whole poem could not be published until the Revolution of 1905 abolished censorship in his country, he included parts of it in the *Journey*.

Catherine's reaction to these lines largely explains his arrest. The 'ode [is] most clearly manifestly revolutionary,' the Empress observed with distress; 'Tsars are threatened with the block. Cromwell's example is cited and praised.'[34] She was not entirely accurate. Radishchev had portrayed an evil monarch, whose abuse of power had led to his overthrow; then comes his trial and execution at popular behest.

What the ode does, therefore, is to praise Cromwell for 'teach[ing] peoples how to avenge' their wrongs. It then goes on to criticize 'the great man' ('velikii muzh') for 'destroy[ing] the citadel of liberty' he had helped to build. Robespierre is then reproached for duplicating the earlier 'perfidy,' which consisted in Cromwell's failure to set 'a great example.'[35]

At the time Catherine read the *Journey* she was in no mood to see the subtleties of Radishchev's tightrope act. Her instinct, despite what some commentators have said on the subject, was not entirely unsound. The lines from 'Liberty' were perhaps included in the book to complement the dream sequence in 'Spasskaya Polest',' where the author imagines that he himself has become monarch. He sees the people, whose 'trembling silence assured me that they were all subject to my will. On the sides, upon a somewhat higher level, stood a great number of charming, splendidly garbed women. Their glances expressed their delight upon seeing me, and their very wishes strove to anticipate mine ere they arose.'[36] Suddenly, in the midst of royal rapture, Truth appears in the guise of a pilgrim. She removes the cataracts from the emperor's 'blind' eyes, revealing the true state of his nation and the true feelings of his people. 'Thy faithful subjects,' Truth tells him, 'love not thee, but their country; who are always ready for thy defeat, if it will avenge the enslavement of men.'[37]

This allegorical masterpiece constitutes an appeal to end serfdom, but together with the ode to liberty it could be construed as something rather more threatening. And Catherine may have recalled that when loyalists such as Derzhavin mentioned Cromwell or Mirabeau, they did so with unequivocal horror. In Derzhavin's rhetorical obloquy the Lord Protector is Julius Caesar and Nero incarnate, while Mirabeau is likened to Catiline.[38]

Would the Empress have overlooked Radishchev's bravura performance if the timing of his book had been more fortunate? Although he had worked at it for more than ten years, Radishchev published it only in 1790. In one of his few references to the French Revolution, Radishchev then compounded the *faux pas* over Cromwell by calling Mirabeau a great orator. Catherine, ever on her guard against the contagion emanating from France, was furious at even so tame an allusion. Mirabeau, she noted, 'deserves not once but many times over to be hanged.'[39] After adding copious exclamatory annotations to the book, she then decided that Radishchev deserved the same fate. Late in the summer of 1790, he was arrested while serving as chief of the St Petersburg Custom House and imprisoned in the Peter and Paul Fortress.

Milton's influence on the *Journey* is twofold. From both Radishchev himself and his sons we know that he read Milton and had the highest opinion of him. Indeed, Milton, Shakespeare, and Voltaire (in that order) are described in the *Journey* as the three supremely great writers. From Milton Radishchev drew support for his theories on prosody – discussed in the chapter on Tver'. The other influence is political. The longest chapter in the *Journey* – which like Karamzin's *Letters* owes much to Sterne – contains a historical account of the origin and development of censorship. This represents, when seen in its Russian context, as bold a defence of freedom of the press as Milton's *Areopagitica* during the English Revolution. Karamzin's attitude to autocracy, which he came to admire and uphold, was quite contrary to Radishchev's, but both writers were sentimentalists. Karamzin shed tears over *The Messiah* in Westminster Abbey and over Adam's transgression, while Radishchev wept at the sight of brutalized serfs. Pushkin did not side with Karamzin, whose obsequious many-tomed eulogy to the Russian state repelled him. He saw in Karamzin a terrestrial version of those 'Arselickers of the Almighty' caricatured by Pushkin in his parody of *Paradise Lost*, in which Milton's Satan for the first time in Russian letters quite definitely carries the stamp of poetic approval.

1 Opening page of a 'satanic' manuscript translation-adaptation of
Paradise Lost from which God and Christ are excluded

2 Vasilii Petrov, Catherine the Great's 'pocket poet,' as portrayed during his stay in England (artist unknown)

3 Eve tempting Adam, from the first Russian illustrated edition of 1795

ВОЗВРАЩЕННЫЙ РАЙ.

КНИГА ПЕРВАЯ

Прежде воспѣтъ мною погубленный рай преслушаніемъ непокориваго Адама; нынѣ пою рай возвращенный для спасенія рода человѣческаго твердымъ послушаніемъ новаго Адама; послушаніемъ всѣми образы искушеннымъ, и всегда побѣдоноснымъ надъ ухищреніями искусителя духа. Еммануилъ посрамилъ древняго змія; восторжествовалъ надъ нимъ; и ужасная пустыня нѣкоторымъ образомъ чрезъ его побѣду превратилась въ рай сладости.

Душе

4 Opening page of Ivan Greshishchev's translation of *Paradise Regained*

ИСТИННЫЙ СВѢТЪ,

ПОЕМА
ВЪ
ДЕВЯТИ ПѢСНЯХЪ,
СОЧИНЕННАЯ
НА РОССІЙСКОМЪ ЯЗЫКѢ.

Печатана въ Университетской Типографіи у Н. Новикова, 1780 года.

5 Title page of the Masonic *True Light*

6 The sole surviving portrait of Mariya Khrapovitskaya, one of Russia's first woman poet-translators (by an unknown artist)

7 M.M. Kheraskov at the time he wrote his Miltonic *Universe* (by an unknown artist)

8 Adam and Eve – a tender moment in Eden, from the first illustrated Russian edition of *Paradise Lost*, 1795 (unsigned)

9 Pugachev, the peasant rebel, displaying an appropriate reaction (from a contemporary painting by an unknown artist)

10 A politicized devil spying on Pugachev (detail), by an unknown serf artist

11 Milton as he appears in the frontispiece to the 1824 Russian edition of the epics

12 Vasilii Zhukovsky in his Romantic phase (by an unknown artist)

13 Self-portrait by Lermontov

PARADISE LOST.

BOOK I.

Of Man's first disobedience, and the fruit
Of that forbidden tree, whose mortal taste
Brought death into the world, and all our woe,
With loss of Eden, till one greater Man
Restore us, and regain the blissful seat,
Sing, heav'nly Muse, that on the secret top
Of Oreb, or of Sinai, didst inspire
That shepherd, who first taught the chosen seed,
In the beginning how the Heav'ns and Earth
Rose out of Chaos: Or if Sion hill
Delight thee more, and Siloa's brook that flow'd
Fast by the oracle of God: I thence
Invoke thy aid to my adventrous song,
That with no middle flight intends to soar
Above th' Aonian mount, while it pursues
Things unattempted yet in prose or rhyme.
And chiefly Thou, O Spi'rit, that dost prefer

14(a, b) The opening pages of the Delille-Milton *Le Paradis perdu / Paradise Lost*, 1805, in an early bilingual edition familiar to the Russian Romantics

PARADIS PERDU.

LIVRE I.

Je chante l'homme en proie aux pièges tentateurs,
Et le fatal péché de nos premiers auteurs
Qui, par le fruit mortel privés de l'innocence,
Nous léguèrent le mal, le crime et la souffrance,
Jusqu'au jour où, calmant le courroux paternel,
L'homme-dieu nous rouvrit les demeures du ciel :
Sujet vaste et sacré, dont jamais le génie
N'enchanta les bosquets des nymphes d'Aonie.
Toi donc qui, célébrant les merveilles des cieux,
Prends loin de l'Hélicon un vol audacieux ;
Soit que, te retenant sous ses palmiers antiques,
Sion avec plaisir répète tes cantiques ;
Soit que, cherchant d'Horeb la tranquille hauteur,
Tu rappelles ce jour où la voix d'un pasteur
Des Hébreux attentifs ravissant les oreilles,
De la création leur contoit les merveilles ;
Soit que, chantant le jour où Dieu donna sa loi,
Le Sina sous tes pieds tressaille encor d'effroi ;
Soit que, près du saint lieu d'où partent ses oracles,
Les flots du Siloé te disent ses miracles :

15 The Devil and Kiukhel'beker, Pushkin's Decembrist friend (unsigned)

PART TWO

Satan as Romantic and Marxist Idol

'Twentieth century ... Now the gloom
Is still more frightening.
Even more black and sweeping looms
The shade of Lucifer's vast wing.'

Alexander Blok, 'Retribution' (1910–11)

SIX

The Demonic Tradition from Zhukovsky to Pushkin

'A dungeon horrible, on all sides round
As one great furnace flamed; yet from those flames
No light; but rather darkness visible
Served only to discover sights of woe.' (PL I. ll 61–4)
                      Lines in Milton that Pushkin particularly admired

'ARSELICKERS OF THE ALMIGHTY'

Mirsky compares Zhukovsky's influence up to about 1820 to that of Spenser or Ronsard, which gives some notion of the relative youth of Russian poetry, since Zhukovsky (who was born in 1783) is the accepted patriarch of its Golden Age. He still believed in the epic, and advised the young Pushkin to devote his talent to the genre, advice the young poet spurned after writing 'Bova' in 1814. At the age of fifteen Pushkin felt, as Zhukovsky did not, that the future of heroic verse was uncertain, and he did not want to follow 'the all-wise German Klopstock, [whom he] could not understand.' Nor did Pushkin feel tempted to imitate Milton and Camoëns:

Za Mil'tonom i Kamoensom
Opasalsia ia bez kryl parit';
Ne derzal v stikhakh bessmysslennykh
Kheruvimov zharit' s pushkami ...[1]

(I hesitated to coast in the cloud-land of
Milton and Camoëns.
Did not dare in senseless verses
To fry Cherubim with cannon.)

Pushkin's instinct was sound, as the failure of Shikhmatov's *Peter the Great* and sundry *Suvoriades* and *Alexandriades* proved. *Evgenii Onegin*, by contrast, took something from the epic but at one leap formed a poetic vehicle that moved Russian verse closer to the spirit of the modern novel. Since the Karamzinians and Arzamasians (to whose number Zhukovsky, Batiushkov, Pushkin, and some of the foremost poets of the time belonged) cultivated the 'fugitive' verse introduced by M.N. Murav'ev, one might therefore have expected a decline in the literary status of *Paradise Lost*. But this did not happen, partly because it was not regarded as a conventional epic (which indeed it was not, despite Pushkin's reference to its cherubim and cannons). Partly it seems also to have been Satan's reputation that pulled it through into the Romantic era, at a time when the casualty rate among 'national' epics was very high.

In the battle between the classicists and the enthusiasts of the new sensibility, many of the older generation's literary models suffered an eclipse. Pushkin and his friend P.A. Viazemsky found themselves defending what Pushkin called 'genuine romanticism' ('istinnyi romantizm'), although few of their countrymen agreed about what this meant. Viazemsky, in his foreword to Pushkin's *Fountain of Bakhchisarai* (1824) advanced the view that romanticism involved not so much the breaking of fixed rules as the recognition of authentic emotion. He praised Schlegel and Mme de Staël for recognizing this; and in Viazemsky's general reflections on contemporary literature he followed Mme de Staël rather than Chateaubriand, who regarded Christianity as the key to Western culture. Like Mme de Staël, Viazemsky preferred to put the emphasis on national character, and in this sense 'Homer, Pindar, Sophocles, Euripides, etc., were in their own time in a certain sense Romantics, for they sing of the doings of their own Greeks, not of the Chaldeans; just as Milton sang not of Homer's superstitions, but of the Christian tradition.'[2]

It was possible, of course, to combine the Christian with the national theme, as Zhukovsky, who was very devout, tried to do in his epic on St Vladimir. But most poets and critics of his and Pushkin's generation were more concerned with *narodnost'*, that is, with the problem of erecting an autonomous literature. It was in this context that the example of England was considered interesting, since there the conflict between French and the vernacular was not settled until Chaucer's time: and the rise of a national literary idiom in England was not (as it was thought to be in France) tied to classical models. Originality was considered by Zhukovsky and others as one of the main issues in the contest with the new sensibility, and for some time Russian readers would have found it hard to know to which side of the barricades Milton belonged.

At the end of the eighteenth century both Shakespeare and Milton were regarded as classics. One journal at that time even suggested that Milton was no longer read in England; he had become as remote as Voltaire.³ Then where did the break with classicism occur? Nikolai Ivanovich Nadezhdin (1804–56), the first Russian critic to examine the origins of romanticism, included the Middle Ages in its realm and made Shakespeare and Milton into its pioneers. In 'De Origine, Natura et Fatis Poeseos Quae Romantica Audit,' a doctoral dissertation presented at Moscow University in 1830, his conclusions met with such applause that it was promptly serialized in the *Vestnik Evropy*. Its readers, Zhukovsky among them, had no difficulty, it seems, in seeing 'Shakespeare, Milton, Thomson, Scott, [and] Southey' as part of an identical ongoing tradition, checked at times by the neoclassical surge of writers such as Dryden, Pope, and Dr Johnson.⁴

Nadezhdin was far from being the first to identify *Paradise Lost* as a Romantic work. Nor was he the earliest critic to discern the seeds of the modern movement (now transforming the character of Russian poetry) in English literature. In his lectures on the history of poesy at Moscow University Shevyrev, who had befriended Pushkin after his return from exile in 1824, tried to relate the innovative direction taken by literature in England to the 'moralizing' character of its people. According to him, *Paradise Lost* was the embodiment of this religious and didactic vein, and it could also be seen in its latest manifestation in Byron's *Don Juan*, 'the Odyssey – as Shevyrev calls it – of the nineteenth century.'⁵

Yet there is an interesting distinction between the way Nadezhdin and Shevyrev each come face to face with Byronism and the figure of Milton's Satan that lurked behind this alarming literary phenomenon. Vast as Byron's influence was on the Continent, it was nowhere more marked than in Russia. In the 1830s poets and critics were still fighting over his legacy. Shevyrev, who unlike Nadezhdin had welcomed Pushkin's break with tradition, felt more and more deeply drawn to romanticism, his 'dramatic piece' on Adam and Eve's expulsion from Eden (1828) being a characteristic expression of the new sensibility.⁶ He saw no difficulty in reconciling the sublime in Milton or the 'ideal lyre of Byron and Moore' with what he saw as the peculiar and wholly laudable mission of English literature 'to return European poetry onto the path of friendship with life and Nature.'⁷

Examined more closely, Shevyrev's judgment, as displayed in his own doctoral dissertation, 'The Historical Development of Literary Theory' (1836), is less subtle than Nadezhdin's.⁸ But it was written later, when the triumph of the Romantics was already apparent and the author had clearly joined them. Nadezhdin, on the other hand, had tried to negotiate a compromise between them and the classicists. This is why Nadezhdin's verdict had been awaited with bated breath by both sides. Up to a point each side had reason to feel flattered by his comments. That point was Byronism. In a fascinating manoeuvre, expertly designed to placate opposing factions, Nadezhdin treats Voltaire and Byron as polar opposites, the towering egoists of classicism and romanticism – the movements each incarnated and had brought into a similarly disastrous cul-de-sac. Each had been wholly destructive.

In Voltaire's case, we have 'the sad spectacle of a spirit which, having risen outside itself, into the boundless ocean of existence, and not having before his eyes a pathfinding star in which it can have faith, turns and begins to vent its boundless wandering in comic scoffing and harlequin-like attacks on anything that comes to hand.'[9] Similarly, Byron expresses the 'culmination and distortion of the Romantic spirit, the final eclipse ... of Romantic poetry.' In truth, says Nadezhdin, 'what a terrible spectacle! Like the Cain created by him, Byron reels with the dead bones of existence, from which he himself has extruded all the juices of life. Nowhere does he find peace, he is the ulcer of nature, the horror of mankind, hating the earth, rejecting Heaven.'[10]

In the *Vestnik Evropy* version of Nadezhdin's thesis, Byron is compared with Klopstock's Andremelech, which is strong language indeed.[11] For this fallen angel ends up hating not only mankind, but also both God and Satan. The point of this comparison becomes apparent in the next paragraph where Nadezhdin draws a further parallel between Byron and Milton's Satan; for who can 'resist wondering at his indomitable pride and invincible strength of spirit ... which in its fall ... brings the world with it ... ?'[12] May God save us, says the Russian critic, from 'imitating this model – this dreadful spectre!' ('uzhasnoe strashilishche'). Nadezhdin's vehement assault on the Satanist school, for whose transgressions he makes Byron rather than Milton responsible, was supported by other articles in the *Vestnik Evropy* informing readers of the trends in English literature since Byron's death.

Thus, apart from Shakespeare, only 'Dryden and Milton [were still] called poets.'[13] With the religious revival, Locke was now forgotten and 'is considered a poor ideologue.'[14] Bacon was read only by scholars; while Milton – according to another essay in the same journal – was being imitated by Methodist poets, such as Henry Milman, Montgomery, and Kirke White.[15] None of these forgotten figures appear to have been known to Russian writers of the time, although some Russian writers were aware of Keats and Shelley. The latter is dismissed as 'an Epicurean atheist.' Both are described as the main supporters of the Satanist school, whose 'shameless writings' are seen in the Russian journal as being 'destructive of all human conventions.' Nor was it surprising that the writings of the Satanists were proscribed in England, since their 'aim [was] to undermine everything that exists ... principles, dogmas, customs and traditions, in order to erect on the ruins new dogma, new dispositions, in accordance with ... an imagination dominated by absurd ideas.'[16]

Vestnik Evropy had by this time become (like Nadezhdin and Shevyrev themselves) very much a part of the literary and political establishment. Nor is it entirely surprising that a Decembrist such as Kiukhel'beker should see Satan's rebellion in a different light. Writing from his exile in Siberia, the poet drew a bold distinction between the hero of *Paradise Lost* (as Kiukhel'beker held him to be) and Klopstock's Abbadona, the 'cry-baby demon' ('diavol-plaksa'). The conception of the latter 'was typical of the philosophical tastelessness of the first half of the eighteenth century,' which alone had the dubious distinction of producing this lachrymose and 'sentimental' creature.[17] Milton, by contrast, enjoyed the real honour of having turned his back on the stereotyped devils of Dante and Tasso.

Theirs had been derived from medieval superstition. Milton's Satan, by contrast, was not 'a disgusting monster,' and it was Milton who dared to deviate from popular lore 'before any other poet dared to do so.' His 'Prince of Darkness,' like all Milton's angels after their fall, retained their outer beauty (as did Aretino's Spinello); and Kiukhel'beker was even prepared to praise the allegory of Sin and Death, which he blames Voltaire for misconstruing.[18] At the same time, unlike Nadezhdin, Kiukhel'beker did not consider Milton as being of the same stature as Shakespeare, whom alone he placed next to Homer. Milton came next, with Aeschylus, Dante, Schiller, Derzhavin, and – Byron.[19]

Yet Kiukhel'beker was by no means certain that Milton could be considered a true Romantic. His appreciation for him rested in part on the same qualities that drew many of the Decembrists to Byron, that is, his opposition to the existing social order. As a champion of liberty, however, Milton's status was not quite the same because he appealed also to Orthodox Decembrists, such as Pushkin's friend Fedor Nikolaevich Glinka.[20] Here perhaps lay one of the keys to the way *Paradise Lost* survived the demise of classicism and the rise of romanticism. Sympathy for Satan did not require a religious view of life any more than Byron's *Cain:* but the political implications Decembrists such as Kiukhel'beker drew from Satan's apostasy did not have to be accepted by pious readers.

In Kiukhel'beker's own case the religious and the radical motives combined. As a Protestant, he was better placed than any of Pushkin's other friends to understand Milton, whom he began reading (so Tynianov thinks) at the *lycée* in Tsarskoe Selo.[21] This may have left a lasting impression. Long afterwards in Siberian exile, he wrote this profile of the 'titan' (as Kiukhel'beker calls Milton) in a long poem inspired by *Childe Harold*:

> Velikii *Mil'ton* ...
>   ...
>   No vypal vek emu,
>   Kotoryi ne cheta zhe moemu:
>   Pylal eshche v to vremia very plamen
> I, kak v napitannyi ognem sviashchennym kamen',
>   Tak udarial v serdtsa pevets –
>   I vyleteli iskry iz serdets!
> On Boga vozveshchal: chto zh? i dyshat' ne smeiia,
>   Emu vnimali; slavil krasotu:
> Vliublialsia mir v ego volshebnuiu mechtu;
>   Perunom porazhal zlodeia:
> Zlodei drozhal; ili, proniknut sam
> Ispugom veshchim, dukha otritsaniia
>   Iavlial ispugannym ocham –
> I v dushi prolival potoki sodraganiia.
> Da! ne v metaforu v te dni i smert' i grekh ...[22]

> (Great *Milton* ...
>   ...
>   But the age that was his lot
>   Cannot be compared to mine.
>   At that time the flame of faith still burnt
> And, as with a stone impregnated with holy fire,
>   The bard so struck men's hearts
>   That sparks flew from them!
> He God proclaimed: what of it? and, not daring to breathe,
>   They heeded him: he celebrated beauty.
> The world fell in love with his enchanted vision;
>   With a thunderbolt he routed the evil one:
> [And] the evil one trembled; or, himself imbued
> With prophetic fright, he showed
>   The spirit of negation to frightened eyes,
> Unleashing waves of shuddering in their souls.
>   Yes, in those days no mere metaphors were sin and death ...)

The poet then goes on to say that his age no longer took demons seriously.

As if in confirmation of this, a contemporary caricature shows Kiukhel'beker in the company of an enfeebled devil who looks like one of the playful and naughty demons sketched by Pushkin (see Figure 15). Goethe's 'Geist der stets verneint' had added a gloss to the contest between good and evil that was compatible with *Paradise Lost*, but alien to the Puritanism that had given it birth. Milton's prince of darkness may have had more grandeur than the Mephisto of *Faust*, but the latter's scepticism was more in character with the times.

Yet Satan's change in status was not due to the decline of faith alone. Indeed, in his diary Kiukhel'beker attacks another writer for imagining that the future belonged to science. The times, he said, are essentially religious or 'philosophical-religious';[23] and so the Christian revival that came with romanticism made it seem. Other Decembrists, such as A.A. Bestuzhev-Marlinsky, compared the Romantic explosion to the Reformation; and themselves to its Protestants, who shook off 'the rotten garment of classicism' as the reformers had shaken off Catholicism.[24] But what did all this portend for literature? In 1827 the young Victor Hugo announced in his foreword to *Cromwell* that drama alone corresponded to the spirit of the new age. N.A. Polevoi, for one, vehemently disagreed, arguing that epic genres were equally suitable. The discussion continued, while Lermontov's *Demon*, published only after the middle of the century, proved that while fallen from Heaven, fallen angels did not fall from public favour. Nor, since Milton's epics were largely known to Russian readers in prose, did the contentious future of heroic verse affect their standing in Russia to the degree one might expect, since the continuing interest in the Satan of *Paradise Lost* rubbed off on the personality of its creator.

This is shown by the stark contrast in the attitudes to that epic of Kiukhel'-beker and Pushkin. For the Decembrist, Milton was the prophet of liberty. 'A reverend posterity,' he wrote, now fell on its knees before him because the mob, blind to the ways of destiny, could not heed his prophecies or understand his 'holy, fiery verse.'[25] The mob similarly let down the Decembrists, a verdict shared by Pushkin in his devastating conclusion to *Boris Godunov*, where the appeal to the people also falls on deaf ears.[26] But the poetic seriousness with which Kiukhel'beker viewed Satan was hopelessly undermined for Pushkin by the absurdity – as he thought – of the biblical matter on which *Paradise Lost* is based.

In 'Gavriliada' (1821), a parody of some of its themes that circulated in manuscript to be confiscated by the police and scandalize Nicholas I, the irony of 'Bova' is raised to the level of inspired blasphemy. God is reduced to a cuckolded lecher lusting for the Virgin Mary, who is seduced by Satan. They are surprised by Archangel Gabriel, also her lover, who is abused by Satan as one of 'the Arselickers of the Almighty.' Gabriel then wrestles with the 'rebellious slave' in a mock-Miltonic version of the war in Heaven, only gaining the upper hand after biting Satan's 'puffed-up member.'[27] This painful setback notwithstanding, Satan has all the best lines, which would seem to reflect Pushkin's unwitting admiration for the portrayal of the arch-rebel in *Paradise Lost* despite his reservations about the epic genre.

ZHUKOVSKY AND *PARADISE LOST*

But if for Pushkin Milton's Satan was thus a heroic figure while the poem's biblical baggage seemed absurd, the attitude of Zhukovsky to *Paradise Lost* was quite the opposite. In his case it is clearer than in Pushkin's when he became acquainted with the poem, because Zhukovsky refers to it as early as the beginning of the 1800s. Thereafter it would be cited again and again in sketches and résumés of projected translations,[28] suggesting that the idea of translating *Paradise Lost* stayed with Zhukovsky for much of his life. Indeed, it may have been reawakened in 1837 by the article defending Milton that was left among Pushkin's papers after his fatal duel. Pushkin's criticism of Chateaubriand also no doubt accounts for Zhukovsky's acquisition of that poet's *Le Paradis perdu*,[29] although this would certainly not have been the first translation seen by Zhukovsky. His library, only recently recovered, lists a translation of 1793 in German, a language Zhukovsky had mastered and in which he felt more at ease than in either English or French. Yet at some point, perhaps in 1805, the temptation to tackle Milton's original proved so strong that Zhukovsky acquired Dr Newton's two-volume edition of *The Poetical Works*, containing both Dr Johnson's celebrated *Life* and Addison's no-less-celebrated critical essays.[30]

Interestingly enough, however, the résumé of 1805 contains extracts from two other well-known assessments of *Paradise Lost*. To these Zhukovsky added no comments of his own, but what he then chose to copy out for future reference implies that, like so many Russian Romantic poets (of whom Zhukovsky is usually considered the pioneer), it was Milton's portrayal of Satan that fascinated him.

Presumably this is why Zhukovsky thought it worthwhile to cite Voltaire's strictures on Milton's characterization of Satan, which the sage of Ferney found very much wanting in good taste. Voltaire considered Satan's speeches too long, and some of the episodes in which he is involved, particularly the confrontation with Sin and Death, 'disgusting' and 'abominable.' These criticisms, some of which Voltaire later modified, were familiar to a long line of Russian poets beginning with Prince Antiokh Kantemir, who read the *Essay on Epick Poetry* not long after it appeared in England.[31] The best-known

Russian translation was by Catherine the Great's companion in conspiracy, Dashkova, although Zhukovsky cites a French edition.[32] The Russian poet chose to compare Voltaire's unfavourable assessment of Satan with a later verdict by Hugh Blair, a critic Dashkova herself had met when she was in England. For Blair it was Satan's ambivalence that made his character so absorbing. If Milton erred at times in metaphysics and matters of theology, he never failed to be sublime. For Blair, as it seems for Zhukovsky, if *Paradise Lost* contained faults, in the epic genre its author surpassed 'all poets, both Ancient and Modern.'[33]

This judgment was buttressed by the view of a French pedagogue and aesthetician, Charles Batteux, for whom Satan was the indubitable hero of Milton's poem: for if that were not the case, 'et que ce fût Adam, le dénouement seroit tragique, et nullement épique ...' Verdicts such as this no doubt made an impression on Zhukovsky; otherwise he would not have noted them down. Was he too pious himself to sympathize with Satan's predicament? Two generations later, as we shall see, when Lermontov attended the same school as Zhukovsky, such sympathy was no longer deemed exceptional or extravagant, except by the authorities. But Zhukovsky belonged to a generation whose religious sentiments were supported by the mysticism of the early Russian Romantics, a mysticism nurtured in the Masonic lodges of the Catherinian era and that then reappeared at the turn of the century in the intense interest Russia's writers and intellectuals displayed in German pietism and German philosophical idealism. Zhukovsky represented that swelling trend as well as a spasmodic and not always consistent reaction against French neoclassicism. One of its exponents, Batteux, still enjoyed Zhukovsky's confidence, for he notes the latter's reservations concerning Milton's Satan: no reader of *Paradise Lost* (so the French critic rather innocently asserted) can wish the prince of darkness success.

If Zhukovsky's own sentiments on the subject changed with the years, there is no record of it. For all his admiration of Pushkin, he shared none of his Enlightenment scepticism. It is therefore quite inconceivable for Zhukovsky to have referred to Satan as 'the Arselicker of the Almighty.' Similarly, his faith in the epic remained unshaken even after Pushkin's death, and perhaps it is this commitment to that genre that first prompted the idea of translating *Paradise Lost* in 1805.[34] This intention remained unrealized, and Zhukovsky returned to it in 1812–14, when he expressed it again – this time in a note to himself concerning both Klopstock's *Messiade* and *Paradise Lost*, 'extracts' from which he now wished to translate.[35]

This was a critical period for the poet. In response to Napoleon's invasion Zhukovsky had joined the Moscow militia, witnessing the battle of Borodino, which Tolstoy would so memorably evoke in *War and Peace*. Zhukovsky's passionate response is etched in a patriotic hymn entitled 'A Bard in the Camp of Russian Warriors,' which established his popularity and his reputation as a poet with the public at large. The year 1813 proved a turning-point in his personal life too. He fell in love with the daughter of his half-sister, and even though his affection was returned, the marriage was disallowed. For this and other reasons Zhukovsky moved to St Petersburg, where his long career as perhaps the kindliest courtier of the time began. He became reader to the empress mother and teacher of Russian to members of the imperial family, being promoted in 1825 to be tutor to the future Tsar-liberator, Alexander II. Zhukovsky thus came to be exceptionally well informed about the official status at court of poets such as Pushkin, an issue of some delicacy after the Decembrist insurrection, in which so many of them were directly or indirectly involved. Zhukovsky in no way shared the republicanism of the radicals, but as a man of honour and decency, a living example it has been said of 'die schöne Seele,' he was ideally suited for interceding before the emperor and sundry officials on behalf of both his friends and writers and poets he hardly knew.

He also used his position to introduce the imperial family to several epic poets, among them Camoëns, Dante, Milton, and Klopstock. Of these Dante with his devils had not as yet been translated into Russian, but as we shall see in the following chapter on Milton and Lermontov, the imperial family's response to the latter's *Demon* and even perhaps to *Paradise Lost* was not without influence on the stand taken by government censors. Zhukovsky's authority was not, of course, derived from his status as a quasi-poet laureate, but rather from his tact and unimpeachable integrity, anchored in the conviction that the themes natural to all true poetry were love, Christian faith, chivalry, and loyalty. His affection for the *Messiade* certainly reflected this ideal, which in Klopstock's own case the French Revolution, at least in its initial stages, did nothing to undermine.

Nor does the German poet's guileful portrayal of Satan, who is shown to be unrelentingly and unambiguously wicked, tempt the pious reader into professing anything but conventional Christian sentiment. If this is the reason Zhukovsky turned to the German poem first, he nonetheless chose a demonic part in which the dominant character is Abbadona, a fallen angel who is not wholly committed to the rebellion and is constantly bemoaning his apostasy. In Canto 21 of the *Messias* Klopstock calls him 'the penitent angel.' This aptly captures the note of the Russian version. Zhukovsky would of course have been aware of the German poem's debt to *Paradise Lost*.[36] By that date, ie, by 1812, Zhukovsky had gently begun to turn against French literary models, despite his role in founding Arzamas, the semi-humorous circle of literati who sided with Karamzin in his reform of the language, the purpose of which was to introduce the melodious style and natural grace Karamzin admired in the writers of France.

Romantic disillusionment with French neoclassical rules and political events combined to turn Zhukovsky's attention more and more to German and English poetry. His free translation of Gray's 'Elegy in a Country Churchyard' in 1802 had marked a dramatic new departure in Russian verse, and thus already anticipated his later affection for Southey, Wordsworth, Byron, Moore, and Shakespeare. At a time when Russian society was radiant with the optimism that greeted the coming to the throne of a liberal tsar, it also reflected the young Zhukovsky's support for Gray's populist faith:

> Full many a gem of purest ray serene,
>   The dark unfathom'd caves of ocean bear:
> Full many a flower is born to blush unseen,
>   And waste its sweetness on the desert air.
>
> Some village Hampden that with dauntless breast
>   The little tyrant of his fields withstood,
> Some mute inglorious Milton, here may rest,
>   Some Cromwell guiltless of his country's blood.

During the 1820s Zhukovsky began to translate longer German and English poems, including Byron's 'The Prisoner of Chillon,' Scott's 'Eve of St. John,' and Moore's angelic 'Death of the Peri.'[37]

Kiukhel'beker, writing in 1824, expressed the hope (uttered in jest) that Zhukovsky's emancipation 'from the yoke of French literature' would not end by placing on Russian poets 'chains of German or English sovereignty.'[38] Indeed, most of Zhukovsky's *oeuvre* consists of translations or adaptations; but his great achievement lay in thus endowing the poetic language with a subtlety of feeling and emotional range that, until Pushkin, none of his countrymen quite matched. His translation of *Paradise Lost* would thus undoubtedly have been a major event in Russian literature, comparable perhaps to his life's work, the translation he eventually completed of the *Odyssey*. As it is, all that appears to have survived as testimony to Zhukovsky's oft-repeated intention to translate Milton's epic are the opening lines (the lines in parenthesis were not attempted by the Russian poet):

> Of Man's first disobedience, and the fruit
> Of that forbidden tree, whose mortal taste

92 Satan as Romantic and Marxist Idol

Brought death into the world, and all our woe,
With loss of Eden, till one greater Man
Restore us, and regain the blissful seat,
Sing, Heavenly Muse, that on the secret top,
Of Oreb, or of Sinai, didst inspire,
That shepherd, who first taught the chosen seed,
In the beginning how the Heavens and Earth
Rose out of Chaos; or if Sion hill
Delight thee more, and Siloa's brook that flowed
Fast by the oracle of God, I thence
Invoke thy aid to my adventurous song,
That with no middle flight intends to soar
Above the Aonian mount, while it pursues
Things unattempted yet in prose or rhyme.
(And chiefly thou, O Spirit, that dost prefer
Before all temples the upright heart and pure,
Instruct me,) for thou know'st; thou from the first
Wast present, (and with mighty wings outspread
Dove-like sat'st brooding on the vast abyss
And mad'st it pregnant;) what in me is dark
Illumine, what is low raise and support;

Compare this with:

Grekhopadenie plod zapreshchennyi
Ot dreva [zhizni], koim smert' [na zemliu] [privedena] byla na zemliu
Privedena i s tratoiu Edema
Vse bedstviia liudei, dokol' velikii
Spasitel' ne prishel [ikh] otdat' [im] ikh nebu,
Vospoi [nebesnaia pevitza] sviataia muza, ty izdr [evle]
Na vysotakh Sinaia i Goreva
Vdokhnuvshaia vse pesni pastyriu
Kotoryi pervym izbrannikam raia
Povedal, kak v nachale sozdal nebo
I zemliu Bog. I esli kholm sionskii
Tebe ugoden ili siloamskii
[Kliuch] Prorochestv kliuch, pridi proshu
I ozhivi [menia dlia pesni vdokhnoven'ia] mne golos vdokhnovenn'ia …
Ne chelovecheskim poletom ia
S vysot Anii khochu parit', no [pet']

O nedostupnom znan'iu cheloveka.
...
Ty vedaesh vse tainy, vse tainy neba, vse puti.
...
Ty osveti, chto nizko, podnimi i podderzhi.[39]

This is not a literal translation. Nor would one expect this from Zhukovsky. But even in so slight a fragment there is a major clue on how the Russian poet's treatment of *Paradise Lost* would have differed from the original. Milton refers to Jesus as 'one greater Man,' but for Zhukovsky this is too familiar and he replaces 'Man' with 'Saviour' ('Spasitel' '), a form his Orthodox readers would certainly have found more apt.

What circumstance prompted Zhukovsky to begin the translation? His lines, only recently discovered and first published in 1984, were found in the margin of the poet's edition of Chateaubriand's translation of *Paradise Lost* (in which the French text faces the original). It is quite likely, as a Soviet scholar suggests, that Zhukovsky's attempt was inspired by Pushkin's criticism of Chateaubriand, for it was he who arranged for the posthumous publication of that piece, possibly the last article Pushkin was to write.[40] Its main argument concerning the French version is that:

a sublinear translation can never be accurate. Each language has its own idioms, its own fixed rhetorical figures, its own adopted expressions, which cannot be translated into another language in corresponding words ... If Russian, which is so pliable and powerful in its idioms and resources, so imitative and compliant in its relations with other languages, is not capable of a sublinear translation, of word-for-word rendering, then how will French, which is so cautious in its habits, so predisposed to its own traditions, so hostile even to languages of its own family, survive such an experiment, especially in a struggle with the language of Milton?[41]

Zhukovsky adopted quite a different approach, as we have seen. But to judge by the number of emendations, the effort did not come easily. Yet its particular strengths are more apparent when Zhukovsky's lines are compared with a translation accomplished only a few years earlier by M.P. Vronchenko, who tried to stay closer to the meaning and word order of the original:

Nachal'nuiu oslushnost' cheloveka
I zapovednyi, im vkushennyi plod,
Smert' vnesshii v mir i bedstviia, i Raia
Utratu, vnov' darovannogo moshchnym

Khodataia velikogo posredstvom,
Vospoi, bozhestvennaia Muza, ty,
Ch'iim vdokhnoven'em na vershine tainoi
Khoriva il' Sinaia, drevle Pastyr'
Izbrannym pel vosstan'e iz Khaosa
Zemli i Neba, il', kogda Sion
Ty liubil' bolee, i Siluanskii tok,
U proritzalishch tekshii Boga, i pesni
Tebia otpol' zovu ia smelyi; vyshe
Aonskikh skall vznestis' ona stremitsia
Zane glasit ne petoe donyne,
Ni rech'iu mirnoi, ni prostoi, skazan'e!
...
        zane i Ad i Nebo
Tvoi vzor ot veka zrit
...
        Svet mne v temnom
Poshli, vosstan'e i podporu v nizkom.[42]

Zhukovsky's translation is clearly more 'contemporary' because it avoids Vronchenko's intentional archaisms. It attempts to convey that Miltonic sublimity the Romantics so revered while sacrificing the inversions and the biblical style and character that Vronchenko introduces into his version. Twentieth-century translators of *Paradise Lost* have faced the same problem. Then as now the absence of a historical Russian counterpart to Milton's seventeenth-century idiom has forced translators either to invent an artificial archaic form relying on a Church-Slavonic lexicon, or to 'go modern' (which in excess will also seem contrived).[43]

Vronchenko's translation, although he got much further than Zhukovsky, also remained unfinished. Vronchenko almost gave up on this supreme challenge after completing Book I. He then turned to Book V, which perhaps interested him because it is in this part of the poem that the details of Satan's revolt are first revealed.[44] By then, however, Goethe's Devil had come to rival Milton's for popularity among Russia's Romantic intelligentsia. Vronchenko abandoned *Paradise Lost* for the *Faust* of Goethe, whose verse Zhukovsky had also, of course, found very much easier to translate.[45]

THE DEMONS OF GOETHE AND PUSHKIN

Goethe's Mephisto is commonly perceived as 'the most important literary Devil since Milton's.'[46] But in the Russian context their juxtaposition would not have seemed as stark as in England or Weimar, because in an Orthodox setting both devils were unconventional enough to upset religious susceptibilities. Thanks to the discovery by Zhukovsky's and Pushkin's contemporaries of the *narod*, the commonplace devil of Russian folklore had also begun to make a mark in poetry. He appears, for example, in the guise of a malevolent forest spirit (or *leshii*) in the celebrated prologue to 'Ruslan and Liudmila' together with a mermaid, the traditional Russian witch (*Baba Iaga*), and a magical learned cat: or, by himself, in the company of other devils, in a poem entitled 'Besy,' the vernacular term for demon or devil (which Dostoevsky used as the title for his political novel). Pushkin left a charming sketch of this folk devil, inspired by another of his tales in verse (see page xvi). In 'Besy' the devils choose a winter night to terrify a *barin* and his coachman. They are lost and imagine that they see the other traditional creatures of Russian lore, the *domovoi* or house spirit as well as a sorceress being given away in marriage.[47]

Three-quarters of a century later a visiting English writer, noting how widely *Paradise Lost* was being read by peasants, ascribed its popularity to the fact that the hobgoblins and fairies of Milton's England were still very much alive in the Russian countryside.[48] This was indeed the case, but to the Romantic poets of Zhukovsky's and Pushkin's day the distinction between them and the literary devils of *Paradise Lost* or Goethe's *Faust* was so apparent that the term *besy* was no longer applied to them. Dignity required a more exalted term, *demon* being the neologism coined already in the eighteenth century to express the literary Devil's persona. His fresh neoclassical connections endowed him with a more elegant bearing, which now partly concealed his monkish Christian origins.

In Pushkin's verse the distinction between the folkloric Devil and demons of this type are clear enough, but it is complicated by Pushkin's ambivalence about the existence of the prince of darkness. If like Goethe he refused to believe in the physical reality of the Devil, he did not, like some other rationalists of the age, discount the existence of evil, and in one form or another the demonic theme surfaces again and again in both his verse and prose. The most secular of these, freed of any Christian association, is the semi-Grecian devil of Pushkin's drawings and sketches, whose kinship with Poussin's satyrs or Picasso's is obvious (see page xvi). But the poetic demon who came to obsess the Russian Romantics, particularly Lermontov and the painter Vrubel, has classical trappings only to the degree that Milton's Satan may be said to have them. It would seem that the core of this particular Devil's identity is still Christian, being a far cry from the secular Promethean entity projected by Soviet critics in their reading of *Paradise Lost* after 1917.[49]

By then Goethe the humanist would be ranged on the same side as Milton the poet-revolutionary. But Mephistopheles is very definitely a product of the Enlightenment. The contrast between him and Milton's Devil is not unlike the contrast between the two kinds of poetic *demon*, which (next to the folkloric *besy* or *chertiki* of his sketches) also preoccupied Pushkin's imagination. One is obviously inspired by *Faust* and is represented as such in two of Pushkin's poems, a 'Scene from *Faust*' and a fragment on the same subject. The latter was to be part of a drama he at one time intended to devote to Faust.[50] The direct influence of Milton's Satan is harder to trace. If, like Zhukovsky, Pushkin read *Paradise Lost* both in the original and in French (as well as possibly Russian) translation,[51] Pushkin's Voltairean scepticism and his fondness for Evariste Parny's *La Guerre des dieux* would have undermined the earnestness with which Kiukhel'beker and some of his other friends approached the demonic theme.[52]

At the same time, as Christopher Hill remarks, Milton had indeed 'entered the culture of the European Enlightenment.'[53] The Satan of *Paradise Lost* was transformed by it, losing some of his Christian intensity (thanks to Addison and the Augustan sang-froid of other commentators).

Thus, the attraction that Russian poets felt for Milton's and Goethe's devils reflects to some degree the same Enlightenment ethos, despite the defence of Christianity mounted by poets as influential as Zhukovsky and Chateaubriand. By them Milton was recast to fit a nostalgic and unhistorical view of Orthodoxy and Catholicism. To Chateaubriand, for instance, Dante and Milton were the two Christian poets *par excellence*, and he much regretted that the latter had wasted so much of his life in political engagement. In the Romantic period both Milton's and Goethe's devils took on an independent existence of their own. Both proved to be among 'the most influential literary creations of all time.'[54] Yet both also owed their prominence to their politics, which at times inevitably would be compared to that of their authors.

Goethe himself took an ironically distant Enlightenment view of Christianity – so distant that he would not have considered it worth his effort to give its suppositions the detailed analysis Milton set aside in *De Doctrina Christiana*. But the cosmology adopted in *Faust* is one Milton would have understood. As Goethe later described it,[55] God the Father produced the Son, the Holy Spirit (counterpart to the Holy Ghost, which Milton did not recognize) being produced by Father and Son. Together, in Goethe's half-Christian theology, these three were complete and perfect. They produced Lucifer, who was necessarily imperfect but sufficiently impressed by his own creative powers to mimic God. Milton's Devil questions the Almighty's claims to being author of the creation: Goethe's actually creates the material universe in a feat of self-absorption. This universe would have spiralled deeper and deeper into the abyss of negation if God had not in his mercy decided to open it up to the light. It is from this resultant tension between openness and selfishness, light and darkness, that the forces propelling humanity take their source. Caught between the downward-closing diabolical force and the upward-opening divine force, Goethe's theology is only a secularized version of the Manichean confrontation between good and evil in *Paradise Lost*.

For that very reason, Mephistopheles in *Faust* is much too complex, evasive, and ironical to be identified with the Christian Devil. To the Romantics this made him seem a modern figure, for Goethe even denied Kant's principle of radical evil. To this degree, Mephistopheles is a liberal, who echoes Goethe's shifting views and predilections for alchemy, the Kabbalah, folklore, Neoplatonism, pietism, mysticism, and so on.[56] Milton's Satan, by contrast, is a Puritan revolutionary whose appeal in the context of Zhukovsky's and Pushkin's Russia could be seen as a complement to the slick and superficial Mephisto, who begins by playing the fool in heaven and ends (like Pushkin's Satan in 'Gavriliada') by lusting after angels.

Goethe's *Faust* began to appear in Russian in poetic fragments at the end of the second decade of the century, so that *Paradise Lost* was much better known until Eduard Guber, Vronchenko, and Strugovshchikov came out with their versions of Part I in the late 1830s and 1840s.[57] These decades marked the high tide of Russian interest in Goethe.[58] Pushkin, who is usually credited with introducing the demonic theme into Russian Romantic verse quite independently of the German poet, had certainly read *Faust* long before any of these translations appeared. 'Demon,' a short but haunting poem that came out in 1824, reflects a mentality that is recognizably Mephistophelean. Its protagonist, who is inspired by feelings of freedom, glory, and love, encounters an 'evil genius' ('zlobnyi genii') whose irony and scepticism undermine the romantic hero's faith:

> Ne veril on liubvi, svobode;
> Na zhizn' nasmeshlivo gliadel –
> I nichego vo vsei prirode
> Blagoslavit' on ne khotel.[59]

> (He believed neither in love nor freedom;
> He saw life as a jest –
> And there was nothing in all Nature
> He thought worthy of his blessing.)

The poem was sufficiently disturbing to arouse instant interest, as well as questions about its supposed model. To this Pushkin replied that his poem had 'a more moral aim,' ie,

At the best time of life, the heart has not yet been made apathetic by experience, is susceptible to the beautiful. It is credulous and tender. Little by little the eternal contradictions of reality engender doubt in it – a tormenting feeling, but one of short duration. After destroying forever the best hopes and poetic predispositions of the soul, it disappears. The great Goethe has reason to call the eternal enemy of humanity *the negating spirit*. And didn't Pushkin want to personify this spirit *of negation or doubt* in his demon, and in a compact tableau he traced its distinguishing features and lamentable influence on the morality of our age.[60]

In other words, 'Demon' expressed a state of mind. That it was immoral did not make it less seductive, and in retrospect what made the poem so interesting is that psychologically it seems to catch the pose struck by sundry other poetic demons of the age. Both Lermontov's poem of the same title and Vrubel's obsessive portraits of Demon share this disturbing state. Pushkin himself, however, turned away from this particular vein. His Mephistopheles of 1828, so close in style and sentiment to Goethe's, lacks it entirely. In it Faust, who is plagued by ennui, is assured by Mephistopheles that all 'rational beings' are similarly bored:

> Inoi ot leni, tot ot del;
> Kto verit, kto utratil veru;
> Tot nasladitsia ne uspel.[61]
>
> (Some are bored because they're lazy,
> Others because of what they do;
> Some because they are believers –
> Others because they've lost their faith,
> Another's bored because he hasn't had
> The time to sate his pleasure.)

Faust refuses to be humoured, and in imitation of Goethe's hero recalls his own pursuit of happiness and his failure to find it. He did not, Mephistopheles reminds him, find it even in Gretchen's arms, which Faust at first denies, but is then compelled to concede when in an ironic sally Mephisto recalls the disillusionment Faust felt once his love yielded to his entreaties. The scene ends with the kind of wanton destruction that Mephisto propagates in the German tragedy, the sinking of a ship with its simian and syphilitic human cargo on board:

Na nem merzavtsev sotni tri,
Dve obez'iany, bochki zlata,
Da gruz bogatyi shokolata,
Da modnaia bolezn': ona
Nedavno nam podarena.⁶²

(There are about three hundred scoundrels on it,
Two monkeys, barrels of gold,
And a rich load of chocolate;
And a modern disease, presented to us
As a gift not long ago.)

But this Goethean Devil, with all his repertoire of sophistry and his skill in sowing distrust and disruption, lacks some of the qualities that gave Milton's Satan his appeal. Both are liars and monsters of illusion who shift their shape, flatter, seduce, and promote suffering; but the war in *Paradise Lost* is over higher stakes, not part merely of a predetermined *Naturphilosophie*. In Goethe's Heaven Mephisto is, after all, no more than a jester, whose influence is undermined right at the start by God's admission that evil is intrinsic to his design. He even confesses to fondness for the Devil: 'I have never hated you; of all the spirits who deny me, I blame the rogue the least.'⁶³

All this makes Goethe's Mephisto a less substantial figure than Milton's Satan, devoid both of his passion and of his invincible commitment. What they both share, however, is a resentment of God's tyranny that critics during the Enlightenment tended to see in the same political light. In Russia, however, the disillusionment with absolutism was slower to take root than in Western Europe. When Pushkin was commissioned by Nicholas I to write a history of Peter the Great, he accepted the conventional Voltairean view that progress in his vast country was the result of the battle of Poltava. 'With Peter the Great's victory the European Enlightenment berthed at the shores of the conquered Neva.'⁶⁴

But as Pushkin studied Petrine archives more closely, he drew a distinction between the Tsar-reformer's 'State institutions and his temporary ukases' which were 'written with a knout.'⁶⁵ This duality about the builder of modern Russia is expressed in *The Blackamoor of Peter the Great* and in one of Pushkin's strangest poems, 'The Bronze Horseman.' These reflect both sides of Peter – the progressive reformer and the despotic tyrant subjugating all to his rule. Pushkin placed himself most decisively on the side of the Enlightenment in the sense that he believed that progress could only be achieved through education, reason, and the improvement of morals – not the violent imposition of reforms that go against the traditional modes of a people's life.

100 Satan as Romantic and Marxist Idol

In the introduction to 'The Bronze Horseman,' however, there is also a fatalistic acceptance of autocracy, indeed almost an endorsement of it. Yet at the end the unfortunate Eugene, who perhaps represents the citizenry of Russia, sees the fearsome horseman, the tsar, in a different light:

> On mrachen stal
> Pred gordelivym istukanom
> I, zuby stisnuv, pal'tsy szhav,
> Kak obuiannyi siloi chernyi,
> 'Dobro, stroitel' chudotvornyi! –
> Shepnul on, zlobno zadrozhav, –
> Uzho tebe! ...' I vdrug stremglav
> Bezhat' pustilsia ...[66]

> (He halted sullenly beneath
> The haughty Image, clenched his teeth
> And clasped his hands, as though some devil
> Possessed him, some dark power of evil,
> And shuddered, whispering angrily,
> 'Ay, architect, with thy creation
> Of marvels ... Ah, beware of me!'
> And then in wild precipitation
> He fled.)[67]

In this demonic image the political element is almost openly expressed. There may not seem to be a close relationship between this literary Devil and the Miltonic imagery of an earlier poem:

> V dveriakh edema angel nezhnyi
> Glavoi poniksheiu siial,
> A demon mrachnyi i miatezhnyi
> Nad adskoi bezdnoiu letal.[68]

> (A gentle angel at the gates of Eden
> Shone with his head cast down,
> And a melancholy, rebellious demon
> Flew over the abyss of Hell.)

Both the devil of 'The Bronze Horseman' and the demon of this poem, however, are opposed to authority, terrestrial and divine, and it is this aspect that came to be dominant in the demonic tradition as it developed after Pushkin. For him the moral status of that opposition was still ambiguous because Pushkin was all too well aware that without Peter's brutish energy the Enlightenment would not have 'berthed at the shores of the conquered Neva.' At the same time, when the Romantics in Pushkin's day sympathized with the Satan of *Paradise Lost* or with Goethe's Mephistopheles, it was because they were on the side of feeling against an abstract Old Testament view of divine justice. Satan, and particularly Milton's Satan, came to be identified with the poet's quest for personal freedom. In that sense, the demonic tradition (as the next chapter will try to show) inevitably aroused the interest of tsarist censors. Indeed, by the time Dostoevsky wrote *Besy*, his caricature of the revolutionary movement (which is sometimes translated as *Demons* or more usually as *The Possessed* or *The Devils*), it had come to be associated with the left.

But here too Pushkin forestalled Dostoevsky. 'Demon,' the poem cited above that influenced so much kindred verse of the period, was probably drawn from life. Its original, Alexander Raevsky, was arrested for his involvement with the Decembrists.[69] The poetic heir to Pushkin's 'Demon' was Lermontov's masterpiece, whose hero certainly believed in freedom. It is largely because of this identification that both Lermontov's Demon and Milton's Satan came to be regarded as subversive characters in the reign of Nicholas I.

SEVEN

Milton's Satan and Lermontov

> '... the discourse of the devil is the most perfect of its kind ...'
> Alferoff (1828)

Pushkin has been called a 'very Miltonic poet,'[1] which may be apt in the sense that he could be sublime when he chose to, using the high-flown language (as in *The Demon* or *The Prophet*) with which Milton is most often associated in English poetry. But Pushkin's sublimity is not usually achieved by using blank verse (although he did use it), and as a religious poet he had less in common with Milton than with Byron, whose moral grandeur was based on an exalted view of poetry as a weapon against oppression. For Milton the weapon was derived from God; for Pushkin and Byron, who both loved the Old Testament, its source is still Christian, but shrouded in a Romantic aesthetic to which Lermontov also subscribed. Both Lermontov and Pushkin followed the pattern set by Radishchev in seeing literature not as a form of entertainment, but as a morally absorbing and responsible vocation. This anti-frivolous and anti-aesthetic attitude, expressed by Belinsky and shared by so many Russian writers, did not have Puritan roots, but it produced an ideal of the poet and of his prophetic role in society that has much in common with Milton's.

Mikhail Yur'evich Lermontov believed in this ideal with his whole heart, and he leapt into fame and notoriety in an appropriate manner after Pushkin's burial in 1837 by circulating a poem ('Death of the Poet') in which high society was accused of being a sordid accomplice in the duel that ended the great poet's life. The last sixteen lines of the manuscript, in which 'malicious and vulgar gossips' (whom readers associated with the court) were described as the 'executioners [of] Freedom and Genius,' earned Lermontov not only fame but exile. His military service in the Caucasus was cut short four years later by a duel, also in suspicious circumstances. Thus, the destiny of Pushkin and Lermontov was similar. Both were proscribed and exiled by a government convinced that their message was subversive. Both men, profoundly aristocratic in origin and in social attitude, shared a similar conception of poetry. Yet for all their apparent similarities, of which the most visible was their affection for Byron, Pushkin's art marked the end of an epoch; Lermontov's inaugurated another, that of the post-Decembrist generation, which produced writers, critics, and revolutionaries such as Gogol, Belinsky, Herzen, and Bakunin.

For this generation *Paradise Lost* had become a classic, and one that was perhaps as familiar in Russian as in French translation. For Lermontov, reading it would have been a particularly significant experience because at the age of fifteen (he was born in 1814) the young poet became obsessed with the satanic theme. This is reflected in 'Demon,' his most celebrated poem, which was begun in 1829 and completed a decade later. Considered one of the three major works of Russian classical literature, it was published in Russia only in 1860, almost twenty years after the author's death, but circulated in his lifetime through hand-written copies of some of its drafts. Of these there were eight in all. Belinsky, who read one of them, acclaimed *Demon* in 1841 for the splendour of its imagery, its sumptuous poetic animation, its superb verses, and the vitality of its thought.[2] Such was the poem's reputation even before Belinsky's review appeared that members of the tsar's family requested a copy, and it was for them that Lermontov wrote one of the final drafts, although censorship prevented its publication.

This may seem odd, since the story of *Demon* is not overtly political, nor do the final drafts seem to offend religious susceptibilities. Nor is its hero, a fallen angel, a novel literary figure in a period that saw the publication of Byron's *Cain* and *Heaven and Earth*, Alfred de Vigny's *Eloa*, and Tom Moore's *Lalla Rookh*. All these poems owed something to *Paradise Lost*, the debt being usually explicitly acknowledged, and they were known in turn to Lermontov.[3] Indeed, Byron's influence on the Russian poet was not, as in Pushkin's case, a passing phase, for he was fascinated as much by Byron the man (or legend) as the poet. His image of Byron – 'outcast as he and driven from home'[4] – was one Lermontov applied to himself and psychologically may help to explain his early attraction for the figure of the fallen angel, the outcast from Heaven.

What was novel about *Demon* when compared with foreign verse of this genre is the final setting of the Russian poem, which Lermontov elaborated after his experience in the Caucasus in 1837. The details of *Demon*, as the poet added them in the final drafts, come from Georgian and Ossetian folklore.

Like Radishchev's Angel of Darkness in *Ermak*, Lermontov's satanic hero is transported from his Miltonic milieu as 'Eden's outcast' to Russia, although Lermontov uses the Caucasus rather than the Urals as the romantic backdrop for the tale.[5] There, in a verdant valley sheltering an earthly paradise where nightingales sing, the Demon sees Tamara, a Georgian princess, who is about to marry Gudal, the prince of Sinodal. As the wedding festivities are prepared in the palace of Tamara's father, the bridegroom is seen approaching with his lordly caravan in tow, but is killed en route by a mountain bandit.

Tamara is inconsolable and withdraws to a convent, to which the Demon pursues her. Passionately in love with Tamara's dark-eyed beauty, he harbours the inexplicable hope that this human attachment will free him from his burden of despair and eternal loneliness. Finally, entering Tamara's cell, he declaims his love for her in what must be one of the most moving passages of its kind in European literature, and she is both drawn to him and repelled by the foreboding of God's judgment. Torn by compassion and desire, she yields to the Demon's entreaty to be his companion in eternal damnation. As she does so, Tamara dies at the moment of the Demon's triumph.

Tamara is then buried by her grieving father, who builds a chapel on a granite promontory in her memory, which only vultures haunt; but the conclusion of the poem differs in the final drafts. In the sixth, the last to come down to us in a copy authorized by the poet, Tamara is defiant and irredeemable to the very end. When Lermontov learnt that 'the highest circles' (that is to say, the empress and her daughters) wished to read the poem, he drafted two further versions, which brought the ending more in line with conventional Orthodoxy. In the last extant copy, written early in 1839, Tamara's guardian angel declares that she has won redemption by her death. Her soul is saved and is borne to Heaven. The Demon fails to retrieve Tamara (as he does in earlier versions), and is left, as at the beginning of the poem, 'bereft of hope, of love, [and] of paradise.'[6] He is condemned, rather like Satan in *Paradise Lost*, to bear the burden of his guilt and pride 'unpitied and alone.'[7]

The theme of human attachment is also prefigured by Milton in Book IV of the epic where Satan, after alighting on Mount Niphates, is overcome by the beauty of Eve when he sets eyes on her in Eden. It is out of envy for Adam, so Chateaubriand supposed, that Satan contrives the downfall of our first parents. The other important element in *Demon* that may be traced to *Paradise Lost* is the sexuality of the angels, a characteristic that had earlier shocked Amvrosii but that poets of the Romantic era seized on to exploit for their own purposes. Alfred de Vigny explicitly refers to Milton's precedent here in order to justify the plot of *Eloa*, in which an innocent angel from

Heaven is seduced by Satan and (like Tamara in the sixth draft of *Demon*) joins him in his eternal damnation.[8] In Byron's *Heaven and Earth*, in which Anah, a woman, falls in love with Azaziel, an angel, Milton's sexuality is also permitted to cross the boundary between mortals and celestial beings (as in the Russian poem).

Lermontov would have been aware of all these precedents. Indeed, in the 1831 draft of his poem he even cites some lines of *Cain* with the implication that his 'melancholy Demon' bears more than a passing resemblance to Byron's Miltonic Lucifer.[9] It has also been pointed out that the subtitle of the final draft, 'Vostochnaia povest' ' or 'Oriental Romance' was almost certainly suggested by the one Thomas Moore used in his exotic *Lalla Rookh*, in which a 'disconsolate' fallen angel tries to regain entry to Eden and the gates of Heaven. Yet in the discussion of these and other Romantic parallels with the Russian poem, Lermontov's direct debt to Milton has so far been overlooked. V.D. Spasovich before 1917 saw *Demon* as being essentially a 'poetically and philosophically weakened variant' of *Paradise Lost* and Byron's *Cain*, a verdict that B.T. Udodov and Elena Loginovskaia in their interesting recent studies of Lermontov reject. But neither Udodov nor Loginovskaia (or Spasovich before them) actually attempt to ascertain when Lermontov read Milton or what *Demon* may owe to *Paradise Lost*.[10]

This hiatus in Lermontov scholarship is all the more surprising when it is recalled that Pushkin and the author of *Demon*, apart from many other shared characteristics, both had teachers who translated *Paradise Lost*. Efim Liutsenko, whom Pushkin (as we have seen) first came to know in his *lycée* at Tsarskoe Selo, translated Milton's two epics in 1824 and brought them out in a second edition in 1827.[11] That was also the year in which Lermontov's wealthy grandmother, Mme Arsen'eva, enrolled him (as a non-boarder) in the Pension Noble, which contemporaries considered to have the best teachers of the day, equal and perhaps superior to those in Pushkin's prestigious *lycée*. It had a particularly strong literary tradition, Fonvizin, Chaadaev, and Griboedov being former pupils. Arsen'eva, who spared no expense on Lermontov's private education before sending him to the Pension Noble, had acquired the services of Aleksei Zinov'evich Zinoviev as a tutor for her grandson; and it was Zinoviev who later brought out the first full and thorough translation of *Paradise Lost* into Russian from the original.[12]

Whether Zinoviev was interested in Milton in 1827, the year in which he began tutoring Lermontov, we cannot be certain. Zinoviev, then twenty-six, was not only a classical scholar but himself a writer and poet, and had ties through M.P. Pogodin and S.P. Shevyrev with the circle gathered around the *Moskovskii Vestnik*, and through Semën Egorovich Raich, also a poet and translator, with another journal called *Galateia*.[13] *Galateia* published a poetic translation of a passage from *Paradise Lost* in 1830, and Stepan Shevyrev a much longer poem inspired by the expulsion of Adam and Eve from Eden in 1828.[14] The latter appeared in the proceedings of the Society of Russian Literature,[15] to which Zinoviev belonged, so it is not unlikely that he would have been *au courant*. He is known to have been interested in English poetry at that time, but it was Russian literature, as well as Greek and Latin, that Zinoviev was supposed to teach Lermontov.

Their connection continued over the next three years until 1830. These were formative ones for Lermontov, after which he left the Pension Noble for Moscow University, the institution at which Zinoviev had completed his magistral work. Since Zinoviev set down his views on education, the way he taught the young poet is not entirely obscured by time. It seems that Zinoviev did not believe in excessive emphasis on grammar, and preferred to immerse his pupils as soon as possible in a reading of the 'classics' themselves, a method favoured at the Pension Noble,[16] where Zinoviev was also a master. Whether *Paradise Lost* was included among these classics can only be surmised. Shakespeare was then the rage at the school;[17] and it is probable that, before he entered Moscow University, Lermontov was also introduced to Byron's verse.

By then the Russian poet had been taught excellent French and good German by a succession of tutors, who also guided him in other subjects. Thereafter, according to Zinoviev's own reminiscences, Lermontov 'soon learnt English from his new governor Winsun,' the last teacher to be employed by Mme Arsen'eva.[18] This gentleman, about whom little is known, was subsequently engaged as a house tutor by Count S.S. Uvarov, Nicholas I's minister of education. Winsun also taught at the Pension Noble until it was closed down at the Emperor's behest, and it may be assumed therefore that whatever Lermontov picked up of English literature in the years when he became preoccupied with the demonic theme would have been either through Winsun or Zinoviev. Unfortunately, although much has been written about Lermontov's youthful studies, nothing has apparently come down to us of his English curriculum, the only enlightening piece of evidence (so far ignored) being a speech that Alferoff, one of Lermontov's classmates, delivered on *Paradise Lost* in 1828.[19]

None of Lermontov's biographers mention it,[20] yet it was published in the journal, bound in green silk, that the masters of the Pension Noble brought out as a testament to their pupils' accomplishments. These were indeed noteworthy, and compare favourably with those of students at Harrow in Byron's day. Thus, the boys at the Russian school were expected to execute translations of literary pieces by critics such as Hugh Blair[21] and to deliver public orations in foreign languages. From the subjects chosen some idea can be formed concerning the literary preoccupations at the Pension Noble. An Italian oration, for example, was devoted to Boccaccio, while other students spoke about Alfieri and Tasso's *Gerusalemme Liberata*.[22] Another oration compared Lomonosov to Jean-Jacques Rousseau, whose ideas on education Zinoviev very much admired.[23] Ivanenko (also a contemporary of Lermontov's) discussed Steele and Tom Moore.[24] Lermontov is known to have recited Russian poetry on one of these public occasions; the oration on Milton is, however, of particular interest, because it anticipated by a few months the young poet's first draft of *Demon*. And it so happens that in his speech Alferoff treats Satan as 'the principal actor and the real hero' of Milton's poem. While assuring his parental audience that 'in all the speeches of Satan, wherever he breaks forth into impiety and imprecations, Milton has judiciously mingled so much absurdity as to render them incapable of shocking the most pious reader,' it is obvious from the rest of Alferoff's address that he found the more conventional passages, such as the dialogues between God and Christ, 'the weakest part of the poem.' This is where Milton's 'majesty abandons him,' while 'the discourse of the Devil is the most perfect of its kind; for all his perverseness and evil propensities are displayed in a masterly manner.'[25]

Was this verdict an echo of the views of Winsun himself, an early Satanist dispatched *in partes infidelium*? Or were the pupils of the Pension Noble expected to show some personal initiative in their literary judgments? Whatever the case, the Romantic consensus had by now tilted in Satan's favour, as Byron so characteristically suggested not long before his own death. Milton, he then said, 'certainly excites compassion for Satan, and endeavours to make him out an injured personage – he gives him human passions too, makes him pity Adam and Eve, and justify himself much as Prometheus does.' Then why was Milton 'never' blamed for this? 'I should be very curious to know,' Byron added, 'what his real belief was.'[26] Alferoff's forgotten oration adopted this line of interpretation too, without of course actually questioning Milton's own piety, and it may therefore shed some light on Lermontov's own obsession with Satan.

The young poet's poetic preoccupation with the satanic theme began, as we have seen, in 1829, and from the first draft it is clear that just as the line 'Pechal'nyi demon, dukh izgnan'ia' / 'the melancholy demon, spirit of exile' remained unchanged in all subsequent versions of *Demon*, so too did the theme of the fallen angel's mortal attachment. In the first draft of the poem written at the Pension Noble it is expressed incompletely by the following alternatives: the Demon discovers that an angel loves a woman, and he then seduces her. She dies and becomes one of his minions in Hell. The Demon then tells her how 'unjust God is, etc.'[27] In the other version, the Demon falls in love with a nun, but on confronting her guardian angel, he decides to encompass her ruin. The nun dies (as Tamara would in her convent), and her soul is received in Hell. The Demon, encountering the guardian angel, 'upbraids him with a taunting smile.'[28]

Of these two plots the second is more Byronic than Miltonic, although what lies at the source of both projected narratives is Satan's moment of weakness for Eve in Book IV of *Paradise Lost*. The imprecations against God, which impressed Alferoff, and to judge by Lermontov's first variant, impressed Lermontov too, could equally well have come from the same source, or from Byron's *Cain*, in which Lucifer echoes the rebellious sentiments of Milton's Satan.[29] But *Cain* crops up only in a later (1831) draft of the Russian poem, so it is rather unlikely that the original evocation of Demon's satanic character was suggested by Byron rather than the Miltonian source.

On the other hand, it could have been influenced by other demonic poems with which Lermontov also became familiar at an early age, such as Klopstock's *Messias* or Goethe's *Faust*, although the precise date at which he came to read them is just as difficult to pin down as his first acquaintance with *Paradise Lost*. The only *terminus post quem* is a passage in *Vadim*, a 'demonic' novel Lermontov 'finished' in 1833–4, although it is unclear when he began it. *Vadim* deals with the Pugachev Rebellion, to which Lermontov shows himself more sympathetic than Pushkin in *The Captain's Daughter*. The hero, a peasant and a hunchback, conceives a monstrous hatred for Palitsyn, the philandering landowner who attempts to seduce Vadim's sister, with whom Yurii, the son of Palitsyn, is also in love. The novel, which Lermontov did not complete, ends with Vadim and Pugachev's Cossacks (with whom the former secretly collaborates) searching for Palitsyn and his son, who both go into hiding. Before this point is reached, Yurii (whose character anticipates that of Pechorin in *Hero of Our Time*) begins to reminisce about his other female conquests.

It is in this unlikely-seeming context that Lermontov copies a Russian translation of those lines in *Paradise Lost* where Satan's followers, having been transformed into serpents,

>   Greedily ... plucked
> The fruitage fair to sight, like that which grew
> Near that bituminous lake where Sodom flamed. (x. ll 560–2)

Yet interestingly enough, Lermontov's source is not Liutsenko's 'literary' translation of *Paradise Lost*, but one of the older editions of 1820, which still used much of Stroganov's Church-Slavonic idiom.[30] This does not necessarily mean that Lermontov read Milton long before writing *Vadim*, but it is certainly possible that he made notations (as was his wont) from *Paradise Lost* while he was still at Moscow University or the Pension Noble. He would then later have inserted the lines above into his novel.[31]

This supposition may seem all the more likely because, according to Shan-Girey, Lermontov's cousin, the poet's reading of English 'soon' became so fluent that he began to read Shakespeare and Milton in the original.[32] Yet Lermontov never made any attempt to translate them. He did translate Moore, Burns, and Byron, however, and we are told that he acquired a real feeling for the language by immersing himself in the latter's poetry. He did this by acquiring the 1823 edition of Byron's works and Moore's two-volume *Life* (1830) of the poet, which consists of correspondence and journals Byron had willed to Moore prior to his death at Missolonghi in 1824. Since Lermontov so much admired Byron, and for a while modelled himself on him, it is also likely that the Russian poet would have learnt of Byron's attitude to Milton. Sometimes this was gently ironic, as in the biographical allusions to the 'first Mrs. Milton' whose behaviour would perhaps have reminded readers of Lady Byron's conduct:

> The only two that in my recollection
>   Have sung of heaven and hell, or marriage, are
> Dante and Milton, and of both the affection
>   Was hapless in their nuptials, for some bar
> Of fault or temper ruin'd the connexion
>   (Such things, in fact, it don't ask much to mar);
> But Dante's Beatrice and Milton's Eve
> Were not drawn from their spouses, you conceive.[33]

Or again in the same poem, where the allusion is to Dr Johnson's vindictive biography of Milton:

> Milton's the prince of poets – so we say:
>   A little heavy, but no less divine:
> An independent being in his day –
>   Learn'd, pious, temperate in love and wine;
> But his life falling into Johnson's way,
>   We're told this great high priest of all the Nine

> Was whipt at college – a harsh sire – odd spouse,
> For the first Mrs. Milton left his house.³⁴

But Byron, when in a more serious vein, loved Milton as both a man and a poet, as Lermontov and his Russian contemporaries would have realized from other passages in *Don Juan*, such as the following stanza:

> Think'st thou, could he – the Blind Old Man – arise,
>   Like Samuel from the grave, to freeze once more
> The blood of monarchs with his prophecies,
>   Or be alive again – again all hoar
> With time and trials, and those helpless eyes,
>   And heartless daughters – worn – and pale and poor;
> Would *he* adore a sultan? *he* obey
> The intellectual eunuch Castlereagh?³⁵

Byron believed that it was Milton's politics that had 'kept him down,' but of course he himself shared Milton's passion for freedom, and it is this muted note that inevitably found its way into *Demon*, mingled (as in Byron himself) with scepticism and pride. The literary Satan created by Lermontov has his moment of weakness for Tamara as does Milton's Satan for Eve, but in *Paradise Lost* Satan triumphs with her transgression in Book IX, while Demon is defeated:

> I vnov' ostalsia on, nadmennyi,
> Odin, kak prezhde, vo vselennoi
> Bez upovan'ia i liubvi.³⁶

(And again he stood all alone in the universe, arrogant, without love or hope.)

Here Demon may recall the Satan of Book I after his expulsion from Heaven, but Lermontov's hero in his hopelessness and desperate frustration seems to give vent to a feeling shared by Pechorin, Arbenin, and the other 'superfluous' heroes of the period. Milton's Satan is made of sterner stuff, as is reflected in his resolution 'To claim our just inheritance of old' (II. l 38). Equally, his boast that 'the mind is its own place, and in itself / Can make a Heaven of Hell, a Hell of Heaven' (I. ll 254–5) strikes a posture of defiance of which Demon is incapable. This is why Lunacharsky, Lenin's commissar for enlightenment, thought the Russian poem so inferior to Milton's.³⁷

This criticism, reminiscent of Franz Mehring's preference for *Paradise Lost* over Klopstock's epic, because it too was more revolutionary than the *Messiade*, was made before and after the Bolshevik Revolution. Boris Eikhenbaum, for example, whose scholarship on Lermontov has proved so valuable, suggested in 1924 that there were simply 'no sufficiently strong traditions in Russian poetry for the kind of abstract-metaphysical poem, which ... Lermontov envisaged in his portrayal of *Demon*.'[38] This may be true, but the demonic tradition on Russian soil is older than the distinguished scholar imagined, for (as we have seen) in reality it stretches back to the Stroganov-Milton in the middle of the eighteenth century.

Vigorous minds of Alferoff's and Lermontov's day were certainly perceptive enough to understand the philosophical issues underlying Satan's rebellion, for even *Demon* constituted a challenge to conventional Orthodox feeling. The contrast in militancy between its hero and Milton's Satan may be due, as Lunacharsky implies, to the historical fact that the middle class of seventeenth-century England was more forceful, enterprising, and politically mature than the pusillanimous gentry of Lermontov's time. Milton's portrayal of Satan also anticipated a trend Pushkin found so admirable in English literature as a whole when he said that its heroes were (it seemed to him) invariably more 'concrete' and more real than the characters of French fiction.

This certainly differentiates the Satan of *Paradise Lost* from Demon or the dandyish Satan of *Eloa*. Yet it is also true that with the decline in the aftermath of the Enlightenment of the idea of Hell, Satan's attributes had simply ceased to impress. This is reflected rather comically in the untranslatable lines someone added to an 1847 manuscript copy of *Demon*:

> Demon, demon rifmobes'ia,
> Otleti daleko proch';
> V podzemel'e, v podnebes'ia
> Ty menia ne uvlechesh'.[39]

Poets were therefore compelled to adopt a less literal presentation of the traditional Satan, and this was as true in Russia as elsewhere on the Continent. Goethe's Mephistopheles notably marks the change, for he does not even pretend to be a rival to God. In other words, Milton's grandiose conception of Satan as the adversary of God and man no longer exercised quite the same power over the imagination. This being the case, Lermontov's Demon was bound to be only a weakened image of the original.

If the literary appeal of Milton's Satan survived the decline in revealed religion to which Chatskii, Evgenii Onegin, Pechorin, and most of the secular heroes of Russian drama and fiction in the first half of the nineteenth century bear witness, it is because there are so many more dimensions to Satan's character than to the devils and fallen angels derived from him in the Romantic era. Thus, to state the most obvious, Satan in *Paradise Lost* appears in at least three distinct guises – as prince of Hell, archangel, and tempter.[40] Yet Lermontov's contemporaries were by and large far less interested in his primary manifestation than were the readers of Kheraskov's and Derzhavin's day.[41] With the exception of the scene in Hell depicted by Byron in *Cain*, most of the demonic poems Lermontov would have read, from *Eloa* to Moore's *The Loves of the Angels*, were concerned in one way or another with the exclusion from Heaven. For the Romantics this was the symbolical analogue to the poet's own exclusion from society, a theme with which both Byron and Lermontov were so much concerned.

They were also preoccupied with Satan's role as tempter, which Milton explains at the beginning of Book IV preceding the Mount Niphates speech:

> for now
> Satan, now first inflam'd with rage, came down,
> The Tempter ere th' Accuser of mankind,
> To wreak on innocent frail Man his loss. (IV. ll 8–11)

Thereafter his degradation begins when Satan is compared first to a 'prowling Wolfe' (l 183), 'a Thief' (l 188), 'A Cormorant' (l 196), and then 'A Toad' (l 800). Finally, he and his accomplices become serpents (as in the scene recalled in *Vadim*). Yet this is an aspect of Satan the tempter that Lermontov wholly ignored in *Demon*, just as he ignored the prince of Hell and his bold counter-offensive against God described in the opening two books of *Paradise Lost*.

This is why Lermontov's characterization of Demon is both less rebellious and less supernatural than that of Satan in *Paradise Lost*. Tamara, in the sixth draft of the Russian poem, shows more courage than Demon is ever called upon to demonstrate. But this decline in Demon's prowess also reflects the irrelevance of God in the secular world-view of Byron's contemporaries. 'Who are thou?' asks Cain in the lines Lermontov copied out in 1831. 'Master of Spirits,' Lucifer replies. 'And being so, canst thou / Leave them, and walk with dust?' asks Cain. 'I know the thoughts of dust,' Lucifer answers, 'and feel for it, and with you.'[42] In the Russian poem the philosophical analogue to this is the following exchange between Demon and Tamara, when she at first resists his advances:

Tamara: And God?

>   Demon: His glance on us will never dwell,
>   His realm is Heaven,
>   He scarce can spare for Earth a Thought.[43]

Thus, the titanic adversary of God and man in *Paradise Lost* is reduced in *Demon* to the scale of a fugitive lover, pleading that God will neither care nor notice.

GERMAN DEVILS

If Demon is feeble, so were his literary predecessors. Thus, the sceptical Mephisto of Goethe's *Faust* has all the marks of the *Aufklärung* but none of the indomitable will of Milton's Satan; but poets and translators were often attracted by both Satans. Vronchenko, for example, who translated parts of Book I of *Paradise Lost* in 1831 (which Lermontov could have seen),[44] later translated *Faust*; so did Kholodkovsky.[45] Yet Goethe's *Faust* had not yet reached the peak of its popularity, so that apart from Milton's epics the only foreign demonic poem that would have been as freely available to Lermontov in Russian translation as in the language of the original was the *Messiade*.

'Farting Klopstock,' as Blake called him, was very highly thought of in Russia in Pushkin's and Lermontov's time, although Kutuzov's translation was not. But in 1814, as we have seen, Zhukovsky translated parts of Book II of the *Messiade* into verse, and entitled it *Abbadona*, Abbadon the 'destroyer' being the Hebrew name for the Greek Apollyon, whom Klopstock calls 'death's dark angel.'[46] There was also a very full manuscript translation of the German poem, dating from the same period; and although this represents the only exemplar of its kind seen by the present author in Soviet archives, the existence of the formidable text (which has sixty-eight rhymed sections) is enough to suggest that some Russian readers took the *Messiade* very seriously indeed.[47] Lessing came to consider the poem a bore, but Zhukovsky was perhaps even more inspired by it than by *Paradise Lost*. Nonetheless, his fragment is rather less accurate than the manuscript version.

For instance, when Satan leaves Hell with Andremelech, whom Klopstock represents as 'the enemy of God, greater in malice, [and] ... a fiend more curst, a deeper hypocrite,' Zhukovsky puts far more emphasis on Satan's might and power than is to be found in the original. In the Russian version all the devils of Hell join Satan as he leaves for Earth. Herzen in his romantic youth was impressed;[48] and to judge by his diary, Zhukovsky himself was moved by profound religious motives when he undertook the translation. The opening of Klopstock's poem, with its council in Hell and the central role allotted to Satan, was clearly indebted to Milton. Thereafter, as Satan and his acolytes appear on Earth, the narrative follows the New Testament and has no resemblance at all to *Demon*. But it does contain a passage in which Abbadon regrets his apostasy, the consequence of his contrition being that he is rejected by both God and Satan.

Klopstock's fallen angel is too repentant to be considered a likely original for Lermontov's poem, although the opening line of *Demon* does recall the beginning of Zhukovsky's *Abbadona*.[49] Lermontov may also have read Kutuzov's cumbersome translation, which was reissued in 1820–1.[50] By then the *Messiade*'s debt to *Paradise Lost* was well recognized by Russian critics, the English and the German epics being regarded together with Dante's *Inferno* as the three great Christian poems. As such, it was thought that they complemented each other, Dante having based himself on the Church Fathers, Milton on the Old Testament, and Klopstock on the New.[51] And, as in Milton's case, there was the attempt to present the *Messiade* as being intimately connected with Orthodoxy. Indeed, so much so that when Sergei Pisarev completed a new verse translation of Klopstock's poem in 1868, he dedicated it to the tsar,[52] a procedure Pisarev did not follow with his translation of *Paradise Lost*.

Does this mean that the *Messiade* was regarded as more conventional or 'safe' than the English poem that inspired it? Probably, but its vogue, which did not long survive the 1860s, also says something about the extraordinary longevity of Milton's epics, whose popularity (to judge by the number of new translations and editions) continued to increase so dramatically right up to the First World War. Klopstock's narrative deals with the life of Jesus, which was no doubt even more familiar than the themes of *Paradise Lost*. Indeed, Klopstock's poem was thought especially suitable for reading side by side with the Bible.[53] Yet this did not save it from being forgotten. Nor, in the case of Milton's epics, can Satan take the credit for their longevity in Russia, although, as the country moved closer to revolution, as a literary and political figure he seems to have become more relevant where Klopstock's Devil was too closely tied to conventional religion.

Thus, the demonic tradition associated with *Paradise Lost* proved more durable than one might have expected. After Lermontov, it found its most gifted exponent in Vrubel, who moved from realistic religious painting to experimentation in the impressionist manner and to a long artistic quest focused on representing Demon in canvases of magnificent colour. His mystical depiction of Lermontov's Miltonic hero (see Figure 24) shows how far Satan had evolved from the very sober and resourceful character of *Paradise Lost*. Demons in one shape or another also continued to inhabit Russian prose. Sometimes they appeared as folk devils, as in Gogol's *Evenings on a*

Farm near Dikanka or in the *poshlyi* and unheroic guise evoked by Sologub; but here there was no connection with Milton, whose Satan survived rather through the biblical tradition kept alive by a succession of religious Russian writers from Dostoevsky to Remizov and Mikhail Bulgakov in *Master and Margarita*. In poetry he found his most characteristically Romantic expression in Elizaveta Zhadovskaya's adaptation of *Paradise Lost* and *Paradise Regained*, which appeared in 1859, a year before the publication in Russia of *Demon*.

THE TEMPTER'S TRIUMPH

Zhadovskaya (not to be confused with Iuliia, her more talented namesake) surely did not possess the ability to turn both Milton's epics into verse in their entirety; nor did she know English.[54] Yet her *Poteriannyi rai* and *Vozvrashchennyi rai* are in fact presented on the title page as translations 'from the prose.' Dobroliubov, the radical critic who collaborated with Chernyshevsky on Pushkin's old journal, the *Contemporary*, thought Zhadovskaya's procedure disgraceful. So it is, for nothing on the title page alerts the reader to the fact that the Russian text covers only four books of *Paradise Lost* (and one of its sequel). Dobroliubov assumed that Zhadovskaya intended to mislead the public, and he calls her strange production a commercial 'speculation' designed to cash in on Milton's reputation.[55]

This may well have been the case, but the intent is more likely to have been the publisher's rather than the author's, who supplies some introductory verses dedicated to Milton the 'Divine Writer,' in which her purpose is partly revealed. Her opening line ('Mil'ton Bozhestvennyi Pisatel'') is obviously taken from the epigraph accompanying Milton's portrait in earlier popular prose translations.[56] So is part of the third line: 'Serdets i dush ocharovatel'' / 'Enchanter of hearts and souls'; but the next line 'Dai povtorit' mne pesn' tvoiu' hints that she intended to 'repeat [Milton's] song,' not necessarily to 'translate' it. In these dedicatory lines Zhadovskaya also announces her intent to start with the 'fourth theme,' eg, Book IV of *Paradise Lost*. Thus, any unwary reader turning past the title page should have been warned what to expect.

Nonetheless, Zhadovskaya's work is not a mere adaptation. Where she does not omit, she clearly made the attempt to follow the narrative closely. What therefore is interesting about her hybrid translation-adaptation is not the verse itself, which is commonplace, but the taste that dictated her omissions. She was evidently not greatly interested in *Paradise Regained*, part of which is added only as an afterthought to the main part of the Russian book (spliced in with a section of the earlier epic). Most of her verse is devoted to *Paradise Lost*.

Anyone considering abridgment of the latter has to decide what constitutes the most important or appealing part of the long narrative. Vasilii Petrov made an easy choice in 1777 by translating only the first three books, which, by making Satan in his guise as prince of Hell the centre of attention, also concentrates on one of the explosive issues of the poem as a whole: the consequences of his rebellion against God. As such, the opening books are in a sense self-contained, although they do not describe at any length how the rebellion came about.

The chronological beginning of the poem, is narrated in books v and vi, where Milton deals with Satan's apostasy and the resulting war in Heaven. Zhadovskaya's Romantic predecessors were not, to judge by the poetic fragments that appeared in the journals of the time, particularly attracted to this part of *Paradise Lost*. Sometimes they were drawn to the blind poet's moving invocation to light in Book iii, which Gnedich translated in 1805 and Pavel Petrov attempted anew in 1833;[57] or, like Vronchenko in 1831, they turned to the very opening of the epic, where Satan is shown in his most striking posture, challenging God. Milton's description of Eden also perennially attracted translators and illustrators, but Zhadovskaya was drawn by the same theme that obsessed Lermontov: Satan as tempter.

Indeed, this is the title she gives the 'First Song' of her opus (which largely corresponds to Book iv in the original). Her 'Third [and final] Song,' which covers Book ix in *Paradise Lost*, ends with the tempter's seduction of Eve. Throughout her poem, in which the speeches of Milton's characters are apportioned as in a play, Satan is described as 'Iskusitel'' ('The Tempter'). Her 'Second Song' is taken up with Book vii, the shortest of her three 'Songs,' in which she omits many of the most memorable passages in Raphael's dialogue with Adam but not his injunction to 'be lowly wise.' On the other hand, Adam's description of 'this Earth a spot, a grain / An atom, with the Firmament compared' (viii. ll 17–18) is one Zhadovskaya could not match, and she leaves it out. She also omits much of the cosmological argument, focusing instead on Eve's creation from Adam's rib.

Similarly, the depiction of the transgression is also considerably shortened, and the subtlety of Satan's flattery of Eve lost. Instead of 'Wonder not, sovran mistress ... that I approach thee,' there is the uncalibrated directness of the Russian: 'O krasota zemnykh krasot!' / 'O beauty of earth's beauties!' And the conclusion of Book ix, represented in Zhadovskaya's version as the conclusion of *Paradise Lost*, is rather less sophisticated. Compare,

> Thus they in mutual accusation spent

The fruitless hours, but neither self-condemning
And of their vain contest appeared no end. (IX. ll 1187–9)

with

Obidy byli ikh serdechny
Oni ukor v ukor veli
I ukorizny bezkonechny
Vse napolniali zhizni dni.[58]

Yet there is a certain logic to Zhadovskaya's abridgment. The crucial seduction in the Garden becomes in her version the culmination of Milton's narrative, and although this is possibly the best-remembered episode in the poem, Satan thereby inevitably dominates the action. In his guise as tempter he thus becomes the unchallenged hero of the piece in the same sense as Demon is in Lermontov's poem. Of Satan's degradation there is in Zhadovskaya's verse almost no hint, but at the same time the colossal figure who hurls imprecations at the Almighty at the outset is also reduced to a more human scale.

Hence, the invocation to the Sun at the beginning of Book IV, in which Milton portrays Satan as a heroic Elizabethan cast almost in the magnificent mould of Marlowe's Faust, is diminished into a rather whimpering speech in which the tempter's self-pity drowns out the breath-taking defiance of the original. 'Me miserable! Which way shall I fly?' (l 73) becomes 'O gore mne! o gde ukrytsia / ot gneva vechnago Tvortsa?' (p 12). And the next line: 'Which way I fly is Hell; myself am Hell' has an equivalent no less feeble: 'Vstrechaiu vsiudu bezdnu ada' (p 12). Satan's invocation ends on a note of bravado:

So farewell hope, and with hope farewell fear,
Farewell remorse! All good to me is lost
Evil be thou my good ... (ll 108–10)

For this the best Zhadovskaya can do is weak:

Likuite uzhasy muchen'ia, –
Dobro pogiblo navsegda!
O zlo! ty radost' – ty otmshchen'e,
Sostav'te shchastie moe![59]

She misses many of the philosophical nuances of Satan's speech, and adds some of her own, such as Satan's admission that as a 'freethinker' ('vol'nodumets') he deserves his divine punishment.[60] Satan also admits to being an atheist ('Ia Satana, ia ateist!'), a notion Derzhavin and Kheraskov both expressed during the French Revolution, but which in the context of Milton's poem is surely absurd.

Thus, consciously or unconsciously, Zhadovskaya's translation-adaptation follows the same trend as *Demon*. Would she have read Lermontov's masterpiece? It was first published in Russian in Karlsruhe in 1856 by one of the poet's relatives, so she could have seen this and certainly the fragments that had already appeared. Or she could have seen a manuscript copy. If so, her Milton does not quite deserve the neglect that has been meted out to it ever since Dobroliubov wrote his angry review. For her version does, after all, show Milton's Satan at a historical watershed: an enfeebled atheist, lachrymose and sensual, this 'Angel of Darkness' (as she calls him) is one Radishchev (who used the same term) would have spurned.[61]

Yet the political compromise her Satan represents in the difficult years of Nikolaevan reaction may not have been entirely of Zhadovskaya's own choosing. She would almost certainly have known of the scandal surrounding Lermontov's *Demon*. If her aim was to get her book approved by church and state, Zhadovskaya had to present Satan in a suitably contrite and conventional light, irrespective of Romantic predilections. Indeed, at the time that she began her book, neither of Milton's epics nor Lermontov's poem were permitted to be published as their authors intended. By an interesting twist of fate, both *Demon* and *Paradise Lost* were proscribed by Nicholas I's censors. Both came to be regarded as subversive.

EIGHT

Banning and Reviving Satan

> 'Even more black and sweeping looms
> The shade of Lucifer's vast wing.'
>
> Alexander Blok

While Byron may have thought of Satan as an Englishman, he was uncertain to what degree Milton himself was in sympathy with the towering figure of *Paradise Lost*. For it was only in 1825 that Milton's heterodoxies were revealed in broad daylight by the publication of the *De Doctrina Christiana*, providing supporters of the Satanist argument with fresh ammunition to bolster their cause. By then Byron, who placed Milton above Shakespeare, was dead: nor is it probable that Lermontov and the other Romantic poets we have dealt with so far were aware of the time bomb Milton's work on Christian doctrine turned out to be. In Russia the Satanist controversy evolved not so much around variant readings of *Paradise Lost* or its author's politics and his true intentions as a Christian, but in the context of a demonic tradition that, with the publication of Lermontov's poem in the second half of the century, came to encompass both art and music. The aim of this chapter is to show how this occurred, although it is a moot point whether Russian Satanism as it shot upward from the seeds planted in *Paradise Lost* was any closer in spirit to Milton's intent than the German devils discussed above.

SCANDALS OVER DEVILS

Inside the poet's native country only fragments of *Demon* were allowed to see the light of day before 1860. Despite initial approval, the authorities banned the poem after the alarm sparked by the dialogue about God between Tamara and Demon. *Paradise Lost* and *Paradise Regained* seem to have met similar obstacles, religious and political, for the two epics were also subjected to censorship and banned. Indeed, as early as 1838, the year before Lermontov completed *Demon*, a Moscow newspaper commemorating Baron Stroganov's translation of *Paradise Lost* suggested that Orthodox scruples were responsible for the manuscript's failure to get published.[1] Why did this Christian poem seem 'corrupting' ('soblaznitel'noiu')? The critic, who left his suspicions on this score unsigned, did not discuss Satan's role in *Paradise Lost*, but it is possible that his comment about 'that century of cautious Orthodoxy' was Aesopian in intent. The author may well have known that Milton's proscription had begun anew under a tsar who identified the Enlightenment with the French Revolution. Rebellion, celestial or otherwise, was to be discouraged at all cost. By both the authorities and the radicals literature came to be perceived as a model or inspiration for social conduct. As such, literature was now too serious a matter to be left to the Muses: if it failed to meet certain ideological tests prescribed by the tsar, no aesthetic virtues were thought adequately redemptive. Thus, Lermontov had first attracted Nicholas's disapproval with his poem on the death of Pushkin, the conclusion of which was described by Count Benckendorff as 'shameless freethinking, more than criminal.'[2] Nicholas concurred, dispatching someone to inspect Lermontov's papers, as well as a medical officer to ascertain whether the poet was not 'deranged.' A similar procedure had been employed in the case of Chaadaev, one of the most brilliant thinkers of the time, who was pronounced insane by imperial decree.

It is as a result of this that Lermontov was exiled to perform his military service in the Caucasus, and through his unrepentant conduct there he drew the attention of tsarist officials on subsequent occasions. Nicholas's unfavourable impression of the poet, however, was countermanded in part by the empress's interest in *Demon*. As noted in her diary, she read one of the drafts Lermontov had prepared for the occasion in 1839;[3] armed with this knowledge, a friend of the author submitted the poem to the St Petersburg Censorship Committee with a view to publication. After making certain cuts, the committee gave its assent, but for some reason unclear to this day Lermontov did not proceed to publish. Possibly, as V.E. Vatsuro has recently suggested, he was incensed at the cuts.[4] Meanwhile, the mood of the censors had been transformed by the scandal involving A.A. Bestuzhev-Marlinsky, the convicted Decembrist whose portrait they had in error allowed to appear in print. This led to the resignation of the head of the Third Section, and at the end of the year a new and significant ruling was issued insisting that in future all literature with 'a spiritual' ('dukhovnyi') content was to be read by both religious and secular censors.

This affected *Demon* as well as the publication of other work by Lermontov. For example, *Mtsyri* (another major poem in which a monk flees his monastery and declares himself ready to exchange 'Paradise and Eternity' for a few moments of freedom) was expressly proscribed. The proscription of Milton began even earlier and stretches over many years. According to the Leningrad archives of the Holy Synod it was the Chief Censorship Directorate that was first approached about *Paradise Lost* and *Paradise Regained*. The affair began in April 1834, being prompted by a new single-volume edition of the two poems printed for an unnamed publisher. Since the institution of censorship had not in essence changed since Radishchev's time, such submission of printed matter had, of course, by now become a routine affair. Despite Amvrosii's theological reservations when he brought out the first full edition of *Paradise Lost* in 1780, Milton's poem had appeared no less than a dozen times since then. As far as is known, *Paradise Regained*, published half a dozen times in the same period, met with no criticism either.[5] It might even be argued that selective editing of *Paradise Lost* (eg, 'Think only what concerns thee and thy being' VIII. ll 173–4) could have served to endorse the Nikolaevan policy of social differentiation. Had influential personages changed their attitude towards Milton's work since 1825?

Where Milton's reputation was concerned, that year was crucial (as we have seen) in another context; but the censors could not have been immediately affected by the controversial work on Christian doctrine because an edition of *Paradise Lost* saw the light only two years after the Decembrist Rebellion. Following that, if we exclude solitary editions of the epics in 1835 and 1842–3, another one in 1850, and one of *Paradise Regained* in 1848, nothing of Milton's was published until Zhadovskaya broke into print with her adaptation-translation. These gaps in publication are all the more surprising in view of what happens thereafter. For between the early sixties and the Revolution of 1905, either the epics or some other work of Milton appeared in Russia on average almost every year.[6] Was the earlier hiatus due entirely to censorship? The surviving records do not tell the whole story of Milton's proscription in the Nikolaevan era, but what they do reveal is that both church and state censors were concerned by Satan's disturbing example. The parallel between his conduct and Milton's own unsavoury reputation as a regicide and republican was too close to overlook, and the only reason a final decision over what to do with the epics took so long to arrive at was Count Sergei Uvarov's reluctance to act.

Uvarov's claim to fame rests on the trinity he proclaimed as the source of Nikolaevan ideology: 'Orthodoxy, Autocracy, and Nationality.' Without much formal education Uvarov rose to high office at a young age, becoming both minister of public education and president of the St Petersburg Academy of Sciences.[7] In his published papers he dealt with a variety of topics, from pre-Homeric mythology to Oriental studies, which he wished to see more intensively developed in Russia; but the principal preoccupation of his official reports was to dam the flood of dangerous Western ideas into Russia. Among his legacies (he resigned as minister in 1849 at a time when the failure of this policy could not be overlooked) was a multi-tiered censorship system. It covered every aspect of scholarly and literary activity, giving the mechanisms for controlling opinion unprecedented amplitude. In view of the influence on him of Joseph de Maistre, who saw a connection between Satan's Pandemonium and the ranting of the National Assembly,[8] it might be thought that Uvarov's attitude to Milton should have been equally reserved. Indeed, he did follow Maistre in seeing Baconian science as essentially a 'Protestant' creation, and as such the main source of modern materialism and republicanism. But instead he appears to have enjoyed the sparring between government officials and those of the Holy Synod over Milton's epics. For nobody was quite certain in whose bailiwick they belonged. The minister himself insisted on precedent: since they had never before been assigned to the 'theological' category, why do so now? Through Winsun, the English tutor Uvarov's household shared with Lermontov, the minister would have been fully aware of the awesome reputation Milton's epics had now acquired 'as Classics in the History of Letters.'[9] Uvarov may therefore have been simply too embarrassed to follow the dictum of lower officials who wished to see the poems banned. For them Milton's Satan had no possible connection with Christian doctrine, and they described Milton's influence as potentially very menacing because of the 'demand' for the epics among 'the simple uneducated class.'[10] And making that danger all the more tangible were the 'khodebshchiki,' a peculiarly Russian phenomenon, although their counterparts had existed in Milton's England too. They peddled Milton's books throughout the empire's 'towns and ... villages' and lay therefore, unlike urban booksellers, outside police control.

    The minister who replaced Uvarov took the bull by the horns with a verdict worthy of Solomon. All prosaic translations of *Paradise Lost* and *Paradise Regained* were henceforward proscribed, but verse translations were to be exempted. It is this class-ridden loophole Zhadovskaya exploited when the official Moscow police publisher brought out her rhymed version of Milton. Did she know of the heretical passages censors had criticized earlier? Her adaptation certainly seems to avoid them, but her contrite and feeble Satan, the censors may have concluded, could hardly be perceived as a political threat. Accordingly, in June 1858, her work received the imprimatur Milton's works were now required to carry from both the government *and* the spiritual ('dukhovnyi') censors. But suspicions at this point about Satanism as a literary and ideological phenomenon were dormant, not dead. It is therefore odd that the period's vociferous 'civic' or 'radical' critics ('democratic' in Soviet usage) also proved either unsympathetic or oblivious to the politics of Milton's Satan, whose credentials as a rebel were after all as authentic as Milton's own.

'APOTHEOSIS OF REBELLION'

Ever since 1855 the radical critics had conducted a guerrilla war against the literary establishment. This is the year N.G. Chernyshevsky joined the staff of the *Contemporary*. When he relinquished his post of literary critic, he passed it on to Nikolai Dobroliubov, a devoted disciple who (like Chernyshevsky himself) was the son of a clergyman and an ex-seminarian. Dobroliubov had thus probably also read Milton's epics before Zhadovskaya's translation gave him the opportunity to attack that kind of literature. Yet Dobroliubov's motives are not entirely clear.

'Previous translations of *Paradise Lost*,' he observed, 'had been in prose.' Now 'Mme Zhadovskaya conceived the notion that Milton's poem will have an even greater success among us if she turns it into verse.'[11] The result, according to Dobroliubov, was both deplorable and misleading. Since she translated from only three of the books in *Paradise Lost* and from only one in *Paradise Regained*, Zhadovskaya had no business covering her production with Milton's mantle. Dobroliubov was also able to show how the lines that offended him were not from the original but from the earlier Russian translation in prose.[12]

That such translations had in fact appeared before 1810 the influential young critic was apparently unaware, but his familiarity with a later edition of the Amvrosii-Milton enabled him to spot Zhadovskaya's misrepresentations. It was this that triggered his gravest charge. Her translation was simply unworthy of the English poet. Zhadovskaya and other 'Muscovite publicists' like her would do well in future to leave such feeble efforts alone: 'Do not get us wrong. It is not that we are mocking Milton, or poetry, as if to say that we do not need any translations, or that the ones we already have are more than adequate. No. It is not that we are condemning Elizaveta Zhadovskaya for translating Milton, but for doing it badly, for not translating everything she should have, and then conveying the impression that what she did translate was all [there is to translate in the original].'[13] Beneath these justified charges lay a new offensive in criticism: the utilitarian heresy that the Russian *muzhik* needed a good pair of shoes a lot more than fine verse by Pushkin. Inspired by Belinsky's didacticism, this departure expressed a fresh social awareness and an uncompromising insistence on activism, which in turn was fired by the dream of a 'new man' to which Chernyshevsky devoted his Utopian novel *What Is to Be Done?*[14] In theory, Milton could easily have been accommodated to this anti-aesthetic credo, as indeed he would be after 1917. But at this juncture the conflict between the Radical Democrats and the supporters of 'l'art pour l'art' (such as Botkin, Druzhinin, and the Slavophile Apollon Grigor'ev) was played out within a more familiar literary context. To the reading public at large little was as yet known about the English Revolution or the heroic part John Milton had played in it. The 'Ioann' Milton of popular perception had a biblical aura about him that the Christian baggage of the epics only enhanced. All this proved an obstacle to understanding him for a generation of intellectuals reared on Büchner's *Stoff und Kraft* or *The Origin of Species*.

Even the status of Goethe's *Faust* was now in doubt. Turgenev, accused of sympathizing with the nihilists for his portrayal of Bazarov in *Fathers and Sons*, was seen as perpetrating a disservice to those who defended Goethe 'the uncommitted artist.' For Turgenev Mephisto became a convenient springboard from which to launch 'his criticism of the superfluous man.'[15] The lack of compassion and social consciousness that Turgenev discerned both in Mephisto and in so-called superfluous people stands in sharp contrast to the Russian discovery, as revolution approached, that, unlike Goethe's devil, Milton's Satan and the Prometheus of Aeschylus shared a common mission to liberate mankind. Byron and others in the heyday of romanticism had said as much. Indeed, Belinsky had also been aware of Milton's politics in a way that the young Dobroliubov evidently was not. Writing not long before his death in 1848, the 'father' of Russian criticism described Milton's poetry in lines Blake or Shelley or Byron would have approved. For Belinsky Milton was 'the apotheosis of rebellion against authority.'[16] Yet nihilists who had taken a comparable stand in their rejection of established literary and aesthetic canons paid no attention to Satan's characterization in *Paradise Lost*. Only one talented poet of the period did in fact do so, and his politics, ironically enough, were conservative.

SLUCHEVSKY'S SATAN

As a poet, Konstantin Sluchevsky, who was born the year Pushkin died, acquired his reputation as early as the 1850s when Turgenev and Grigor'ev greeted his literary début with extravagant praise. A decade later he turned to Milton, and it is possible that his translation of *Paradise Lost* would have got much farther if it had not been for the vendetta initiated against him by the Radical Democrats. Sluchevsky, who was connected with the court and rose to influential positions in government, then retreated from the literary scene rather like Fet for almost twenty years.

When this remarkable poet began publishing again, the prevailing aesthetic favoured 'art for art's sake.' This had been at the core of Sluchevsky's bitter dispute with Chernyshevsky and D.I. Pisarev. The sometimes morose and melancholy themes of Sluchevsky's own poetry, which Dostoevsky appreciated for its genuine religious awareness, may have prompted his choice in turning to Satan's encounter with Sin and Death. The symbolism of this meeting was lost on Voltaire, who thought that scene in Book II so deplorable that his strictures themselves became a touchstone of taste in the early Romantic period. To those reared on neoclassical prejudice, the almost gothic element in Satan's encounter with Sin and Death was hard to stomach. But Book II also presents a challenge to the translator, for any change of inflection can push what teeters on the outer edge of the sublime into the ridiculous. Yet to a Romantic, which Sluchevsky remained even during a period that generally ridiculed the sublime, the flight from Hell was one of Milton's great achievements. And like Byron or Lermontov he felt an instinctive sympathy for Satan's predicament. The action takes place when 'the Adversary of God and man' seeks an escape from Hell 'with thoughts inflamed of highest design.' As he 'explores ... sometimes the right-hand coast, sometimes the left' in a motif reminiscent of Willoughby's and Chancellor's quest for a northeast passage, Satan 'soars / Up to the fiery concave towering high' (II. ll 634–5). It is at this point that he encounters Death guarding the egress from Hell:

> Satan was now at hand, and from his seat
> The monster moving onward came as fast,
> With horrid strides; Hell trembled as he strode.
> The undaunted Fiend what this might be admired,
> Admired, not feared; God and his Son except,
> Created thing nought valued he nor shunned;
> And with disdainful look thus first began:
>   'Whence and what art thou, execrable Shape
> That dar'st, though grim and terrible, advance
> Thy miscreated front athwart my way
> To yonder gates? Through them I mean to pass,
> That be assured, without leave asked of thee.

126 Satan as Romantic and Marxist Idol

> Retire, or taste thy folly, and learn by proof,
> Hell-born, not to contend with spirits of Heaven.' (II. ll 674–87)

Sluchevsky omits some of Milton's detail, such as 'disdainful look' and the full sense of 'nought valued he nor shunned'; but as a whole the Russian does catch Satan's audacity:

> Zavidev Satanu, s siden'ia svoego
> Podnialos' chudishche s kop'em emu na vstrechu:
> Pod nim, treshchia vsei tverd'iu, vzdrognul ad
> I Satana pred nim ostanovilsia,
> O, net, ne strakh, – vo vsem, chto sushchestvuet
> Otsa i Syna lish' boitsia on!
> On tol'ko udivlen, nezhdano ozadachen.
> I obratias' k chudovishchu skazal;
> 'Kto ty? otkuda ty, prokliatoe viden'e,
> Chto smeesh' stat' pregradoiu na puti,
> I tvoi uzhasnyi lik, tvoi nenavistnyi obraz,
> Urod, osmelilos' vozdvignut' u vorot
> Peredo mnoi! Ia pronesus', konechno,
> Bez razreshen'ia i soglas'ia tvoego!
> Nazad! kol' net, ty dorogo zaplatish'
> Za opyt tvoi, poznavshi, adskii oblik,
> Chto boi ne boi s tsarem, s nerukotvornym mnoi!'

Satan's language here is rather more powerful than the original and the insults weightier, although for a Russian translator the tone of the exchange is complicated by the reversal of genders, Sin ('Grekh') being masculine and Death ('Smert''') feminine. Nonetheless, here is the way Sluchevsky renders the dramatic imagery Voltaire found so offensive. Compare:

> Pensive here I sat
> Alone, but long I sat not, till my womb,
> Pregnant by thee, and now excessive grown,
> Prodigious motion felt and rueful throes.
> At last this odious offspring whom thou seest,
> Thine own begotten, breaking violent way
> Tore through my entrails, that with fear and pain
> Distorted, all my nether shape thus grew
> Transformed; but he my inbred enemy

Forth issued, brandishing his fatal dart
Made to destroy. I fled, and cried out *Death!* (II. ll 777–87)

with

     Zdes' u poroga
Sidela ia, zadumchiva, odna,
Poka v moei rasshirennoi utrobe,
Toboiu oplodotvorennoi, neskazalis'
Dvizheni'ia strashnyia, neistovye muki,
Terzavshiia, poka vot etot gnusnyi plod,
Tvoi syn, kotoryi pred toboiu, ne iavilsia,
Ne vyrvalsia na svet, menia vsiu iskalechiv;
S kop'em v rukakh, na veki smertonosnym,
Iz chreva moego on vyshel. Ia bezhala,
Ispugana v konets, i zakrichala –
     'Smert''![17]

The Russian misses some of the original's nuances, such as 'with fear and pain' and, more significantly, the potent ring of 'inbred enemy.' Compared with Zhadovskaya's effort, Sluchevsky's translation, which ends with the lines above and appeared in print only in 1897, can only seem masterly. He was not at all interested in Milton's politics, even if his admired translation unwittingly underlined them, since by then Satan had come close to regaining the political recognition the French Revolution had imposed on him. A popular Milton biography, which came out only a few years before Sluchevsky's fragment on Satan, revived the Promethean parallel favoured by the Romantics. The author of the book was a Legal Marxist interested in both the English Revolution and the condition of the Russian worker.[18] He accepted the argument, often heard in Britain and on the Continent but not before advanced in Russia, that Satan's rebellious conduct was inspired in part by what Milton saw and knew of Oliver Cromwell.

This approach to *Paradise Lost*, adopted by Lunacharsky after the Bolshevik Revolution, would make the poem palatable to Russian socialists otherwise disposed to dismiss the epic as Christian – that is to say, reactionary – propaganda. But the mystical quests and speculative flights of Russia's more influential poets and writers in the 1880s and 1890s were not conducive to literalism such as this. The pastoral and lyrical side of *Paradise Lost*, which had also appealed so much to the Romantics despite their infatuation with Milton's Satan, now found new admirers with the revival of a kindred aesthetic.[19] Satanism was now again in vogue, but it was not at first a poetic or literary event. Its revival was due to one of the most original artists of the nineteenth century whose obsession with Lermontov's Demon led to madness and untimely death.

VRUBEL'S DEMONIC OBSESSION

When the eleven-year-old Vrubel was still in Saratov, he made a copy of Michelangelo's *Last Judgement*, which is the earliest evidence we have of the future artist's extraordinary visual retention. Like Picasso, who was to 'stand for hours on end' before Vrubel's paintings when they were shown in Paris in 1906,[20] the Russian innovator whose work inspired the symbolists began his career with a deep commitment to academic painting that in his case was accompanied by a passionate interest in literature. He read Gogol's *Dead Souls* as a schoolboy and became enamoured of the novels of Turgenev, whom he much preferred to Dostoevsky, a writer he disliked even more than Tolstoy. Chekhov he came to love, and he learnt enough German in his *lycée* to read *Faust* in the original. He spoke French, studied English, and had a good enough command of Latin to teach it. As a young man Vrubel became deeply interested in Proudhon, Lessing, Goethe, and Kant. Of the Russian poets, Pushkin and Lermontov meant most to him. Critics and biographers tracing Vrubel's obsession with the demonic to its literary sources agree that Milton, Goethe, and Lermontov played a part in influencing the artist, but no one is sure what weight to attach to each.[21] For this there are two reasons.

Vrubel began working on his image of the Demon as early as 1885. In one form or another it continued to haunt him until the end of his working life when, prior to his commitment to an asylum, he caused a sensation in St Petersburg by working on his unfinished version of *The Demon Downcast* on the premises of the World of Art Exhibition in 1902. During those seventeen years the Demon would re-appear in his *oeuvre* in various forms; but, in his continuous and perturbing quest for the image that would express his shifting vision of Lermontov's hero, many of the likenesses he drew, painted, and sculpted were destroyed by the artist himself. That is why we do not have a record of Vrubel's involvement with the demonic theme to match that of Lermontov, in whose case the drafts of the poem survived. Yet the superficial parallels between the poet and the artist are obvious enough. The theme, once they were attracted to it, remained with them for the rest of their lives.

The other difficulty in isolating influence is due not to the absence of material, but to its abundance. As a recent revisionist Soviet essay on the artist rightly suggests, there is nothing very remarkable in the fact that 'a profound and dramatically inclined artist' such as Vrubel should have become interested in 'the grandiose image of the spirit of Evil.'[22] That image did, after all, represent a focal point in the classical literature to which highly educated artists of Vrubel's generation were all exposed. Nor was the general public unaware of Satan, despite the antipathy of the radicals of the sixties. From the time Vrubel began working on Demon to his death in 1910 there were no less than thirty-four editions of *Paradise Regained* and almost as many translations and editions of *Paradise Lost*. Most of these were illustrated, the most familiar illustrator being Gustave Doré, who it seems was similarly struck by two of Vrubel's favourite themes, Satan after the expulsion from Heaven and Satan in flight after escaping Hell.

Such subjects, long traditional fare for Milton's many illustrators, were usually treated in the popular editions of *Paradise Lost*. Indeed, the adoption of chromolithography by Russian publishers, who introduced it somewhat later than in the West, made dramatic coloured reproductions of Satan an added attraction for buyers of the ubiquitous and inexpensive prose versions of Milton's epics (see figures 16 and 30). But Vrubel, whether aware of these illustrations or not, is unlikely to have been inspired by them. His Demon from the very outset was associated with Lermontov's poem as well as with Anton Rubinstein's opera of the same name. Indeed, this is borne out by a letter Vrubel's father wrote at the end of 1885 where he alludes to a tetralogy his son had in mind: 'The Demon, Tamara, The Death of Tamara, and *Christ at Tamara's Grave.*'[23] But Christ does not appear in Lermontov's poem despite the piety of the draft intended for the empress's eyes. For Vrubel, by contrast, the underlying Christian motif had a profound symbolic meaning, which may have had its roots in his experiences as a young man and the religious revival that came to affect the intelligentsia as a whole in the 1880s. In 1873, when Vrubel was first introduced to the changing world of contemporary art through the Society for Travelling Exhibitions (its members were generally known as the Itinerants), he was deeply impressed by Kramskoi's painting of *Christ in the Wilderness*. After he moved to St Petersburg and then made the first of many journeys to Italy in 1875, his own devotional strain was duly reflected in a series of sketches and paintings on biblical subjects; these took a fresh turn when Professor Adrian Prakhov introduced him to Byzantine art. The murals Vrubel was then commissioned to do for the ancient St Vladimir's Cathedral in Kiev presented him with new opportunities, which were given yet another direction when the painter visited Venice to study the Santa Maria Assunta mosaics on the island of Torcello. He also visited Rome, much as Milton had done two and a half centuries earlier, being particularly attracted by Giovanni Bellini, Tintoretto, Tiepolo, and Cima da Conegliano. On his return to Russia Vrubel did several paintings on religious subjects, including one of *Christ*.

But the most extraordinary of this series was his *Virgin and Child* (see Figure 17). Unmistakably the face of the madonna bears a resemblance to the wife of Adrian Prakhov's son, Emil'ia Prakhova, with whom the artist was infatuated. That face is also recognizable in an androgynous head of the *Demon* begun in 1890 (see Figure 18), although at that point this image's further development in Vrubel's art is complicated by a commission he received to illustrate the jubilee edition of Lermontov's *Collected Works*. Yet Lermontov's poem could no longer, it seems, contain the complexity the theme had acquired for Vrubel himself. In *Tamara's Dance* (see Figure 19) and *Tamara and the Demon* (Figure 20), the exotic and melancholy 'Eastern' countenance of the hero, reminiscent perhaps in mood of Moore's *Lalla Rookh*, betrays little of the inner fire of the original Demon Vrubel had conceived or of the ambiguity of the Demon's later manifestations. Indeed, the Demon of 1890 was so striking and novel in conception that, according to one of Vrubel's most recent admirers, it 'undoubtedly unlocked the door to symbolism in Russian art.'[24] It left Vrubel's father in a quandary. 'Misha,' he wrote in the first of hundreds of mystified ruminations on his son's obsession, 'says that the Demon is a spirit uniting both male and female elements in itself. It is not so much an evil spirit, as it is a dolorous one, but nevertheless, an overbearing spirit ... a grandiose one.'[25] Yet Colonel Vrubel, whose precise habits of mind had been bolstered by his legal training and profession as a judge, felt that 'all this' was not present in what he had seen in his son's work.

There are obviously similarities between Vrubel's mature painting and symbolism as it had already taken shape in the West. Yet in Russia what Vrubel was trying to do was long rejected by artists of the academies, a rejection that may have added to his conception of the Demon an outsider's psychological insight. If the original inspiration for the subject was literary and biblical, the expressive treatment it received at his hands in turn influenced the poetry and theatre of the *fin-de-siècle*. Yet Vrubel himself is difficult to place in the effervescent art world of St Petersburg and Moscow. He did not himself describe his art as symbolist, even if his use of colour is at times similar to that of Odilon Redon. Nor did he see himself as a 'decadent,' an appellation relished by some of his Viennese contemporaries who exhibited Vrubel's work at the Secession. Like many of them, he was attracted by hedonism – Vrubel referred to the pleasures of the senses as 'Homerism' – but in him this urge was in continuous tension with his spiritual quest, of which his Demon became the visible expression. Like Vladimir Soloviev, the religious philosopher idolized by the Russian symbolists, he wanted 'art to be a real force, enlightening and remolding all of mankind.'[26] Perhaps it is this striving that gives some of his portrayals of the Demon their intangible heroic quality, although they may seem today as distant from Lermontov's more muted vision as they are from the Satan of *Paradise Lost*.

In *Demon* Lermontov's hero simply lacks the rich and ornate imagery of Vrubel's later invention. He too is weighed down by 'the bitter shame of sin,' but the despair of Vrubel's Demon is both more vague and more all-encompassing. Interestingly, the artist did not believe in original sin. Nor did he like to hear his demons described as devils. '*Daimon*' in Greek means 'soul' or 'spirit,' and Vrubel enthusiastically proposed that this is what his portrayals represented. But what kind of *daimon*?

The *Demon Seated* (see Figure 21), one of Vrubel's best-known canvases, carries little suggestion of the supernatural, being best described in the words the artist wrote to his sister: 'That is [,] not that sort of monumental Demon I'll paint later, but a "demonic" semi-nude, winged, young, dejected, and pensive figure sitting, with his hands hugging his knees, against the background of the setting sun, and looking at a blossoming field from which there stretch branches bending under the weight of flowers.'[27] But the sculptured head of the Demon of tinted plaster, cast in the same year, with its burning eyes and sensual downturned lips produced quite a different impression (see Figure 22). The enormous shock of hair (it has been pointed out) may have been suggested by Iokhim Tartakov, who sang the role of Demon in the Kiev Opera, an actor whose 'lion's mane of curly hair and face ... were reminiscent of Anton Rubinstein.'[28] Indeed, on the operatic stage a certain stereotype of the Demon already existed. If Vrubel borrowed from it – some of the same features reappear in the pensive 'Head of the Demon' used to illustrate Lermontov's poem (see Figure 18) – its theatricality has been refined to an intensity that reminded observers of the thirty-year-old Alexander Blok. This symbolist poet's tormented features came to be identified by Vrubel's contemporaries with the abstract ideal of the poet. This face, 'at once ascetic and tainted by earthly desires [and] effusing a sense of gigantic power' is far removed from the energetic leader we encounter in the opening two pages of *Paradise Lost*. Milton's Satan is presented from the first as a mighty antagonist whose power, heroic self-assertion, self-reliance, and self-deification are aesthetically and intellectually exciting. What undermines this magnificent impression is the reader's gradual realization that Satan's seductiveness is linked to deceit, tyranny, and destruction.

Vrubel's Demons are varied enough in mood and temper to capture some of the qualities of Milton's Satan, but they are never presented by the Russian painter in his earlier uncorrupted state as Lucifer, the prince of angels, or as the titanic adversary of God in the war in Heaven. Vrubel's Demon, like Zhadovskaya's Satan, is above all the tempter, whose ennui and gloomy intensity carry the contradictory marks that gave Russian pre-revolutionary culture its disturbing edge. That contradictory character, epitomized by the most influential critic of the era as being one both of 'great power and great impotence,'[29] also gives some of Vrubel's portrayals of Demon a sense of tragic futility that is alien to Milton except at the very end of *Paradise Lost* with Satan's grotesque transformation into a toad and serpent. Such a mood is most hauntingly conveyed in one of Vrubel's last canvases, *The Demon Downcast* (Figure 23). It reminds one of the moment in Milton's poem where Satan after he is expelled from Heaven awakens stunned in Hell. But Satan, even at his most despondent, does not project quite the same sense of tragic isolation: he is, after all, even in defeat supported by his angelic fellow rebels. Thus, the closest the Russian painter comes to catching the traditional image of Satan in *Paradise Lost* is in his *Demon in Flight* (see Figure 24). Vrubel did several versions of this, a theme to which Alexander Blok added the appropriate apocalyptic note. For in *Paradise Lost* Satan's escape from Hell and his flight towards earth also prefigure mankind's doom. To Blok Lucifer's flight spells cosmic catastrophe:

> Twentieth century ... Now the gloom
> Is still more wide and frightening.
> Even more black and sweeping looms
> The shade of Lucifer's vast wing.[30]

Blok's *Retribution* remained unfinished: epic poetry, it has been suggested, did not agree with the era. This did not affect the popularity of *Paradise Lost* and *Paradise Regained*, but the revival of religion and of romanticism in literature and art inevitably affected the intelligentsia's image of Milton. Nor is its association with Satanism really surprising, since the tendency to confuse Satan's character and the author's has persisted to this day. What is more surprising is the turn Vrubel's demonic obsession took in the last years of his life, before he was struck down by blindness. It was complicated by the intelligentsia's *fin-de-siècle* flirtation with Nietzsche. The artist's recorded allusions to the German thinker do not occur until 1902, the period of his first mental breakdown, but there seems little doubt that his disillusionment with Christianity in those years was affected by this encounter.[31] Indeed, it was the Nietzschean loathing of the 'herd' that inspired Vrubel to attack

Tolstoy, whose notorious article on art in 1898 questioned the 'greatness' of the likes of Michelangelo, Shakespeare, Goethe, and Beethoven, because they failed to arouse 'either a religious perception of universal brotherhood or a feeling of common humanity.'[32] Following Nietzsche, Vrubel had by this time come to think of Christianity as an outworn creed, and he despised the 'herd' instinct that he believed had prompted Tolstoy's defence of popular Orthodoxy and the 'people.'

By then, Nietzsche's view of the artist's tragic sense of life coincided not only with Vrubel's vision of his own isolation in philistine society but the image he projected of *The Demon Downcast*. Nietzsche, it has been suggested, is one of the keys to this startling canvas (which preoccupied Vrubel throughout the autumn of 1901 and the spring of 1902); the other is 'Milton's God from *Paradise Lost*.'[33] If this is so – for we are told that it is Milton's 'image of the fallen Satan [that] Vrubel borrowed for his rebellious Demon'[34] – the pathos of this tormented figure was surely accentuated by the artist's own final crisis, his rejection of faith. In this godless context it may seem incongruous to describe the Demon as Nietzsche's Antichrist – the Antichrist who relishes 'struggle [and] resistance.'[35] For without God, the rebellion in Heaven becomes meaningless. But after the October Revolution there was a fresh approach to this metaphysical predicament, which the hapless Zhadovskaya had first naïvely unearthed when she made Satan proclaim his atheism.[36] Some such tack could have been taken by Marxist critics. Instead, they rescued Milton's Satan from the isolation to which Vrubel's Nietzschean élitism had confined him by providing him with a tangible earthly foe. Despite the opposition that would greet his promotion to revolutionary status after 1917, Satan's new opponent materialized in the shape of imperialism. In the collectivist view that marked so much Marxist criticism, the Satan of *Paradise Lost* came to be perceived as a leader of the people 'in a new form.' This at least bore some connection, however far-fetched, with the Cromwellian revolution. Under Brezhnev he would thus acquire a Soviet personality to match the social ethos of twentieth-century totalitarianism; but this modern Miltonic Satan would be a far cry from the anti-social individualist of Pushkin's and Lermontov's day, whom Vrubel in the end had transformed into a demonic *Übermensch*.

NINE

1917 and After: The Triumph of Milton's Satan

> 'In relating Satan's rebellion against God, Milton is writing the apologia of the English bourgeoisie.'
> Lunacharsky, *Istoriia zapadno-evropeiskoi literatury* (1924)

Those who identified Satan with Oliver Cromwell did not necessarily also assume that the author of *Paradise Lost* belonged to the Devil's party. Nor did Jacobin sympathizers necessarily admire the Lord Protector. Robespierre himself, for example, thought him a tyrant – as did Alexander Radishchev, although for the Russian radical Cromwell's great service to mankind lay in the first part of his political career, when he taught the Stuarts a lesson in popular sovereignty.[1] But as depicted in *Paradise Lost*, Satan's politics cannot so easily be divided into a progressive and a negative part. After the decline of romanticism his stand against the absolutism of the Almighty, enlightened or otherwise, came to engage the intelligentsia's sympathy only when there was general awareness of its connection with the English Revolution.

Thanks in part to Nikolaevan censors, such awareness was long postponed. But in the 1860s the liberal political climate that came with the great reforms enabled *Areopagitica* to appear in a Russian version, thus adding an explicitly radical dimension to Milton's earlier reputation as a Christian poet. Readers also learnt, thanks to the translations of Macaulay and particularly of Guizot – the first historian to depict England's seventeenth-century crisis as a modern revolution – that the historical background to *Paradise Lost* was not irrelevant to the revolutionary movement then taking shape in their own country. Lermontov's tutor, Z.Z. Zinoviev, whose accurate translation of *Paradise Lost* came out long after the poet's death, cited Macaulay's celebrated defence of Milton's credentials as a revolutionary in his introduction.[2] But this connection was made in a Whig context; the first critic to promote this relationship in a Marxist one did not appear until the 1890s.

He would be better known today if he had joined the Bolshevik faction of the Russian Social-Democratic Labour Party after its split in 1903. As it is Evgenii Andreevich Soloviev died in 1905 at the age of forty-two, just as his gifts were becoming more widely recognized. He was not the earliest Marxist critic in Russia, for Plekhanov had already written on literary subjects, but he was one of the first to become associated with Legal Marxism, a phenomenon denounced by the young Lenin only a few years after Soloviev began his career as a writer in the early 1890s. *Oliver Cromwell* (1893) was his second book, followed a year later by a biography of Milton. He also wrote on a wide range of other writers and poets, such as Pushkin, Karamzin, Turgenev, Sen'kovsky, and on his own contemporaries, Chekhov and Gorky, his biography of Dostoevsky being translated into English. One of his more original works was a series of reflections, *Working People and the New Ideas*.[3] As a literary critic Soloviev sympathized with D.I. Pisarev, one of the best-known radicals of the 1860s, whose writings he brought out in a six-volume edition. Its publisher, F.F. Pavlenkov, also commissioned the books on Cromwell and John Milton.

A MARXIST SATAN

Soloviev's books on Cromwell and Milton were designed as part of an ambitious series of biographies, selling for twenty-five kopecks, which came as close as any publishing venture before the Russian Revolution to realizing Tolstoy's project for an Everyman's library. *Cromwell* and *Milton* would have been read by a very wide public, which is one of two reasons why these popularizations are of some importance. The other is that they were still being widely read after 1917, and may well have influenced Lunacharsky's defence of Milton's Satan. Soloviev was not a historian by training, but both his biographies are well informed, leaning on both Cromwell's own *Letters and Speeches* and Guizot's history of the English Revolution. He also cites Macaulay, Ranke, and Gardiner, whose multivolume work on the period from 1603 to 1656 tried to break with the whole conception of a Whig and Tory history. Like Gardiner's great work, Soloviev's interpretation constitutes a rehabilitation of Cromwell; indeed it was the first sustained attempt in Russian to erase the stain that had long marked Milton's association with this 'son of Beelzebub.' In this sense, the two biographies complement each other.

To Soloviev the ideals of the two men were identical, his verdict on Cromwell being affected more by Carlyle's view of the role of the hero in history than by Plekhanov's critique of that view. To Carlyle, the first historian to compile Cromwell's letters and speeches, the Lord Protector was not a hypocritical religious fanatic propelled by personal ambition (as Victor Hugo and so many others presented him), but a pragmatic idealist cast in the heroic mould. This is essentially the interpretation Soloviev adopts. His Milton is cut of the same cloth. He assumes that the Satan of *Paradise Lost* represents Cromwell at least in the opening books; nor has he any difficulty in also identifying him with Aeschylus' Prometheus and with the author himself. The epic poem becomes the key to all that Milton had 'lived through and experienced between 1641 and 1661,'[4] and Satan is the poet's most successful characterization. He 'impresses by his immensity, an immensity of physique and passion, [and] his pride, for whom freedom is everything.' Forgetting for the moment Satan's later degradation, Soloviev sees him as a noble character, in whom low instincts of any kind that 'might evoke dislike' are wholly absent.[5] The thought that Charles Stuart could have been the original for Satan's duplicity, another reading favoured by some Miltonists, is not even mentioned by the Russian writer. For him Oliver Cromwell's opposition to Charles I acquires something of Milton's own nobility of mind, although Milton placed freedom higher than the existence of the republic.

Yet Soloviev's perspective is a Russian one, with many of the Aesopian allusions one might expect – to 'Eastern despots' who rule their countries like Charles I.[6] Milton's struggle against censorship is all the more admirable, he hints in another passage, in view of the revival of censorship in the author's own lifetime 'in several European countries.' He sees Milton's and Cromwell's belief in individual freedom, although based on a religious foundation, as in no way different from the one animating the Russian intelligentsia of the day. And Milton acted in its best tradition in self-abnegatingly postponing his ambition to become 'England's Dante and Tasso' by hurling himself into the life of a revolutionary. What matters is that he did his duty as *grazhdanin* (which may loosely be translated as 'civic-minded patriot').[7]

These perceptions of the English Revolution, shared by many socialists and liberals, should have helped Milton's Satan to accommodate himself to 1917 much as he had so skilfully come to terms with 1789. For the French Revolution had also brought his politics to the fore, as did the rise of the Chartist movement in England. Similarly, it was, above all, Milton's standing as a radical and revolutionary that largely interested Russian liberals and Marxists in 1905. Lunacharsky's view of Milton seems to have been shaped at this time. When Lenin's commissar for the enlightenment devoted a play to Cromwell in 1918, he portrayed the poet-revolutionary much as Soloviev might have done, standing to the left of a progressive Lord Protector.[8] Nonetheless, Lunacharsky was criticized by left-wing Bolshevik critics for depicting the popular hero of his drama – only a 'bourgeois revolutionary' after all –

too favourably.[9] Lunacharsky rejected these criticisms and, as Russia's Civil War came to an end, used the podium provided by a workers' university to tell his listeners that the Satan of *Paradise Lost* shared the 'invincible' sentiments of its author's own 'revolutionary heart.'

This verdict, when Lunacharsky's lectures were published in what turned out to be the first authorized post-revolutionary treatment of English literature, carried much weight. But this significant step of Milton's Satan towards official approbation was undermined by the popular association of *Paradise Lost* and *Paradise Regained* with Christianity. In the quarter-century before the First World War, the two epics sometimes appeared as often as three or four times a year, being often read *en famille* together with the Bible.[10] Of this Bolshevik censors were well aware, which explains why Milton's poems were proscribed by the new atheist regime. Had the 'new Presbyters' been aware of tsarist proscription, Milton's fate after 1917 would have been less complex.

MAYAKOVSKY AND BLOK

As it is, the Christian association at first outweighed both Satan's revolutionary credentials and Milton's own. This is amusingly reflected in the prologue to Mayakovsky's *Mystery Bouffe*, the play the Bolshevik poet began just after the February Revolution. There *Paradise Lost* and *Paradise Regained* are consigned to perdition. The place these epics had attained in Russian culture is intimated by the fact that they are grandly condemned along with the Bible and the Koran as symbols of the 'Old World.' This world, together with its capitalists, Christians, and Moslems, is demolished in Mayakovsky's drama with the help of a biblical device – the Flood. Non-Bolshevik critics have not been deterred from discovering Christian symbols in Mayakovsky's verse, despite his professed loathing of Christianity. Nor, if the analogy is not far-fetched, is it difficult to see in Milton's Puritan writings the ties that still bound him to the Elizabethans and the society the English Revolution overturned. In the first years of the new regime, the same kind of link tied many artists to the Bible, in which they sought keys to the apocalyptic events taking place before their own eyes.

The most famous example of this is the revolution's poetic masterpiece, *The Twelve*, which is a response to the experiences of the first weeks of January 1918. The twelve Red Guards who dominate the action, and from whom the poem takes its name, reflect the militant secular order imposed by the Bolsheviks; but Blok's poem culminates with the perplexing appearance in the final stanza of Jesus Christ at the head of the marauding Red Guard brigade. Religious symbolism such as this and the controversy aroused by it proved that, for all their hostility to religion, the Bolsheviks could not rout the Christian way of seeing things by decree. Milton's message, like Blok's, would be understood in many ways, and the millenarian vision they shared could even be turned to support the goals of the revolution.

Milton's Jesus in *Paradise Regained*, for example, has (like the Christ of *The Twelve*) been likened to Lenin, the new Messiah, whose presence at the head of the Red Brigade could be read as Blok's approval of the Bolshevik regime.[11] To judge by his diary Blok's meaning was not that simple, but most Bolsheviks were uncomfortable when anyone tried to demonstrate that revolution and religion were not incompatible, the prevailing view on the left after 1917 being best expressed not by Blok, the last great poet of imperial Russia, but by Mayakovsky. To Lenin's discomfiture, this was the poet who, as most established writers fled, appointed himself the literary tribune of the Bolshevik Revolution. Although he had joined the Bolshevik party as early as 1908, at the surprisingly young age of eleven, many of the party's members found his work distastefully strident and common.

Rising to prominence as one of the leaders of Russian futurism, Mayakovsky demanded the rejection of traditional art and literature, glorifying the virtues of industrialism that would sunder Russia's links with a past Mayakovsky considered entirely deplorable. This is the key to *Mystery Bouffe*, his first major post-revolutionary work, which was completed only after the Bolshevik coup in October.[12] The plot, which pits seven pairs of the unclean (representatives of the proletariat) against seven pairs of the clean (cosmopolitan members of the bourgeoisie and aristocracy) was appropriate to the occasion. The clean attempt to control the unclean by establishing a monarchy and then a republic, but the unclean finally assert themselves and guide the ark they had built through Heaven and Hell until they finally reach the promised land, a workers' paradise where machines produce all that is needed for the good life.

The biblical influence on Mayakovsky's play, with its saints and Beelzebubs (whose defeat by the workers the author celebrates) is obvious. So is the contrast between his Devil and Blok's Lucifer or the Demon of Vrubel. *Mystery Bouffe*, which is called 'an heroic, epic, satirical, portrayal of our epoch,' was supposed to represent in dramatic allegorical form the triumph of the new over the decrepit civilization of the past, to which the poet readily consigned Holy Mother Russia as well as the international bourgeoisie. But Mayakovsky's Devil is a mere caricature by comparison with the Satan of *Paradise Lost*. He is a shallow and peevish trickster of the kind to be found in Russian tales of everyday life before Milton gave this shallow creature philosophical and political significance. The purpose of the caricature in *Mystery Bouffe*, however, was obvious enough: in the new world Mayakovsky celebrated there was to be no place for evil or original sin. And the removal of deity from popular culture now faced Satan with a problem he had faced only once before during the French Revolution: if there was no God, against whom was the prince of darkness supposed to stage his rebellion?

SATAN AS PROMETHEUS

Mayakovsky, whose notion of good was Benthamite pure and simple, thought evil too trivial an entity to give the matter much thought. But evil returned in the work of one of the most original novelists of the next generation. In Mikhail Bulgakov's *Master and Margarita*, the Devil takes over Moscow while Stalin's infernal powers bewitch Soviet society: but the official recognition bestowed by Lunacharsky on Milton's Satan did not at first inspire contemporary readings. Nor was his policy of bringing out the literary masterpieces of the bourgeoisie in massive and inexpensive editions at first affected by the new restrictions placed on writers under Stalin. The vast rise in literacy being one of the Soviet government's proud achievements, the party was equally keen to assure comrades abroad that the threat posed to so-called bourgeois culture by *Proletcult* and its offspring had been overcome. Lenin (as D.S. Mirsky noted) had been distrustful of those 'who promised to effect a cultural revolution in Russia overnight.'[13] The bridges of a true proletarian culture could be built only after mastering 'the culture created in the course of mankind's entire development,'[14] a statement that legitimized the reaction against experimentation and ultra-modernism in art that had marked the first years of Bolshevik power.

This should have guaranteed safe passage for *Paradise Lost*, if not for *Paradise Regained*. Gorky, now the best known of Russia's living writers, had also provided an argument in its support, bizarre as it may seem today, when he said that *Paradise Lost* was not the product of individual genius, but of 'the creativity of the masses.'[15] This proposition, so consonant with the Stalinist ethos of the thirties, was one Gorky in fact first uttered before 1914. In 1925 Denis Saurat, in a book that would be read by Miltonists everywhere, applied a similar notion with great effect to the study of Milton's beliefs: 'Thought does not go from great men to great men, but flourishes on its own – and occasionally a great man establishes a connection with the people.'[16]

This was the key to Saurat's major thesis: that Milton owed his ideas on the creation, the soul, the Trinity, the resurrection, and much else, to the mortalists. The poet's heretical views had, of course, been known to the general public since the publication of *De Doctrina Christiana* exactly a century earlier; but Saurat's work was part of the 'New Movement' in the West that tried to shift the attention away from questions of style and art to Milton's ideas. This movement began not long after the First World War, but there is no evidence that it had any influence on Gorky or on Lunacharsky, whose treatment of religion and myth was inspired (as Lunacharsky himself admits) by another Frenchman, Paul Lafargue.

Lafargue, whose funeral Lenin had attended in 1911, set out to prove that Christianity and monotheism were both economically determined, like all abstract ideas. Here he was an elegant exponent of the approach advanced by his father-in-law, Karl Marx.[17] Lafargue's writings, highly praised by Lenin, were published in Russia in the twenties and thirties, Lunacharsky being particularly impressed by his analysis of the myth of Prometheus.[18] Milton refers to this demigod several times, but without any distinctive additions to the two legends associated with him. Prometheus stole fire from Zeus and gave it to man, and, according to a separate legend, he was punished for doing this by Zeus, who tortured him by having him chained to a rock, where an eagle fed daily on his liver. Lunacharsky perceived a relationship between Prometheus and Milton's Satan, a parallel that Shelley, another favourite poet of Lunacharsky's, had suggested in the preface to *Prometheus Unbound*.[19]

This idea, restated by some modern critics such as Werblovsky, made Satan the hero of *Paradise Lost* in much the same way that he had been for William Blake and so many of Milton's Romantic readers. For Soviet critics it became the key to interpreting the poem as a whole, as is reflected in that monument to Marxist erudition the *Literaturnaia entsiklopediia* (*Literary Encyclopaedia*), which was launched by Lunacharsky and edited by him until his death in 1933. Had he lived, the entry on Milton would presumably have been written by him. As it is, it was entrusted to two critics, Vasiutinskii and Lavretskii, both of whom followed Lunacharsky's view of Satan as a 'cosmic revolutionary.'

In his retelling of the myth of Prometheus, Aeschylus, an aristocrat and conservative, could not be identified politically with his hero, as Lunacharsky well realized. Milton's views, on the other hand, could be linked to Satan's sentiments more easily; for in *Paradise Lost* 'it is as if Milton were ... reliving the pain of the revolution's defeat: this is the poet's own drama and that of his friends. In relating Satan's rebellion against God, Milton is writing the apologia of the English bourgeoisie.'[20] Yet Satan is also the traducer of mankind. His insurrection against the heavenly host can be seen, so Vasiutinskii argues, as an attack on the revolutionary Puritans. Hence the ambivalence of *Paradise Lost*, for Milton was compelled to invest the traditional biblical context with his own contradictory experience. In real life the revolution was aborted because of the unwillingness of the class to which Milton belonged to push the revolution beyond a certain self-serving point. Satan's rebellion, however, knew no bounds. The lower classes, therefore, became identified in Milton's mind with Satan since it is they who wished to carry the revolution further by threatening private property.

Paradise Regained is seen by the Soviet critic as a continuation of the same internal conflict. The poem's essential idea – 'seeing the coming revolution in terms of man's spiritual rebirth' – is realized in Christ's triumph over Satan. Thus, Adam and Eve's transgression is redeemed; but symbolically the redemption is for the errors committed in the revolution. Yet if this is so, why did Milton feel that Adam and Eve were worth saving? Vasiutinskii earlier in his analysis says that they merely represent 'the ideal of the bourgeois Puritan family in the seventeenth century.' Was this all that Milton really desired to salvage?

Vasiutinskii's reply is that Milton in fact never sold out. He still held on to a belief in the possibility of a new society, despite his class background. Christ therefore established the 'kingdom of God' not in Heaven, but on earth. This is achieved in *Paradise Regained* not by overt action, but by persuasion and conviction. Belief in 'the light within' also, therefore, becomes a political course of conduct, particularly since Christ is presented as not a divinity but a 'Greater Man.' He symbolizes, Vasiutinskii insists, the 'chosen' leader of the future revolution overcoming reaction. In *Paradise Regained* Satan, by the same token, represents the Restoration; and he is painted in the familiar Stuart colours of 'treachery, duplicity and cunning.'[21]

This interpretation, Vasiutinskii concludes, is confirmed by Milton's final masterpiece. Unlike many Western commentators, Vasiutinskii refuses to see *Samson Agonistes* as a pessimistic work. In retelling the biblical story Milton found in Samson the symbol of the Puritan cause. The Puritans had learnt much in the period of reaction. If Milton believed in the necessity of a moral rebirth (eg, in *Paradise Regained*), then with *Samson* he must have become convinced that 'without revolutionary force no victory of the new society was possible.'[22] Samson, in overcoming his passions by the power of reason, having been spiritually reborn, struggles actively against reaction (the Philistines), and triumphs only by using force. Thus, Vasiutinskii argues, at the very end of his life Milton's faith in the strength of the young bourgeoisie was rekindled – 'he saw its successes, but he knew that he would not live to see the ultimate triumph of its cause: Samson – there are autobiographical lines in him – goes down at the same time as his enemies.'[23]

Samson's isolation and loneliness reflect Milton's own. This is one of the few points on which the pre-revolutionary Russian encyclopaedia and Vasiutinskii's interpretation of the poet's life and work are in accord. He was forgotten by all, *Paradise Lost* receiving its due only with the French Revolution and in eighteenth-century Germany, where it exerted 'an enormous influence on the literature of the rising bourgeoisie.'[24] Vasiutinskii also describes Milton's impact on English writers – on Cowper, Young, Shelley, Ebenezer Eliot, and George Meredith, this being one of the few sections of the two articles on Milton in the *Literary Encyclopaedia* where dependence on Western scholarship is evident. Vasiutinskii had clearly read Havens's study on Milton's influence on English literature,[25] his arguments in support of Milton's materialism being derived from the two pioneering studies by Denis Saurat.

Otherwise Vasiutinskii seems to have arrived at his interpretation of Milton's life and work unaided. It does not wholly agree with the shorter accompanying article by Alexander Lavretskii, which concentrates on Milton's style. For the latter, *Paradise Lost* reflects above all the genesis of capitalist society, just as Dante's poem mirrored 'the completed life of the feudal-Catholic Middle Ages.'[26] He explains the ambiguity of Satan's characterization in terms of the 'aging poet's disillusionment with revolution ...' Nor does he subscribe to Vasiutinskii's view that the 'spiritual' revolution to which Milton at the end aspired was also in a sense 'more real,' since this did not involve an abandonment on Milton's part of a belief in violence.

Lavretskii also accepts the more traditional view that the portrayal of Satan, being based in part on Cromwell, reflects Milton's ambivalent attitude to the Lord Protector, whose love of freedom was corrupted by his lust for power. It is this, according to Lavretskii, that makes Satan into 'a truly demonic being, doomed to fall.'[27] His view of the English poet is therefore politically a shade more moderate than Vasiutinskii's, and could be read as a reflection on what was happening in the Russia of Stalin, after collectivization. As far as *Paradise Lost* was concerned, however, there seemed to be no actual taboos against its publication, its path having been paved by approval in the *Literary Encyclopaedia*, the authority of which was then taken very seriously indeed.

SATAN AS *VOZHD'*

How exactly the new translation was begun is not revealed in the surviving Soviet archives, but they do show that in 1934 S.N. Protas'ev, an otherwise little-known poet, approached Academia about bringing out the first post-revolutionary translation of *Paradise Lost*. Founded by Gorky, Academia was the most prestigious of the country's publishing houses, and it is perhaps not insignificant that Protas'ev's approach coincided in time with the publication of volume eight of the encyclopaedia, where the author of *Paradise Lost* was so enthusiastically endorsed as 'the first bard of revolution.' By then, however, party control of literature and the arts had made publishers particularly cautious about accepting outside proposals, and evidently this also applied to Milton. As M. Rozanov, a senior editor at Academia would put it, although *Paradise Lost* was certainly a classic, it was also 'idiosyncratic,' a characterization that could be interpreted in many ways. Above all, the epic seemed 'so out of harmony with our epoch' that 'the most thorough attitude' would need to be exercised 'in rendering it in the Russian language.'[28]

Fortunately for all concerned the ideal person to see that this would be done (as it must have seemed to Rozanov) had not long ago returned from England, and he accepted the invitation to supervise the new edition. Prince D.S. Mirsky, the son of a prominent liberal minister under the tsarist regime, had begun his writing career at the age of twenty-one with the publication of a collection of poems. These were written during his student years at the University of St Petersburg before 1914, when war and revolution upset his literary ambitions. Like most of the country's intellectuals, he opposed the Bolsheviks. As an exile in Paris and then in London, where he lectured at the School of Slavonic Studies, he soon became one of the leading authorities on Russian literature and the Soviet scene. Mirsky's biography of Pushkin, published in 1926, had been the first serious work on Russia's great poet in English, and it was probably not long after its completion that Mirsky began to acquaint himself with the Milton scholarship to which Soviet archives today testify.

Three years later, he came out with a charmingly illustrated edition of Milton's *Brief History of Moscovia*, which had not been published separately since the seventeenth century. By way of supplement to his elegant introduction Mirsky added a Latin epistle, signed by Tsar Alexis Mikhailovich, that excoriated Milton the regicide and insulted Oliver Cromwell.[29] Since the letter is a forgery, its historical interest is slight, but it does reveal something of Mirsky's own state of mind before he returned to the Soviet Union. He suggests that the letter should be compared with 'certain more recent declarations of anti-revolutionary governments denouncing other "Sowers of infand wickednesse" and attempting to fight "universal contagions" that have in more recent times "poysoned and infected most parts of Christendom!"'[30] Before publishing the *Moscovia* Mirsky became a Marxist, the outcome (according to Muggeridge) of a commission to produce a book on Lenin, whom he came to see 'as an enlightened saviour rather than, as heretofore, a degraded villain.'[31]

To Mirsky, who returned to Russia in 1932, Milton was the most heroic figure in English literature, by comparison with whom the intellectuals and literati he met in and around Bloomsbury sank into total insignificance. He was to chronicle some of these feelings in a satirical exposé of Britain's 'intellidzhentsia,' a theme already explored by Harold Laski and, in another key, by D.H. Lawrence, to whom Mirsky devoted many pages. Where Milton was concerned, his sympathies lay not with his modernist detractors but with the 'New Movement,' which tried to shift the attention from questions of style and art to that of Milton's thought. He took his cue from Saurat by telling one of his Russian colleagues that at the source of *Paradise Lost* lay a philosophical conception 'fundamentally very far removed' from orthodox Christianity. C.S. Lewis, who vehemently disagreed with this view, nonetheless gave Saurat the credit for 'rescu[ing] Miltonic criticism from the drowsy praise of his "organ music" and babble about the "majestic rolls of proper names," to have begun the new era in which readers take him (as he wished to be taken) seriously ..."[32] Despite the fact that much of what Saurat wrote about Milton's ideas has been either revised or contradicted by later scholarship, the very fact that he adopted a 'non-theological' approach to Milton's work was, then, of particular comfort to Marxists such as Mirsky.

It would also have been of comfort to Rozanov at Academia, whose confidence in Mirsky's good judgment may have been buoyed by the latter's outburst against the 'brazen religious propaganda of the priesthood' in England, whose effect on the masses is contrasted with the 'subtle, slippery, eely, "refanned and enlightened" ' idealism of a whole range of British intellectuals, from Bertrand Russell to Keynes, I.A. Richards, Middleton Murry, and G.K. Chesterton. Their poison, according to Mirsky, was more effective.[33] Moscow archives do not reveal how exactly Mirsky became involved in the Milton project, but as chief editor it was his responsibility to pass judgment both on the translation and the commentary, and he soon developed his own ideas on how the translation should be done.

He was critical of Protas'ev's archaisms, offering various suggestions that the translator probably found singularly unhelpful. Mirsky's fond allusions to Latin and Italian poetry, models for Milton's own, were of the kind T.S. Eliot (following Dr Johnson) disparaged in 1936; but how could these help Protas'ev to find a corresponding Miltonic manner in Russian? Mirsky begged Protas'ev to be less 'poetic' and less 'harmonious,' but the only specific instructions (those relating to the introduction of Soviet vocabulary into the text) were also perhaps the most questionable. For Mirsky the translation was justified by the parallels between the English and the Russian revolutions.

Although no less critical of the extreme left than Lunacharsky had been, in a literary sense Mirsky was more radical. He saw Milton's language as being not only 'highly original, but ... entirely *new.*'[34] For Eliot this was no recommendation. Indeed, his chief argument against Milton in 1935 was the linguistic one; the poet's style is so mannered or learned that it sunders the connection that should exist between verse and the spoken language. Mirsky, by contrast, saw Milton's verbal innovations as a reflection of the revolutionary times. By analogy 'the contemporary political, military, and other words that Milton introduced' into *Paradise Lost* were to be rendered not by archaic expressions, but by the Soviet speech of the day.

Indeed, there were several instances where Milton's vocabulary corresponded rather more closely with Soviet usage than the Church-Slavonic-based words in the translation Mirsky was asked to evaluate. Thus, where Satan is referred to either as 'general' or 'commander' (*PL* I. ll 337, 359), the translator rendered these by the archaic 'vladyka' or 'vlastelin';[35] but Mirsky suggests that today's Russian equivalent, 'general' or 'komandir,' is preferable. Similarly, 'squadron' (I. l 357) and 'brigade' (I. l 675) are translated as 'opolchen'i' and 'sotnia,' whereas Mirsky suggests 'eskadron' and 'brigada.'[36] Such terms (says Mirsky) reminded Milton of the Civil War – an association enforced by the election to Pandemonium, which recalls 'very specifically the elections to the "soviet" or soldiers' "soviets" of the republican army.'[37]

One difficulty with Mirsky's proposal, however, is obvious. When Milton uses the term 'brigade' to describe a detachment of Satan's followers –

> Thither winged with speed
> A numerous brigade hastened: as when bands
> Of pioneers with spade and pickaxe armed
> Forerun the royal camp, to trench a field.
> Or cast a rampart. (I. ll 674–8)

– the associations he had in mind were certainly not shared by the Soviet reader of the 1930s. A 'brigade' then was a group of workers directed to meet the goals of the Five Year plans. They 'hastened' but they did not 'wing.'

And were the soldiers' councils of the English Revolution really the equivalent of the soviets of the 1930s? Of 1905 perhaps: but, by the time the party had taken control, their political meaning (and therefore their general association in the reader's mind) was no longer the same. Sometimes this projection into the seventeenth century of contemporary values is committed by the translator himself. For example, where Satan is referred to in *Paradise Lost* as 'their great Sultan' (I. l 348) the word used in the translation is 'vozhd',' a perfectly respectable ancient Russian term for leader. Yet by the

1930s – certainly by 1934 – it had become the sanctioned term for Stalin's dictatorial ascendancy over other party leaders. Soon 'vozhd'' would come to acquire a similar connotation to 'Führer' in the Third Reich.

Thus, Mirsky's insistence on finding a relevant lexical equivalent for *Paradise Lost* could also lend the seventeenth-century English poem unexpected contemporary political overtones. The problem was not, of course, new. It had faced Milton's translators throughout the two centuries in which Russians had now known *Paradise Lost*, the absurdity of dressing Milton up in 'modern' garb being demonstrated spectacularly by the illustrations appearing during the French Revolution (see Figure 26). Satan in a centurion's guise urging rebellion on his fellow Romans is just as ridiculous as a Georgian Pied Piper leading workers and *muzhiks*. But where should the line be drawn? In his book on Milton in 1964 Douglas Bush makes 'Great Sultan' into the 'seventeenth-century equivalent of Führer or Commissar,'[38] which suggests how hazardous such updating can be. Mirsky and his collaborators on the Academia edition of *Paradise Lost* felt it at first hand. Equating Stalin with Satan surely entailed some risk. During the great purge Mirsky and others involved in the unpublished translation were arrested, Mirsky dying after horrible suffering in a concentration camp. But the appetite of Milton's Satan for relevance, as surely the present study has shown, is inexhaustible. This is demonstrated, perhaps rather alarmingly, by his recent sighting in Kiev.

TEN

Satan as Anti-Imperialist

'[T]he liberation struggle against imperialist-colonizers continues [because] Milton's ... poem has not yet lost its revolutionary sound.'

Klimov et al *The Art of John Milton* (1977)

The style of Brezhnev's rule, which lasted for almost two decades, has been compared to Stalin's, but in parodic form. The shade of Stalin, after being denounced by Khrushchev and his associates at the Twentieth Party Congress in 1956, returned to semi-official favour before being again denounced, in instalments, by Gorbachev. In the light of *glasnost'* and *perestroika*, the Brezhnev years were labelled by the party as the 'period of stagnation,' which is certainly valid in a cultural sense, since the prevailing ideology was neo-Stalinist. Its relationship to the original rhetoric of the Bolshevik Revolution was as hollow (for all its sporadic successes) as Napoleon's III's exploitation of the Napoleonic legend. This is why the fate of Milton's Satan in Soviet schools is symbolically so interesting. His Brezhnevite profile represents the end of the line for a revolutionary ideology that, as in Napoleon III's time, was largely kept alive by military pomp and circumstance. In retrospect, it seems that this was now all that was left of the idealism of 1917 and of the commitment that had led to victory in the Patriotic War. Soviet schools and universities were the captive receptacles of the bombast and clichés fathered by the official need to maintain the memory of these two events. Perhaps this is why in 1977 the Ministry of Education in the Ukrainian capital approved a *Pedagogic Analysis of the Art of John Milton*, although the subject may at first glance seem far removed from either war or revolution.

It is by way of *Paradise Lost* that Satan acquired a foothold in the upper reaches of the Kievan educational system. He had, of course, been seen in the Ukraine before. Gogol had introduced his leering grimace into the village of Dikanka, an image that some of its terrified inhabitants never forgot. That particular devil came in the traditional, popular guise, which was still thriving in the second half of the nineteenth century. Thus *lubki* (copper- or woodcut prints) were still being hawked at that time depicting the Devil's traditional torments (see Figure 32). This devil had no intellectual pretensions, and his tortures were of a kind Hieronymus Bosch or Martin Luther would immediately have recognized as standard-international.

Thus, in the central part of the *lubok* men and women are being broken on a wheel, while a couple of wingless *chertiki* are adding to their pain by stoking a fire under it. A winged Satan (his rank is revealed in the accompanying verses) is seen presiding over the bisexual tortures with appropriate commanding gestures. This popular view of Hell survived the Bolshevik Revolution, and even colours – as we have seen – Mayakovsky's caricature of it. But in Satan's academic incarnation no Soviet caricature is intended: it bears all the fraudulent earnestness and pathos of the 'stagnant' years.

EMBODIMENT OF LOVE OF FREEDOM?

Soviet students opening *The Art of John Milton* would have learnt that: 'The image of Satan in Milton's poem represents not only the embodiment of love of freedom, but of the ideas of humanism [and] truth ...'[1] Several hands were responsible for this portrait, including T.N. Glebova, N.P. Klimov, and B.B. Remizov, although the instigator of the enterprise appears to have been N.M. Matuzova, who taught English and American literature at the Kiev State Pedagogical Institute for Foreign Languages.

The pretext for *The Art of John Milton* is revealed in the introductory pages, where scholars abroad are castigated for their preoccupation with linguistic analysis at the expense of Milton's views and his defence of the English Republic. But the source for this charge is not, as one might too hastily conclude, the Kiev collective itself. The complaint was made by E.M.W. Tillyard, master of Jesus College, whose biography of Milton has been reissued several times. In 1940, although it first appeared a decade earlier, the book was damned with faint praise as 'earnest and useful' by an expatriate American who suspected its author of sharing the same prejudices against Milton as F.R. Leavis.[2] The misunderstanding is not unnatural, because the biography does contain odd readings, such as the belief that 'Lycidas' was inspired by hydrophobia. Tillyard's purpose, however, was not to disparage but to probe. Like his other Cambridge contemporaries obsessed with peering *behind* received judgments and opinions, he grew more concerned with Milton's state of mind than with what the poet actually said. Tillyard reproaches his predecessors for not paying enough attention to Milton's intent. He even expresses surprise than anyone should ever have taken the poet's stated purpose in the very opening lines of *Paradise Lost* at face value. 'Such simplemindedness can ill satisfy a generation which is sceptical of professed motives and which suspects the presence of others.'[3]

To Tillyard it seemed obvious that 'Milton did partly ally himself with Satan, that unwittingly he was led away by the creature of his imagination.' So insistent is he on this that he attacked Saurat for suggesting that Satan represents only a part of Milton's mind, 'a part of which he disapproved and of which he was quite conscious.'[4] Such unequivocal support of the satanic school would certainly have been read with interest by the Kievan Miltonists. It should be noted at this point that Tillyard is the only foreign authority on the subject they acknowledge and that in an edition of 1930.[5] This detail has some bearing on their remarkable commentary, for they appear wholly unfamiliar with more recent literary criticism in the West.[6] They are aware of Blake, who made the neatest statement of Tillyard's case when he said that the author of *Paradise Lost* was of the Devil's party without knowing it; and they praise Byron, whose rebellious Lucifer they rightly relate to the Satan of Milton's poem. But they are quite unaffected by the recent literature on the subject, which, since A.J.A. Waldock's study in 1947, has produced a host of modern restatements and as many rebuttals or qualifications.

Given their contempt for textual and verbal analysis it is a moot point whether the Kievans would have gained much by reading such criticism. Besides, their commentary may have been intended as a supplement to the Soviet Milton anthology of 1976, or more likely perhaps, as a corrective, although it should be added that Dr Anikst also touches on the satanic interpretation in his introduction to the anthology. Milton's 'poetic feeling,' he says there, and 'the emotions of a citizen and revolutionary' prompted him 'against his will to make Satan more attractive than God,'[7] but the Moscow critic does not confuse Milton's character with the Devil's. Rather, he goes out of his way to suggest (as others in the West have done) that the Jesus of *Paradise Regained* has equal claims to being considered autobiographical. This possibility is not even entertained by the Kievans.

To arrive at the vivid portrait of Satan as anti-imperialist all the Miltonists of Kiev had to do was to add Marx and the insights provided by Tillyard to their own view of the party and state. Satan, it transpires, next to his well-known traditional attributes, embodies the idea of 'unity of leader and army, as well as of the idea of the leadership of the people in a new form.'[8] To support this belligerent interpretation, readers are referred to books I and II of *Paradise Lost*, a favourite quotation being those lines where Satan, after being hurled from Heaven, looks back on what he has lost and utters this challenge:

> Farewell, happy fields,
> Where joy for ever dwells! Hail, horrors, hail,
> Infernal world, and thou, profoundest Hell,
> Receive thy new possessor: one who brings
> A mind not to be changed by place or time,
> The mind is its own place, and in itself
> Can make a Heaven of Hell, a Hell of Heaven.
> ...
> Better to reign in Hell than serve in Heaven. (I. ll 249–55, 263)

According to *The Art of John Milton* the last line is still to be heard wherever 'the liberation struggle against imperialist-colonizers continues' – because 'Milton's ... poem has not yet lost its revolutionary sound.'[9]

It might be tempting to dismiss this as simply political propaganda, but William Empson, as a refugee with the combined North-East China universities in 1938–9, gives equally strong testimony to the reaction Satan can evoke in 'a non-European audience.'[10] The purpose of Empson's autobiographical digression was to demonstrate that Milton's style could achieve what T.S. Eliot asserted it was too artificial and too far removed from common speech to do. The Kievans would evidently side with Empson, as their variant on Empson's Chinese experience suggests. Like Empson, they assume that Milton, after trying sincerely to present God in the best biblical light, finds God too nasty for this to work in *Paradise Lost*.

That contradiction, due to the impossible theological problems Milton was stuck with, crept into the poem, which ended up better (as a work of art) but more antitheistic than Milton ever intended. This is why (in Empson's view, since the Kievans do not elaborate on this) a non-European audience, not being Christian, responded so positively to Empson's rendition of Satan. In other words, anyone whose vision is not blurred by Christian prejudice, will 'not require a separate theological argument' before they can sympathize with Satan.[11] With the proper modifications, Empson's argument can thus be fitted to the Marxian view that Puritans like Milton *used* the illusions of the Old Testament to camouflage their class aims, which the Kievan exegesis of course advocates.

For the authors of *The Art of John Milton* there is, therefore, no logical necessity to be too scrupulous over the complex issue of Milton's intent.

History, not intricate textual analysis (which they disdain), supplies the key, although this does not absolve the Kievans from examining the poem and posing some of the same questions that commentators before them have asked. The most crucial of these concerns Satan's rebellion. What caused it? At the beginning all the reader is told is that his motive was pride, but the actual reasons for the revolt are only revealed much later. This being so, Empson's non-Christian may justly suspend judgment. As Sir Herbert Grierson put it in the courteous idiom of his time: 'if the third part of a school or college or nation broke into rebellion we should be driven, or strongly disposed, to support some mismanagement by the supreme powers.'[12] The alternative he prescribed would be to 'attribute to the rebels a double dose of original sin,'[13] an explanation no Marxist or atheist will accept.

The Kievan Miltonists prepare a more modern potion. Equal to God in strength, wisdom, and might, Satan rebels against the tyranny of the celestial monarch because 'he cannot continue living the life of a slave, and does not wish others so to do.'[14] To this unsupported rationalization there are a number of objections, the main one being that slavery has no parallel in Heaven; and C.S. Lewis paints a rather different view of Satan's original condition: 'he was not hungry, not over-tasked, nor removed from his place, nor shunned, nor hated ... in the midst of a world of light and love, of song and feast and dance ... he could find nothing better to think of or more interesting than his prestige.'[15]

But the Kievans see this otherwise. According to them Milton reconsidered the biblical account of conflict between God and Satan, and transformed it from a mere confrontation of personalities into 'a juxtaposition of ideas, of world-views, social forces.' The biblical Satan 'persuades' the other angels to rebel by craft, cunning, and wiles. 'But with Milton, Satan's appeal to the angels is to fight for liberty and equality, and this appeal immediately provides him with the support of an enormous army,'[16] on whose size Milton focuses the reader's attention in order to convey some impression of the extent of God's tyranny. Thus, Satan acquires a following that has faith in him, and while 'inspiring, [and] organizing the rebellion Milton's Satan bec[o]me[s] the leader in the struggle of the masses against the tyranny of God.'[17] With all the 'courage, will power, sang-froid, endurance, [and] determination' that are ascribed to him, Satan could well be confused with the *vozhd*'[18] of another epoch. Yet he appears to have some grasp of collective leadership too: 'he understands that decisions determining the future must be discussed and taken together, and that the fundamental responsibility for executing them rests on the shoulders of the rank-and-file participants of the insurrection.'[19]

Satan, oddly enough, thus appears to believe in free will while God only makes a pretence of doing so. While Satan is concerned over 'his responsibility to his comrades,' God is motivated only by a lust for power, and in his despotism creates Adam and Eve only to compensate for 'the moral blow suffered to his pride and vanity by Satan's rebellion.'[20] God's thirst for blind obedience and flattery are only exceeded by his hypocrisy, which is shown in the poem by his treatment of our first parents. They are expected to worship him while he predicts, and encompasses their doom. The temptation in the Garden of Eden, thus becomes not a test of Eve's virtue, but proof of God's evil. Satan's role in the unfortunate business is to strike a blow for freedom – an attempt to liberate her and 'millions yet unborn' from the bondage of ignorance imposed by a capricious and vain despot.

As Eve puts it in the Kievan version: 'Is it a sin to know?' Hence, Satan's 'main motive' is his 'ambition to awaken the reason that lies dormant in the first people on earth, their thirst for knowledge, their freedom of thought.' His purpose is to prevent the 'celestial tyrant' from reducing these 'thinking beings into non-rational creatures,' which God intends to do 'in order to gratify his power hunger.'[21] Thus, for Milton the temptation of Adam and Eve 'acquires the same revolutionary connotation' as 'Satan's rebellion.' In dealing with the 'transgression' (for which the Kievan commentators always supply the appropriate inverted commas) Milton is really 'anticipating the Enlightenment' when 'all social phenomena, all religions and all knowledge, all dogmas and all laws' will be subjected to the 'Judgment of Reason.' That this is what Milton meant to do is further indicated, say the Kievans, by the contrast between the biblical Eve and the way Milton portrays her. His Eve's primary characteristic is not her beauty but her 'curiosity.' Apart from this, she is diligent, loves her husband dearly, and is prepared for the great sacrifice in the name of love. 'She understands that although she faces punishment, she will acquire the priceless gift of knowledge.'[22]

Adam's conduct deserves equal praise. He is the 'first gentleman' on earth, but when he hears of the divine retribution his reaction is the only honourable one: 'How could this be? All people are born free ...' Indeed, add the Kievans, Adam is right: why should mankind be made to pay for the fault of one person? Mark Twain, whose spoof of Eden the Soviet critics cite fondly, is commended for following Milton in developing a similar scepticism about the dubious procedures of the Almighty.[23] The fall is to them (as to Twain) a travesty of justice.

Milton's intent, therefore, is to expose God's ways to man, not to explain them. The celestial scene in which Christ alone takes up the invitation to save mankind becomes one such well-placed hint: the angelic host show what they feel for their boastful deity by silence. And the Kievans further suggest that

Jesus does so only because his own prestige, as the Son of the Father, is inevitably involved in the manoeuvre. There is even the insinuation that once the offer is redeemed, the Almighty may leave his only begotten son in the lurch.[24]

Are any of these insights or aspersions, taken by themselves, new? Nineteenth-century critics had made most of them, and modern atheists like Empson have enriched this tradition with sophisticated observations of their own.[25] In Empson's view God is not good, which is where his argument and that of the Kievans converge. However, Tillyard says that if Milton had been in the Garden he would immediately have eaten the apple and written a pamphlet to prove that he was justified in doing so. If we accept this, it is unfair to charge Satan with trickery: his intentions are the author's, and it is only a step from there to the Kievan identification of Milton with Satan. Had Satan rather than Milton written the pamphlet, would it not sound like the Kievan commentary?

That an atheist's reading of *Paradise Lost* should thus lead into the same corner as a Soviet-Marxist one may not in itself seem surprising. But it is surely startling to find the Jesuit Gerard Manley Hopkins explaining the fall much like this in 1883: 'Eve taking it as a challenge on God's part which it was the most subtle and refined morality in her to accept by an act of outward disobedience; Adam, not deceived about that but still deluded into thinking God would admire his generosity in sinning out of charity to his wife.'[26] The main issue here is the one in *The Brothers Karamazov*: the limits of human freedom. Dostoevsky like Hopkins regarded God's logic as a firm framework imposing a clear if difficult obligation on man. This the Kievans flatly reject by supporting Satan's challenge, but their alternative had also been thoroughly explored by Milton's earlier admirers. Thus, William Blake in *The Marriage of Heaven and Hell* (1793) declined to accept the theological system that enabled Milton to call God 'good' and Satan 'evil.' Milton's God becomes Blake's version of the Devil – the eternal negation – and Milton's Satan, his Messiah.

In his *History* Lunacharsky, who probably had not read Blake, arrived at a similar reading of *Paradise Lost*: 'the great revolutionary heart of Milton is so full of rebellion, so full of protest against the established order, that his most interesting character is the Devil.' What *The Art of John Milton* does, however, is to produce the satanic argument in its most secular and didactic form. In doing so it breaks one of the few conventions of literary criticism, which is to weigh the countervailing argument, or at least give the appearance of doing so. The Kievan Miltonists do not attempt to do this, although even the most superficial reader of *Paradise Lost* must be aware that it comes to a Christian conclusion. This is one powerful reason why the editor of an authoritative and recent English edition of Milton's verse repudiates the satanic interpretation. He does not go as far as C.S. Lewis, who in a prophetic vein declared that 'to admire Satan ... is to give one's vote not only for a world of misery, but also for a world of lies and propaganda.'[27]

16 Satan in space, as seen in an early Russian chromolithograph, from a popular prose edition of *Paradise Lost*, 1892

17 Vrubel's *Virgin and Child* (detail), 1895

18 Vrubel's *Head of the Demon*, 1890–1 (illustration for Lermontov's poem *Demon*)

19 Vrubel's *Tamara's Dance*, 1890–1 (illustration for Lermontov's *Demon*)

20 Vrubel's *Tamara and the Demon*, 1890–1 (illustration for Lermontov's *Demon*)

21 Vrubel's *The Demon Seated* (detail), 1890

22 Vrubel's *Head of the Demon*, 1890 (tinted plaster cast)

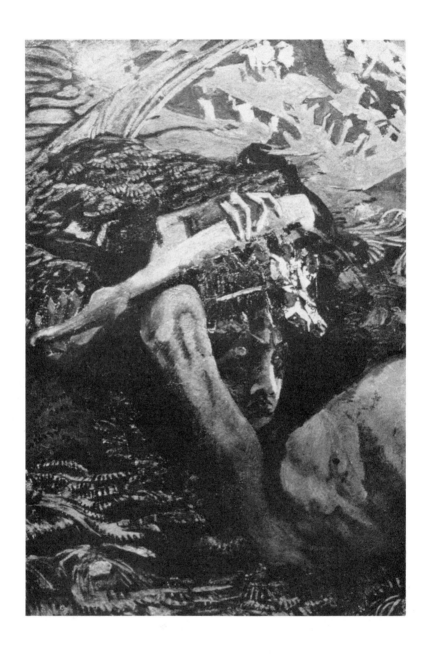

23 Vrubel's *The Demon Downcast*, 1902

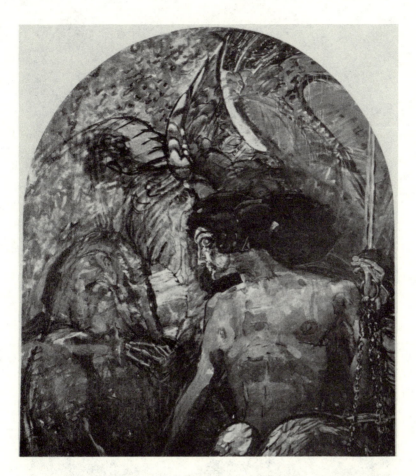

25 Vrubel's *The Prophet*, 1898, inspired by Pushkin's poem of that title

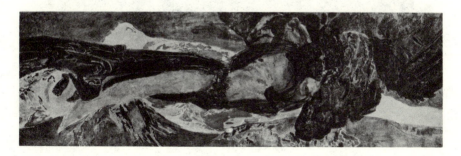

24 Vrubel's *Demon in Flight*, 1899 (unfinished)

26 Satan summoning to revolution: frontispiece to Jacques Delille's 1805 translation of *Paradise Lost*

27 Lunacharsky, Lenin's commissar for enlightenment, on the podium lending Bolshevik support, from a contemporary poster (unsigned)

28 Satan, Sin, and Death, from the 1850 popular edition of *Paradise Lost*

29 Satan and his minions being cast out of Heaven, from the Zagorsky edition of *Paradise Lost*

30 Satan addressing supporters in Pandemonium: chromolithograph from the 1901 edition of *Paradise Lost*

31 A popular Russian Satan in Roman garb, from the Sytin edition of *Paradise Lost*, 1901

32 a *lubok* (or popular print), 1860, depicting the Devil's tortures

33 A Russian view of Kaiser Wilhelm as Satan, from the print room of the Saltykov-Shchedrin Library in Leningrad

34 The folkloric Devil in 1911, as drawn by Aleksei Tolstoy (with his self-portrait)

CONCLUSION

Prince of Darkness, Prince of Light

'God is a plus sign, the Devil is minus.' Albert Einstein

'There are things that are known and things that are unknown, in between the doors.'
William Blake

Attitudes to good and evil define society. Literature, no less than theology, law, or folklore, reflects our attempts to come to terms with them. But that most literary of all characters (as he has been called), the Devil, enjoys a global presence that evades national boundaries. Yet Russian culture, it has been suggested by the brilliant Soviet Slavist Yurii Lotman, is particularly susceptible to the Manichean polarities of good and evil.

According to this view, maximalism and the contempt for compromise, which have so often characterized Russia's religious and political attitudes, are due to the fact that concepts accommodated in Western societies – for example, Purgatory and the attendant way stations between Hell and Heaven that modulate the progress to salvation of even so fanatical a Puritan as John Bunyan – are simply alien to the Russian mind. Is this why the belligerent Satan of *Paradise Lost* found so receptive an audience in Russia?

Joseph Brodsky, no foe himself of sweeping generalizations such as this, argues just as elegant a case for the contrary. In his view it is 'ambivalence' that 'is the chief characteristic of [his] nation.'[1] In fact, Milton's Satan can be both ambivalent, as befits a parliamentary creature of compromise, and implacably determined. Romantics and Bolsheviks were drawn to the latter persona, whereas during the Enlightenment many preferred the reasoned, guileful rhetoric of the politician who in the most adverse of circumstances brings his defeated supporters in Pandemonium around to an extraordinarily successful strategy – the transgression of mankind.

If it was Milton's most original achievement to give Satan a persuasive case, did it seem doubly so in eighteenth-century Russia? Certainly, no comparable figure in polite literature prepared readers there for the appearance of evil in the guise of so beguiling an intellectual. Why did Russian translators simply ignore the great baroque devils (as conceived, for example, by Grotius or Calderon)? The fact is, they did. The literary Devil – as distinct from popular tales of biblical or apocryphal provenance – had made no mark on Russian letters previous to Stroganov's translation of *Paradise Lost*.

Even in manuscript form (as we have seen) there appears to be only one eighteenth-century work prior to 1745 that is wholly devoted to the literary Devil.[2] This Polish creature is so bestial and trivial that, despite the anonymous author's belletristic pretensions, he still belongs more to folklore than to literature. By comparison, the diabolical creatures in Torquato Tasso's *Gerusalemme Liberata* and Giambattista Marino's *La Strage degl' Innocenti* had far more substance. But, like Klopstock's *Messias*, these poems – so influential elsewhere – became known to readers in Moscow and St Petersburg only a decade or so before the French Revolution. By then, Milton's Satan had left his impression both on popular culture and on formal literature, and no diabolical creation would rival him in influence until Goethe's Mephisto aroused the enthusiasm of educated readers in the nineteenth century.

To those familiar with Dante, Marlowe, Tourneur, or Vondel, this may seem surprising. Yet none of the many poets who made the Devil at home in the secular literature of Western Europe was translated into Russian before Milton. If his influence was also sometimes felt indirectly through imitators such as Klopstock, none of the ersatz Satans matched the original either in grandeur or in that peculiarly Puritan amalgam of valour and self-righteousness.

Masonic writers and poets were the first in Russia to endow the Devil with un-Orthodox literary attributes. The Masonic conception of good and evil appealed to those secular pilgrims in Moscow and St Petersburg who had left conventional religion behind them. Their quest for truth and personal salvation aroused Russia's embryonic intelligentsia from philosophical sleep. The Masonic awakening helped divest Milton's Satan of traditional theological prejudice. If the Satan of *True Light* is still to some extent a bloody and vengeful trickster, for Kheraskov and even for Derzhavin he is also a serious intellectual antagonist, embodiment of the Voltairean scepticism that, after the French Revolution, Russian writers and poets joined the empress in denouncing.

But the celebrated reactionary characterization of Satan as the world's 'first Freethinker' anticipates his next astonishing promotion. It is true of course that the traditional Prometheus had much in common with the enemy of God and man. Both rebelled against divine authority. Both suffered an inevitable defeat and eternal punishment. But as an eminent scholar who has long studied the Devil suggests, 'the merging of Prometheus and Satan was one of the crucial symbolic transformations.'[3] It would eventually enable Bolshevik critics to triumph against those who, like Mayakovsky, persisted in seeing *Paradise Lost* as a reprehensible adjunct to the Bible.

Satan in his Promethean guise has had a long innings, but is he likely to survive the collapse of Communism in its Marxist form? His trail can be pursued from the Decembrists to the partial revival of their Romantic interpretation after the Bolshevik Revolution by Lunacharsky and D.S. Mirsky. Before this promotion, Milton's Satan seems in his Russian setting to be at first no more than a mere usurper. As Pugachev's instigator he is not bereft of a certain nobility. But his appeal to arms in Kheraskov's *Universe* – 'And we shall not be slaves, but Gods and Tsars' – contains no hint (as in *Paradise Lost*) that the rebellion may have been justified.[4] Radishchev probably thought otherwise. This may explain why the threatening shadow of his Miltonic 'Angel of Darkness' seems to carry the author's endorsement. Yet Radishchev, Russia's first political thinker, never finished this work nor did his immediate successors produce any serious treatment of good and evil. Is this to be explained by the lack of a mature political culture of the kind that had given rise to *Paradise Lost*?

So Boris Eikhenbaum suggested when he tried to account for the failure of Lermontov's generation to produce 'the abstract metaphysical poem' Lermontov himself envisaged after *Demon* but never wrote. If Milton so magnificently succeeded in doing so, according to Lunacharsky this was because the middle class of his day had the economic and political self-assertiveness its Russian counterpart in the nineteenth century still lacked. Reflecting this fact, Milton's Satan has all the accoutrements of a great leader, one who simply overshadows his Russian imitators because none can match his heroic self-reliance.

In a philosophical sense, however, the motives of Kheraskov's or Lermontov's demons are similar to those of Milton's Satan. Theirs is the familiar Christian theme of the creature attempting to exalt itself above its created place under God – the temptation that leads step by step to the misery and guilt of human life. If Milton and the Russian poets shared this Christian vision, were their attitudes to sin bound by quite the same conventions?

Orthodoxy, as outside observers have so often noted, made confession the key to salvation. This is why Russians did not usually internalize their guilt or sense of sin to the same monstrous proportions as Puritans were liable to do. One might expect to see this contrast reflected in literary representations of the Devil, which is indeed the case. For next to the demonic tradition described in this book, there was the *poshlyi* or shabby demonry associated with prose writers like Gogol and Sologub, whose 'petty demon' ('melkii bes') accommodates himself to the banalities of everyday life and has no aspirations to the sublime. He is earth-bound and second-rate, like the Devil in *The Brothers Karamazov*.

In *The Possessed* (entitled *Besy* in the original, a pejorative word for demon that has no precise English equivalent), Dostoevsky used this devil's contemptible motives to impugn the revolutionary movement; but the emotional source of the Romantic rebellion lay in a sensibility Dostoevsky himself shared in his youth. There is some presentiment of its arrival in Russian letters in Kheraskov's treatment of Satan's escape from Hell. This is reminiscent not only of *Paradise Lost* but of Lermontov's celebrated lines on the Romantic hero who only in tempests seeks calm – 'A on miatezhnyi ishchet buri / Kak budto v buri est' pokoi.' Similarly, Kheraskov's descriptions of nature, wild and uncontrolled, not only bears the stamp of Milton's imagery, but also of *das Wunderbare* – the element that Bodmer and Klopstock found so uplifting in *Paradise Lost*.

Thus, quite apart from his Promethean politics, Satan became identified with the author's vision of nature, unfettered and sublime, that the Romantics made their own. Their dream landscapes resembled those of a Golden Age in which Satan seems to have felt at home no less than our first parents. This idealized vision of evil did not filter down into the illustrations to the popular editions of Milton's epics that were read so widely in imperial Russia.

There Satan is almost invariably shown in standard Roman garb (see figures 30 and 31). His facial expression is never lascivious, but is usually rather stolid and is quite unmarked by the yearning that gives away the Romantic Satan. In his angelic Roman form there is certainly no hint of sexuality. This was an upper-class discovery, which in part explains why the young of Lermontov's day were so fascinated by Milton's Satan.

To the Romantics he became one of the earliest symbols of the generational strife that would become so much a part of Russian social and intellectual history. To Alferoff, representing the young generation, it must have felt doubly sweet to announce, in English, to those doting parents who came to admire the accomplishments of the *jeunesse dorée* at Lermontov's school that the dialogues between God and Christ were 'the weakest in the poem.' By contrast it seemed to him that the Devil's discourse (with its attacks on divine authority) seemed 'the most perfect of its kind.'⁵ Milton's Satan now absorbed the educated reader's perception of *Paradise Lost*.

In Lermontov's case the demonic image obsessed his entire poetic life. Attacks on Satanism for its 'corrupting and antisocial' proclivities are unlikely to have had much effect. Zhukovsky, Polezhaev, Ryleev, Podolinsky, Kiukhel'beker, and even to some extent Pushkin (who is usually credited with introducing the theme into Russian lyric verse) were all inspired by it. In England the demonic theme did not long survive the passing of Byron and his so-called fellow Satanists. In Russia its decline was slower. Its demise is vividly etched in Zhadovskaya's adaptation of Milton's epics in 1859, in which her Satan is stripped of his defiance and is transformed into a lachrymose and feeble tempter.

Observing a comparable change in Lermontov, Lunacharsky challenged national *amour-propre* with his preference for the Satan of *Paradise Lost*. It was a courageous stand to take at a time when *Demon* was considered (as it usually still is) as one of the greatest poems in the language. If he preferred Milton's poem, it was because there 'protest against the established order' is expressed with all the fervour of the poet's 'great revolutionary heart.'⁶

Thanks to the authority of Lenin's commissar for enlightenment, Soviet critics accepted this verdict, together with Lunacharsky's explanation for the retrogression of the demonic tradition in Russian literature. To him it lay in the failure of the Decembrist revolt. Was this yet another Marxist mythopoeic invention? Even Pushkin's interest in the demonic theme hardly antedates 1825. Yet it is a fact that some of his earliest verse on the subject does appear to have a Decembrist connection.⁷ Moreover, Kiukhel'beker (who was sent to Siberia for his complicity in the rebellion) drew a similarly unfavourable parallel between Milton's Satan and Klopstock's 'cry-baby' demon. For this Decembrist poet, whose fiery profile of Milton dates from his Siberian exile, the change was due to religion's decline. 'The flame of faith' that had burnt in 'the time of the Titan' (as he calls the English poet-revolutionary) had died in his. *Faust* expressed the changing times. No longer conceived as God's rival, in Goethe's hands Mephisto had been reduced to negative status as 'Der Geist der stets verneint.'

This was indeed a contrast to the heroic energy of Milton's Satan. It was made sharper by Mephisto's lack of any discernible biblical connection, although to the Romantics such matter in *Paradise Lost* aroused conflicting emotions. To Kiukhel'beker, a Protestant, it seemed dated and absurd. But to Orthodox Decembrists such as F.N. Glinka, whose own verse drew so richly on the Scriptures, the Bible was a source of inspiration. The young Pushkin, a child of the French Enlightenment, agreed with Kiukhel'beker.

'Bova' pokes fun at cherubim being 'fried by cannon.' The blasphemous 'Gavriliada,' in which Satan's 'puffed-up member' becomes a casualty in a mock-Miltonic version of the war in Heaven, ridicules Christianity and heroic verse. Pushkin was equally unreceptive to A.A. Bestuzhev-Marlinsky's religious conception of the Romantic explosion as *the* Reformation of the nineteenth century. Indeed, it may be thought remarkable that Milton's art was so unreservedly appropriated by the new aesthetic.

Was this because his treatment of Hell and Satan set him in a central tradition of our culture to which Dante, Tasso, and Goethe – to name its most influential representatives – also belong? Romantics, even when they spurned Orthodoxy, shared Milton's vision of a long-lost paradise, a vision that inspired Heine and other so-called Utopian radicals as well, of course, as Marx.[8]

After the Enlightenment the problems of Milton's Satan with tsarist censors began with the suspicion that the 'uneducated' reader might take the Devil's seditious example to heart.[9] Since the Bible did not become widely known in Russia until the second half of the nineteenth century, there was some support for this view, particularly since prose versions of *Paradise Lost* were sometimes mistaken for it.[10] If so, did the common reader respond as Belinsky did when he characterized the epic as the 'apotheosis of rebellion'? He and Gogol could not agree on whether the Russian people were, as the Slavophiles maintained, the most pious on earth; but the evidence (where readership of the epics is concerned) does suggest that for the middle class and perhaps for the intelligentsia at large, even as late as the beginning of the twentieth century, Milton remained the conventional 'divine poet' of Victorian imagination.[11]

What undermined the traditional Christian view of Satan as the harbinger of evil was the secularization of Russian society, which, although it came later than in the West, also made the Promethean perception of Milton's hero more acceptable. There was also another change that can be traced to the Romantics. Kiukhel'beker congratulates Milton, it may be recalled, for divesting a lowly and snivelling creature immured in medieval superstition of the 'disgusting' characteristics attributed to the Devil in popular lore.

But in fact the folkloric Devil proved his vitality by surviving the nineteenth century. He continued to inspire poets and writers, as we see by comparing Pushkin's drawing of him (see page xvi) with that of Aleksei Tolstoy, which was done in the twentieth (see Figure 34). The outward appearance of their *besy* is almost the same: both have horns, tail, and bestial features. Tolstoy's Devil, it is true, has lost his hooves, that is to say, he has shed this noble link with pagan antiquity (which is still retained by Pushkin's satyr-like *bes*). But this change is insignificant, except for what it tells us about the demise of classicism. For the folkloric Devil has become part of global literary convention, as essential to Salman Rushdie as he is to political satirists. Thus, to cite one of this Devil's most recent sightings in the Soviet Union: he appeared in Vilnius University in a puppet play by Vytantis Landsbergis, the son of Lithuania's president. Inspired by *Spitting Image* (the British TV program that burlesques current affairs) Landsbergis casts Mikhail Gorbachev in the role of the witch who sends a devil with the fairy-tale apple to poison Snow White. Snow White represents Lithuanian independence and freedom.

This use of Satan is both folkloric and Manichean, being reminiscent of his employment during the First World War by tsarist caricaturists, to whom the 'evil empire' was represented by Kaiser Wilhelm (see Figure 33). The Satan of *Paradise Lost* is too lofty and too abstract in his thinking to fuel political caricature or nationalist loathing such as this. The connection with the Scriptures endowed him with a seriousness that served Milton's high purpose, but also – precisely because of his seriousness – led to proscription and tsarist censorship. If Russians had taken poetry less literally or didactically, this would never have happened: but here the Puritan view of life and Russian attitudes to literature struck the same chord. *Paradise Lost* was not written to entertain but to instruct. Most Russian readers were prepared to accept this. Hence it was not Satan's rebellion alone that aroused passionate strictures, but his sexuality, a side of Milton's hero that long remained concealed or camouflaged.

It is true that the Satan of *Paradise Lost* does not dwell on carnal matters. But Milton did anticipate the Romantic poets by having his angels make love. Moreover, there is more than a hint in the epic of Satan's physical attraction for Eve. This taboo – the taboo restraining mortals from sexual congress with Christian deities (even lapsed ones) – was not really breached in Russian literature until Lermontov's *Demon*. It is this infringement of the taboo, rather than the poem's admittedly dubious mixture of Christian and pagan symbols, that prompted the strong reaction of the authorities. Indeed, the disturbing consequences of physical intimacy with Satan, mocked to such pornographic effect by Pushkin, were still being felt by Vrubel's contemporaries. The androgynous ambiguity of some of the artist's early portrayals of Demon was compounded by Vrubel's moral dilemma. He could not decide whether Lermontov's figure represented evil – the guise in which he appears in the illustrations to the poem (see figures 19 and 20) – or whether he stood for the demonic, a life force Vrubel associated with classical Greece. Milton had yielded to the same pagan embrace in describing the bewitching dance of Juno and Pan in the Garden:

> The birds their choir apply; airs, vernal airs
> Breathing the smell of field and grove, attune
> The trembling leaves, while universal Pan,
> Knit with the Graces and the Hours in dance,
> Led on the eternal spring. (PL IV. ll 264–8)

A mixture such as this of Athens and Jerusalem was offensive to 'Christian feelings' in Lermontov's day.[12] But a similar Christian sense of sin overwhelms Tamara and prompts her suicide. Despite his protestations to the contrary, shame also pursues her diabolic seducer. Today both reactions might seem somewhat excessive.

Yet the Soviet regime, which before *glasnost'* and *perestroika* retained an almost Victorian attitude towards any public expression of sexuality, continued to subject that particular stream in Russian art and literature to undefined cultural controls.[13] Surprisingly, despite the so-called sexual revolution that would later transform popular culture in the West, the pundits who defended the values of Western civilization during the cold war felt a similar unease. The classical and Christian roots on which Milton the humanist and Puritan drew produced a duality that even radical modernist critics found distasteful. Edmund Wilson, for example, thought the 'trouble' with Milton was that the Puritan elements in him 'fought and partly destroyed the classical and Catholic mythologies upon which he was hoping to build.'[14]

It was this (and other real and imagined transgressions) that Ezra Pound, T.S. Eliot, and F.R. Leavis were to seize on during the 'great Milton controversy,' after which Soviet critics took it upon themselves to defend the poet-revolutionary from his 'bourgeois' foes.[15] Thus, the belligerent Puritan Satan of the English Revolution found a new revolutionary Hell.

By the 1930s Marxists like D.S. Mirsky had blazed the trail in divesting *Paradise Lost* of any overt Christian connection. Satan's brigades became eager pioneers in overfulfilling the Five Year plans. Mirsky's Soviet edition of the epic did not, it is true, see the light of day: and Mirsky himself perished in the Gulag. But undaunted, Milton's Satan resurfaced after Stalin's death. In his passage through schools in the Brezhnev era he attained his highest rank.

Now Milton's Devil came to represent not only 'love of freedom' but 'the ideas of humanism, truth, and unity of leader and army, as well as of the ideas of the leadership of the people in a new form.'[16] In that capacity the Satan of *Paradise Lost* led the struggle against imperialism, a promotion as remarkable as the Romantic confusion of the Christian Devil with Prometheus. In an atheist setting the prince of darkness had become – as befits a Puritan and Marxist hero – a militant prince of light.

Has any other major literary creation since the seventeenth century shown such an astonishing adaptability to changing times? Satan's Soviet career is not entirely without precedent. For is not Satan's image under Brezhnev reminiscent of the frontispiece to a Napoleonic edition of *Paradise Lost* in 1805, when Bonaparte was already betraying the ideals of the French Revolution? Satan here is portrayed as an upright centurion, fully clothed, summoning his fellow-revolutionary angels to battle for the rights of man (see Figure 26).

If this pose is as hollow as the fraudulent revolutionary rhetoric of the Brezhnevian Satan, the parallels between the two do have a common historical source. Both the French and the Russian revolutionaries adopted some of the ideals proclaimed by Milton's Satan. Thus it is that Soviet assessments of *Paradise Lost*, despite certain changes between 1917 and the 1980s, continued to be tied to prevailing Marxian analyses of England's 'bourgeois Revolution.' This historical connection was ultimately responsible for giving Milton both his pre-eminent place in Soviet criticism and the peculiar approbation the Satan of *Paradise Lost* came to enjoy as the quasi-official embodiment of totalitarian humanity and freedom.

With *glasnost'* and *perestroika* this prestigious phase in Satan's career as an intellectual pillar of the Marxist-Leninist establishment has come to an end. The decline of Communism will give good and evil a new home in the hiatus left by the ideological collapse of dialectical materialism, a new home that may come to look very much like the one 1917 destroyed. Religion and nationalism, both supposedly expunged by the October Revolution, have already paved the way for their return. In the official revolutionary dispensation, the juxtaposition between good and evil was supposed to disappear with the dictatorship of the proletariat and the triumph of scientific socialism. Yet on logical grounds it was foolish for atheist ideologues to idolize Milton's arch-rebel – for without the existence of God, Satan's rebellion is pointless.

Now that the head of the Russian Orthodox church is challenging the Soviet government to demonstrate its commitment to democratization by allowing optional religious education in Soviet schools to replace official atheism, it is surely unlikely that the militant Marxist exegesis represented by *The Art of John Milton* could pass unchallenged in the changing Soviet educational system today.[17] The reading of the Bible, now for the first time countenanced on Soviet television, will instead once again place religious works like *Paradise Lost* and *Paradise Regained* in a Christian context. This revival of traditional values, advocated in Russia on both the so-called democratic left and the patriotic right, has already affected theatrical portrayals of the Devil. We see its resurrection in an arresting Moscow drama on Stalin and Beria, *Chernyi chelovek ili ia, bedny, Soso Djugashvili*.[18] In this play, which is in verse, a Romantic devil shares titular credits with the 'Great Leader of Mankind.' The idea of fusing the banalities of the *Short Course* (the odious Communist Party history everyone after 1938 was required to read) with the lofty language of Pushkin and Lermontov, is brilliantly original. In the narrow literary sense, Victor Korkia's play is a *tour de force*. But is Romantic or Byronic irony an apt device for exploring the dark psychological forces underlying the monstrous crimes of the Stalin era? If the answer is no, it is because the enormity of human suffering in the Gulag dwarfs Marxist explication. Angelica Balabanova, who worked with Lenin but left the USSR prior to collectivization and the purges, could still describe the tarnished hero of October in poetic Goethean terms as one who 'desired the good and created evil.'[19] But Stalin today, while so often likened by the Soviet press (under *glasnost'*) to Satan, evades the traditional measures used by Milton and the Romantic poets to weigh good and evil.[20] The Soviet unveiling of the unspeakable horrors of Stalinism has not only shattered a faith, but has revived an older one, which before 1917 most of Milton's readers took for granted. Russia's religious awakening may make *Paradise Lost* and *Paradise Regained* relevant again in a Christian, rather than an atheist, setting. Yet whatever the future has in store for the Russian people, the shifting career of Milton's Satan among them confirms Alexander Solzhenitsyn's perceptive observation about the historical boundary between good and evil; it 'oscillates continuously in the consciousness of a nation, sometimes very violently, so that judgements, reproaches, self-reproaches and even repentance itself are bound up with a specific time and pass away with it, leaving only vestigial contours behind to remind history of their existence.'[21]

APPENDIXES
ABBREVIATIONS
NOTES
BIBLIOGRAPHIC NOTE
BIBLIOGRAPHY
INDEX

APPENDIX ONE

Milton's Interest in Russia

1 THE RUSSIAN THEME IN MILTON'S VERSE

Of the various conjectures advanced to explain the genesis of *Moscovia*, the most interesting is the suggestion that Milton was considering the possibility of writing an epic poem about the English discovery of Russia. Like the *Lusiade*, in which Camoëns recounts the voyage of Vasco da Gama around Africa to India and back at the end of the fifteenth century, Milton's projected poem would have dealt with the heroic voyages of English seafarers and their valiant attempts to find a northeast passage to China and the East Indies. Thus, according to Heinrich Mutschmann, the *Moscovia* is nothing but a pilot project, Milton's way of exploring the terrain for a Muscovite epic, for which the poet prepared with his customary thoroughness. Once this poetic idea was abandoned, it was commuted to prose history, but (as Mutschmann goes on to say) the Russian theme was not forgotten, which explains – as we shall see – its later re-emergence in *Paradise Lost*.[1]

Like some more recent speculations about Milton's purpose in writing the *Moscovia*, Mutschmann's theory would substantiate the view that it was written early in the poet's life. The continuing controversy over its date of composition has a direct bearing on the diverse hypotheses still being proposed to explain Milton's true motives. By the author's own admission, the preface to the *Moscovia* was written years after the posthumously published text, in which the *terminus post quem* is 1625, the year of the first edition of Purchas (of which Milton makes extensive use). D.S. Mirsky suggests that the preface dates from before the English Civil War, and thus before Milton's journey to Italy in 1638, since it was the Civil War that interrupted Milton's foreign travels. If so, the history itself was compiled in the early 1630s, at a time when Milton had already conceived the notion of writing a national epic.[2]

Thus, Mirsky's dating is not incompatible with the German theory concerning the *Moscovia*, and it is supported more recently by an American Miltonist, Lloyd E. Berry, who narrows down the date to the Horton-Hammersmith period in Milton's life (1632–8) when he was consumed with his own program of reading, largely historical in character. By then Milton would already have been familiar with the work of Giles Fletcher. As Berry further suggests, another clue in its preface confirms the assumption that the *Moscovia* was written before the history of Britain, for which (it is known) Milton began to read on his return from Italy in 1639.[3]

The clue – Milton's reference to Paulus Jovius, who also confined himself to describing 'only *Muscovy* and *Britain*' – would seem conclusive, at least about the order in which the two histories were composed. In the next sentence Milton then informs the reader that 'Some such thoughts, many years since, led me at a vacant time to attempt the like argument; and I began with *Muscovy* ...'[4] But Patrick, Parks, and others, place more faith in the publisher's advertisement to the *Moscovia*, which discloses that 'This Book was writ by the Author's own Hand, before he lost his sight. And sometime before his death dispos'd of it to be printed.'[5] Thus, the preface, according to Patrick, would have been written some time after 1660 and perhaps as late as the 1670s, while he ascribes the *Moscovia* itself to the years between 1645 and 1649.[6]

Parks also puts more credence in the publisher's advertisement, which at least dates the *Moscovia* to the period before Milton went blind in 1652. But when was the 'vacant time' to which Milton alludes? Parks follows Hanford in assuming that it was written at a time of leisure during the Commonwealth or early Protectorate (1653–9). In accepting this premise, he thus reverses the order of the two histories by 'presuming' that Milton finished the first four books of his British history by March 1649. Thereafter, as he took up his duties as Latin secretary, the closest thing to a 'vacant time' that Milton might have had was the period between the publication of *Eikonoklastes* on 6 October 1649 and his commission to respond to Salmasius on 8 January 1650.[7]

Precise as Parks's estimate may seem, not only does it disregard the evidence of Milton's preface, but his assumption about the composition of the *History of Britain* is almost as difficult to sustain as the chronology of the *Moscovia*. Indeed, W.R. Parker places the composition of the former in 1648, after the completion of the *Moscovia*,[8] while others believe it was begun even earlier, between 1645 and 1647.

Robert R. Cawley, another authoritative voice in the dispute over the *Moscovia*'s chronology, also believes that it was written in the 1640s, which would support Mutschmann's view about the link between it and the epic Milton may have conceived on the lines of an English *Lusiade*. Indeed, similarities between the Portuguese poem and *Paradise Lost* have often been explored by scholars quite unaware of Mutschmann's suggestive hypothesis, which in a sense sustains it.⁹ For if the 'discovery' of Muscovy by the courageous adventurers of the previous century was one of the many epic themes eventually abandoned by Milton when he finally settled on the fall of man as the subject of his poem, some of the parts discarded found their place in his later verse when, blind, he recalled what he had read in the 1630s and 1640s. This may be the most plausible explanation for the scattered allusions to Russia and the mysterious lands beyond in *Paradise Lost*.

The blind poet would draw on the vast treasure-house of geographical and historical knowledge he had accumulated in his youth, the outcome being magnificent passages such as the one in Book XI, where Michael shows the first Adam how Satan will tempt 'our second Adam' in the wilderness:

> all Earth's kingdoms, and their glory.
> His eye might there command wherever stood
> City of old or modern fame, the seat
> Of mightiest empire, from the destined walls
> Of Cambalu, seat of Cathaian Chan,
> And Samarkand by Oxus, Temir's throne,
> To Paquin of Sinaean Kings; and thence
> To Agra, and Lahore of Great Mogul,
> Down to the golden Chersonese; or where
> The Persian in Ecbatan sat, or since
> In Hispahan; or where the Russian Ksar
> In Moscow; or the Sultan in Bizance,
> Turkestan-born. (XI. ll 384–96)

Here Russia is merely a detail in the great pageant of future historical splendour, reminiscent of the exotic imagery of Coleridge's 'Kubla Khan.' But in another passage the context is closer to *Moscovia* (where the hostilities between the Russians and the Tartars are discussed at some length):

> As when the *Tartar* from his *Russian* foe
> By *Astracan* over the Snowie Plaines
> Retires; or Bactrian Sophi, from the horns
> Of Turkish crescent, leaves all waste beyond
> The realm of Aladule, in his retreat

> To Tauris or Casbeen; so these, the late
> Heaven-banish't host, left desert utmost hell
> Many a dark league, reduced in careful watch
> Round their metropolis, and now expecting
> Each hour their great adventurer[,] from the search
> Of foreign worlds. (x. ll 431–41)

The *'Tartar'* makes an earlier appearance in Milton's verse in 'Il Penseroso' (ll 114–15) as a figure of romance on his wondrous horse of brass: but in *Paradise Lost* the 'roving Tartar' (III. l 432) adopts the belligerence and craft attributed to him in the *Moscovia*.

Milton's evocative use of names, drawn in part from the same source, is also to be found in the passage where Satan searches for the animal into which he will creep, to accomplish man's fall:

> Sea he had searcht and Land
> From *Eden* over *Pontus,* and the Poole
> *Maeotis* up beyond the river *Ob;*
> Downward as far Antarctic; and in length
> West from *Orontes* to the Ocean barred
> At *Darien,* thence to the Land where flowes
> *Ganges* and Indus. (IX. ll 76–82)

The juxtaposition of the River Ob with the classical terms for the Black Sea (Pontus) and the Sea of Azov (Maeotis) is startling. If it serves Milton's poetic ends, it would also have reminded readers (as Cawley observes) of the English search for a northeast passage.[10]

This particular parallel with the *Moscovia,* however, is not impressive. For there the River Ob is not represented as a kind of Ultima Thule but rather as a boundary to yet another Shangri-La: 'Russians ... report ... that there is a Sea beyond Ob so warm that all kinds of Sea-Fowl live thereabout as well in Winter as in Summer.' This, Milton believed in his youth, is what lay in the 'Lands between *Russia,* and *Cathay.*'[11] Perhaps, by the time he wrote *Paradise Lost* such sanguine expectations had been dissipated by fact.

Thematic parallels between the *Moscovia* and the epic poem are, however, more arresting than the purely verbal ones. There is, for example, the comparison between Satan's unforgettable flight through Chaos and the English voyages along the storm-ridden coast of Norway and Lapland through the polar circle into the unknown seas north of Archangel. There is the one between the opulence of Satan's retinue in Hell and the gaudy magnificence of the Muscovite court. The bridge from Hell to earth is also reminiscent – at least to Mutschmann – of the bridge erected 'three waies, 150 fathom long' over the crowds at the coronation of Theodore to conduct the Tsar from one church to another.

2 WILLOUGHBY-SATAN'S EXPEDITION

Cawley, the only Miltonist who has taken the German scholar's suggested parallels to heart, also inadvertently reveals why the latter's conjectures have suffered such neglect. Most of his more fanciful ones – such as the view that Milton was an illegitimate child and an albino (which supposedly explained his blindness) – have been rather ostentatiously cold-shouldered by scholars.[12] This did not prevent Cawley from developing Mutschmann's suggestion concerning the parallels between *Paradise Lost* and the *Moscovia*, the most curious of these being the textual comparison he draws between an account of the preamble to Willoughby's hazardous voyage and the celebrated council scene in Pandemonium where the 'heroic' Satan volunteers to find a new way to Earth for his companions in adversity. In *Moscovia*, as we have noted above, Willoughby's career is followed in far greater detail than the 'proportions' of the history of Muscovy would warrant. His courage, his discipline, his preparations for the expedition, his behaviour in extremity, and his tragic death at '*Arzina* in *Lapland* near to *Kegor*' are all depicted, as are the circumstances surrounding the discovery of the body by a Russian fisherman, its dispatch back home to England by an English agent, and the sinking of the funeral ship.

Some of these details Milton would have got from '*The Journal* of Sir Hugh Willoughby,' which is noted in Milton's list of sources; others from another account by Clement Adams. The latter's narrative of what happened when the northeast project was broached 'to open a way and passage to our men for travaile to newe and unknown kingdomes' inspired Milton's account in the *Moscovia*:

In this so hard and difficult a matter, they first made choyse of certaine grave and wise persons in manner of a Senate or companie, which should lay their heads together, and give their judgements ...

Sufficient Captains and governours of so great an enterprise were as yet wanting: to which office and place, although many men, (and some voyde of experience) offered themselves, yet one Sir Hugh Willoughbye a most valiant Gentleman, and well borne, very earnestly requested to have that care and charge committed unto him: of whom before all others, both by reason of his goodly personage (for he was of a tall stature) as also for his singular skill in the services of warre, the company of the Marchants made greatest accompt: so that at last they concluded and made choyce of him for the Generall of this voyage, and appoynted to him the Admirall with authoritie and command over all the rest.[13]

All this, as Cawley points out, catches the mood of the scene in Pandemonium where Beelzebub paves the way for Satan's own brave words:

> But first whom shall we send
> In search of this new world, whom shall we find
> Sufficient? who shall tempt with wandring feet
> The dark unbottom'd infinite Abyss
> And through the palpable obscure find out
> His uncouth way ...
>   what strength, what art can then
> Suffice ...
>   Here he had need
> All circumspection, and wee now no less
> Choice in our suffrage; for on whom we send,
> The weight of all and our last hope relies. (II. ll 402–15)

After Beelzebub sits down, none – 'pondering the danger' – volunteer to take the lead, which differs somewhat from Adam's account (in which 'many ... offered themselves'): yet Satan could surely be considered Willoughby *redivivus* in the lines that follow:

> *Satan*, whom now transcendent glory rais'd
> Above his fellows, with Monarchal pride
> Conscious of highest worth, unmov'd thus spake.
> O Progeny of Heav'n, Empyreal Thrones,
> With Reason hath deep silence and demurr
> Seis'd us, though undismaid: long is the way
> And hard ...
> If thence he scape into what ever world,
> Or unknown Region, what remains him less
> Then unknown dangers and as hard escape.
> But I should ill become this Throne ...
>   if aught propos'd
> And judg'd of public moment, in the shape
> Of difficulty or danger could deterre
> Me from attempting. (II. ll 435–50)

After this Satan resumes, as many have contended, something of Cromwell's character as Milton perceived it; but Satan's earliest connection with Russia was perpetrated in the guise – if Cawley is to be believed – of the heroic figure who perished without ever reaching it.

Sir Hugh Willoughby's death points to another link between the *Moscovia* and *Paradise Lost*, where the horrible Night-Hag comes to dance 'with Lapland Witches' (II. ll 664–5). Their domicile had already been more or less established in the *Moscovia*, where Milton speaks of the 'Witches of the *Samoeds*, *Lappians*, and *Tartarians*.'[14] Such sombre associations of the North were evoked in part by the failure of the various English voyagers to find the sought-for northeast passage. Again and again, with repeated loss of life, ships were turned back by impenetrable ice. The despair this evoked is reflected, no doubt, in the scene where Sin and Death are released from their dungeon upon a doomed mankind:

> As when two Polar Winds blowing adverse
> Upon the *Cronian* Sea, together drive
> Mountains of Ice, that stop th'imagin'd way
> Beyond *Petsora* Eastward to the rich
> *Cathaian* Coast (x. ll 289–93)

Gourdon of Hull's *Voiage to Pechora* is another of the sources used by Milton in the *Moscovia*, and the place is mentioned there many times. For English sailors and merchants it had a particularly bleak and frigid reputation; hence its use in *Paradise Lost*.

APPENDIX TWO

An English Oration Concerning Milton's Satan from Lermontov's School*

Almost every country, almost every lettered nation has its epic poem: the English have theirs; among which, as among all others, whether ancient or modern, Milton's *Paradise Lost* stands pre-eminent. Arduous indeed is the task I have imposed on myself, rash indeed my undertaking in endeavouring to point out some of the principal beauties and defects of a poem so great, so sublime, so justly and universally admired. Sensible of my own weakness and limited experience, my courage would totally desert me at the sight of the numerous and enlightened assembly, who honour me with their attention, did I not feel assured of the indulgence and lenity of my judges, many of whom have entrusted to the guidance of our worthy institutions the objects most dear to their hearts; many of whom perhaps are themselves indebted to this establishment for those abilities, by the means of which they have risen to those distinctions, with which they now stand adorned.

Justice and impartiality are the first duty of a reviewer. Without following the judgements and opinions of others I shall endeavour to express the impressions the great work before us produced on my own mind.

Although Milton had previously written several poems of considerable merit, it was not till he had totally lost the use of his sight and had attained his fiftieth year, overwhelmed with domestic and public misfortunes, supported by the strength of his genius alone, that he began his *Paradise Lost*. Deprived of the most useful, the most flattering of the human senses, all Milton's faculties seem from that moment to have concentrated in his mind; he became inflamed with celestial fire, and soaring above this nether world,

---

* *Rechi i Stikhi, proiznesennye v Torzhestvennom Sobranii Universitetskago Pansiona*, po sluchaiu vypuska vospitannikov ... (Moscow: v Universitetskoi Tipografii 1828) 37–43

took his flight into the regions of light, plunged into the realms of darkness, trod the flowery paths of Eden.

[The poem's subject] is the fall of man, occasioned by Satan, who consequently is the principal actor and the real hero of it; and though the Almighty does not occupy so great a share in the action, the whole poem tends to elevate the soul. In all the speeches of Satan, wherever he breaks forth into impiety and imprecations, Milton has judiciously mingled so much absurdity as to render them incapable of shocking the most pious reader ... Milton has perfectly preserved the unity of action throughout the first nine books; but the three last, though they contain many beauties, are far inferior to the preceding ones; and I am at a loss to say to what end, after the principal subject, the triumph of the devil, is exhausted, our author has so much lengthened the episode of the journey of Sin and Death; the description of the Messiah's descent upon earth, and the prophecies of the Archangel Michel [*sic*], revealing to Adam and Eve the evils they and their posterity are doomed to undergo, and giving a prospect of happiness hereafter; for it is not till the end of the twelfth book that Milton at length describes the banishment of our first parents. The long space of time which elapses between the fall and exile is not only contrary to what we find in the Holy Writ, it is also contrary to taste and the rules of epic poetry. According to my opinion, Milton ought to have ended with the tenth book; making Sin and Death accompany Satan, representing God as immediately descending in Paradise in order to condemn, to comfort, and then expel fallen man. Thus, the latter part of the poem, instead of being weakened by useless episodes, would have acquired greater strength by the promptitude and probability of the action.

However, it may be said, that in general the unity of action is well maintained; that it contains no episodes but what naturally arise from the subject, and are of the most beautiful kind: such as the description of heaven and its inhabitants.

The object of most importance in an epic poem, after the plan or fable is without doubt the character of the principal actors. It was very difficult, and one would think almost impossible to treat this subject properly in a work like *Paradise Lost*, in which most of the actors are beings of a nature far superior to that of man; however, Milton's genius is wonderfully successful in this part; he has assigned to every one that which best suits it, and placed them in opposition to each other, as God and Satan, the celestial and the infernal spirits. God the Father and Son are represented as well as they could be by a mortal, although this is the weakest part of the poem, as it naturally must be; for how can human intellect form an adequate idea of the Divine Majesty? The virtues and good qualities of the Angels of heaven, and the perverseness of the spirits of hell, correspond perfectly with their various stations. As on the one hand we behold God Almighty as the most merciful, the most gracious, the most perfect of beings, so on the other we see Satan as the most ambitious, the most proud and the most resentful. The character of our first parents may perhaps appear to many readers much easier to describe. But we may justly ask them the question: What kind of beings were Adam and Eve before the fall? Innocent beings. And is a state of innocence so familiar to us as to render a description of it easy? We must therefore conclude, that if Milton has painted it with great success, it is because he employed all his talents in it. Can we indeed figure to our imagination a more beautiful picture of innocence, than that which Milton gives us in the character of our first parents? Can we represent to ourselves any thing more noble, than the natural dignity of Adam, anything more lovely than the grace, gentleness and modesty of Eve?

... We must now come to those [arts] which enliven and embellish it ... I cannot say anything more ... [in] praise of Milton, than that he is equally successful in striking the mind with terror by the picture he sets before us of the horrors of the infernal regions and the darkness and confusion of Chaos, and in pleasing the imagination by the delightful display of the universe and the blissful abode of our first parents. With regard to the dialogues, they are full of the sublime, and perfectly suited to the different characters of the speakers. If Milton's majesty abandons him anywhere, it is [in] the dialogues between God and the Messiah; for, as I have already said, it was a task too arduous for men; indeed our author seems to tremble himself while describing the sentiments of the Almighty. On the other hand, the discourse of the Devil is the most perfect of its kind; for all his perverseness and evil propensities are displayed in a masterly manner. The machinery would be well constructed, if Milton did not sometimes, to draw too near the marvellous, shock our reason, so for instance in the battles of the Angels, in which there is no probability, and in which the introduction of Artillery, used by the infernal spirits, is an intolerable blemish.

What then are the beauties of this poem so greatly celebrated? Why is Milton ranked among the most sublime, the greatest of poets? since his work contains so many defects. Thinking myself obliged to point out the most remarkable errors, the narrow limits of my essay do not permit me to examine all the beauties, with which the redundant genius of Milton has furnished *Paradise Lost*; but to give some idea of them, in conclusion I must say, that the characters are well drawn, with as much variety as they admit of; that it abounds with most beautiful descriptions, either horrible or pleasing, as the nature of their subject requires, with admirable dialogues, strong and new comparisons; that the style, in blank verse, is rich, energetic and harmonious. So many important qualifications may certainly redeem the defects I have mentioned. Not only pages, but volumes might be and have been written on this sublime poem, but I fear my subject has already led me to trespass too long on the time of my audience, on whose indulgence I rely, and not on my own merits, for a favourable reception of my first essay.

APPENDIX THREE

A Chronological Distribution Table

A Chronological Distribution of Russian Manuscripts and of
Printed Book Translations of Milton's Writings*
prior to the First World War

This list does not include items such as Milton's shorter poems or parts of *Paradise Lost* published in periodicals. Exception has been made in the case of the *Brief History of Moscovia*. The following abbreviations are used: Areop = *Areopagitica*, Mosc = *A Brief History of Moscovia*, Nat = 'On the Morning of Christ's Nativity,' PL = *Paradise Lost*, PR = *Paradise Regained*, SA = *Samson Agonistes*.

1747–9	PL	(Viazemsky-Rychkov)	1778	PR	
c 1750	"	(Suvorin)	1779–84	PL	(Barsov)
? 1753	"	(Pypin)	1780	"	
1754	"	(Vorontsov)	1783–4	"	(Borozdin II)
1754	"	(Zabelin)	1783–5	"	(Fedorov)
1756	"	(Rumiantsev)	1785	"	
1760	"	(Volynsky-VonLiar-Larsky)	1785	PR	
1761–3	"	(Titov-Davydova)	1787	"	
1762–3	"	(Zabelin II)	1795	PL	
1764–5	"	(Chertkov)	1795	"	
1774	"	(Borozdin)	1796	"	
1777	"		1803	PL&PR	
1778	"		1810	" "	
1778–80	"	(Khrapovitskaya)	1810	" "	

* The manuscript copies are identified in parentheses as indicated in this volume and *Prophet*.

Appendix Three 179

1810	" "		1895	" "
1820	" "		1895	" "
1820	*PR*		1895	" "
1824	*PL&PR*		1896	" "
1827	*PL*		1896	" "
1835	*PL&PR*		1896	" "
1839	" "		1896	" "
1842–3	*PL*		1897	" "
1848	*PR*		1897	" "
1850	*PL&PR*		1898	" "
1859	" "†		1899	" "
1860	" "		1899	" "
1861	" "		1900	" "
1861	" "		1901	" "
1864	" "		1901	" "
1868	" "		1903	" "
1871	*PL*		1904	" "
1871	*PL&PR*		1905	" "
1872	" "		1905	*Areop*
1875	*Mosc*		1906	"
1876	*PL&PR*		1906	"
1878	" "		1906	*PL&PR*
1881	Nat		1907	*Areop*
1882	*PL&PR*		1907	*Mosc*
1882	" "		1907	*PL&PR*
1884	" "		1908	" "
1884	" "		1910	" "
1888	" "		1910	" "
1890	" "		1911	*SA*
1891	" "		1911	*PL*
1891	" "		1912	*PL&PR*
1891	" "		1913	" "
1892	" "			
1893	" "			
1894	" "			

* The manuscript copies are identified in parentheses as indicated in this volume and *Prophet*.
† Translation-adaptation

Abbreviations

DRKGBL	Dom redkikh knig, Gosudarstvennaia ordena Lenina Biblioteka SSSR imeni V.I. Lenina (Rare Book House, Lenin Library, Moscow)
DZGBL	Dissertatsionnyi zal Gosudarstvennoi ordena Lenina Biblioteka SSSR imeni V.I. Lenina (Dissertation Hall, Lenin Library, Moscow)
GPB	Gosudarstvennaia ordena Trudovogo Krasnogo Znameni Publichnaia Biblioteka imeni M.E. Saltykova-Shchedrina (Saltykov-Shchedrin Public Library, Leningrad)
ORBAN	Otdel rukopisei, Biblioteka Akademii nauk SSSR (Manuscript Section, Library of the Academy of Sciences of the USSR, Leningrad)
ORGBL	Otdel rukopisei, Gosudarstvennaia ordena Lenina Biblioteka SSSR imeni V.I. Lenina (Manuscript Section, Lenin Library, Moscow)
ORGIM	Otdel rukopisei, Gosudarstvennyi istoricheskii Muzei (Manuscript Section, State Historical Museum, Moscow)
ORGPB (L)	Otdel rukopisei, Gosudarstvennaia ordena Trudovogo Krasnogo Znameni Publichnaia Biblioteka imeni M.E. Saltykova-Shchedrina (Manuscript Section, Saltykov-Shchedrin Public Library, Leningrad)
PL	*Paradise Lost*. As in Douglas Bush's Viking-Penguin edition of Milton (1978) unless otherwise stated
PR	*Paradise Regained*. As above unless otherwise stated
Popular Culture	V. Boss *Russian Popular Culture and John Milton* (forthcoming)

Prophet	V. Boss *Poet-Prophet: Milton's Russian Image from the Enlightenment to Pushkin* (forthcoming)
PSS	A.S. Pushkin *Polnoe sobranie sochinenii v desiati tomakh* 10 vols (Moscow-Leningrad: Izdatel'stvo Akademii nauk 1950–1)
SK	*Svodnyi katalog russkoi knigi grazhdanskoi pechati XVIII veka 1725–1800* ed I.P. Kondakov et al 5 vols (Moscow-Leningrad: Izdanie Gosudarstvennoi Biblioteki SSSR imeni V.I. Lenina 1962–7)
TSGADA	Tsentral'nyi arkhiv drevnikh aktov (Central State Archives of Ancient Manuscripts, Moscow)
TSGALI	Tsentral'nyi Gosudarstvennyi arkhiv literatury i iskusstva (Central State Archives of Literature and Art, Moscow)
TSGIAL	Tsentral'nyi Gosudarstvennyi istoricheskii arkhiv v Leningrade (now TSGIA SSSR) (Central State Historical Archives, Leningrad)

Notes

INTRODUCTION

1 Some of the Old Testament apocrypha reached the Eastern Slavs through the Bogomils, who made the Devil into a co-creator and contaminator of the world. On this, see Obolensky *The Bogomils*, especially Appendix IV where some of the literature on Bogomilism in Russia is noted.
2 Danilov, the demon in Vladimir Orlov's recent novel *Danilov the Violist*, for example, is closely modelled on Lermontov's hero.
3 See, for instance, Jeffrey B. Russell's interesting 1986 study *Mephistopheles, the Devil in the Modern World*, where there is mention of Moussorgsky's *Night on Bald Mountain* and Shostakovitch's *War and Peace* quartet in the demonic context, but no discussion at all of the Devil in Russian literature. An earlier book by Maximillian Rudwin, *The Devil in Legend and Literature* (1959), is in this respect no different.
4 As late as 1958 this brilliant scholar was criticized for turning to Western sources in discussing the origins of *Demon*. Yet Eikhenbaum's 1924 study of Lermontov and his discussion of Satanism, 'O demonologicheskoi traditsii v russkoi poezii 20–30kh godov XIX v.,' are still invaluable: see ch 6 below.
5 The controversy over Milton and the English Revolution in the Communist Party was triggered by the production of Lunacharsky's play *Oliver Cromwell* during the Russian Civil War; the author's view of Milton's Satan is discussed in the final chapter of this volume.
6 Of the pre-revolutionary literature discussing *Demon*'s possible sources, the most knowledgeable are Dashkevich's contributions. These and later scholarship are discussed below: see ch 6.
7 See Pypin *Dlia liubitelei knizhnoi stariny* 48ff. The eighteenth-century transcriptions of Baron Stroganov's original translation that I found in Moscow and

184 Notes to pages xx–xxvi

Leningrad archives are described in *Prophet*. However, the first manuscript adaptation of *Paradise Lost* to make Satan into the hero and central character of the story is analysed in ch 2 below.

8 Entitled 'The Book about Satan's Ejection from Heaven' ('Kniga o sverzhenii s neba Satany'), it was transcribed in 1740, and is to be found in ORGBL, Muzeinoe sobranie no 10954. The manuscript is discussed below in ch 2.
9 Some of the more interesting literature is itemized in the archival section of the bibliography below as well as in the opening chapter.
10 See, for example, the *Povest' o Savve Gruditsyne*, the writing of which in the 1660s coincides in time with the publication of *Paradise Lost*. In it the Devil helps Savva, the hero, to seduce an old man's young wife; but generally the Dark One was considered woman's ally, the accomplice of Eve. This is duly reflected in that chauvinist sample of popular wisdom: 'Gde satana ne smozhet, tuda babu poshlet' / 'Where the Devil's beat, he'll send a bitch to do it.' See Dal' *Tolkovyi slovar' zhivogo velikorusskogo iazyka* 139, 'Satana.'
11 Avvakum *The Life Written by Himself* 87. Avvakum's Devil wears several mantles, the most fearsome being that of Antichrist. But to any reader of Christopher Hill's fascinating study *Antichrist in Seventeenth-Century England* it must be apparent that, apart from Muscovite syntax, little differentiates Avvakum's Antichrist from the being whose coming is foretold in *Paradise Lost*.
12 Staehlin *Original Anecdotes of Peter the Great* 41:243. The Tsar also commented ironically on the freshness of the inkstains.
13 Saint-Martin influenced Novikov, the foremost journalist and publisher of the Russian Enlightenment under whose aegis the first full translation of *Paradise Lost* came out: see ch 2 below and Longinov *Novikov i Moskovskie Martinisty*.
14 Zhirmunskii's classic study, *Gëte v russkoi literature*, has not been made redundant by the more recent two-volume work on the same subject published by the University of Pennsylvania Press: but neither Zhirmunskii nor André von Gronicke discusses Milton's influence. For a recent Soviet treatment of Goethe's Russian translators that also touches on some who tackled *Paradise Lost* see Iu.D. Levin's outstanding monograph *Russkie perevodchiki XIX veka*.
15 See Klimov et al (eds) *Pedagogicheskaia razrabotka po tvorchestvu Mil'tona* 13.
16 Hill *Milton and the English Revolution* 439
17 Bulgakov's Azazello is reminiscent of Satan's standard-bearer in Milton's epic, but Ellendea Proffer in her biography of Bulgakov rejects the influence of *Paradise Lost*: see my comment on this in the bibliographic note below.
18 Kolakowski 'Three Motifs in Marxism' 159

19 On this see 'Milton in Russia,' my letter to the editor of the *Times Literary Supplement* (24 Sept 1984) 1037.

1 SATAN AND THE FIRST TRANSLATION OF *PARADISE LOST*

1 On this remarkable *pesn'*, which represents the first poetic defence of the heliocentric theory in the Russian language, see the appendix to *Prophet*.
2 On Kantemir and Milton's influence on his own verse and prosodic views, see chs 2 and 3 in *Prophet*.
3 See Gillet *Le Paradis perdu dans la littérature française* 116–17; Gillet notes that 'on ne peut ni accepter ni démentir sans réserves cette histoire.'
4 Lewis *A Preface to Paradise Lost* chs 7 and 8
5 Poets before Lomonosov used Church-Slavonic words to 'elevate' poetic idiom, but Lomonosov elaborated such usage into a formal system in his *Predislovie o pol'ze knig tserkovnykh* (1757).
6 Stroganov 'Predislovie ...' in 'Pogublennyi rai, chrez Ioanna Mil'tona geroicheskoi poemoi predstavlennyi, s Frantsuzskago na Rossiiskii perevedennyi Tainym Sovetnikom, Eia Imperatorskavo Velichestva Deiistvitel'nym Kamer-Gerom i Ordena Sv. Aleksandra Nevskago Kavalerom Baronom Aleksandrom Grigor'evichem Stroganovym ...' 2. The references in this chapter are to the Viazemskii copy of the manuscript, F.48 (Rychkov) in ORGPB, unless otherwise stated.
7 Although 'pogublennyi' can (like 'poteriannyi') have an abstract connotation too, Dal' gives the following synonyms for 'gublenie': 'paguba,' 'trata,' 'izvod,' 'gibel,' 'porchia,' 'ubiistvo.'
8 Unlike other copies of the Stroganov-Milton that I have seen, the Novosil'tsev manuscript (ORBAN Ustiuzhskoe sobranie, no 57) remained with the same family for close to a century: see ch 4 in *Popular Culture*.
9 See 'Starinnyi perevod Stroganova' *Moskovskie vedomosti* 39 (14 May 1838) 316 (unsigned).
10 Ie, the 1820 Russian edition of *Paradise Lost*, which Lermontov read: see ch 7 below.
11 See D'Israeli *Curiosities of Literature* 193. D'Israeli was probably unaware that this folly made commercial sense. According to Ants Oras (who cites D'Israeli's essay in another context) the common reader liked this prose paraphrase, and it was republished several times.
12 'Mais la presse est si gênée en France, & au contraire elle est si libre en Angleterre, qu'on ne sera pas surpris que le Traducteur ai été obligé de retrancher bien des endroits de cet admirable Poëme, pour obtenir la permission

de le faire imprimer ...' See Dupré's 'Avertissement' to *Le Paradis perdu, poëme heroïque de Milton ...* vol 1 (The Hague 1730) 1.
13 See '*Le Paradis perdu, poëme heroïque de Milton.* Traduit de l'Anglois conformement à l'Original. Avec les Remarques de Mr Addison. Nouvelle Edition. Augmentée du *Paradis Reconquis,* & de quelques autres Pièces de Poësie du même Auteur' (The Hague 1740).
14 'Predislovie k blagosklonnomu chitateliu,' in the Stroganov-Milton 'Pogublennyi rai ...' 2. (The citations in this chapter are from the Viazemskii copy of the translation, which is discussed in the next chapter.)
15 Ibid 1
16 Ibid, ie, 'On perevel knigu, sochinenuiu Gugonom Trotslem o istine blagochestiia khristianskago; vtoruiu, sochinenuiu Mil'tonom, imenuemuiu 'Rai pogublennyi,' tret'iu – o supruzhestve, i drugiia mnogiia.' None of these were published.
17 'The possibility is not to be excluded that he was familiar with some translation of Milton's *Paradise Lost* and *Paradise Regained;* there are separate parallels to be found in the poems of both poets.' (See Berkov ed *Virshi* 242.) This supposition has been reiterated by the late Professor Dmitrii Chizhevskii, but in the absence of textual parallels (which neither Berkov nor Chizhevskii demonstrate) or of any other evidence of a biographical nature about Buslaev's interest in Milton, it is difficult to ascertain which editions the Russian poet might have used. There are references in 'Spiritual Speculations' to Virgil, Ovid, and Homer, but to no modern poets. Although Church-Slavonic in tone, the poem does contain neologisms of recent vintage, such as 'instrumenty,' 'elementy,' 'koncerty,' etc, the literary origin of which is not necessarily Miltonian. About Buslaev, authorities such as Smirnov, Filaret, Gennadi, etc, have little to say. He earned his livelihood as deacon at the Uspenskii Cathedral in Moscow, having attended the Moscow Theological Academy.

The full title of Buslaev's poem reads: 'Umozritel'stvo dushevnoe, opisannoe stikhami o preselenii v vechnuiu zhisn' prevoskhoditel'noi baronessy Marii Iakovlevny Stroganovoi ... ,' which may be inexactly anglicized as: 'Spiritual Speculations, Described in Verse Concerning the Migration to Eternal Life of the Most Excellent Baroness Mariia Iakovlevna Stroganova ...' The poem, which contains one hundred syllabic lines, was known to Novikov, who endorses the flattering portrait of Mariia Iakovlevna's exemplary Christian character in Buslaev's poem. He also cites Trediakovsky's high praise of it. See Novikov *Opyt istoricheskago slovaria* 23–7. Buslaev, says Novikov, 'was a learned man, who knew all the best Ancient writers and poets.' His work cannot be described as an epic in any sense, but it does contain narrative, the most moving being the poet's lines on the crucifixion.
18 Note to the 'Second Epistle' in 'Dve Epistoly' in P.N. Berkov (ed) *A.P. Sumaro-*

kov – *Izbrannye proizvedeniia* (Leningrad 1957) 128. An attempted translation of the *Two Epistles* into English may be found in the first volume of *The Literature of Eighteenth-Century Russia* by Professor Harold B. Segel of Columbia University. It is, however, inaccurate. The names of Milton and Shakespeare, for example, are omitted in the English text. Some of Sumarokov's plays may also be read in a recent translation by Richard and Raymond Fortune, *Selected Tragedies of A.P. Sumarokov* (introduced by John Fizer), published by Northwestern University Press (Evanston 1970). Possibly the most interesting of these is the Russian dramatist's version of *Hamlet*, which was first published in the same year as the *Two Epistles*. It then disappeared off the Russian stage in 1762, when the circumstances of Catherine II's ascent to the throne with the murder of her husband, the reigning tsar, made performance of Sumarokov's adaptation of Shakespeare politically inexpedient. See also Pokrovskii (ed) *Aleksandr Petrovich Sumarokov*.

19 Alekseev 'Pervoe znakomstvo s Shekspirom v Rossii' in Alekseev (ed) *Shekspir i russkaia kul'tura* 19–22

20 It is conceivable that Sumarokov may have been familiar with the famous Shakespearean allusion in 'L'Allegro' through the French translation of the poem included in the 1740 edition of Dupré's translation of *Paradise Lost*. See 'L'Allegro de Milton. Traduit de l'Anglois' in *Le Paradis perdu ...* (The Hague: Chez M.G. Mervile 1740) 94–7. Compare with the original:

  Then to the well-trod stage anon,
  If Jonson's learned sock be on,
  Or sweetest Shakespeare, Fancy's child,
  Warble his native wood-notes wild
  And ever, against eating cares,
  Lap me in soft Lydian airs,
  Married to immortal verse,
  Such as the meeting soul may pierce,
  In notes with many a winding bout
  Of linked sweetness long drawn out
  With wanton heed and giddy cunning,
  The melting voice through mazes running,
  Untwisting all the chains that tie
  The hidden soul of harmony ...('L'Allegro' ll 131–44)

21 Orell's edition, *Johann Milton verlohrnes Paradiese*, in 1754 was a reissue of Bodmer's earlier translation, and it was reprinted again in 1759, 1769, and 1780. There were also partial translations of the epic by Hermann Brockes (1740) and Karl Wilhelm Müller (1755, reprinted 1761), and an important verse translation of the whole poem by Friedrich Wilhelm Zachariä in 1760 and 1763

(reprinted 1763–4, 1778–83). *Paradise Regained* and *Samson* appeared in 1752 (in translations by Simon Grynaeus, who included other Miltonian poems in his edition, reprinted in 1781, 1782, and 1791).

22 Dupré's translation, the most popular of the century, came out on several occasions: in this period in 1743, 1749, 1753, and 1762 (published either in Paris or Amsterdam). Paolo Rolli's translation was also republished in this period in 1740, 1742, and 1758 (while at the end of the century a poet turned his *versi sciolti* into French).

23 See ch 9 in *Prophet*.

24 'V etot vek ostorozhnogo pravoslaviia poema Mil'tona pokazalas' soblaznitel'-noiu.' See 'Starinnyi russkii perevod Mil'tonova *Poteriannogo raia*' *Moskovskie vedomosti* 39 (14 May 1838) 316.

25 See Pypin *Dlia liubitelei knizhnoi stariny* 48ff.

26 See Speranskii *Rukopisnye sborniki XVIII Veka*. Speranskii refers to a *sbornik* (GPB Viaz F.139) that includes an alphabet by Karion Istomin in English translation and 'Eksplikatsii' by Kantemir together with his translation of Boileau.

2 INTRODUCING MILTON'S SATAN TO THE COMMON READER

1 The Barsov manuscript (ORGIM F.450 no 3386) has a Pro Patria watermark. It corresponds to no 772–5 in Klepikov, for which the dates are 1779–84. Since part of the Russian translation, however, is taken from the 1780 printed text (as is shown below), I assume the date of the transcription to be closer to 1784, the other reasons for this hypothesis being discussed below. Owing to the vagaries of Nikolai Pavlovich Barsov's academic life – he was born in 1839 and died in 1889 – it is impossible to ascertain where he acquired the manuscript. From 1869 to 1871 he was connected with the history faculty at St Petersburg University, becoming librarian at the University of Warsaw in 1871. As professor at that institution, he also taught Russian history there after 1873. Barsov's chief opus is the *Ocherki russkoi istoricheskoi geografii*. Barsov ms, top of page 32: 'Spisanno po liubopytstvu dlia znaniia.'

2 Barsov ms 1: 'Satana plaval desiat' dnei mezhdu ognennymi volnami sovsem svoim prokliatym voinstvom.' This manuscript is unusual in that Milton is nowhere mentioned; nor does the title recall *Paradise Lost*. It is simply entitled (on the first page, above the transcription itself) 'Iz knigoi pervoi povest' ' / 'novel [or 'telling'] from the first book.'

3 'Ponarecheniiu filistinov vposledniia [*sic*] vremena, vel'zevul emu byl napersnik' ibid

4 Ibid

5 For example, in the Barsov version, Eve's speech beginning 'Adam, well may

we labor still to dress / This garden, still to tend plant, herb, and flower ...'
(IX. ll 205–6) repeats Amvrosii word for word: 'Liubeznyi Adam[e]!' [there is no 'e' in the printed text]. My tshchimsia vsemerno opravliati vertograd sei[.] i smotreti za drevami i tsvetami, poruchennymi nam ot Boga' (Ibid 18). The next lines are then omitted in the manuscript, but are resumed with 'Thou therefore now advise / Or hear what to my mind first thoughts present ...' (IX. ll 212–13) / 'Skazhi ty svoe mnenie, ili poslushai, chto mne razum preustavliaet ...' The punctuation in Barsov is not quite the same as in Amvrosii, and occasionally 'sem' is omitted, 'prochie' inserted, and so on.

6 See Obolensky *The Bogomils*, especially Appendix IV, where some of the literature on Bogomilism in Russia is noted.
7 See 'Kniga o sverzhenii s neba satany, zelo polezna' ORGBL no 10945, 'O khitrom prel'shchenii Adama' 7v–15.
8 'Kako demony zhalobu prinosiat na gospoda Boga i sovetuiut' ibid 15–21
9 'O demonskom sobranii i dume' ibid
10 'O voine khristove i o pobede na ada' ibid 77–90
11 'O demonskom sobranii i dume' ibid 97–105
12 'Kuiu silu demony imut [sic]' ibid 116–20
13 'O priznakakh i fantaziiakh besovskikh' ibid 120–3
14 'O ved'makh prokliatykh i charovnikakh besovskikh i o vorozheikakh' ibid 124–7
15 'Obraz na strakh, izhe liubiat zagadyvati' ibid 128v
16 Especially in those about Antichrist, which are well represented in the Barsov collection in ORGBL F.17 nos 6, 29, 32, 238, 338, 414, 483, 525, 622, 678, 813, and 824. Most of these tales of Antichrist, however, are of late-eighteenth- or nineteenth-century vintage.
17 Eg 'Rodoslovie ot Adama, v krugakh' (second half of 18th c) ORGBL no 10300; 'Rodoslovie ot Adama, v krugakh' (also 18th c) ibid no 9615; and see Shchapov *Opisanie rukopisei sobraniia Moskovskoi dukhovnoi akademii po vemennomu katalogu* 77, where the apocryphal manuscript of Adam's compact with the Devil is described. The sixth-century cosmography of Cosmas Indikopleustes was still popular in some parts of Russia in the nineteenth century: see ORGBL no 10336. See also 'O sotvorenii mira' ibid no 1092 (dated 17th or 18th century).
18 A record of their reading has survived in inventories to be found in various *sborniki*.
19 Ie *The True Light*; see ch 4 below.
20 See ch 3 below.
21 See SK 7157.
22 Ibid 4049
23 The success of the historical epic in Russia proved equally ephemeral, Kheraskov's *Rossiada* being the best known.

24 *La Strage* was translated into English by Crashaw in 1646: but Milton expressed his admiration for Marino several years earlier in *Mansus*, which is dedicated to Giambattista Manso, the patron of both Tasso and Marino. Also in the *Defensio Secunda* Milton tells how he visited Manso and discussed epic poetry with him.
25 The parallel is suggested by Golenishchev-Kutuzov in his chapter 'Poeziia ital'ianskogo barokko – Marino i ego shkola' in *Romanskie literatury – Litteratures Romanes* 260–1. The author leans to some extent on Mirollo *The Poet of the Marvelous*, but points out that the latter omits to cite the Russian translation.
26 The 197 copies that were left in bookshops in 1787 were destroyed, like the copies of the Masonic imitation of *Paradise Lost*, also published by Novikov: see ch 6 below.
27 See ch 5 *Prophet*.
28 See Eisenstein *Film Form and Film Sense* 58–62.
29 Barsov ms 1
30 Ibid
31 Ibid
32 Ibid 2. See:
    The great Seraphic Lords and Cherubim
    In close recess and secret conclave sat,
    A thousand demi-gods on golden seats ...(*PL* I. ll 794–6).
33 Ibid 2
34 See:
    and next to him Moloch, sceptred king,
    Stood up, the strongest and the fiercest spirit
    That fought in Heaven, now fiercer by despair.
    His trust was with the eternal to be deemed
    Equal in strength ...(*PL* II. ll 43–7)
35 Ie 'Pervyi Molokh derzha v rukakh skipetr[,] iavostneishi l'stets ... na lugakh empiriskikh, otchaianie pache umnozhilo estestvennuiu ego zlobu derznul sravniati sebia vsemogushchemu ...' Barsov ms 2
36 Ie 'Liubeznyia klevrety [sic]; ia ves'ma sklonen k voine i nenavisti [sic] nikomu ne ustupaiu' ibid 2
37 Ie 'svergnut' bozhestvennogo monakha ... Polozhim chto on umilitsia i ob'iavit vse obshche [sic] proshchenie' ibid 2
38 'The Argument' to *PL* Book II
39 Ie 'Ia sam poidu skvoz' temnyia zaputeniia' Barsov ms 2
40 Ie 'svoi bystriia [sic] kryl'ia, i letit ko vratam adskim puskaias' inogda napravo, inogda nalevo' ibid 2v
41 Ie 'Vidit Uzhasnye vrata tri zatvora byli iz medi; tri iz zheleza i tri iskamnia [sic] adamantovykh neprokhodimyia nikakoiu siloiu ograzhdenny ognem v

segda [sic] goriashchim ... Dva prestrastnyia chudovishcha ... stoiali edinodos-
rediny tela podobilos' zhene prekrasnoi, snizhe zmieiu uvivaiushchuiusia vok-
rug poiasa, adskie psy neprestanno ... est'li chto prinudit ikh udalitsia to skry-
vaiutsia [sic]' ibid 2v

42 Ie 'Vtoroi obraz podobilos' teni i chernost'iu temnee bylo nochi, iarosten kak 10 furii uzhasen' ibid 2v
43 Ie 'Satana tot chaz razsudil chto delat [sic] nadlezhalo: utisha eia otvetstvoval laskatel'nym glasom: liubeznaia dshcher' moia; ponezhe ty menia za ottsa priznavaesh' ibid 3
44 Ie 'sniala ot poiasa svoego zlopolochny kliuch ... podniala velikuiu Reshetku kotoruiu bez neia sily Adskie nemogli by pokolebit'; Zamki poslushali i zapory-zheleznyia otpali pervym dvizheniem Ruki Eia' ibid 3
45 Ie 'Rychanie burei podobnoe gromu potriaslos' samuiu glubinu Ereba' ibid 3
46 Ie 'Orkus adskii, i prestrastnyi demagorgon' ibid 3
47 'The Argument' to *PL* Book III
48 Ie 'Beshenstvo eto mshchenie obladaet im setuia opogublennykh [sic] minutakh, prodolzhaet on s zharom put' svoi' Barsov ms 3v
49 Ie 'dostig togo mesta ot kuda velikoe svetilo dnei daleko svet svoi razlivaet' ibid 5
50 Ie 'Kniaz tmy [sic], nizshedshi na shar eto [sic] uchinil soboiu takoe piatno kakoe mozhet byt' niodin [sic] zvezdochet chrez zritel'nyia truby nikogda ne vide'l' ibid 5
51 Ie 'Satana poklonilsia unizhenno pred velikim arkhangelom poobychaiu [sic] ustavlennom mezhdu nebesnymi dukhami' ibid 5
52 Ibid 17v
53 'Sledstvennaia Razluka! Votshche neshchastnaia Eva! Votshche laskaesh ty sebia priiatnym vozvrashcheniem! Uvy!' ibid 19v
54 Ie 'Satana s osobennym udivleniem smotrel na mesto ... no ona est' naiprelest-neishii predmet pred ochami on nakhodit v glazakh eia vse priiatnosti soedineny. Takovo bylo udovol'stvie Satany' ibid 19v–20
55 Ie 'Vysokaia dusha ego uteshala sebia luchshimi nadeianiami' ibid 30v
56 Ie 'I derzhas' ruka za ruku poshli oni tikhimi i somnitel'nymi stopami po uedinennym poliam Edemskim' ibid 40v

3 MONKS AND 'POCKET POETS': PUBLICATION

1 The fullest account of Petrov's life is I.A. Shliapkin's article in *Istoricheskii vestnik* 31 (1885), which may also be found in Vengerov's *Russkaia Poeziia* vol 1. See also the articles on the poet in *Moskvitianin* 1:1 (1841); 6:12 (1841); 2:9 (1849).
2 Dmitriev *Melochi iz zapasa moei pamiati* 9–10. On the other hand, Novikov

(in his *Opyt istoricheskago slovaria o rossiiskikh pisateliakh*) has a much lower estimate, politically tinged no doubt, of Petrov's talents. It should be added that Petrov's translation of the *Aeneid* was highly praised by contemporaries.

3 Eg 'Skol' sila velika Rossiiskago iazyka! / Petrov lish zakhotel, Virgilii stal zaika.' Petrov returned to his unfinished translation of the *Aeneid* after *Paradise Lost*, the last part being published in 1786.

4 Petrov '*Poteriannyi rai poema Ioanna Mil'tona* perevedena s aglinskago' (St Petersburg 1777) intro np

5 On Sichkarev, see the preceding chapter: and sk item 6485 and Novikov *Opyt istoricheskago slovaria* 205.

6 Petrov *Oda na velikolepnyi karrusel'*

7 Novikov *Opyt istoricheskago slovaria* 162-3

8 'Zhizn' Vasiliia Petrovicha Petrova' in *Trudy Vol'nogo obshchestva sorevnovatelei prosveshcheniia i blagotvoreniia* 1:1 (1818) 129, as quoted by Cross in his most recent article dealing with Petrov's sojourn in England, 'Petrov v Anglii' in Makogonenko (ed) *Sbornik XVIII Vek* 231. Petrov, who is one of the many Russians whose fate in eighteenth-century England Professor Cross has pursued, stayed (as Cross shows) for a period of three years – not two as is commonly stated in Russian sources.

9 See, for instance, part of the epistle included in Gerbel's *Russkie poety*, 30. Gerbel considers 'K***, iz Londona' Petrov's best poem.

10 Karamzin 'Pis'ma russkogo puteshestvennika' in *Izbrannye sochineniia* vol 1:545. These lines of the future historian were written after reading Hume.

11 See the discussion of this in Cross 'Petrov v Anglii.' Blagoi (unlike G.A. Gukovskii) would agree with the generous assessment by Professor Cross. For Gukovskii's verdict, see his *Istoriia russkoi literatury XVIII veka* 337-8. Pushkin called Petrov one of 'Catherine's gray eagles.'

12 In the eighteenth century alone there were more than a hundred publications of *Paradise Lost* (compared with fifty editions of Shakespeare's plays).

13 Demidov *Zhurnal puteshestviia* ... , entry for 24 May 1772:51

14 Mavor *The Virgin Mistress*. I owe this reference to Cross 'Petrov v Anglii' 234. On Petrov see also Serman (ed) *Poety XVIII veka* 321.

15 Petrov *Poteriannyi rai* ... intro np. Petrov does, however, mention Milton's blindness: 'Porazhennyi slepotoiu, umel on pol'zovatsia mrakom.'

16 For a discussion of Petrov's translation, see Maksudova's dissertation 12-13.

17 'Preduvedomlenie' to Amvrosii *Poteriannyi rai* (Moscow 1780). The identity of the translator is indicated at the end of the dedication: MAPA (Moscow Academy Prefect Amvrosii).

18 *Raut, Istoricheskii i literaturnyi sbornik* 3:139-40

19 See Bantysh-Kamenskii *Slovar' dostopamiatnykh liudei russkoi zemli* 3:503–8.
20 Makarov 'Mariia Vasil'evna Khrapovitskaia' 98–9 See also Mordovtsev *Russkie zhenshchiny novago vremeni* 160–75.
21 Her translation of Marmontel, *Inni ili razrushenie peruanskoi imperii*, was especially successful, being republished by Novikov in 1782. See SK no 4070-71. See also Makarov 'Mariia Vasil'evna Sushkova' 145–6.
22 Eg 'Perevod s Aglinskago *Poteriannyi Rai*,' which is contained in a *sbornik* in the manuscript collection of the Saltykov-Shchedrin Library in Leningrad, F.15:50. See *Otchet Imperatorskoi Publichnoi Biblioteki za 1889 god 5 Priobreteniia Biblioteki* 143, where the transcription of the *sbornik* is assigned 'to the last years of the xviiith century.' Khrapovitskaya's translation (114–33) concludes with the notation: 'Perevod M.S. r.Kh.,' ie 'Mariia Sushkova, née Khrapovitskaya.' Her translation of *Paradise Lost* precedes a well-known version of the *Tale of the Host of Igor*, here rendered into contemporary Russian not long before the publication of the controversial first published edition in 1800. That is to say, the *Tale* is the latest item in the *sbornik*, the earliest being a translation from the French ('Philosophers – a comedy') of 1773. But all this is of little help in establishing the actual date of the Miltonic translation.
23 See Khrapovitskaya '*Poteriannyi Rai*' ORGPB F.15:50 n;117v. In this, the only explanatory note to be found in the manuscript transcription of Khrapovitskaya's translation (which thus reveals its source) the reference is to Newton's gloss to Moloch's speech:
   But see the angry Victor hath recalled
   His ministers of vengeance and pursuit
   Back to the gates of Heaven ...(PL I. ll 169–71)
Here, the Russian translator follows Bishop Newton in laying bare Moloch's distortion of the truth (repeated in Book II) in suggesting that the angels rather than Christ defeated Satan's legions: 'no v shestoi knige Rafail' povestvuet, chto oni byli prognanny edinym Messieiu.' Of course, Khrapovitskaya adds, 'Raphael's account is true ... the demons do not want to acknowledge that the Messiah alone defeated them.' Would she have made the allusion to Book VI if she had not intended to complete the translation?
24 This may partly be attributed not only to the fact that Khrapovitskaya belonged to a younger generation than Petrov (a generation whose literary idiom tended to be less Latinate) but also to her training in modern languages, whose influence on Russian as written in the last decades of the century was profound. Nor did she feel constrained to follow Milton by staying close to his word order and punctuation. Thus, the opening lines of *Paradise Lost* –
   Of man's first disobedience, and the fruit
   Of that forbidden tree, whose mortal taste

> Brought death into the world, and all our woe,
> With loss of Eden, till one greater man
> Restore us, and regain the blissful seat,
> Sing heavenly Muse, that on the secret top
> Of Oreb, or of Sinai didst inspire
> That shepherd, who first taught the chosen seed,
> In the beginning how the heavens and earth
> Rose out of chaos: or if Sion hill
> Delight thee more, and Siloa's brook that flowed
> Fast by the oracle of God; I thence
> Invoke thy aid to my adventurous song,
> That with no middle flight intends to soar
> Above the Aonian mount, while it pursues
> Things unattempted yet in prose or rhyme. (ll 1–16)

– are faithfully rendered by Petrov in one sentence. Khrapovitskaya sensibly divides this passage into two (with 'chaos' in l 10); eg: 'Preslushanie pervozdannogo, plod zapreshchennogo dreva, koego snediiu smert' i vse bedstva izliialis' vo vselennuiu, i lishenie Edema dopole velichaishii Muzh, vozstavia nas, ne vosvratil nam blazhennago sego zhilishcha: vospoi nebesnaia Musa, na tainstvennykh vershinakh Khoriva i Sinaia prosvetivshaia pastyria, vozglasivshago izbrannomu plemeni, kako v nachale nebo i zemlia proizoshli iz Khaosa. Est'li zhe tebe bolee ogodny Sionskii kholm i Siloamskii istochnik, tekushchii bliz meste [sic] ot kuda iskhodili Bozhii proveshchanii, ia otpole tebia prizyvaiu: vspomoshchestvui otvazhnoi moei pesni, stremiashcheisia vysokim pareniem vosnestisia prevyshe gory Ioniiskoi, i povedati dela do dnes' eshche neopisannye ni prostoiu rechiiu, ni v stikh ne vmeshchennye' (ms cit, p 114).

25 Makarov 'Mariia Vasil'evna Khrapovitskaia' 10
26 See, for example, Brokgauz-Efron *Entsiklopedicheskii slovar'* vol 2 (St Petersburg 1890) 621 (see 'Amvrosii'), and vol 19 (St Petersburg 1896) 317–18 (see 'Mil'ton'); Vengerov (ed) *Russkii biograficheskii slovar'* vol 2 (St Petersburg 1900) 91 (see 'Amvrosii'); Lunacharskii and Mikhailova (eds) *Literaturnaia entsiklopediia* 315–16 (see 'Mil'ton'); SK vol 2 (Moscow 1964) item 4253; Mel'nikova *Izdaniia napechatannye v tipografii moskovskogo universiteta XVIII veka* item 1239, and elsewhere.
27 For a list of Amvrosii's writings see Vengerov *Kritiko-biograficheskii slovar' russkikh pisatelei* vol 1:496–500, where the principal sources on his life are also cited, with the exception of a short anonymous biography published in Poltava by N. Pigurenko in 1884.
28 See also chs 1 and 2 in *Prophet*.
29 Amvrosii *Kratkoe rukovodstvo k oratorii rossiiskoi*. See SK no 123.

30 As quoted by Sukhomlinov *Istoriia rossiiskoi akademii* 1st ed:194
31 Ibid 195. Examples such as 'tiun, gorvol', slana, shamad, bresh,' which Amvrosii cites, prove his point, but not 'samostoiatel'nost' – now a part of the language.
32 But on the title page of the second edition of Amvrosii's translation (published in 1795 by A. Reshetnikov in Moscow), it is said to have been made from 'a foreign tongue' ('s inostrannago iazyka') rather than French (as indicated in the first edition and the reprint of 1785).
33 Thus, if we take the opening lines from Amvrosii's translation –

Poiu preshlushanie pervago cheloveka, pagubnoe
deistvo zapreshchennago ploda
poterianie raia i zlo smerti, torzhestvu-
iushchiia na zemle: dokole Bogochelovek pri-
idet sudishi narody, i nas paki pri-
vedet v blazhennoe zhilishche!

Nebesnaia Muza, Vsevyshniago dshcher'! sni-
di so uedinennykh vysot Khoriva i Si-
naia, gde ty vdokhnoveniem svoim nauchila
pastyria pokazati izbrannomu plemeni,
rodu Evreiskomu, kako nebo i zemlia pro-
izoshli iz neustroennago smesheniia; uzheli
ty bolee liubish' goru Sionskuiu i iasnye
istochniki Siluamskie, tekushchie bliz
tekh mest, gde Vechnyi otkryval Svoi
predvozveshchaniia? Ia ottuda ozhidaiu
tvoeia pomoshchi. Peniia moi, smelo voskhodia
prevyshe gory Aoniiskiia, obvimut veshchi, ko-
torykh eshche nikto he derzal kosnutisia,
ni svobodnym slovom, nizhe stikhami.

– and compare them with Stroganov's version, there are less than a dozen words that are substantively different in the later translation. The most significant of these is the reference to the 'loss of Eden,' which is in turn reflected in the title chosen by Stroganov, ie *'Pogublennyi rai.'* Its connotation of destruction and unredeemable loss is stronger than the term 'poteriannyi' (from 'teriat' – literally 'to lose'), which both Petrov and Amvrosii preferred to use – hence in l 3 above 'poterianie raia' rather than Stroganov's 'pogublenie.' But Amvrosii did use the same word to qualify 'deistvo' in l 2.

Another significant change by Amvrosii is the Russian equivalent introduced for 'Heavenly Muse.' Although Milton's meaning was explained by Dupré and the note translated by Stroganov, the latter interestingly enough declined to use the identical Russian equivalent – 'Muza' – although Kantemir and others had already employed the term. His translation – 'Bozhestvennaia Smysle' or 'Divine Intent' – would have had, of course, less of a pagan ring. Since Stroganov justified his undertaking by stressing the dependence of *Paradise Lost* on Holy Writ, his choice is understandable. Petrov, Khrapovitskaya, and Amvrosii all restored Milton's Muse to Mount Sinai.

The other changes brought in by Amvrosii merely reflect the increasing inroads of the vernacular at the expense of Church-Slavonic. 'Vsevyshnaia dshcher' would thus have been more acceptable to the Russian public in 1780 than 'Vsevyshnee chado.' Similarly, 'the heavens and earth' arising 'out of chaos' (rendered accurately by Stroganov as 'bezdna') is altered by Amvrosii to take into account the mentality fostered by modern science: 'neustroennoe smeshenie,' literally 'unstructured mixture.'

The remaining alterations of Amvrosii are quite minor. He prefers 'iasnyi' to Stroganov's 'svetlyi' in l 13, 'otkryval' to 'ustroil' in l 15, 'ozhidaiu' to 'trebuiu' in l 16, and the more modern 'ne derzal' to 'nepokusilsia.' Finally, Amvrosii prefers 'svobodnoe slovo' (literally 'free word') as an equivalent for Milton's 'prose' in l 20. Stroganov's 'prostaia rech',' however, does not have the same ambivalence.

Comparison of other passages in the two translations yields similar results. Amvrosii 'modernized' Stroganov's text, excising Church-Slavonic endings and vocabulary that would have seemed archaic to readers in the 1780s. But the credit Amvrosii is invariably given for completing so 'difficult' an undertaking belongs elsewhere.

34 See *Sanktpeterburgskii vestnik* 453ff.
35 Amvrosii *Poteriannyi rai* ... 178, as quoted in translation by Clarence Manning. In passing judgment on the Russian translation, Manning criticized the inadequacies of Amvrosii's version by translating the Russian prose back into the original language of the poem and then comparing this with what Milton wrote. Thus, he takes the scene where Satan unleashes 'devilish engines' of his own invention against Michael and his angels:

'So warned he them, aware themselves, and soon
In order, quit of all impediment;
Instant without disturb they took alarm,
And onward move embattled; when behold
Not distant far, with heavy pace the foe
Approaching gross and huge; in hollow cube
Training his devilish enginry, impaled
On every side with shadowing squadrons deep,
To hide the fraud. At interview both stood
A while, but suddenly at head appeared

Satan: and thus was heard commanding loud.
  ' "Vanguard, to right and left the front unfold,
That all may see who hate us, how to seek
Peace and composure, and with open breast
Stand ready to receive them, if they like
Our overture, and turn not back perverse,
But that I doubt; however witness Heaven,
Heaven witness thou anon, while we discharge
Freely our part. Ye who appointed stand
Do as you have in charge, and briefly touch
What we propound, and loud that all may hear."
  'So scoffing in ambiguous words, he scarce
Had ended; when to right and left the front
Divided, and to either flank retired;
Which to our eyes discovered new and strange,
A triple mounted row of pillars laid
On wheels (for like to pillars most they seemed,
Or hollowed bodies made of oak or fir.
With branches lopped, in wood or mountain felled),
Brass, iron, stony mould, had not their mouths
With hideous orifice gaped on us wide,
Portending hollow truce. At each behind
A seraph stood, and in his hand a reed
Stood waving tipped with fire ...' (PL VI. ll 547–80)

Manning then compares these lines with his own translation of Amvrosii's translation from the French of the corresponding passage in English: 'So he ordered them to be in readiness; but they are already prepared; their ranks are drawn up. They come holding their weapons high in martial order. Our foes approached, heavily dragging many weapons, surrounded by serried regiments, hiding their cleverness from our eyes. We were looking at them, when Satan appeared before his regiments and gave a command.

'Suddenly the first ranks of the army parted; the regiments were doubled on both wings. We saw a strange, new sight; a triple order of columns one above the other, lying on wheels; since these things were like columns, or hollow oaks or pines felled in the forests or on the mountains with their branches lopped off. Seraphim, holding in their hands a reed burning with fire, stood behind every weapon.'

One obvious problem with such a procedure is that the modern English prose does not, in fact, correspond to Amvrosii's eighteenth-century Russian. But a more serious objection is that Manning simply failed to check the French translation, to which, as it turns out, Amvrosii was meticulously faithful: 'Il les avertit ainsi de se tenir sur leur gardes: mais ils sont déjà préparés: leurs rangs se trouvent formées. Ils s'avancent, les armes hautes, en ordre de bataille. Nos ennemis s'approchoient, traînant pesamment leur nombreuse artillerie entourée d'escadrons épais qui déroboient l'artifice à nos yeux. Nous les observions, quand Satan parut à la tête des siens, & donna l'ordre.

'A l'instant le front de l'armée s'ouvre, les troupes se replient sur les deux flancs. Nous découvrons un spectacle étrange & nouveau: une triple rangée l'une sur l'autre de colonnes posées sur des roues, car ces pièces ressembloient à des colonnes ou à des troues creux de chênes & de sapins, abbattus dans les forêts ou sur les montagnes, après que les branches en ont été coupées. Un Séraphin, portant en sa main un roseau armé de feu, étoit posté derrière chacune de ces machines' '*Le paradis perdu* de Milton, Traduit de l'Anglois; Avec les remarques de M. Adisson [sic]. Nouvelle Edition, revue & corrigée.' vol 2 [Paris 1765] 30–1).

Clearly Dupré, given his neoclassical tastes, was not impressed by the war in Heaven: nor was Voltaire. Other passages in the French are closer to the original, and so, therefore, are the Russian. Take, for example, the following lines in Book v, where Raphael meets Eve: 'They entered the village solitude which now charmed the eye, as the shadow of Pomona, adorned with flowers and sweet fragrances. Eve, more attractive in her beauty alone than Diana and more beautiful than any one of the three goddesses, in the tradition of the mythologer, who once revealed their charms on Mount Ida; Eve, to honour the heavenly guest, stood before him. She had no need of clothing, but she was sufficiently clad in her virtue. No licentious smile changed the colour of her cheeks. The Angel greeted her with the sacred kiss, which in later times prepared the Daughter of Jesse to receive within her womb the Eternal Son.' As Manning correctly points out, this is certainly rather feeble when compared with the original.

> [So to the sylvan lodge]
> They came, that like Pomona's arbor smiled
> With flowerets decked and fragrant smells, but Eve
> Undecked, save with herself more lovely fair
> Than wood-nymph, or the fairest goddess feigned
> Of three that in Mount Ida naked strove,
> Stood to entertain her guest from heaven; no veil
> She needed, virtue-proof, no thought infirm
> Altered her cheek. On whom the angel 'Hail'
> Bestowed, the holy salutation used
> Long after to blest Mary, second Eve. (*PL* v. ll 377–87)

Yet here again Amvrosii did not stray far from the translation of Dupré, which

Manning once more neglected to compare with the Russian text: 'Ils entrèrent dans leur champêtre retraite, qui réjouissoit la vue comme les berceaux de Pomone, ornés de fleurs & de parfums. Eve, plus charmante par sa seule beauté que (1) la Déesse des bois, ou que la plus belle de (2) ces trois Divinités qui, suivant la fable, exposèrent toutes leur grâces sur le mont Ida; Eve (1) se tuit debout, pour faire honneur à son hôte céleste. Elle n'avoit pas besoin de voile; sa vertu la voiloit assez. Nulle pensée déréglée n'altéroit les coloris de ses joues. L'Ange lui donna la salutation, la sainte salutation qui prépara, dans la suite des tems, la fille de Jessé à recevoir en ses flancs le Fils de l'Eternel' (*Le Paradis perdu* ... vol 1: 254–5).

36 Sukhomlinov *Istoriia rossiiskoi akademii* vol 1:196
37 See Helsztyński, 'Milton in Poland' 148.
38 Ie Count Tarnowski, rector of the University of Cracow: see ibid 147.
39 Another point held against the *Essay on Man* was Pope's support of the heliocentric theory, a matter concerning which *Paradise Lost* is more ambivalent. For an account of this episode see Raikov's admirable study, *Ocherki po istorii geliotsentricheskogo mirovozzreniiia v Rossii* 287–99 (based on N.S. Tikhonravov's earlier essay). It says something of Amvrosii's tolerant intellectual interests that he read Pope's work and approved of it: his brief review of the *Essay on Man* was published posthumously in *Bibliograficheskie Zapiski* (1858) 490–1. At the same time Amvrosii's membership of the Holy Synod made him acutely aware of what was permissible and what was not. Apart from its intellectual content, the Russian translation of the *Essay on Man* is interesting in another respect: there are still some syllabic verses in the body of a translation that is largely syllabo-tonal. This gives some idea of how long the syllabic tradition survived in secular poetry.
40 See the introduction to Amvrosii *Poteriannyi rai* ...1.
41 Eg 'Siia poema perevedena byla eshche v 1745 gody g. tainym sovetnikom i deistvitel'nym kamergerom, grafom Aleksandrovichem Sergeevichem Stroganovym i nyne pis'mennaia nakhoditsia v biblioteke ego siiatel'stva g. tainago sovetnika, senatora i kavalera kniazia Petra Nikiticha Trubetskogo ...' *Sanktpeterburgskii vestnik* 483
42 On Ruban, see Modzalevskii *V.G. Ruban* and A.N. Neustroev, who gives a chronological list of Ruban's extant writings in *V.G.R.* Novikov noted Ruban's poetic promise in his *Slovar'* (191). He was born only a short while before Stroganov's translation of *Paradise Lost* was made, and would therefore not have known its author, but he would perhaps have heard of the translation in his youth. The reference to Prince Trubetskoi's copy suggests yet again how alive the manuscript tradition of Milton's work appears to have been even at this late date.
43 For instance, the Fedorov (ORGBL, F.313 no 42 M.2959); and the Borozdin

(ORGPB, NSRK, F.905) copies, which, according to the watermarks were transcribed not earlier than 1783–5 and 1783–8 respectively. Moreover, the Novosil'tsev copy may have been transcribed more than a decade *after* the publication of the first edition of *Poteriannyi rai*. These manuscripts are discussed in chs 4 and 5 of *Popular Culture*.

44 Which is where Petr Gerasimovich Novosil'tsev purchased his family's copy of 'Pogublennyi rai'
45 See ch 2 above.
46 Novikov began his own *Selected Library of Christian Readings* in 1784 after he moved to Moscow. For a recent and well-informed discussion of his activities see Walicki *Rosyjska Filozofia i Myśl* 32–48.
47 Amvrosii's translation of *Paradise Lost* was published seven times in all, for the last time in 1860. The first nineteenth-century edition came out in 1803 (and not 1801 as indicated by Sopikov *Opyt rossiiskoi bibliografii*, see no 8714; or 1802 as noted by Gennadi *Spravochnyi slovar' o russkikh*, see vol 1:24). Moreover, Efim Liutsenko in the introduction to his translation of *Paradise Lost* and *Paradise Regained* in 1824, also refers to this non-existent edition of 1801: see *Poteriannyi rai poema Ioanna Mil'tona s priobshcheniem poemy Vozvrashchennyi rai* ... (St Petersburg: V Tipografii N. Grecha 1824) vii.
48 Parker *Milton* vol 2:1200, ie '*Paradise Lost* was translated from French into Russian by Ivan Greshischev in 1778.' There is no mention of Stroganov's, Petrov's, or Amvrosii's translations. Parker's error is reiterated by Gillet, Tisch, and others.
49 Pierre de Mareuil 'Le Paradis reconquis, et quelques autres ouvrages de Milton, traduit de l'anglais' (Paris 1730) preface ix, as quoted by Gillet *Le Paradis perdu dans la littérature française* 144
50 Ibid xiii
51 Ibid xiv
52 Ibid vi
53 Novikov *Opyt istoricheskago slovaria* 48
54 This too was the criticism made by Nikolaevan censors in banning both epics: see ch 3 in *Popular Culture*.
55 Ellwood *History of the Life of Thomas Ellwood* 233. But Ellwood's story is doubted by, among others, Tillyard: see n56 below.
56 Tillyard *Milton* 336
57 Warner *John Milton* 83
58 Coleridge in appendix to *Lectures and Notes on Shakspere* 527. This passage is not included in Wittreich's recent compendium, *The Romantics on Milton*, which contains an anthology of Coleridge's comments on Milton.

59 Chateaubriand in *Essai sur la littérature anglaise* (ed Desbarres 1863) 167, as quoted by Telleen *Milton dans la littérature française* 131
60 Hill *Milton and the English Revolution* 389. The author's comparison rests on some lines in Book III, where Christ expects to be tried by

> things adverse
> By tribulations, injuries, insults,
> Contempts and scorns, and snares, and violence,
> Suffering, abstaining, quietly expecting
> Without distrust or doubt. (*PR* III. ll 189–93).

61 See Praz 'Milton et Poussin' 200–1.
62 Pierre de Mareuil '*Le Paradis reconquis*, traduit de l'anglois de Milton ... avec six lettres critiques sur le Paradis perdu et reconquis' (Paris: Chez Garneau 1749) 2. (This is the edition Ivan Greshishchev is most likely to have used.)
63 Greshishchev *Vozvrashchennyi rai* (Moscow 1778) 6
64 See Efim Liutsenko's comments in the preface to *Poteriannyi rai poema Ioanna Mil'tona s priobshcheniem poemy Vozvrashchennyi rai ...* (St Petersburg: N. Grecha 1824) xi–xii.
65 Liutsenko was also working from a French translation of both poems: see ch 5 in *Prophet*.
66 The actual origin of the translation is not indicated, but a note at the end reveals that it was made 'from the French'; see 'Il Penseroso, ili Mysli Mil'tonovy' *Sanktpeterburgskii vestnik* 6:124.
67 The latest of these that Beketov is likely to have used is the edition of 1765 in four volumes in octavo: '*Le Paradis perdu de Milton*, Poëme Héroïque, traduit de l'anglois; Avec le Remarques de M. Addisson [*sic*]. Nouvelle Edition, revue & corrigée. A Paris. Chez Nyon, Quai des Augustins, à l'Occasion.' The third volume also contains *Le Paradis reconquis* in the translation by Pierre de Mareuil (although his name is nowhere mentioned), followed by translations of 'Lycidas' (199–210), 'L'Allegro' (211–17), 'Il Penseroso' (218–26), and 'On the Morning of Christ's Nativity' (227–31). The fourth volume contains Pierre de Mareuil's 'Six Lettres Critiques' (1–218) and the 'Remarques' culled from Addison's *Spectator* (221–375).
68 This is discussed in *Imaginary Conversations: Southey and Landor* (1846) as quoted by Joseph Anthony Wittreich 338, where Landor cites Marsand, an editor of Petrarch, who used both 'pensiero' and 'pensero.' See '*L'Allegro et le Pensieroso de Milton*. Traduits en vers François. (A Londres: Chez Messrs Becket & de Hondt, Dans le Strand 1766) preface vii. (Ribouville's name does not appear on the title-page.)
69 In his introduction the French poet accounts for the omissions of his version,

among the most striking being the passage at the outset invoking the Goddess Melancholy:
> Whose saintly visage is too bright
> To hit the sense of human sight;
> And therefore in our weaker view,
> O'erlaid with black staid Wisdom's hue.
> Black, but such as in esteem
> Prince Memnon's sister might beseem,
> Or that starred Ethiop queen that strove
> To set her beauty's praise above
> The sea-nymphs ... ('Il Penseroso' ll 13–22)

These lines Ribouville disliked, and he describes Milton's comparison 'du sombre de la mélancolie, au teint d'une Ethiopienne' as 'feeble and puerile.' He makes a second notable omission beginning with l 109 where the English poet refers indirectly to Chaucer:
> Or call him that left half-told
> The story of Cambuscan bold
> Of Camball, and of Algarsife,
> And who had Canace to wife,
> That owned the virtuous ring and glass,
> And of the wondrous horse of brass,
> On which the Tartar king did ride; (ll 99–116)

This excision is justified in the following words: 'J'ai cru pouvoir aussi supprimer les noms de *Cambuscan le hardi, d'Algarsife* & autres Héros chantés par *Chaucer* Poéte célébre [sic], mais inconnu en France, & que peu d'Anglois entendent aujourd'hui, a cause de la vétusté de son langage, & je l'ai fait d'autant plus hardiment que cela n'otoit rien de la pensée de mon Auteur.' But perhaps the real reason Ribouville omitted the Chaucerian lines is that he found them too hard to render in verse. Is it a coincidence that Pierre de Mareuil in his earlier translation also omits this passage? But the latter's prose translation had less excuse for taking such barbarous liberties (to which he also gave vent in the other passage on the Goddess Melancholy). This explains why both sections suffer a similar fate in the Russian translation.

70 See Beketov 'Il Penseroso ili mysli Miltonovy' 120; *L'Allegro et le Penseroso de Milton* 30. The Russian translation should not be compared with the original without looking first at the French text from which it was taken: '(Il ne me reste plus, chère Déesse, que deux choses à te demander;) c'est de pouvoir fréquenter les cabinets des curieux; d'aller, de tems à autre, considérer ces temples augustes, dont les voûtes semblent monter aux nues, dont les piliers massifs prouvent l'antiquité, dont les vitrages précieux n'admettent

qu'une lumière sombre, qui, par-là, inspirent une religieuse horreur; vitrages dont les peintures son comme autant de fastes des siècles passés, & le précis des annales du vieux tems. Ah! mon âme est ravie en extase toutes les fois que j'y entends cet harmonieux mélange de voix & d'instrumens de musique, qui portent aux Cieux les hommages des humains' (*Le Paradis perdu* vol 3:225–6). Is Ribouville's verse rendering really closer to the spirit of the original?

> Mais, surtout pensive Déesse!
> Fais que mes pas cherchent toujours
> Des cloitres les tristes entours
> Séjours de la sainte Sagesse;
> Pleins d'un zéle respectueux
> Qu'ils pénétrent souvent sous ses voutes antiques,
> Monumens sacrés, magnifiques
> De la pieté de nos ayeux!
> Que j'aime ces vastes enceintes
> Où l'astre brillant des cieux
> Verse à-travers des vitres peintes
> Un jour sombre & religieux!
> Et la que du plain chœur les chants mélodieux
> Et l'Orgue majestueux
> Par leur divine harmonie,
> Fassent a mon âme ravie
> Gouter les plaisirs des cieux!

This passage is not in the Russian translation, and Beketov also leaves out the allusion to Spenser that follows the Chaucerian lines:

> And if aught else, great bards beside,
> In sage and solemn tunes have sung,
> Of tourneys and of trophies hung;
> Of forests, and enchantments drear,
> Where more is meant than meets the ear ... ('Il Penseroso' ll 116–20)

This passage is not omitted by Mareuil, but the Russian version resumes again only with the unforgettable lines near the poem's conclusion:

> But let my due feet never fail,
> To walk the studious cloister's pale,
> And love the high embowed roof,
> With antique pillars' massy proof,
> And storied windows richly dight,
> Casting a dim religious light.
> There let the pealing organ blow,
> To the full-voiced choir below,

In service high and anthems clear,
As may with sweetness, through mine ear,
Dissolve me into ecstasies,
And bring all Heaven before mine eyes. (ll 155–66)
71 In Sichkavev *Zritel' mira i deianii chelovecheskikh* 103

4 MASONIC DEVILS AND THE LIGHT WITHIN

1 I go by the watermark of the manuscript, which bears no date: see ORGPB *Sobranie Andreia Alesandrovicha Titova,* no 265. Titov was a nineteenth-century Rostov bibliophile, which would suggest a provincial provenance for this copy. One of its early owners – to judge by the unskilful signature – was 'Ekaterina vikhtorovna [*sic*] Davydova,' of whom nothing has come down to us.
2 Ibid 142
3 Ibid
4 Ibid 143
5 Ibid 143v. The moral intruction, entitled 'Teologicheskoe nravouchenie razsuzhdenie o Adamii padenii,' begins on page 142 and ends on page 152. It is not in the same hand as the transcription of the Stroganov-Milton, but is on the same paper and is bound together with *Pogublennyi rai*.
6 Semeka 'Russkoe masonstvo' 139. Elagin's role is thus misconstrued, for instance, in Billington's *Icon and the Axe* 246–7, in which the importance of the Masonic movement, however, is rightly stressed. In eighteenth-century Russia it represents the first intellectual manifestation with socio-political overtones.
7 Elagin 'Zapiski Elagina' 597, as quoted by Semeka 'Russkoe masonstvo' 139–40
8 See Longinov *Novikov i moskovskie martinisty*. In the more recent Soviet studies of Novikov by Makogonenko (*Nikolai Novikov*) and Malyshev (*N.I. Novikov*), Novikov's Masonic interests and activities are neglected.
9 Longinov *Novikov i muskovskie martinisty* 126ff. As Novikov put it rather touchingly: 'Odnazhdy, prishel ko mne Nemchik, s kotorym ia, pogovoria, sdelalsia vsiu zhizn' do samoi ego smerti nerazluchnym.' See also Tukalevskii 'N.I. Novikov i I.G. Shwarts' 175–226.
10 Barskov *Perepiska moskovskikh masonov,* xvii, and ch 8 in Pypin *Russkoe masonstvo*
11 Anon '*Istinnyi svet poema v deviati pesniakh,* sochinennaia na rossiiskom iazyke. Pechatana v universitetskoi tipografii u N.I. Novikova (1780 goda)' 9:148–9. 'True light' is not an entirely satisfactory translation of the title, since 'istinnyi' has a more spiritual connotation than 'true.'

12 Ibid 48
13 Semennikov *Knigoizdatel'skaia deiatel'nost' N.I. Novikova v tipograficheskoi kompanii* 29
14 G.P. Makogonenko, the outstanding Soviet specialist on Novikov and his circle, was not familiar with the poem when I discussed its origins with him in Leningrad, but he is surely right in suggesting that it could only have been written by a poet of considerable education, someone no doubt connected with Moscow University. There is no literature on the work: I cite the copy to be found in the Rare Book House (Dom Redkikh Knig) of the Lenin Library.
15 Novikov *Istinnyi svet* 3:56–8
16 Ie Francesco Algarotti; on Algarotti and his activities as a popularizer of science in St Petersburg, see my *Newton and Russia*, 124–6.
17 On the poet's views on astronomy, see Kester Svendsen *Milton and Science*, and McColley 'The Astronomy of *Paradise Lost*' *Studies in Philology* 34 (1937) 209–47. There are also illuminating comments on the subject in Camé *Les structures fondamentales de l'univers imaginaire miltonien*.
18 Satan's lines about earth in Book IX, ll 104–7, seem to endorse the geocentric view, but even there Milton leaves the heliocentric option open. On Newtonian additions to this by Kantemir see ch 2 in *Prophet*.
19 In *Paradise Lost* Milton was ambivalent about the heliocentric system as he was about its corollary: the infinity of the universe. Philosophically he denied it, but 'aesthetically Milton was as responsive as Henry More to the vastness of a universe in which Infinite God was reflected in Infinite Space.' See Nicolson *Mountain Gloom and the Mountain Glory* 274.
20 Zemnyi ne mozhet um nash' kogda postignut',
   Gde kroetsia sei punkt, soboi chto mozhet dvignut',
   Razrushat' estestvo, i sferu vsiu potriast' [.]
   Raztorgnuv krasotu, vo smed' obratno spast'. (*Istinnyi svet* 3:ll 569–72 p 57)
21 The *Opyt o cheloveke* in N.N. Popovskii's translation was first published in 1757 and reprinted in 1763 (as well as 1787 and 1791): see SK nos 5494–7. On the scandal surrounding it, see Raikov *Ocherki po istorii geliotsentricheskogo mirovozzreniia v Rossii* 285–94.
22 In the sense that in *Micromégas* we have the first visit by an alien to our world; see Kingsley Amis *Maps of Hell* 29.
23 Amvrosii's translation of Dupré-Milton soon superseded it, but see notes 6 and 7 to the Introduction above.
24 Riazanovskii *Demonologiia v drevne-russkoi literature* 125–6
25 See (in its non-Russian context) Mueller *Die Gestalt Lucifers*. Mueller also devotes a chapter to Klopstock's variant of Milton's Satan.

26 Ie 'Messiia poema, sochinennaia g. Klopshtokom. Perevod s nemetskago Alekseia Kutuzova.' See SK no 2938. The translation is, of course, in prose. Kutuzov knew both Karamzin and Radishchev.
27 Quoted by Tisch 'Irregular Genius' 307
28 Franz Mehring 'Friedrich Gottlieb Klopstock' in Gesammelte Schriften vol 10:3–7. Mehring wrote this characteristic essay in 1903. Later he was even harsher towards Klopstock, denying the author of the Messias, which ultimately comprised more than 20,000 verses, 'jede Spur ... epischer Begabung.' And he goes on to say that the poet 'hat es schwer genug büssen müssen, dass er dem Rat der Bodmer und Breitinger gefolgt war und sein Leben an eine Schulaufgabe, an ein religioses Epos gesetzt hatte ...' See 'Deutsche Geschichte vom Ausgange des Mittelalters' in Gesammelte Schriften vol 5:62–3.
29   Vladeiia vsem on im, na goru uzhe voskhodit,
   I deistvom chudnym tam zhelan'e proizvodit,
   Imeia polnu vlast' nad tsarstvami zemli,
   Izvodit on pred vzor sokryty chto vo tli
   Glazam predstavia vse poriadkom to tekushchim,
   Vo svete sem' veshchei nachalom prisnosushchim.
      Sei chudnyi uzh vostal v Egipte Labirint,
   Derzhava vsekh tsarei krasu ego khranit.
   Kolosy divnye i slovny Piramidy,
   Ne vidny berega uzh ozera Meridy.
   Nauki iz tekli [sic], nachalo vospriiav',
   Zakony mudrye otpol' priiav ustav.
   Tam vidom Vavilon Atlantu ves' podoben.
   Mogushchii on tsvetet, i krasotoi ispolnen,
   Sto glav chto podnial vdrug vratami okruzhas',
   Uzh gordo tol' v nem tsar', bezumno voznosias',
   Statui stavia vid on gordostiiu smelo
   Tak khitrostiiu ruk, chto izvaianno delo,
   V Dierne pole sei zlatyi uzhe istukan,
   Pochten narodom vsem nechuvstvennyi bolvan.
   Verkhi zlaty blestiat, palaty ukrashaia,
   Sady zelenye grazhdan uveseliaia ...(ll 332–54)
30 For a recent edition of Der Messias see Klopstock Ausgewählte Werke. See also Dilthey Milton und Klopstock 122–8; and Murat Klopstock, Les Thèmes principaux
31 John Pordage, who was a contemporary of Milton and deeply influenced by Boehme, is not to be confused with his son, Samuel Pordage, who in 1661 published a long poem whose theme has affinities with Pilgrim's Progress and

Paradise Lost. John Pordage's *Metaphysica vera et divina*, the best known of his mystical writings, was translated into Russian from the German edition in 1786. On this, see Sakulin, *Iz istorii russkogo idealizma Kniaz' V.F. Odoevskii* 422–3. It is not clear to what extent Prince Odoevsky was familiar with Milton, but through German translation he became acquainted with English mystical writers of the seventeenth century who had themselves been exposed to the influence of Boehme and his German disciples. See also Bailey *Milton and Jakob Boehme*.

32 Eg, 'Vselennaia' in *Tvoveniia M. Khevaskova* 3:90:
   Kak raia ot chuzhden, kak pal nash praotets,
   V zlatykh stikhakh vospel Britanskii nash pevets.
   V voztorgakh liru ia Miltonovu lobzaiu!
   No sledovat' emu v sikh pesniakh ne derzaiu.
The edition cited here is aptly described by Longinov as 'scandalous' since it excludes more than a quarter of Kheraskov's writings; but unfortunately, the Soviet edition is even more exclusive. See Sukhomlinov *Istoriia rossisskoi akademii* 509–10.

33 Gukovskii (ed) *Poety XVIII veka* 12ff

34 Tukalevskii 'N.I. Novikov, I.G. Shwarts' 209

35 See, for instance, Hill's discussion of this in *Milton and the English Revolution*, which compares the Milton of *Paradise Regained* to Lenin in 1905 – 'lest we should think of Milton's lines too passively' 389. Earlier Marxist critics, such as Christopher Caudwell, on the other hand, see the poem as 'defeatist' and lacking 'the noble defiance' of *Paradise Lost*. See Caudwell *Illusion and Reality* 82–3.

36 See the servility of this couplet in Kheraskov *Piligrimy, ili iskateli shchastiia*: 'Tsariam sovetov ne daiu, / Tsaria menia umnei, ia slavu ikh poiu' (p 5). Kheraskov's panegyrical odes are almost as unctuous as those of Petrov, although this was typical of the period.

37 Ibid 4:101. But Kheraskov makes fun of Rousseau earlier in the poem (p 5) for saying: 'je n'aime pas le vieillard avec une plume.' Yet when Rousseau wrote this 'emu bylo ot rodu 60 let!'

38 Ibid:
   Moi Pansof mudrogo Sokrata preziral,
   Gomera bakharem v Il'iade nazyval;
   On Lokka ne liubil, prenebregal Nevtonom
   Rugalsia Tassom on, i Iungom, i Mil'tonom.
   Kazalis' Kant emu i Viland bez uma;
   U Lomonosova kazalas' v odakh t'ma;
   Emu kazal'sia plokh vo pritchakh Sumarokov ...(p 126)

39 Ibid: 'Ko liubopytstvu byt' ne sleduet pristrastnym' (p 20)
40 Mirsky *A History of Russian Literature* 48
41 Ie *Vladimir vozrozhdennyi*, which was published six years after the *Rossiade* in 1785, but did not enjoy the same success
42 Kheraskov 'Vzgliad na epicheskie poemy' 281
43 Kheraskov 'Vselennaia' in *Tvoreniia* 3:np preface
44 Nicolson *The Breaking of the Circle* 172–4
45 'Vselennaia' in *Tvoreniia* 92
46 Lewis *Preface to Paradise Lost* 97–8. Lewis ridicules Satan's argument on logical grounds, but is it not possible that by putting these words in Satan's mouth, he was merely inverting the idea he himself held, ie, that God created the universe out of himself? This notion, that God drew on the prime matter of Chaos, and that therefore matter was good, is also associated with Samuel Pordage, and others who thought they understood Boehme.
47 'Vselennaia' in *Tvoreniia* 91
48 See ch 7 below.

5 SATAN, PUGACHEV, AND THE FRENCH REVOLUTION

1 Newton's *Principia* was known in Peter the Great's entourage as early as 1698, but public awareness of its philosophical implications came only much later: see my *Newton and Russia* Part II.
2 See Teplova ' "Vestnik Evropy" Karamzina o velikoi frantsuzskoi revoliutsii i formakh pravleniia,' in Berkov, Makogonenko, Serman (eds) *XVIII Vek. Sbornik 8* 269–73ff.
3 Kheraskov 'Vselennaia in *Tvoraniia* 48 etc.
4 Ibid 55
5 Ibid 48
6 Ibid 55
7 See Derzhavin 'Kliuch' in *Sochineniia Derzhavina* vol 1:80.
8 The celebrated ode to God ('Ty byl, Ty est', Ty budesh' vvek') was partly lifted from Klopstock's *Der Erbarmer* ('Du warest, du bist, wirst sein!'); see Derzhavin 'Bog' in *Sochineniia Derzhovina* 197.
9 See Ivanov 'Derzhavin i Novikov' in Makogonenko (ed) *XVIII Vek. Sbornik 11* 78ff.
10 See Derzhavin's letter to P.S. Potemkin of 2 Aug. 1774, in *Sochineniia Derzhavina* vol 5:155–6, in which the poet uses the same noun to describe Pugachev ('zlodei') that had been used to describe Cromwell.
11 See Tiander's revealing tribute, 'Dzhon Mil'ton' 13–26.
12 Derzhavin 'Na kovarstvo frantsuzskago vozmushcheniia i v chest' kniazia Pozharskago' in *Sochineniia Derzhavina* vol 5:317

13 Ibid
14 Ibid
15 Ibid: Predosmotria svoiu vygodu,
   I sdelat' nuzhnym chtob obia,
   Nevinnost', ravenstvo, svobodu,
   Pokoi i schast'e istrebia ...(p 318)
16 Derzhavin's explanatory note to l 3 of the stanza above, ibid p 318
17 Radishchev 'Angel T'my' 389
18 Ibid where Zapadov takes the following passages in *Paradise Lost*:

>   ... But his doom
>   Reserved him to more wrath; for now the thought
>   Both of lost happiness and lasting pain
>   Torments him; round he throws his baleful eyes,
>   That witnessed huge affliction and dismay
>   Mixed with obdurate pride and steadfast hate. (I. ll 53-8)

And

>   As when a spark
>   Lights on a heap of nitrous powder, laid
>   Fit for the tun some magazine to store
>   Against a rumored war, the smutty grain
>   With sudden blaze diffused, inflames the air;
>   So started up in his own shape the Fiend. (IV. ll 814-19)

which he compares to the following lines in 'Angel T'my' (the title being either suggested by 'apostate Angel' in l 125 or by Amvrosii's rendering of Dupré's translation of 'Fiend,' ie 'angel t'my'): 'Razvesistye brovi zakryvaiut sverkaiushchie ochi, na koikh obitaet lest', neistovstvo, obman, isstuplenie, lzhesmekhi, kovarstvo i iarost'; izrygaiushchie, edva veshchaet, lozh', smert' i prokliatie; ezhe zazhaty zhitel' vsegdashniia noshchi i otets prizrakov, terzaemyi bessonitseiu vechnoiu, edva vozmogaet otvykshie ot sveta razverzsti vezhdy ...' And 'No iako strela, moshchnoiu drevnego Parfianina rukoiu na luke zaderzhannaia, mgnovenno izletaet, parit po vozdushnoi doline, edva okom v polete presleduemaia, ili pache, iako zakliuchennyi v mednoe zherlo sharovidnoi chugun vnezapno gromozhdaiushchim gromovym treskom i blistaniem molnii soputstvuemyi, svistit, nesetsia, vizzhit, rassekaet vikhriashchiisia vozdukh okrest ego, uskol'zaia ot presleduiushchego emu oka; i edva voobrazit' vozmozhem, on mety uzhe dostig' (II. pp 167-8).

These lines Zapadov then compares to the following lines in Amvrosii's translation: 'Iarost' nebesnaia ostavila emu besmertie dlia viashchshshego vozdaianiia ego prestupleniem. Prishel v sebia i uzhasom ob'iat stal. Proshedshee ego terzaet, budushchee v otchaianie privodit. Oziraetsia povsiudu plamennymi ochami. V mrachnykh ego vzorakh vidimy pechal', smushchenie, gordost', nenavist'. Pronitsaiushchee ego zrenie, podobnu tomu, kakoe imeiut angely, vdrug ob'emlet vse mesto onoe, prokliatoe, uzhasnoe i prestrashnoe' (p 3). And 'Kak kogda iskra padaet na mnozhestvo selitry i porokhu, ugotovennoe dlia sobliudeniia i khranilische, onym napolniaemo, po ikhu nastupaiushchiia voiny; vdrug chernyi sostav vzryvaet, bleshchet i vosplameniaet vozdukh; tako zlobnyi dukh vosstal s iarost'iu i pokazalsia sushchim angelom t'my' (p 143; the references are to the 1785 edition of the Russian translation). Indeed, even when Radishchev's opening is compared directly with Book 1 of *Paradise Lost*, where Satan is found lying 'thunderstruck' on the burning lake, the thematic congruence is obvious. Thus, the Russian text opens with 'se drevni vozmutitel' nebesnykh sil' arousing himself to the use of his 'ogromnoe chelo ... dosiazaiushchie zybiami svoimi do dna moria pri napriazhenii buri i vikhria ...' Milton also has Satan 'rolling in the fiery gulf' and 'o'erwhelmed / With floods and whirlwind of tempestuous fire ...' (ll 76–7). The Russian 'vikhri' was used by Kantemir as an equivalent for Cartesian vortices. If Radishchev had the English poem before him, 'buri i vikhri' would have been a vivid rendering of 'whirlwinds and tempestuous fire.' But it is not necessary to assume that Radishchev was concerned with verbal equivalence. If his opening sentence is read side by side with Milton's description of Satan –

> With head uplift above the wave, and eyes
> That sparkling blazed; his other parts besides,
> Prone on the flood, extended long and large,
> Lay floating many a rood, in bulk as huge
> As whom the fables name of monstrous size,
> . . . .
> Created hugest that swim the ocean stream: (1. ll 193–7, 202)

– then the source of Radishchev's powerful image is surely apparent: 'I se drevnii vozmutitel' nebesnykh sil pod'emlet iz mrachnogo svoego obitaniia ogromnoe svoe chelo, izluchistymi morshchinami prepoisannoe, no iako volny obshirnogo Okeana, to dosiazaiushchie zybiami svoimi do dna moria pri napriazhenii buri i vikhria, to izglazhaiushchiesia pri otishii i zertsalovidnye' (p 168).

19 Eg Lang *The First Russian Radical*, and McConnell *A Russian Philosophe*
20 The painting of Pugachev and the Devil shown in Figure 9 was completed some time in the mid-1790s by a serf artist on the estate of Prince P.I. Panin, who was largely responsible for crushing the rebellion. It hangs in the Historical Museum in Moscow, from which the reproduction here is taken. Soviet specialists on eighteenth-century painting consulted by the author (at the Istoricheskii Muzei in Moscow, and at the Russian Museum and the Hermitage in Leningrad) were not able to recall an earlier appearance of the Devil in *secular* realistic Russian portraiture.

21 As well as some concluding verses from *The Seasons* by Thomson: see Rothe *N.M. Karamzin's europäische Reise* 54–5.
22 Although 'Poeziia' was published in 1792, there is some doubt about the actual year of composition, 1787 being the year indicated by the poet. The epigraph to the poem (see Karamzin *Izbrannye sochineniia* vol 2:7) is taken, interestingly enough, from Klopstock: 'Die lieder der göttlichen Harfenspieler schallen mit Macht, wie beseelend.' It is quite possible that he read Klopstock before turning to Milton, but the Miltonic strain in some of his early verse is unmistakable – and unmistakably bad. There are also biblical references in 'Poeziia.' Karamzin's translation of Klopstock has not survived: see Rothe *Karamzin's europäische. Reise* 49.
23 See ch 1 in *Prophet*.
24 Karamzin *Izbrannye sochineniia* vol 2:7
25 Ibid 11
26 I cite the translation in Kochetkova *Nikolay Karamzin* 26.
27 See R.D. Keil 'Ergänzungen zu russischen Dichter-Kommentaren (Lomonosov und Karamzin)' 380–3, and the review by Cross of N.M. Karamzin *Polnoe sobranie stikhotvorenii* in *Slavonic and East European Review* 45:105 (1967) 547.
28 I cite the Russian edition of the *Letters* in Karamzin *Izbrannye sochineniia* vol 1:525.
29 Karamzin *Tvorenie, Sochinenie Gaidna*. Slova perevedeny s nemetskogo Karamzinym (Moscow: Universitetskaia tipografiia u Khristofora Klaudiia 1801)
30 Ie *'Sotvorenie mira. Oratoriia. Muzyka U. Gaidna* (Moscow: tipografiia F. Drekslera 1811); there was another translation in 1888, entitled *Mirozdanie* and published in St Petersburg.
31 See 'Tvorenie mira' in Radishchev *Polnoe sobranie sochinenii* vol 1 (1938) 18–21. The dramatis personae consist of God, a chorus, and parts thereof. Originally Radishchev's 'Creation of the World' was included in drafts of the *Journey* (on which see below), but it was then left out of the published version – probably for fear of offending the censors: see ibid vol 1:448.
32 Babkin (ed) *Biografiia A.N. Radishcheva napisannaia ego synov'iami* 51
33 Semennikov *Radishchev ocherki i issledovaniia* 17–18
34 Catherine's notes to the *Journey* have been translated in their entirety by Leo Wiener as an addendum to his translation of this work cited below, 36. Oliver Cromwell is also mentioned in the 'Zhitie F.V. Ushakova' which is included in the *Polnoe sobranie sochinenii*.
35   Velikii muzh, kovarstva polnyi,
     Khanzha i l'stets i sviatotat',
     Odin ty'v mire sei blagotvornyi
     Primer velikii mog podat'.

212 Notes to pages 77–83

    Ia chtu, Kromvel', v tebe zlodeia,
    Chto vlast' v ruki svoei imeia,
    Ty tverd' svobody sokrushil;
    No nauchil ty v rod i rody,
    Kak mogut mstit' sebe narody:
    Ty Karla na sud kaznil.
36 Radishchev *Journey* 67
37 Ibid 71
38 Eg 'Na kovarstvo frantsuzskogo vozmushcheniia ...' *Sochineniia Derzhavina* vol 1:320:
    Razstrigi, Kromveli, Nadiry
    Vel'mozhi zlye i tsari
    Dlia khval zvoikh imeiut liry
    Dlia obozhan'ia altari ...
Later in the poem Derzhavin makes an equally uninformed attack on Mirabeau and Lafayette:
    Pust' Katiliny, Bedemery
    I Mirabo i Lafaiet,
    Gotovia skrytye udary,
    Kramolami kolebliut svet ... (*Sochinenii Derzxhavin* 331)
39 See 'Empress Catherine's Notes' in *Journey* 249.

6 THE DEMONIC TRADITION FROM ZHUKOVSKY TO PUSHKIN

1 Pushkin *Polnoe sobranie sochinenii v desiati tomakh* vol 1:60. In *Evgenii Onegin* Pushkin refers to 'northern poems' ('Chital, zabyvshis', mezhdu tem, / Otryvki severnykh poem)' which Yu. Tynianov thinks is an allusion to the epics he read at Tsarskoe Selo, as did Kiukhel'beker, his school friend; see Tynianov's *Pushkin i ego sovremenniki* 282–3.
2 As quoted by Gillel'son in *P.A. Viazemskii – zhizn' i tvorchestvo* 105–6. Gillel'son, whose interesting study is based in part on the Ostaf'evo papers of the family, refers to the inventory of books in A.I. Viazemskii's library (dating from 1780), which includes Milton among its authors, together with D'Alembert, Helvétius, Voltaire, Diderot, Fénelon, Lafontaine, La Rochefoucauld, Boileau, Scarron, Crébillon, Marmontel, and J.-J. Rousseau, but only a scattering of English writers (ibid 10). By the end of the Romantic period, very few of these authors were still being read in Russia, Milton being one obvious exception. Shakespeare's flowering in Russia only really starts with the Romantics.
3 See the comment in *Novosti* 2 (June 1789) 129–47: 'V Anglii zabyli Mil'tona

i vo Frantsii chitali Vol'tera. No my rodimsia tak pozdno, chto i o Mil'tonakh i Vol'terakh nachinaem vspominat', kak uzhe o drevnikh.' This was no doubt taken from a French source.

4 The dissertation, entitled in the Russian translation: 'O proiskhozhdenii, prirode i sud'bakh poezii, nazyvaemoi romanticheskoi,' is now included in the volume of Nadezhdin's literary criticism, Nadezhdin *Literaturnaia kritika estetika*, expertly edited by Yurii Mann.
5 Shevyrev *Istoriia poezii* 63
6 Shevyrev 'Pervyi vecher po izgnanii iz raia,' which was published in the works of the *Obshchestvo liubitelei Rossiiskoi slovesnosti* as *Sochineniia v proze i stikhakh* vol 7 (Moscow: Universitetskaia tipografiia 1828) 151–4. The poem was directly inspired by Book XII of *Paradise Lost*. It was republished in *Atenei* the same year; and again in *Literatura pribaltiki* 34 (1833). It may also be found in Shevyrev's *Stikhotvoreniia*, which includes an essay on his verse by M. Aronson.
7 Shevyrev *Istoriia poezii* 64
8 Shevyrev 'Teoriia poezii.' Here Shevyrev arrives at this curious assessment of Johnson's *Life* of Milton: 'Ne smotria na to, chto on, vernyi torizmu, nemilserdo [sic] presleduet Mil'tona za ego politicheskiia mneniia, on umeet otdat' spravedlivost' emu, kak Poetu' (205).
9 'O proiskhozhdenii ... poezii, nazyvaemoi romanticheskoi' in Nadezhdin *Literaturnaia kritika* 240
10 Ibid
11 Ibid. The variations between the *Vestnik Evropy* version and the original dissertation are noted by Mann.
12 Ibid 241
13 *Vestnik Evropy* 11 (June 1829) 260. Interestingly, the comment is taken from a review of Chateaubriand's *History of English Literature* (which is discussed in the next section) in the *Mercure du XIX siècle*.
14 'Idéologue' in *Vestnik Evropy* 11 (June 1829) 260
15 'O sushchestve angliiskoi literatury XIX-go stoletiia' *Vestnik Evropy* 13 (July 1829) 17. The article (a continuation of the earlier item noted in n 13) does not indicate which Montgomery is meant; presumably, Robert Montgomery, the natural son of a professional clown and a schoolmistress, who (says Havens) 'shot like a comet across the heaven of popular favor.' He is the author of several poems influenced by Milton, including *Satan, or Intellect without God* (1830, 10th ed 1842) and *The Messiah* (1830, 8th ed 1842). The latter was torn to shreds by Macaulay, but neither of the works had appeared at the time of the French review. H.H. Milman, another imitator of Milton, was praised by Southey for his *Samor, Lord of the Bright City* (1818), but is better

remembered today as Gibbon's editor and historian of Latin Christianity and the Jews. Henry Kirke White, praised even more highly by Southey, is dismissed by Havens as a 'pathetic, overrated consumptive' who imitated the 'Allegro-Penseroso' form; Havens *Influence of Milton on English Poetry* 472.

16 *Vestnik Evropy* 13 (July 1829), 20
17 Kiukhel'beker *Polnoe sobranie stikhotvorenii* vol 3:38
18 Ibid n 4 to 'Vechnyi Zhid' 37–8
19 Kiukhel'beker 'Literaturno-kriticheskie stat'i' in *Puteshestvie, dnevnik, stat'i* 467. Kiukhel'beker's assessment of Byron, at one time rather low, changed after the latter's death.
20 Glinka (1786–1880) presided over the *Obshchestvo liubitelei rossiiskoi slovesnosti* from 1819 until his arrest in 1825, in which capacity he would certainly have become acquainted with Milton's epics. He belonged to the more moderate wing of the Decembrist movement, and after being exiled to Petrozavodsk (until 1830), he lived in Tver', Moscow, and St Petersburg. In the 1830s he sympathized with the Slavophiles, collaborating with M.P. Pogodin and S.P. Shevyrev on the *Moskvitianin*. He is perhaps best remembered for his *Stikhi* (1839) and *Iov* (1859), which, like *Paradise Regained*, owed much to an epic tradition inspired by the Jobean model. See Shavrov *Iov i druz'ia ego*. See also Kostin 'Dekabrist Gedor Nikolaevich Glinka' unpublished diss (Saratov 1972). Glinka's selected verse has been brought out in the Soviet period in the 'Biblioteka poeta' series in 1961. V. Bazanov in his interesting chapter on Glinka in *Ocherki Dekabristskoi literatury* 139–64, suggests that some of the poet's religious verse has much in common with Sergei Murav'ev-Apostol's 'Orthodox catechism.'
21 See Tynianov *Pushkin i ego sovremenniki* 282. Tynianov suggests that Kiukhel'beker read Milton in a manual used at the *lycée*.
22 Kiukhel'beker *Polnoe sobranie stikhotvorenii* vol 3:26–7
23 See the entry for 29 Mar 1834 in Kiukhel'beker's *Dnevnik* in ibid 299–302.
24 Bestuzhev-Marlinskii 'O romane N. Polevogo ...' in *Sochineniia v dvukh tomakh* vol 2:581 (the article was first published in *Moskovskii Telegraf* [1833] under a pseudonym). Polevoi's novel *Abbadona* was published in Moscow in 1834.
25 See 'Poety' in Kiukhel'beker *Izbrannye proizvedeniia v dvukh tomakh* vol 1:128–33, especially ll 18–33.
26 See Christopher Hill's interesting comment on this with reference to *Samson Agonistes* in *Milton and the English Revolution* 489.
27 Ie 'Gavriliada' in Pushkin *pss* vol 4:149:
Ne trepetal ot vashikh ia pridvornykh,
Vsevyshnego prisluzhnikov pokornykh,

Ot svodnikov nebesnogo tsaria!

The poem has recently been translated in a fresh and forthright manner by D.M. Thomas, and it is his words I cite in translation here: see Pushkin *The Bronze Horseman*. 'Nadmennyi chlen' is not, of course, the same as 'puffed-up member,' but 'haughty' here would not do either, so Thomas does catch a part of Pushkin's *double-entendre*.

28 As noted in Ianushevich 'V.A. Zhukovskii' 481–91
29 Ibid 483. On Pushkin and Chateaubriand see ch 6 in *Prophet*.
30 The London edition of 1803. The German translation was by S.G. Bürde: see Ianushevich, 'V.A. Zhukovskii' 483.
31 Voltaire first brought out the *Essay* in an English edition while he was in London. On Kantemir's familiarity with it and the polemic it aroused between the author and Paolo Rolli, see ch 2 in *Prophet*.
32 A French edition first became available in St Petersburg in 1739; Dashkova's translation, published in the journal *Nevinnoe uprazhnenie* in 1763, was followed by other translations, including the one that was published as a book in 1781.
33 The extract from Blair (as copied out and translated into Russian by Zhukovsky) is quoted by Ianushevich 'V.A. Zhukovskii' 482
34 Thus, in the *konspekt* Zhukovsky made up of 'the best books' for his own edification that year, a whole section is devoted to this poem: ibid 481.
35 This was the prelude to Zhukovsky's growing interest in epic poetry: see Ianushevich's other brief article in the same volume, 'Obraztsy epicheskoi poezii v chtenii i osmyslenii V. A. Zhukovskogo' 479–81. Later the Russian poet would extend this interest to non-European heroic verse. Thus, during the 1830s and 1840s he completed his translations of epics and episodes 'Nal and Damayanti' from the *Mahabharata* and 'Rustam and Zorab' from Firdausi's *Shah-Name*.
36 As acknowledged by Klopstock himself. Abbadona, however, does not appear in *Paradise Lost*, although Milton does employ Abbadon as the name of a place in *Paradise Regained* (IV. l 624). (Abbadon is Hebrew for the Greek Apollyon, 'angel of the bottomless pit' – as in Revelation 9:10.)
37 In Persian myth the Peri are beautiful but malevolent angels who are excluded from Paradise until penance is accomplished. (In Catholic doctrine, however, a sinning angel is fixed eternally in evil.)
38 V. K. Kiukhel'beker, 'On the Trend of our Poetry, Especially in the Lyric, in the Past Decade' in Proffer (ed) *Alexander Pushkin* 269
39 As quoted by Ianushevich 'V.A. Zhukovskii' 488. Bracketed words and phrases indicate alternative versions by Zhukovsky.
40 Ibid 485. See also the discussion of this in ch 5 of *Prophet*.

41 I cite the late Carl Proffer's translation of Pushkin's essay 'On Milton and Chateaubriand's Translation of *Paradise Lost*' in his *Alexander Pushkin* 220.
42 The translation of Book I appeared in the *Moskovskii Telegraf* 37:1 (1831) 35–48, and is cited by Ianushevich. His article appeared before the publication of the excellent Levin monograph *Russkie perevodchiki*, which contains some most interesting reflections both on Vronchenko and on Zhukovsky.
43 See the discussion in ch 9 below on D.S. Mirsky's attempt to bring out a Marxist edition of *Paradise Lost*.
44 Originally Vronchenko intended to translate all of *Paradise Lost*, an achievement that (as he observed in his letter to Iu.I. Poznanskii at the beginning of the 1830s) 'would serve as my memorial for a while at least among lovers of Russian poesy' (as quoted by A.V. Nikitenko in 'Mikhail Pavlovich Vronchenko [Biograficheskii ocherk]' in *Zhurnal Ministerstva Narodnogo Prosveshcheniia* 136:10 (1867) 12 in Levin *Russkie perevodchiki* 36 n 42). According to the same letter, Vronchenko had by then translated Book V too, which, however, has remained unpublished.
45 The translation of Part I of *Faust* and extracts from Part II appeared in 1844. As well, Vronchenko translated Schiller, of whom Zhukovsky was also fond. See Levin *Russkie perevodchiki* 36.
46 Russell, *Mephistopheles* 167
47 Beskonechny, bezobrazny,
v mutnoi mesiatsa igre
Zakruzhilis' besy razny,
Budto list'ia v noiabre ...
Skol'ko ikh! Kuda ikh goniat
Chto tak zhalobno poiut?
Domovogo li khoroniat,
Ved'mu l' zamuzh vydaiut? (Pushkin PSS vol 3:178)
48 Baring *The Mainsprings of Russia* 43. Here Baring compares the universal belief among the Eastern Slavs in the house spirit to the common belief in Milton's day in the 'drudging hobgoblin,' whom the English poet thought of as having a hairy hide just like the *domovoi*.
49 See chs 8 and 9 below.
50 See 'Szena iz Fausta' and 'Nabroski k zamyslu o Fauste' in Pushkin, PSS vol 2:286–90, and 308–10. The former was published in 1828.
51 Pushkin's reading of Milton is discussed in ch 6 of *Prophet*.
52 Parny's parody of Christianity reflects the criticisms that had been directed at it by Holbach and Voltaire, whom he much admired. Book VII, which describes the unfortunate expansion of Christianity in a spirit Gibbon would have approved, characterizes the Bible as the source of superstition and ignorance.

Chateaubriand's *Génie du Christianisme* (1802) was in part inspired by the desire to challenge Parny's witty critique. For an illuminating recent commentary to the poem (perhaps published in the USSR to augment atheist views), see E.G. Etkind's notes to the Soviet edition of *Voina Bogov* (1970).
53 Hill *A Tinker and a Poor Man* ch 28. I am grateful to the author for letting me see part of this work in typescript.
54 Russell (*Mephistopheles*) is referring here to Goethe's Mephistopheles (157), but the verdict also applies to Milton's Satan, who not only had a longer historical innings in Russia, but enjoys the further advantage of having his political life extended after the Bolshevik Revolution: see ch 8 below.
55 See Goethe's autobiographical *Dichtung und Wahrheit* as cited by Cottrell in *Goethe's View of Evil* 28–30.
56 Goethe began to work on *Faust* in about 1770 and was still working on it before he died in 1832: it represents therefore several decades in the author's protean creative life. *Faust: Eine Tragödie* consists of parts I and II, the first being written between 1787 and 1806 and published in 1808. The second part was written in 1825 and 1831 and came out in 1832. Curiously, in the youthful version, the *Urfaust* (which was begun more than a decade and a half earlier than Part 1), Mephisto does not appear at all, his closest simulacrum being the *Erdgeist* or Earth-Spirit. (The *Urfaust* was not published until the end of the nineteenth century.) Goethe had, of course, read and admired *Paradise Lost*.
57 On Guber see ch 3 in Levin *Russkie perevodchiki*. Levin also discusses other nineteenth-century Russian translations of Goethe.
58 See Zhirmunskii *Gëte v russkoi literature* 332. This valuable monograph has since been reproduced in the West.
59 Pushkin *PSS* vol 2:155: the poem was published in 1824
60 This response, written in 1825, remained unpublished in Pushkin's lifetime. I cite the translation in Carl Proffer's edition of Pushkin's critical prose 8–9.
61 Pushkin *PSS* vol 2:236
62 Ibid 290
63 Goethe *Faust: Eine Tragödie* II:337–40
64 Ilia Feinberg 'Istoriia Petra I' *Nezavershennye raboty Pushkina* 3rd enlarged ed (Moscow 1982) 58, as quoted in Riasanovsky *The Image of Peter the Great* 91
65 Ibid Feinberg 58–9 as cited by Riasanovsky 91
66 Pushkin *PSS* vol 4:393
67 Oliver Elton's graceful but not always faithful translation is quoted extensively by Riasanovsky in his interesting discussion of Pushkin's changing attitude to Peter the Great, and is cited here: see Riasanovsky *The Image of Peter the Great* 96

68 Pushkin *PSS* vol 3:16
69 See Chereiskii *Pushkin i ego okruzhenie* 339. As we have seen, Pushkin himself denied the likeness, as he was no doubt bound to do given that his note was intended for publication. But there are in fact two other poems – so it has been suggested – that were also inspired by Raevsky: 'Kovarnost'' (1824) and 'Angel' (1827).

7 MILTON'S SATAN AND LERMONTOV

1 Hill *Milton and the English Revolution* 439. Presumably this comment was inspired by Maurice Baring, who in his well-known sketch of Pushkin says that at times the great Russian poet attained 'the sublimity of a Milton.' See *Landmarks in Russian Literature* 196.
2 Later, in a letter to a friend, Belinsky qualified this enchantment by calling the poem 'childish' and 'immature' yet a 'tremendous creation.' See *Polnoe sobranie sochinenii* vol 4:544 and vol 12:85–6.
3 For an informed discussion of the sources associated with *Demon*, see B.T. Udodov *M. Yu. Lermontov Khudozhestvennaia individual'nost* 265ff.
4 The line is from the celebrated and prophetic poem Lermontov wrote in 1832 (see Lermontov *Sobranie sochinenii v chetyrekh tomakh* 361):
   Net, ia ne Bairon, ia drugoi,
   Eshche nevedomyi izbrannik.
   Kak on gonimyi mirom strannik,
   No tol'ko s russkoiu dushoi.
   Ia ran'she nachal, konchu rane ...
5 On Radishchev's 'Angel of Darkness' and its debt to Milton's Satan, see ch 5 above.
6 Lermontov *Sobranie sochinenii* vol 2:539:
   Odin, kak prezhde, vo vselennoi
   Bez upovan'ia i liubvi! ...
7 This Miltonian motif is echoed, of course, in most of the demonic verse of the period, eternal solitude rather than torment in Hell becoming Satan's apt punishment. This change was due perhaps as much to Romantic psychology as to the decline of belief in Hell.
8 Vigny *Eloa* in *Oeuvres complètes* vol 2:12:
   Car ce peuple d'Esprits, cette famille aimante
   Qui, pour nous, près de nous, prie et veille toujours,
   Unit sa pure essence en de saintes amours:
   L'Archange Raphaël, lorsqu'il vint sur la Terre,
   Sous le berceau d'Eden conta ce doux mystère.

9 See n 29 below. In the preface to *Cain*, completed after the poet's exile in Ravenna in 1821, Byron says that he had not read Milton since he was twenty, 'but I had read him so frequently before, that this may make little difference.' *The Poetical Works of Lord Byron* (London, New York, Toronto, Melbourne: Oxford University Press 1912) 511

10 See Spasovich *Baironizm u Pushkina i Lermontova* 74–5 (which had earlier appeared in *Vestnik Evropy* 4 [1888]); Udodov *M.Yu Lermontov Khudozhestvennaia individual'nost'*; and Loginovskaya *Poema M.Yu. Lermontova 'Demon'* section 3, where one might expect some discussion of *Paradise Lost*.

11 On Liutsenko, see chs 5 and 6 in *Prophet*.

12 Zinoviev's translation was published only in 1861.

13 See Maiskii 'Iunost' Lermontova' 185.

14 For a discussion of these verse translations, see ch 5 in *Prophet*.

15 Ie *Sochineniia v proze i stikhakh* 151–3. This is the society Pushkin had sometimes attended, as had many of the leading poets and writers of the time, Efim Liutsenko being one of its founders. Vasilii Petrov's partial translation had been read, as we have seen, at one of its sessions; and the society possessed a copy of the Stroganov-Milton, now lost.

16 See Viskovatov 'Vospominaniia A.Z. Zinov'eva v pereskaze P.A. Viskovatogo' 57. For a fuller discussion of Zinoviev's pedagogic views at first hand, see Zinov'ev 'O vospitanii' 371–84. From this it appears that the author was a Platonist who sought to reconcile his classical views on education with those of Rousseau. See also Iazykov's essay on Zinoviev, 'Uchitel' Lermontova-Zinov'ev' 605–10.

17 Maiskii 'Iunost' Lermontova' 233. Dante, Tasso, and Ossian were also admired.

18 See Viskatov 'Vospominaniia A.Z. Zinov'eva v pereskaze P.A. Viskovatogo' 56. Or was it *Whinson*? In Russian sources the name is unfortunately always given in Cyrillic.

19 See Appendix II.

20 The post-revolutionary scholarship on Lermontov is listed in Miller's recent *Bibliografiia literatury o M.Yu. Lermontove*. Of the pre-revolutionary literature discussing *Demon*'s possible sources, the most knowledgeable is N.P. Dashkevich's 'Motivy mirovoi poezii v tvorchestve Lermontova' (in his *Stat'i po novoi russkoi literature*), where the author does mention *Paradise Lost* as one in a long line of other candidates (from Vondel to Lamartine); see 453ff. He does not, however, discuss when or where Lermontov would have read Milton. Here Udodov (in *M.Yu. Lermontov* 262ff) follows Dashkevich; indeed, his treatment of the subject is more thorough than any other Soviet study, but his references to *Paradise Lost* do not inspire confidence. Thus, on page 265 Udodov refers to Amvrosii's translation of 1780 and that of Efim Liutsenko in

1824; and is apparently unaware of all the other Russian translations and editions of the time. Similarly, Udodov neglects to mention the reference to Milton's poem in *Vadim*, and cites Maiskii's excellent article ('Iunost' Lermontova' see n 13 above) as a source: 'o ser'eznom izuchenii v Moskovskom Blagorodnom Pansione tvorchestva Mil'tona.' In fact, however, Maiskii has very little on Milton, and although he studied the journals brought out by the Pension Noble, neither Maiskii nor any other Lermontov specialist refers to the Alferoff speech. Its timing must reopen the question of Milton's influence on Lermontov's *Demon*, although I have not been able to ascertain whether Alferoff was one of the 'bande joyeuse' to which Lermontov belonged. Maiskii, who has many interesting things to say about the poet's friends (see his 'Novye materialy k biografii M.Yu. Lermontova' in Brodskii, Tolstoy et al (eds) *Zhizn' i tvorchestvo M.Yu. Lermontova* 634ff), does not mention Alferoff at all. Nor does Brodskii in his article 'Lermontov – student i ego tovarishchi' (in the same volume, 40–76), in which the discussion of Zinoviev's literary interests also leaves much to be desired. Was his interest in Milton, for example, literary, religious, or political in character? Iazykov, who provides a bibliography of Zinoviev's extant writings, notes the appearance in 1883 of a translation (from the English) of a religious work; in the following year, when Zinoviev died, he also brought out Alexander Adam's volume on Roman antiquities. Though much has been written on the demonic theme in Russian Romantic literature, Milton's influence on both the major and the minor poets of the period has been almost wholly neglected. So has Winsun's role in Lermontov's familiarity with English literature, although the poet's Byronism has been well and truly dealt with.

21 The translation of Blair (from the French) may be seen at ORGBL Muzeinoe sobranie F. 178 no 8223: 'O nachale i proiskhozhdenii iazyka i o izobretenii pis'ma' [vospitannikov Universitetskogo blagorodnogo pansiona kn. Grigoriia Gagarina i Petra Likhacheva].

22 The quality of these public orations varies, as one might expect, being comparable perhaps to the Apposition Day addresses that used to be 'de rigueur' in English public schools. On the other hand, some of the polyglot speeches in the *Rechi i stikhi ... Universitetskato Blagorodnago Pansiona* are too fluent, it seems to me, to have issued unassisted from their young authors.

23 He also deferred to the judgment of Addison: see Zinov'ev 'O vospitanii' 384.

24 Ivanenko, whose acquaintance with Lermontov is documented, gave his speech in Russian. Moore was clearly popular.

25 I have spotted only a couple of idiomatic *faux pas* in Alferoff's oration and must assume that the answer to the query posed in the next sentence must be positive.

26 'Reminiscences of Medwin' 20 Nov 1821–28 Aug 1822, as quoted by Wittreich *The Romantics on Milton* 522
27 Lermontov *Demon* in *Sobranie* vol 2:546: 'chto bog nespravedliv i proch.'
28 Ibid 547
29 The influence of Milton's Satan on Lucifer in *Cain* is discussed by Friedrich Blumenthal in *Death of Abel*, his monograph on *Cain, Paradise Lost*, and Gessner's *Death of Abel*, as well as by Ioto ('The Two Devils') in the *Knickerbocker Magazine*.
30 The parallel between Lermontov's lines – 'No chto emu ostalos' ot vsego etogo? vospominaniia? da, no kakiia? gor'kiia, obmanchivyia, podobno plodam, rastushchim ne beregakh Mertvago moria, kotorye, blistaia rumianoi koroiu, taiat pod neiiu pepel', sukhoi, goriachii pepel'!' (*Vadim*, end of ch 19, Lermontov *Izbrannye proizvedeniia* vol 2:189) – and the *Poteriannyi rai* of 1820 is analysed in Semenov *M. Yu. Lermontov stat'i i zametki* vol 1:251–2.
31 As Udodov points out in his detailed discussion of Lermontov's creative methods, he tended to hoard what he wrote, polishing and improving and making use of notes compiled over a period of time. The genesis and gestation of *Demon* was in this sense characteristic.
32 As quoted and discussed by Semenov *Lermontov* 254–5. As in Pushkin's case, the various bits of evidence concerning Lermontov's degree of mastery of English are inconclusive and can be read many ways. Smirnova, cited by Semenov, says: 'On khorosho vladeet angliiskim iazykom i teper' chitaet romany Bul'vera.' In 1840, writing from the Caucasus, the poet requested 'polnago Shekspira *po-angliiski*.'
33 Byron *Don Juan* Canto III (1819) ll 73–80
34 Ibid ll 817–24
35 Ibid Dedication (1818) ll 81–8
36 Lermontov *Demon* in *Sobranie* vol 2:539
37 Lunacharsky first expressed his admiration for Milton in the lectures he gave before students of a new Bolshevik university in 1923–4, which were published soon after as the first authorized Marxist *History of Western European Literature* to be written after 1917: *Istoriia zapadno-evropeiskoi literatury v ee vazhneishikh momentakh* in *Sobranie sochinenii* vol 4:172–3.
38 Eikhenbaum *Lermontov* 97. The interesting essay on the demonic tradition, 'O demonologicheskoi traditsii v russkoi poezii 20–30kh godov XIX v.,' was later denounced when Eikhenbaum came under attack as a formalist. As late as 1958 D.A. Gireev had Eikhenbaum in mind when he attacked those who, in discussing the sources of *Demon*, usually turned to Western European literature. 'This theoretically [printsiapial'no] mistaken tendency in Lermontov scholarship has its beginning with bourgeois scholars of the nineteenth century' (Gireev

Poema M.Yu. Lermontova 'Demon' 43). The fact is, however, that in comparing Milton's Satan with Demon, Lermontov specialists before 1917 are often to be found wholly in agreement with Lunacharsky's verdict. Spasovich, for example, after emphasizing Satan's defiance in *Paradise Lost*, says that Lermontov's Demon 'seems almost to proclaim himself tsar of knowledge and freedom in vain: for he has not demonstrated his might in the realm of intellect, and has much more in common with the Satan of Alfred de Vigny' (*Baironizm u Pushkina i Lermontova* 75). Dashkevich, whose work Lunacharsky would surely have known, reached the same conclusion. For him Milton's Satan is 'an indomitable, proud, revolutionary-republican, beaten but not broken,' by comparison with whom both Demon and the Satan of *Eloa* are flimsy creatures indeed. The controversy, as Udodov's interesting study shows, continues.

39 See TSGADA Lermontov (Demon) Muzeinoe Sobranie F.178 vol 3 no 4609:iii. The date of the transcription is 30 Nov 1847; it is signed 'M.F.K.'
40 Kastor, for example, sees Milton's Satan as a 'trimorph,' and discusses the three aspects of his character (archangel, prince of Hell, and tempter) as quite separate entities, an approach that would be more interesting if the author had also attempted the link with the Satan of *Paradise Regained*; see *Milton and the Literary Satan*. Elizaveta Zhadovskaya, in translating a part of *Paradise Regained*, chose to focus again on Satan the tempter, as if in continuation of the role he plays in Book IV of *Paradise Lost*. It would be difficult to see any real continuity between the two epics in Satan's other incarnations.
41 See chs 4 and 5 above.
42 Lermontov *Demon*, in *Sobranie* vol 2:567. Lermontov does not indicate the Byronic edition he consulted – presumably that of 1823, which also contains the author's preface and the allusion to Milton: see n9 above.
43 The translation cited here is that of Alexander Condie Stephen, whose *The Demon* was published in 1875 by Trubner and Co (London) 65. It comes nowhere near doing justice to the spell-binding original, but is far superior to Avril Pyman's recent translation, which is included in the English edition of Lermontov's *Selected Works* brought out by Progress Publishers, Moscow, in 1976 and reissued in 1978.
44 It was published in Polevoi's *Moskovskii Telegraf* 37:1 (Jan 1831) 38–48, the most enterprising literary journal of the time.
45 Kholodkovsky, unlike Vronchenko, avoided blank verse in translating Milton.
46 *Abbadona* first appeared in another popular journal, *The Son of the Fatherland* (*Syn otechestva*) in 1815, no 22; it is included in Zhukovsky's *Sobranie sochinenii v chetyrekh tomakh* vol 2:231–6.
47 See TSGADA Klopstock 'Messiia poema v dvukh otdeleniiakh' Muzeinoe sobranie 5889 no 11057. The manuscript, which consists of 177 pages, is unsigned and

undated, but was probably written after 1812 (since the *sbornik* of which it is a part contains a piece devoted to Napoleon's defeat that year).
48 See Gertzen *Polnoe sobranie sochinenii i pisem'* 366.
49 Ie:
   Sumrachen, tikh, odinok …
        Pechal'noi
   Mysl'iu brodil on v minuvshem.
50 Published by the press of Moscow University, it begins in what might seem a suitably Miltonic strain, but soon becomes quite unwieldy: 'Vospoi bezsmertnaia dusha iskuplenie greshnykh chelovekov, Messieiu v chelovecheskoi ploti na zemle sovershennoe, stradaniem, muchenicheskoiu konchinoiu, preobrazheniem I izliiannoiu za nas kroviiu liubov' Bozhestva Adamovu plemeni vnov' dorovsvavshee. Tako ispolnilas' volia Prevechnago. Tshchetno vozstaval satana protivu Bozhestvennago Syna; naprasno Iudeia Ego opolchalas'; Ono preiprinial i sovershil velikoe primirenie.' 'Primirenie' catches the mood of the entire poem.
51 See the piece on Klopstock in *Syn otechestva* 62:3–14. The article is a translation of a section of Mme de Staël's *De l'Allemagne*, where the contest between the English and German Muse is described largely in terms of the contrast between *Paradise Lost* and Klopstock.
52 See Klopstock *Messiada*.
53 The manuscript version of Klopstock's poem, cited in n47, even has an *'ukazatel'* ispol'zovannykh tekstov sv. pisaniia …'
54 Apart from her Milton translation-adaptation, Elizaveta Zhadovskaya is also known for *Pesni i stikhotvoreniia, Pervoobraz smerti i bratoubiitsa*, and *Dve Legendy*, also published in Moscow, in 1860, and apparently her last book.
55 Dobrolivbov *Sovremennik* (1859) in *Sobranie sochinenii* vol 78 no 12:248
56 The prose editions of Milton's epics, some of them brought out by peasant publishers, were extraordinarily popular and at this time were still more widely disseminated than the Bible.
57 On Gnedich and his translation of Milton, see ch 5 in *Prophet*.
58 'Poteriannyi rai. Poema Ioanna Mil'tona … v stikhakh Elizavety Zhadovskoi' (Moscow 1859) 99
59 Ibid 15
60 Ibid 14
61 See ch 5 above.

8 BANNING AND REVIVING SATAN

1 'Starinnyi russkii perevod Mil'tonovo *Poteriannogo raia*' *Maskovskie vedomosti* 39 (14 May 1838) 316

2 See Manuilov *Letopis' zhizni i tvorchestva M. Yu. Lermontova* 77.
3 Gershtein *Sud'ba Lermontova* 69ff, and Naidich 'Posledniia redaktsiia "Demona" ' *Russkaia Literatura* 76ff
4 In my summary of the problems encountered by *Demon* I rely on Vatsuro's article, which adds some new details to an otherwise well-known story; see 'K tsenzurnoi istorii *Demona*' 410–14. Next to Lemke's account, which also deals with Lermontov, the least unsatisfactory historical treatment of censorship is Skabichevskii's *Ocherki istorii russkoi tsenzury*' which covers part of the same ground in greater detail.
5 Milton's censorship as described here draws on the Holy Synod reports, which have not previously been cited by Soviet scholars or, indeed, before 1917. This is not the first time that *Paradise Lost* fell foul of the censorship authorities in Russia; the story, interesting in itself, spans both the eighteenth century and the Soviet period. For a more detailed account of how tsarist censors responded to the popularity of the epics see my *Russian Popular Culture and John Milton*.
6 These editions are described in my *Russian Popular Culture and John Milton*. Properly speaking, the Milton 'revival' began with Zinoviev's publication in 1861 of what remained for many decades the most faithful prose translation of *Paradise Lost*. But Lermontov's old tutor did not live to see the massive popularization of the two epics, which publishers began a decade later.
7 On Uvarov see Cynthia Whittaker's study *The Origins of Modern Russian Education*.
8 See Maistre *Considerations on France* 75. For the author, 'the sublime bard's imaginary world' was realized when 'mankind's enemy' seated himself in the Riding School and, 'calling every *evil spirit*,' proclaimed the Declaration of the Rights of Man and Citizen.
9 See TSGIAL F.722 Opis' no 1, Delo no 2798:1.
10 Ibid, letter from the chairman of the Moscow Committee, 9 Apr 1852:2v
11 I cite from the *Sovremennik* article 'Poteriannyi rai Poema Ioanna Mil'tona,' as reprinted in Dobroliubov *Sobranie sochinenii* vol 5:532.
12 Ibid 533
13 Ibid 534
14 This was one of the young Lenin's favourite novels; he used it for the title of one his best-known political tracts.
15 Gronicka *The Russian Image of Goethe* vol 2:17
16 Belinskii 'Vzgliad na russkuiu literaturu 1847 goda' in *Sobranie sochinenii v trekh tomakh* 792, as quoted by Samarin in 'Tvorchestvo Dzh. Mil'tona v otsenke V.G. Belinskogo' 432. The late Professor Samarin, an eminent Soviet Miltonist, exaggerates Belinsky's priority and ignores the many critics and poets in the

West who had made the same valuable point. Nor was Samarin aware of the censorship records discussed above or of Milton's proscription in the Nikolaevan era.

17 Published as 'Satana, Grekh i Smert' ' in *Vestnik inostrannoi literatury ezhemesiachno-literaturno-istoricheskii zhurnal* 7 (Dec 1897; St Petersburg) 5–9. The translation was probably made around 1866, but is not included in any of the published editions of Sluchevsky's verse.

18 See Solov'ev *Mil'ton – ego zhizn' i literaturnaia deiatel'nost'*. Soloviev sees *Paradise Lost* as the culmination of 'twenty years given to the service of the Good Old Cause' and attacks those (like Chateaubriand) who felt Milton had wasted them on politics. Writing in a spirit the radicals of the sixties would have found thoroughly congenial, he goes on to say: 'Let us not therefore feel sorry about the melodious poems [Milton] did not write: besides written poems, there are many others unwritten in the poem of life, of action and struggle, and these are no less enlightening.' Ibid 43

19 Likhachev, for example, made Milton's description of the Garden the pretext for a moving fragment entitled 'Noch v Edeme' ('Night in Eden'): see *Vsemirnaia illiustratsiia* 54 (1894) 25. On Likhachev, one of several translators of Milton at this time, see Vengerov *Istochniki slovaria russkikh pisatelei* vol 3:489.

20 As noted by Sergei Sudeikin, a Russian artist then living in Paris: see, Mikhail Vrubel *Perepiska* 295.

21 This is apparent from Suzdalev's study *Vrubel': Lermontov*, which recapitulates two interesting articles by the same author: '*Demon* Vrubelia' and 'O mirovozrenii Vrubelia.'

22 See Mikhail Guerman's introduction to Guerman et al *Mikhail Vrubel* 20.

23 Vrubel *Perepiska* (1976) 116

24 Guerman et al *Mikhail Vrubel* 20

25 Vrubel *Perepiska* (1976) 118

26 Solov'ev, *Sobranie sochinenii* vol 3:173

27 Vrubel *Perepiska* (1976) 55–6

28 Ibid 194

29 Merezhkovskii *Polnoe sobranie sochinenii* 249, as quoted by Guerman *Mikhail Vrubel* 28

30 The lines are from Blok's 'Vozmezdie'; see *Izbrannye stikhotvoreniia* 269.

31 See Aline Isdebsky-Pritchard 'Art for Philosophy's Sake: Vrubel against the "Herd" ' in Rosenthal *Nietzsche in Russia* 246.

32 Lev N. Tolstoi 'What Is Art?' in *The Novels and Other Works* trans Aylmer Maude, 22 vols (New York, 1902) vol 18, as quoted by Aline Isdebsky-Pritchard, ibid 227

33 Isdebsky-Pritchard 'Art for Philosophy's Sake' in Rosenthal *Nietzsche in Russia* 236

9 1917 AND AFTER: THE TRIUMPH OF MILTON'S SATAN

1. Radishchev's attitude to Cromwell, revealed in his ode 'Liberty' ('Vol'nost' '), displeased Catherine and perhaps contributed to the harsh sentence he received following the publication of *The Journey from St. Petersburg to Moscow* in 1790.
2. Zinoviev's translation, which was in prose, appeared in 1861, but was probably begun many years earlier.
3. Published posthumously as *Rabochie liudi i novyia idei* in St Petersburg in 1906. This book carries a portrait of the author by way of frontispiece.
4. Solov'ev *Mil'ton* 58–9
5. Ibid 62
6. Ibid 37. The phrase he uses – 'vostochnyi despot' – refers of course to Alexander III, the reactionary autocrat who died in the year Soloviev's biography of Milton was published.
7. Ibid 42. The word was introduced into the language in the Petrine period, but by the end of the nineteenth century (thanks in part to the 'civic' poets) had reacquired radical overtones.
8. The play was written at a time when Lunacharsky expected Soviet power to be overthrown, Cromwell in the play clearly being likened to Lenin, while the author identified himself with his conscience – John Milton. 'I want to be told,' says Cromwell in the play as he foresees the Commonwealth's end, 'that it *all* did make sense after all.'
9. Lunacharsky was accused of having glorified the Danton of the English Revolution – Oliver Cromwell – and in so doing was 'sullying its Marat-Levellers.' See Kerzhentsev's attack on the play in *Pravda* 263 (20 Nov 1920).
10. As pointed out by Kaspari, the publisher of Ol'ga Chiumina's translation of *Paradise Lost* and *Paradise Regained* (St Petersburg 1899) in the preface he inserted to this sumptuous edition
11. Or as a parody of the conventional notion of Christ. The various interpretations are discussed afresh by Pyman in *The Life of Aleksandr Blok*. A similar parallel is invoked by Christopher Hill with reference to the Jesus of *Paradise Regained* and Lenin: see his *Milton and the English Revolution* 389.
12. The circumstances under which the play was written are mentioned by Lila Brik and Vasilii Kamenskii in Woroszylski's *Life of Mayakovsky* ch 18.
13. Mirsky *A History of Russian Literature* 507. Lenin, as Mirsky rightly says, was far more concerned with the problems created by mass illiteracy than

with the theories proposed by supporters of *Proletcult*, whose influence began to decline with the launching of NEP.
14 Lenin 'Zadachi soiuzov molodezhi (rech na Vserossiiskom s'ezde rossiiskogo kommunisticheskogo soiuza molodezhi 2 oktiabria 1920 g.)' *Polnoe sobranie sochinenii* vol 41:304
15 See Gor'kii 'Razrushenie lichnosti' in *Sobranie trudov v 16 tomakh* 227. This essay, first published in 1909, appeared in a book entitled *Ocherki filozofii kollektivizma*, and was reprinted in 1937.
16 Saurat *Milton Man and Thinker* 287
17 Lafargue's *Causes de la Croyance au Dieu*, first published in Paris in 1905, was partly translated into Russian in 1920 (*Stat'ii o religii* [Moscow]), his selected writings being brought out in a three-volume edition in 1925–31.
18 Compare Lunacharskii 'Mif o Prometee' (*A.V. Lunacharskii ob ateizme i religii* in *Sobranie sochinenii* 272–9) with Lafargue *Le Mythe de Prométhée* (also published separately).
19 Lunacharskii 'Mif o Prometee' *Sobranie sochinenii* 278. The parallel with Milton's Satan is not made by Lafargue.
20 V. Vasiutinskii 'Mil'ton' in Lunacharskii and Mikhailova eds *Literaturnaia entsiklopediia* vol 7:311
21 Ibid 312
22 Ibid 313
23 Ibid
24 Ibid
25 Havens's book *The Influence of Milton on English Poetry*, based on his Harvard dissertation, was published at Oxford in 1922.
26 A. Lavretskii 'Stil' Mil'tona' Lunacharskii and Mikhailova eds *Literaturnaia entsiklopediia* vol 7:315. Lavretskii (ie I.M. Frenkel'), born in 1893, was until recently a member of the Gorky Institute of World Literature in Moscow.
27 Ibid
28 TSGALI file 629 schedule 1, item 1168: 'Primechaniia' by M. Rozanov (14 June 1934) part 8
29 The original item is to be found in the Thomason collection in the British Library.
30 Milton *A Brief History of Moscovia* (1929) 25
31 Muggeridge *Chronicles of Wasted Time* 236
32 Lewis *Preface to Paradise Lost* 92–3
33 Mirsky *Intelligentsia of Great Britain* 151–60. The insertion of 'dzh' into 'intelligentsia' in the original Soviet edition of the previous year was prompted by the Russian transliteration of the first letter of 'gentleman,' thus giving the word an intended pejorative connotation.

34 TSGALI D. M[irskii] ms cit, item 1168, opening page
35 Perhaps both these words could be rendered as 'potentator' or 'governour,' since 'vladet' ' means 'to rule,' while 'vlastelin' is derived from 'vlast' ' – 'power.'
36 A genuine equivalent for 'opolchen'i' is not to be found in English; on the other hand, 'sotnia' is not Church-Slavonic in origin, being derived from the Mongol for 'hundred,' a term dating from the 'Yoke.'
37 I have retained Mirsky's term for 'council' (he is referring to the soldiers' councils in the English Civil War) because to a Russian reader in the 1930s the term would have seemed incongruous too. The equivalent of 'council' is 'soviet,' but 1917 and its aftermath gave it the kind of association that Protas'ev (unlike Mirsky) felt should be avoided at all costs.
38 Bush *John Milton* 149

10 SATAN AS ANTI-IMPERIALIST

1 Klimov et al (eds) *Pedagogicheskaia razrabotka po tvorchestvu Dzhona Mil'tona* 13 (cited hereafter as ... *Po tvorchestvu Dzhona Mil'tona*)
2 Smith *Milton and His Modern Critics* 26
3 Tillyard *Milton* 237
4 Ibid 277
5 Klimov et al (eds) ... *Po tvorchestvu Dzhona Mil'tona*; the edition here cited carries the imprint of the New York publisher, Dial Press.
6 The only other foreign Miltonist referred to is E.S. Le Comte, whose *Yet Once More: Verbal and Psychological Pattern in Milton*, published by the Liberal Arts Press in New York in 1953, is presented as the type of work against which Tillyard issued his warning.
7 Anikst 'Dzhon Mil'ton' 57
8 Klimov et al (eds) ... *Po tvorchestvu Dzhona Mil'tona* 13
9 Ibid 19
10 Empson recounts how during this experience he found himself reciting one of Satan's speeches: 'It was received with fierce enthusiasm, but also with a mild groan from some of the older hands, who felt that they had been having enough propaganda already.' Interestingly he goes on to say that 'the audience ... really did mean to resist to the end however powerless, exactly like Satan and with the same pride ...' See Empson's *Milton's God* 45.
11 Ibid
12 H.J.C. Grierson, as quoted by A.J.A. Waldock in 'Satan and the Technique of Degradation' in Martz (ed) *Milton* 82
13 Ibid
14 Klimov et al (eds) ... *Po tvorchestvu Dzhona Mil'tona* 12

15 Lewis *Preface to Paradise Lost* 96
16 Klimov et al (eds) ... *Po tvorchestvu Dzhona Mil'tona* 12
17 Ibid
18 On Mirsky's use of the term see ch 9 above.
19 Klimov et al (eds) ... *Po tvorchestvu Dzhona Mil'tona* 14
20 Ibid
21 Ibid 17
22 Ibid
23 Ibid 18; 'Eve's Diary' is chiefly memorable for Adam's tribute on her death: 'wherever she was, *there* was Eden.'
24 'K tomu zhe syn byl uveren, chto "Vsemogushchii" papen'ka ne sygraet s nim zluiu shutku i ne ostavit ego na zemle muchit'sia vechno.' Ibid 15. 'Papen'ka' may be translated as 'Daddy,' and carries a connotation that could not be found in any seventeenth-century work.
25 Thus, of Satan's temptation of Eve, Empson thinks 'that ... she feels the answer to this elaborate puzzle must be that God wants her to eat the apple, since what she is really testing is not her obedience but courage, also whether her desire to get to Heaven is real enough to call all her courage out ... As so often in human affairs, her problem is one of Inverse Probability. Thus a candidate in an Intelligence Test often has to think "Which answer is the tester likely to have thought the intelligent one?", and this tends to make him irritated with the whole test. In this case, if God is good, that is, if he is the sort of teacher who wants to produce an independent-minded student, then he will love her for eating the apple' (*Milton's God* 159–60).
26 From a letter quoted by Lorna Sage 'Milton in Literary History' in Broadbent (ed) *John Milton* 336
27 Lewis *Preface to Paradise Lost* 102

CONCLUSION: PRINCE OF DARKNESS, PRINCE OF LIGHT

1 Brodsky *Less Than One* title essay
2 See ch 2 above.
3 Russell *Mephistopheles* 175
4 See ch 4 above.
5 See Appendix II, where Alferoff's English oration on *Paradise Lost* is reproduced in full.
6 See Lunacharsky's sketch of Milton in the *Istoriia evropeiskoi literatury*, which was first delivered in lecture form at the Communist University named after Ya.M. Sverdlov, and had two imprints in 1924 alone.
7 See ch 6 above.

8 On Heine's Russian reception see Ya.I. Gordon's interesting monograph *Geine v Rossii*.
9 Nikolaevan censorship of the epics is discussed in the sequel to the present book: see ch 9 in *Prophet*.
10 Vernacular editions of the Scriptures were first disseminated by the Bible Society. George Borrow, who visited St Petersburg as the society's agent between 1833 and 1835, became, thanks to this visit, the first to make Pushkin known to English readers.
11 For a discussion of the conflicting evidence on this see the conclusion to *Prophet*.
12 These are the lines an ecclesiastical censor found particularly offensive, as he noted in his report for Nicholas's minister of education, Uvarov: 'No ne tol'ko pri opisanii raia a i vo vsei knigi [ie *Paradise Lost*] gospodstvuet snoshenie mifologicheskogo s khristianskim, oskorbitel'ny dlia khristianskogo chuvstva.' ('The mixture of the mythological with the Christian dominates not only the description of Paradise but the entire book, [and] is offensive to Christian feeling.') See page 3 of the report dated 27 Feb 1852, compiled under the auspices of the Moskovskii Komitet dlia Tzenzury Dukhovnykh Knig.
13 The Tretiakov Gallery in Moscow, which houses the largest collection of Vrubel's paintings is still closed for repairs as this book goes to press. On my visits to the gallery it was impossible to overlook the malaise the Demon canvases evoke. Attitudes to erotic or sexual matter have of course changed since *glasnost'* and *perestroika*, at least in Moscow and Leningrad, *Little Vera* (1988) being the first Soviet film to show a naked woman being kissed by a man (dressed). Vrubel's work, long considered 'decadent,' began to be reproduced in the Soviet Union in the 1970s, and assessments of the artist and his work have been drastically revised. In literature the best-known satanic work to be suppressed in the Soviet period is, of course, Bulgakov's *Master and Margarita*. Begun in the late 1920s and completed many years later, it was only recently published in the USSR. The dramatized version, first shown to restricted audiences at the Taganka in Moscow, was hugely appreciated in the 1970s and is still playing (as of January 1990). It has since been produced abroad by Liubimov, the director who first staged it. Some of its underlying erotic themes are echoed in a Soviet ballet film on the life of the dancer Elena Kniazeva, ie *Fouette* (1986) (directed by Vladimir Vassiliev and Boris Ermolaev). For comments on the Miltonic element in *Master and Margarita*, see the bibliographic note below.
14 Edmund Wilson to Stanley Dell, 6 Aug 1925, in Wilson *Letters on Literature and Politics* 124
15 See, for example, Samarin's comments in the introduction to his Milton

biography, *Tvorchestvo Dzhona Mil'tona* 12, and the polemical piece by one of his students, T.I. Paramonova, 'Dzhon Mil'ton v otsenke "Novoi Kritiki," ' in *Vestnik Moskovskogo universiteta* 4(1972), in which she defends Milton against the 'new critics.' Samarin, long a rector of Moscow University, also edited the anthology of Milton that 'Vsemirnaia literatura' brought out in 1976.

16 Klimov et al (eds) ... *Po tvorchestvu Dzhona Mil'tona* 13
17 See Francis X. Clines 'Russian Patriarch Asks Church Role in Schools' *New York Times* 13 June 1990 A19.
18 The title of Victor Korkia's *Chernyi chelovek ili ia, bednyi Soso Djugashvili* is difficult to render in English because 'chernyi chelovek' (which literally means 'black' or 'dark being') has a diabolical connotation in Russian – as, for instance, in Yesenin's poem of that title. It refers to Stalin's *Doppelgänger*, the sinister Romantic Devil of the play who arouses his paranoia and torments the chief of the NKVD too. 'Soso' Djugashvili, of course, is the name by which Stalin was familiarly known in Georgia, which was also the home of Beria. The play was first put on at the Moscow University Student Theatre in the heady spring of 1987 following the xIxth Party Conference.

The unprecedented portrayal on the stage of Stalin as villain aroused excitement of a kind I had never witnessed in a Soviet theatre. But when I saw the play again at the beginning of 1990 the realism (or resignation?) that succeeded the ecstatic early phases of *glasnost'* had no doubt affected the audience's muted reception on this occasion. Ongoing revelations in the Soviet media of the crimes of the Stalin era had also weakened the impact of Korkia's daring idea of tackling the subject at all. In 1987 the effect was sensational: by 1990 Muscovites were neither attentive nor amused. Although circulating in typescript form, the play has not been published. It has some very witty lines, but the most memorable part is the parody of *Boris Godunov*. The author, who is from the Caucasus, had a book of poetry published by Sovetskii Pisatel' in 1988: *Svobodnoe vremia – stikhi i poemy*.
19 Angelica Balabanoff *Impressions of Lenin* 2. She inverts Goethe's meaning.
20 See, for instance, Andrei Vasilevskii's article 'Stalin (li) s nami? Fol'klor o vozhde narodov,' which discusses Stalin's popular standing today: *Literaturnaia gazeta* 18:5292 (2 May 1990) 5. The pretext for the article is Iurii Borev's recent *Staliniade*, which (like Staehlin's eighteenth-century collection on Peter the Great, cited in the Introduction to the present study) contains anecdotes, lore, and legends about the Leader of Mankind.
21 Alexander Solzhenitsyn 'Repentance and Self-Limitation in the Life of Nations' in *From under the Rubble* 109

APPENDIX ONE

1 Mutschmann 'Milton in Russland' 268–75
2 Introduction by Prince D.S. Mirsky to John Milton *A Brief History of Moscovia* (London: The Blackamore Press 1929) 14
3 Lloyd E. Berry 'Giles Fletcher, the Elder, and Milton's *A Brief History of Moscovia*' 154
4 John Milton *A Brief History of Moscovia: And of Other Less-known Countries Lying Eastward of Russia as far as Cathay* (London 1682), as reproduced in Cawley *Milton's Literary Craftsmanship* 43–4; hereafter referred to as Cawley *Moscovia*
5 Ibid 46
6 J. Max Patrick (ed) *The Prose of John Milton* (New York: University Press 1968) 573
7 Parks 'The Occasion of Milton's *Moscovia*' 399
8 Parker *Milton* vol 1: 325
9 For example, after William Julius Mickle had made the comparison in *The Lusiads of Luis de Camoëns* in 1776, the idea has been explored by Bowra (*From Virgil to Milton* 1945), Tillyard (*The English Epic and Its Background* 1954), Letzring ('The Influence of Camoëns in English Literature'), and others. Although the Portuguese epic was Englished by Sir Richard Fanshawe in 1655, the evidence that Milton knew of Camoëns is not conclusive.
10 See Cawley *Milton and the Literature of Travel* 51–2.
11 Cawley *Moscovia* 67
12 In his *Milton and the Literature of Travel,* Cawley cites the 'short pamphlet (eight pages)' by Mutschmann referred to above (as well as the place where the latter makes the suggestion that *Paradise Lost* was originally conceived as an epic about the Armada); see 'Studies Concerning the Origins of "Paradise Lost"' *Acta et Commentationes Universitatis Dorpatensis* B.5 (1924), recently reprinted by Folcroft Library Editions as *Further Studies Concerning the Origins of Paradise Lost.* Cawley goes on to say, however, that 'my own conclusions were drawn and formulated before I had seen Mutschmann's proposal' (60n70). There is, indeed, a striking resemblance in the parallels developed by them both, although I am not aware that Mutschmann's priority has been recognized, or that anyone since Cawley even refers to the brief but suggestive 'Milton und Russland.' Heinrich Mutschmann (1885–1955), who began his professorial career with a doctorate from Bonn on Scottish phonology and was associated for much of his life with the University of Dorpat, wrote a number of studies about Milton in the 1920s and 1930s, but his theories on Milton's blindness, although discussed at the time, were thought extravagant

Miltonists. Parker (*Milton* vol 2: 680) considers them 'perverse,' but while citing some of Mutschmann's other writings, fails to mention 'Milton und Russland.' Since the *History of Britain* has been plausibly linked to Milton's abandonment of the poem on King Arthur (which he also considered writing), the German scholar's connection of the *Moscovia* with a comparable national epic deserves further consideration. Characteristically, however, Mutschmann overdraws his case by perceiving a Russian connection in *Comus* that (to the present writer at least) seems far less convincing. It is also worth noting, since Mutschmann does not, that in the list of possible subjects for his epic poem that Milton drew up before going to Italy, the quest for a northeast passage is not in fact mentioned.

13 The full account of Clement Adams, as 'taken from the mouth of Chancellor,' is to be found in the second volume of Hakluyt *The Principal Navigations*, and is cited here from the extract in Cawley *Milton and the Literature of Travel* 62.
14 Cawley *Moscovia* 80–1

Bibliographic Note

If Milton's Satan is, by common consent, the most important devil in European literature before Goethe's, why has his appearance in Russia so far been overlooked? The influence of Satan and Mephistopheles on Russian literature overlaps, but it is also sequential in the sense that Milton's Satan paves the way for his less heroic but more secular German cousin. About the latter much has been said. V.M. Zhirmunsky's masterly study of Goethe (recently reprinted) shows how Mephistopheles affected the Russian Romantics, and this book has since been supplemented by two volumes on the same subject by an American scholar.

Yet neither Zhirmunsky nor André von Gronicka deal at all with Mephisto's precursor whose influence on Russian poetry (as the present study tries to show) was felt more than half a century before that of *Faust*. There are several reasons for this oversight.

If Baron Stroganov's translation of *Paradise Lost* and the 'satanic' adaptation described in chapter 2 have not been explored by literary scholars, the reasons for this neglect no doubt also prompted Soviet comparativists to avoid *Paradise Lost* and *Paradise Regained*. Until very recently there was a Communist Party taboo on works with a devotional theme. Until 1988 the Bible, closely associated with Milton's two epics before the Revolution, could not be brought legally into the USSR. Nor, before 1988, could it even be borrowed from libraries without special dispensation.

Nor, until the Soviet recognition of Christ's historicity in the 1970s could the Christian tradition in Russian literature be touched on by Marxist scholars except in highly ideologized contexts. Thus, important as Kheraskov or Derzhavin may be in the canon of Russian poetry before Pushkin, their devotional verse (discussed in chapters 4 and 5) has so far been neglected by Soviet scholars. This may also account for the absence of any Soviet discussion of *True Light*, the Masonic imitation of Milton in which Satan first takes wing in Russian verse. (A far more ambitious imitation of the epics, *Paradise Lost and Regained* by Ivan Vladykin, an autodidact of the Catherinian era, does not belong to formal literature as such, and is analysed in my study *Russian Popular Culture and John Milton*.)

Neglect of Milton's Satan by Western Slavists has other causes. To date there is no bibliography of Miltonic translations in Russian, and few of the translations have found their way into Western libraries. The Slavic Library at the University of Helsinki has most of the more important Russian translations of *Paradise Lost* and *Paradise Regained*; Harvard has some, and the British Library one, but only the Lenin Library in Moscow and the Saltykov-Shchedrin in Leningrad have comprehensive collections.

The partial translation by Khrapovitskaya from Thomas Newton's edition of *Paradise Lost* represents the most faithful eighteenth-century rendition, and has so far been ignored. Zhukovsky's connection with the poem is now possible thanks to F.E. Kanunova's recovery of his library. Surprisingly, the larger question of Pushkin's reading of Milton has not so far been properly examined. An attempt to do so is made in *Prophet*. The purpose of the sections on Pushkin above is to show how his protean contribution to the demonic theme widened its poetic range.

Lermontov's ties with Milton have also been overlooked (see chapter 7). Nor has Klopstock, a far less significant source of literary inspiration than Milton but during the Enlightenment often considered his equal, received the attention the many references in the literature of the period suggest he deserves. Satan's politics, of which Russian readers became aware with Pugachev and the French Revolution (see chapter 5) have not, it seems, aroused interest among Soviet scholars.

The affection that the Decembrist Kiukhel'beker and some of Pushkin's other friends felt for Milton has also so far failed to attract attention. The same cannot, of course, be said of the demonic tradition in Russian verse, although the role of Milton's Satan in initiating it in Russia has so far gone unrecognized.

Of Alferoff's links with Lermontov I know no more than the school records imply. That Shakespeare was read at the *lycée* in Tsarskoe Selo and at the Pension Noble is well known, but I have not seen Alferoff's English oration cited anywhere in the voluminous literature on Lermontov's youth. Hence its reproduction in its entirety as Appendix II from the school journal (copies of which are held by the Lenin Library).

Knowledge of Milton's influence in Europe and North America has been much enriched by recent scholarship, little of which seems as yet familiar to Soviet comparativists. Where French intermediaries are concerned I have found Jean Gillet's splendid 1975 monograph most helpful. However, it ends with Chateaubriand, and is thus no guide to Satan's fate at the hands of the symbolists in France, where *Paradise Lost* continued to be influential at the end of the nineteenth century. In Russia Milton's epics reached a far wider audience: how wide is suggested by Appendix III.

It is this availability of the epics (see my *Russian Popular Culture and John Milton*) that makes the specific influence of Milton's Satan on Russian symbolists like Blok or Briusov difficult to gauge. They were all, of course, also familiar with Goethe's *Faust*, some of whose translators (Kholodkovsky, for example) also turned *Paradise Lost* into Russian verse. But the specific influence on symbolist writing of Milton's Satan perhaps deserves a study of its own, although it could not be done (as in the case of Vrubel) without also considering Goethe's Mephisto.

The methodological problem (in separating the two) also affects later pursuits of the demonic theme, as in Ellendea Proffer's impressive biography of Bulgakov, whose exploration of it in *Master and Margarita* is surely one of the most original in twentieth-century literature. Did Mikhail Bulgakov read *Paradise Lost?* I find it hard to believe that he did not. Proffer sees some of the specific parallels (as in the debt to Azazel, one of Milton's fallen angels), but then answers the question in the negative by suggesting that 'a specific example which could come from no other work is required to make the supposition convincing ...' (*Bulgakov* 643).

She then stresses Bulgakov's independence of Goethe: 'Woland differs in important respects from Mephistopheles, the gay and malicious tempter who is very like Dostoevsky's shabby second-rate devil in *Brothers Karamazov*. Woland is majestic, ironic, a genuine fallen angel whose sin was pride.' (*Bulgakov* 556). In doing so, she seems quite unaware that she is describing what Woland shares with Milton's Satan. Bulgakov himself provides the appropriate clue. Woland's kinship with both Milton's Satan and Goethe's Mephisto is inadvertently revealed when he is mistaken in Moscow first for a British subject and then for a German. This also applies no doubt to the most recent manifestation of Satanism on the Moscow stage, Victor Korkia's *Chernyi chelovek,* which I last saw in January 1990. There the Devil owes as much to Pushkin, Lermontov, and Goethe as he does indirectly to the one whose priority in formal Russian literature has been the subject of this book.

The bibliography below is divided into three sections. The first section describes the material in Soviet archives that was found useful in exploring the sources of Russian literary Satanism. The second section takes note of journals, newspapers, and miscellanies (prior to 1900); the third section notes books and articles cited in the text, but not familiar pre-revolutionary encyclopaedias and biographical dictionaries (such as those brought out by Brokgauz and Efron).

Bibliography

I ARCHIVES

Milton manuscripts are noted first: the second section includes the censorship report and is then followed in alphabetical order by other Soviet archives and collections, the arrangement being by topic (ie Adam, Antichrist, Satan) rather than by title.

Milton's Paradise Lost
ORBAN 'Pogublennyi rai' Ustiuzhskoe sobranie no 57
ORGBL 'Pogublennyi rai' Fedorov F.313 no 42: M.2959
ORGIM (No title) Barsov F.450 no 3386
ORGPB 'Pogublennyi rai' Sobranie A.A. Titova no 265

Censorship Report on Milton
TSGIAL F.722, Opis' no 1, Delo no 2798. Delo kantseliariii Ministra Narodnogo Prosveshcheniia. Po predstavleniiu Moskovskogo Tsenzurnogo Komiteta o zatrudneniiakh, vstrechennym sim komitetom pri propuske v pechat' knigi, pod zaglaviem 'Pot. rai' i 'Vozv. rai' soch. *Mil'tona.* Nachato Aprelia 9 dnia 1852. Koncheno Oktiabria 27 dnia 1852 goda

Milton's Dedication to Dr Arnold
DRKGBL 83 Inostrannye Avtografy 9 ed 42

Other Manuscripts
Anon (Adam)
ORGBL 'O khitrom prel'shchenii Adama' Muzeinoe sobranie no 10300
ORGBL 'O sotvorenii mira' Muzeinoe sobranie no 1092

ORGBL 'Rodoslovie ot Adama, v krugakh' Muzeinoe sobranie no 9615
ORGBL 'Rodoslovie ot Adama, v krugakh' second half of 18th c Muzeinoe sobranie no 10300
ORGBL 'Sbornik tolkovanii, izrechenii i khozhdenii' Muzeinoe sobranie no 10261
– (Antichrist)
ORGBL 'Ob antikhriste' 18th–19th c. Barsov F.17 no 6
ORGBL 'Ob antikhriste' 19th c Barsov F.17 no 29
ORGBL 'Ob antikhriste' 18th–19th c Barsov F.17 no 32
ORGBL 'Ob antikhriste' 1763 Barsov F.17 no 338
ORGBL 'Ob Antikhriste i konchine mira' no date Barsov F.17 no 414
ORGBL 'Skazaniia ob antikhriste' 18th–19th c Barsov F.17 no 483
ORGBL 'Skazaniia ob antikhriste' 19th c Barsov F.17 no 338
ORGBL 'O sotvorenii mira' 17th–18th c Barsov F.17 no 1092
– (Satan)
ORGBL 'Beseda chorta s Bonapartom' 19th c Muzeinoe sobranie no 10609
ORGBL 'Kniga o sverzhenii s neba Satany ...' 1740 Muzeinoe sobranie no 10954
ORGBL Blair 'O nachale i proizkhozhdenii iazyka i o izobretenii pis'ma' Muzeinoe sobranie F.178 no 8223
ORGBL Cosmas Indikopleustes, Kosmografiia, Muzeinoe sobranie no 10336
ORGBL Homer 'Iliada ...' trans I. Kondratovich second half of 18th c Muzeinoe sobranie no 2956
TSGADA Klopstock 'Messia poema v dvukh otdeleniiakh' Muzeinoe sobranie 5889 no 11057
TSGADA Lermontov 'Demon' Muzeinoe sobranie F178 vol 3: no 4609
TSGADA Rychkov ['Zapiski o Pugachevskom bunte'] Muzeinoe sobranie no 9636
TSGALI Dmitri Mirsky's [projected] edition of *Paradise Lost* file 629 (see 'Academia')

Dissertations

Kostin, V.I. 'Dekabrist Fedor Nikolaevich Glinka' unpublished diss (Saratov 1972) DZGBL
Maksudova, E.S. 'Iazyk novovremennykh perevodov kontsa XVIII nach. XIX v poeme Dzh. Mil'tona *'Poteriannyi Rai"* (Kazan' 1973) DZGBL

II JOURNALS (ZHURNALY), NEWSPAPERS, AND MISCELLANIES

In this section non-Russian periodicals quoted in the text are omitted: the year(s) given refer to the citations in the text, not the cumulative date of publication. Translations of Milton appearing in periodicals are entered separately in the Index under both Milton's name and that of the translator.

Aglaia (1794-5)
Atenei (1828)
Avrora (1805)
Biblioteka dlia chteniia, zhurnal slovesnosti, nauk i khudozhestv, promyshlennosti, novostei i mod (1835-7)
Blagonamerennyi, zhurnal slovesnosti i nravov (1825)
Chtenie v besede liubitelei russkogo slova (1811)
Chteniia dlia vkusa (1791)
Damskii zhurnal (1830)
Drug prosveshcheniia (1804)
Galateia zhurnal literatury, novostei i mod (1830)
Ippokrena, ili utesha liubomudriia (1800)
Korifei ili kliuch literatury (1802-7)
Literatura pribaltiki (1833)
Litsei, periodecheskoe izdanie Ivana Martynova (1806)
Minerva, zhurnal Rossiiskoi i Inostrannoi slovesnosti (1807)
Molva zhurnal mod i novostei (1833)
Moskovskie vedomosti (1838)
Moskovskii kur'er (1805)
Moskovskii telegraf (1827-31)
Moskovskii zhurnal (1791-2)
Moskvitianin (1843)
Novosti (1789-99)
Novosti russkoi literatury (1803-4)
Opyt trudov (1778)
Panteon inostrannoi slovesnosti (1798)
Panteon russkoi poezii (1814)
Permskiia gubernskie vedomosti (1881)
Raut, Istoricheskii i literaturnyi sbornik (1854)
Russkii invalid (1832)
Russkii vestnik (1858)
Sanktpeterburgskii vestnik (1780)
Sobesednik liubitelei rossiiskago slova (1783-4)
Sobranie russkikh stikhotvorenii, vziatykh iz luchshikh stikhotvorenii rossiiskikh i iz mnogikh russkikh zhurnalov (1811)
Sochineniia i perevody, k pol'ze i uveseleniiu sluzhashchiia (1761)
Sochineniia v proze i stikhakh, Trudy Obshchestva liubitelei Rossiiskoi slovesnosti pri Imperatorskom Moskovskom universitete (1828)
Sovremennik (1838)
Syn otechestva (1812-15)

Taliia ili sobranie raznykh novykh sochinenii v stikhakh i proze (1807)
Testiada ili chtenie dlia pol'zy i udovol'stviia (1807)
Utro (1782)
Vestnik evropy (1802–27)
Vestnik inostrannoi literatury ezhemesiechno-literaturno-istoricheskii zhurnal (1897)
Vsemirnaia illiustratsiia (1894)
Zhurnal priiatnogo, liubopytnogo i zabavnogo chteniia (1803)
Zhurnal razlichnykh predmetov slovesnosti izdavaemyi Liudovikom Ronka (1805)

III BOOKS AND ARTICLES

In this section only those items are entered that are cited in the text, with the exception of modern encyclopaedias (such as the Brokgauz-Efron *Russkii biograficheskii slovar'*, *Bol'shaia sovetskaia entsiklopediia*, and so on). On the other hand, some less common books of reference and bibliographic articles consulted but not quoted are included. Milton editions and translations cited are omitted here; they are cited in full in the Notes and may be located through (brief) entries in the Index.

Alekseev, M.P. 'Problemy khudozhestvennogo perevoda' *Sbornik trudov Irkutsk. Gos. un-ta* vol 18 (Irkutsk 1930)
– (ed) *Ot klassitsizma k romantizmu. Iz istorii mezhdunarodnykh sviazei russkoi literatury* (Leningrad 1970)
– (ed) *Shekspir i russkaia kul'tura* (Moscow and Leningrad: Izdatel'stvo 'Nauka' 1965) 19–22
– (chief ed) *M.Yu. Lermontov – issledovaniia i materialy* (Leningrad: 'Nauka' 1979)
Alferoff 'On Milton's *Paradise Lost*' in *Rechi i stikhi ... Blagorodnago Pansiona* (Moscow 1828) 37–43
Amis, Kingsley *Maps of Hell* (London 1961)
Amvrosii (Serebrennikov or Serebriakov, Avraam) *Kratkoe rukovodstvo k oratorii rossiiskoi, sochinennoe v Lavrskoi seminarii, v pol'zu iunoshestva, krasnorechiiu obuchaiushchagosia* (Moscow 1778)
Anikst, A. 'Dzhon Mil'ton' in Dzhon Mil'ton *Poteriannyi rai. Stikhotvoreniia. Samson-borets* (Moscow: Izdatel'stvo 'Khudozhestvennaia literatura' 1976)
Anon *Istinnyi svet poema v desiati pesniakh* (Moscow 1780)
– 'Starinnyi russkii perevod Stroganova' *Moskovskie vedomosti* 39 (14 May 1838)
Avvakum *The Life of the Archpriest Avvakum by Himself* trans V. Nabokov (New York 1960)

- *The Life Written by Himself* trans K.N. Brostrom (Ann Arbor: University of Michigan 1956)
Babkin, D.S. (ed) *Biografiia A.N. Radishcheva napisannaia ego synov'iami* (Moscow and Leningrad: Akademiia nauk 1959)
Bailey, M.L. *Milton and Jakob Boehme: A Study of German Mysticism in Seventeenth Century England* (New York: Oxford University Press 1914)
Balabanoff, Angelica *Impressions of Lenin* (Ann Arbor: University of Michigan Press 1964)
Bantysh-Kamenskii, D.N. *Slovar' dostopamiatnykh liudei russkoi zemli* Part 3 (St Petersburg 1847)
Baring, Maurice *Landmarks in Russian Literature* (London and New York: Methuen/Barnes and Noble [1910] 1960)
- *The Mainsprings of Russia* (London: Thomas Nelson and Sons 1914)
Barnett, Pamela R. *Theodore Haak* F.R.S. *1605–1690* (-'s Gravenhage 1962)
Barskov, Ia.L. *Perepiska moskovskikh masonov XVIII-ogo veka, 1780–1792 gg.* (Petrograd 1915)
Barsov, Ia.L. 'A.N. Radishchev – "Torzhok" ' in *XVIII vek. Sbornik 2* ed G.A. Gukovskii (Moscow and Leningrad 1940)
Barsov, N.P. *Ocherki russkoi istoricheskoi geografii* (Warsaw: 2nd ed 1885)
Barsukov, N.P. (ed) 'P.N. Radishchev, Aleksandr Nikolaevich Radishchev' *Russkii vestnik*, XVIII (1858)
Bazanov, V.G. *Ocherki Dekabristskoi literatury* (Moscow and Leningrad 1961)
Belinskii, V.G. *Polnoe sobranie sochinenii* 13 vols (Moscow 1953–9)
- *Sobranie sochinenii v trekh tomakh* (Moscow and Leningrad 1948)
Berkov, P.N. (ed) *Virshi. Sillabicheskaia poeziia XVII–XVIII vv.* (Leningrad 1935)
Berkov, P.N. Makogonenko, G.P., Serman, I.Z. (eds) *XVIII vek. Sbornik 8* (Leningrad 1969)
Berry, Lloyd E. 'Giles Fletcher, the Elder, and Milton's *A Brief History of Moscovia*' *Review of English Studies* NS 11(1960)
Bestuzhev-Marlinskii, A.A. *Polnoe sobranie sochinenii* (St Petersburg 1838)
- *Sochineniia v dvukh tomakh* (Moscow 1958)
Billington, James H. *The Icon and the Axe* (New York 1966)
Blagoi, D.D. *Ot Kantemira do nashikh dnei* vol 1 (Moscow 1979)
[Blagorodnyi Pansion] *Rechi i stikhi, proiznesennye v Torzhestvennom sobranii Universitetskago Blagorodnago Pansiona ...* (Moscow 1828)
Blumenthal, Friedrich *Death of Abel* (Oldenburg: G. Stelling 1891)
Boss, Valentin 'Milton in Russia' *Times Literary Supplement* 24 Sept 1984, 1037
- *Newton and Russia – The Early Influence 1698–1796* (Cambridge Mass: Harvard University Press 1972)
Bowra, C.M. *From Virgil to Milton* (London: Macmillan and Co 1945)

Broadbent, John (ed) *John Milton: Introductions* (Cambridge: Cambridge University Press 1973)

Brodskii, N.L. (ed) *Belinskii istorik i teoretik literatury sbornik statei* (Moscow and Leningrad: Akademiia nauk 1949)

Brodskii, N.L., Tolstoy, A.N. et al *Zhizn i tvorchestvo M.Yu. Lermontova sbornik pervyi-Issledovaniia i materialy* (Moscow: Gosudarstvennoë izdanie Khudozhestvennoi literatury 1941)

Brodsky, Joseph *Less Than One* (New York 1986)

Brukhanskii, A.N. 'M.N. Murav'ev i 'legkoe stikhotvorstvo' in *XVIII vek. Sbornik* 4 ed P.N. Berkov (Moscow and Leningrad 1959) 157–71

Bryant, Joseph Allan 'Milton and the Art of History: A Study of Two Influences on *A Brief History of Moscovia*' *Philological Quarterly* 29 (Jan 1950)

Bulgakov, Mikhail *Master and Margarita* (Frankfurt am Main: Posev 1869)

– *Pis'ma zhizn' opisanie v dokumentakh* (Moscow: 'Sovremennik' 1989)

Bush, Douglas *John Milton* (New York: Collier 1964)

Camé, Jean-François *Les structures fondamentales de l'univers imaginaire miltonien* (Paris: Didier 1976)

Caudwell, Christopher *Illusion and Reality* (New York: International Publishers 1963)

Cawley, R.R. *Milton and the Literature of Travel* (Princeton NJ: Princeton University Press 1951)

– *Milton's Literary Craftsmanship* (Princeton NJ: Princeton University Press 1941)

Chateaubriand, François Auguste René, vicomte de *Œuvres complètes* Nouvelle éd revue avec soin ... précédée d'une étude littéraire sur Chateaubriand par Sainte-Beuve, 12 vols (Paris ?1859–61)

Chereiskii, L.A. *Pushkin i ego okruzhenie* (Leningrad: Izdatel'stvo 'Nauka' 1975)

Coleridge, S.T. *Lectures and Notes on Shakespere and Other English Poets* (London: Bell 1904)

Cottrell, A.P. *Goethe's View of Evil* (Edinburgh: Edinburgh University Press 1982)

Cross, A.G. 'Petrov v Anglii' in *Sbornik XVIII vek*. vol 11, ed G.P. Makogonenko (Leningrad 1976)

Curran, Stuart *Le Bossu and Voltaire on the Epic* (Gainesville Fla: Scholars' Facsimiles and Reprints 1970)

Dal', V. *Tolkovyi slovar' zhivogo velikorusskogo iazyka* vol 4 (Moscow 1956)

Darbishire, Helen *The Early Lives of Milton* (London 1965)

Dashkevich, N.P. *Stat'i po novoi russkoi literature* (Prague 1914)

Demidov, N.A. *Zhurnal puteshestviia* ... (Moscow 1786)

Derzhavin, G.R. *Sochineniia Derzhavina s ob'iasnitel'nymi primechaniiami Ya. Grota* vols 1 and 5, ed Ya. Grot (St Petersburg 1864, 1869)

Dilthey, Wilhelm *Milton und Klopstock, Die Grosse Phantasiedichtung und andere*

Studien zur vergleichenden Literaturgeschichte (Göttingen: Vanderhoek und Ruprecht 1954)

D'Israeli, Isaac *Curiosities of Literature* ed Everett Bleiler (New York: Dover Publications 1964)

Dmitriev, M. *Melochi iz zapasa moei pamiati* (Moscow 1854)

Dobroliubov, N.A. *Sobranie sochinenii* (Moscow and Leningrad 1962)

Duganov, R. *Pictorial Souvenirs of Russian Writers from the 17th to the Early 20th Centuries* (Moscow: Sovetskaya Rossia Publishers 1988)

Eikhenbaum, B.M. *Lermontov – opyt istoriko-literaturnogo otsenka* (Moscow 1924)

Eisenstein, Sergei *Film Form and Film Sense* (Cleveland and New York: Meridian Books 1968)

Elagin, I.P. 'Zapiski Elagina' *Russkii arkhiv* vol 1 (1864)

Ellwood, Thomas *History of the Life of Thomas Ellwood* (London 1714)

Empson, William *Milton's God* (Cambridge: Cambridge University Press 1961, 1981)

Evgenii [Bolkhovitinov] *Slovar' Russkikh svetskikh pisatelei* (Moscow 1845)

Fenton, Elijah ' "Zhizn'' g. Mil'tona' trans A.G. Stroganov *Sanktpeterburgskii vestnik* (June 1780)

Firth, C.H. 'Milton as an Historian' *Proceedings of the British Academy* (1907–8)

Fletcher, Harris Francis 'A Note on Two Words in Milton's *History of Moscovia*' *Philological Quarterly* 20:3 (July 1941)

– *The Intellectual Development of John Milton* (Urbana: University of Illinois Press 1956)

Gennadi, G.N. *Spravochnyi slovar' o russkikh pisateliakh i uchenykh, umershikh v XVIII: XIX stoletiiakh i spisok russkikh knig s 1725 po 1825 g*. 3 vols (Berlin-[Moscow] 1876–1908)

Gerbel', N.I. *Russkie poety v biografiiakh i obraztsakh* (St Petersburg 1875)

Gershtein, E. *Sud'ba Lermontova* (Moscow 1964)

Gertzen, A.I. *Polnoe sobranie sochinenii i pisem'* vol 1 ed M.K. Lemke (Petrograd 1915)

Gessen, S., and Modzalevskii, B.L. *Razgovory Pushkina* (Moscow and Leningrad 1929)

Gillel'son, M.I.P.A. 'Stat'ia Pushkina "O Mil'tone v Shatobrianovom perevode Poteriannogo Raia" ' in *Pushkin Issledovaniia i materialy* 9 (1979)

– *Viazemskii – zhizn' i tvorchestvo* (Leningrad: Izdatel'stvo 'Nauka' 1969)

Gillet, Jean *Le Paradis perdu dans la littérature française, de Voltaire à Chateaubriand* (Paris: Klincksieck 1975)

Ginzburg, A. *O lirike* (Moscow and Leningrad 1964)

Gireev, D.A. *Poema M.Yu. Lermontova 'Demon.' Tvorcheskaia istoriia i tekstolog-*

icheskii analiz (Ordzhonikidze 1958)

Gleason, John B. 'The Nature of Milton's *Moscovia*' *Studies in Philology* 61 (July 1964) 640–9

Goethe, Johann Wolfgang *Faust Der Tragödie Zweiter Teil in Fünf Akten* (Stuttgart: Philipp Reclaus Jun 1961)

Golenishchev-Kutuzov, I.N. *Romanskie literatury – Littératures Romanes* (Moscow: Izdatel'stvo 'Nauka' 1975)

Gordon, George, Lord Byron *The Poetical Works* (London 1912)

Gordon, Ia.I. *Geine v Rossii (1830–1860e gody)* (Dushanbe: Izdatel'stvo IRFON 1973)

Gor'kii, Maksim *Sobranie trudov v 16 tomakh* vol 16 (Moscow 1979)

Gorokhova, R.M. 'Obraz Tasso v russkoi romanticheskoi literature' in M.P. Alekseev (ed) *Ot romantizma k realizmu ... iz istorii mezhdunarodnykh literatur* (Leningrad 1978) 117–88

Gronicka, André von *The Russian Image of Goethe: Goethe in Russian Literature in the Second Half of the Nineteenth Century* vol 2 (Philadelphia: University of Pennsylvania Press 1985)

Guerman, M., Gaiduk, A., Senkouskeya, N. (eds) *Mikhail Vrubel', Paintings, Graphic Works, Sculptures, Book Illustrations, Decorative Works, Theatrical Designs* (Leningrad 1985)

Gukovskii, G.A. *Istoriia russkoi literatury XVIII veka* (Moscow 1943)

– *Ocherki po istorii literatury i obshchestvennoi mysli XVIII veka* (Leningrad 1938)

– (ed) *Poety XVIII veka* (Sovetskii pisatel' np 1936)

Hakluyt, Richard *[The] Principal Navigations, Voyages, Traffiques & Discoveries of the English Nation* 12 vols (Glasgow: J. MacLehose and Sons 1903–5)

Havens, R.D. *The Influence of Milton on English Poetry* (Cambridge Mass: Harvard University Press 1922)

Helsztynski, Stanislas 'Milton in Poland' *Studies in Philology* 26 (Jan 1929)

Hill, Christopher *Antichrist in Seventeenth-Century England* (London 1971)

– *Milton and the English Revolution* (New York: Viking Press 1977)

– *A Tinker and a Poor Man: John Bunyan and His Church, 1628–1688* (New York: Alfred A. Knopf 1989)

Ianushevich, A.S. 'Obraztsy epicheskoi poezii v chtenii i osmyslenii V.A. Zhukovskogo' in F.E. Kanunova (ed) *Biblioteka V.A. Zhukovskogo v Tomske* (Tomsk: Izdatel'stvo Tomskogo Universiteta 1984) 479–81

– 'V.A. Zhukovskii chitatel' i perevodchik "Poteriannogo raia" Dzh. Mil'tona' in F.E. Kanunova (ed) *Biblioteka V.A. Zhukovskogo v Tomske* (Tomsk: Izdatel'stvo Tomskogo universiteta 1984) 481–91

Iazykov, D. 'Uchitel' Lermontova-Zinov'ev' in *Istoricheskii vestnik* 6 (1884) 605–10

Ibershoff, C.H. 'Bodmer and Milton' *Journal of English and Germanic Philology* 17 (1918) 589–601

Ioto. 'The Two Devils, or the Satan of Milton and Lucifer of Byron Compared' *Knickerbocker Magazine* or *New York Monthly Magazine* 30 (1847)

Ivanov, M.V. 'Derzhavin i Novikov' in G.P. Makogonenko (ed) *XVIII Vek. Sbornik* 11 (Leningrad 1976)

J.F. *A Brief Historical Relation of the Empire of Russia and of Its Original Growth Out of 24 Great Dukedoms into One Entire Empire since the Year 1514* (London 1654)

Kanunova, F.E. Remorova, N.B. (eds) *Biblioteka V.A. Zhukovskogo v Tomske* (Tomsk: Izdatel'stvo Tomskogo universiteta 1978)

Karamzin, N.M. *Izbrannye sochineniia* 2 vols (Moscow and Leningrad: Izdatel'stvo 'Khudozhestvennaia literatura' 1964)

– *Letters of a Russian Traveller 1789–1790* trans Florence Jones (New York 1957)
– *Polnoe sobranie stikhotvorenii* ed Yu.M. Lotman (Moscow and Leningrad 1966)

Kastor, F.S. *Milton and the Literary Satan* (Keizersgracht: Rodopi 1974)

Keil, R.D. 'Ergänzungen zu russischen Dichter-Kommentaren (Lomonosov und Karamzin)' *Zeitschrift für slavische Philologie* 30:2 (1962) 380–3

Kheraskov, M.M. *Filosoficheskie ody ili Pesni Mikhaila Kheraskova* (Moscow 1769)
– *Izbrannye proizvedeniia* introduced and annotated A.V. Zapadov (Leningrad 1961)
– *Piligrimy, ili iskateli shchastiia* (Moscow 1795)
– *Tvoreniia M. Kheraskova vnov' izpravlennyia i dopolnennyia* (Moscow 1797)
– 'Vzgliad na epicheskie poemy' in V.I. Kuleshov (ed) *Russkaia literaturnaia kritika XVIII veka* (Moscow: Izdatel'stvo 'Sovetskaia Rossiia 1978)

Khodorov, A.E. 'Zachinatel' Dekabristskogo Eposa' in D.D. Blagoi, B.B. Meilakh et al *Dekabristy i russkaia kul'tura* (Leningrad 1975) 143–68

Kiukhel'beker, V.K. *Izbrannye proizvedeniia v dvukh tomakh* (Moscow and Leningrad 1967)
– *Polnoe sobranie stikhotvorenii* (Moscow: Biblioteka Dekabristov 1908)
– *Puteshestvie, dnevnik, stat'i* (Leningrad: Izdatel'stvo 'Nauka' 1979)

Klimov, E.E. *Russkie khudozhniki sbornik statei* (New York: St Seraphim Foundation 1974)

Klimov, N.P., Glebova, T.N., Matuzova, N.M., and Repizov, B.B. (eds) *Pedagogicheskaia razrabotka po tvorchestvu Mil'tona* (Kiev 1977)

Klopstock, Georg Friedrich *Ausgewählte Werke* (München: Carl Hanser Verlag 1962)
– *Messiada* per stikhami Sergeia Pisareva (St Petersburg 1868)
– *Messiia poema* sochinennaia g. Klopshtokom. Perevod s nemetskago Alekseia Kutuzova (Moscow 1785–7)

Kniaz'kov, S.A., and Serbov, N.I. (eds) *Ocherk istorii narodnogo obrazovaniia v Rossii do epokhi reform Aleksandra II* (Moscow 1910)
Kochetkova, Natalya *Nikolay Karamzin* (Twayne Publishers 1975)
Kolakowski, Lescek 'Three Motifs in Marxism' *Kontinent 2: The Alternative Voice of Russia and Eastern Europe* (Sevenoaks and London: Coronet Books / Hodder and Stoughton 1978)
Kuleshov, V.I. (ed) *Russkaia literaturnaia kritika XVIII v.* (Moscow: Izdatel'stro Sovetskaia Rossia 1978)
Lafargue, Paul 'Le Mythe de Prométhée' *La Revue des idées* 12 (15 Dec 1904)
Lang, D.M. *The First Russian Radical: Alexander Radishchev, 1749–1802* (London: George Allen and Unwin 1959)
Lemke, Mikhail *Nikolaevskie zhandarmy i literatura 1826–1855 gg.* 2nd ed (St Petersburg 1909; The Hague 1965)
Lenin, V.I. *Polnoe sobranie sochinenii* vol 41 (Moscow: Izdanie politicheskoi literatury 1964)
Lermontov, M.Yu. *The Demon*, trans A.C. Stephen (London 1875)
– *Izbrannye proizvedeniia* vol 2 (Moscow: 'Khudozhestvennaia literatura' 1973)
– *Sobranie sochinenii v chetyrekh tomakh* (Moscow and Leningrad: Akademiia nauk 1961–2)
Letzring, Madonna 'The Influence of Camoëns in English Literature' *Revista Camoniana* 1 (1964)
Levin, Yu.D. 'Angliiskaia poeziia i literatura russkogo sentimentalizma' in M.P. Alekseev (ed) *Ot klassitsizma k romantizmu. Iz istorii mezhdunarodnykh sviazei russkoi literatury* (Leningrad 1970) 195–269
– *Ossian v russkoi literature konets XVIII-pervaia tret' XIX veka* (Leningrad: 'Nauka' 1980)
– *Russkie perevodchiki XIX veka i razvitie perevoda* (Leningrad: Izdatel'stvo 'Nauka' 1985)
Lewis, C.S. *A Preface to Paradise Lost* (Oxford: Oxford University Press 1977)
Limonov, Yu.L. *Kul'turnye sviazi Rossii s Evropeiskimi stranami v XV–XVII vv* (Leningrad: 'Nauka' 1978)
Loginovskaya, E. *Poema M.Yu. Lermontova 'Demon'* (Moscow: 'Khudozhestvennaia literatura' 1977)
Lomonosov, M.V. *Polnoe sobranie sochinenii* vol 7 *Trudy po filologii 1739–1758 gg.* (Moscow and Leningrad: Izdatel'stvo Akademii Nauk SSSR 1952)
Longinov, M. *Novikov i moskovskie martinisty* (Moscow 1867)
Lunacharskii, A.V. *Istoriia evropeiskoi literatury* (Moscow 1924)
– *Sobranie sochinenii* vol 4 (Moscow 1964)
Lunacharskii, A.V., and Mikhailova, E.N. (eds) *Literaturnaia entsiklopediia* vol 7 (Moscow 1934)

McColley, G. 'The Astronomy of *Paradise Lost*' *Studies in Philology* 34 (1937) 209–47

McConnell, Allan *A Russian Philosophe: Alexander Radishchev, 1749–1802* (The Hague: Martinus Nijhoff 1964)

Maiskii, F.F. 'Iunost' Lermontova (Novye materialy o prebyvanii Lermontova v Blagorodom pansione)' *Acta Universitatis Voronegiensis* tomus XIV, Fasciculus secundus, Contributiones ad Historiam Culturae Rossicae, Curante doc. N.P. Latyshev (Voronegis [USSR] 1947)

Maistre, Joseph de *Considerations on France* trans Richard A. Lebrun (Montreal and London: McGill-Queen's University Press 1984)

Makarov 'Mariia Vasil'evna Khrapovitskaia' *Damskii zhurnal* 29:7 (Feb 1830:yr 8) 98–9

– 'Mariia Vasil'evna Sushkova' *Damskii zhurnal* 29:10 (Mar 1830) 145–6

Makogonenko, G.P. *Nikolai Novikov i russkoe prosveshchenie-XVIII veka* (Moscow and Leningrad 1951)

Malyshev, I. *N.I. Novikov i ego sovremenniki* (Moscow 1961)

Manning, Clarence 'A Russian Translation of *Paradise Lost*' *Slavonic (and East European Review)* 13 (1934)

Manuilov, B. *Letopis' zhizni i tvorchestva M.Yu. Lermontova* (Moscow and Leningrad: 'Nauka' 1964)

Martz, Louis L. *Milton A Collection of Critical Essays* (Englewood Cliffs NJ: Prentice-Hall 1966)

Mavor, E. *The Virgin Mistress: The Life of the Duchess of Kingston* (London 1964)

Mehring, Franz *Gesammelte Schriften* 20 (Berlin 1961)

Mel'nikova, N.N. *Izdaniia napechatannye v tipografii moskovskogo universiteta XVIII veka* (Moscow 1966)

Merezhkovskii, D.S. *Polnoe sobranie sochinenii* vol 15 (St Petersburg and Moscow 1912)

Miller, O.V. *Bibliografiia literatury o M.Yu. Lermontove (1917–1977)* (Leningrad: 'Nauka' 1980)

Mirollo, J.V. *The Poet of the Marvelous, Giambattista Marino* (New York and London 1963)

Mirsky, D.S. *A History of Russian Literature from Its Beginnings to 1900* ed J. Whitfield (New York: A.A. Knopf 1926)

– *The Intelligentsia of Great Britain* trans Alec Brown (New York: Covici, Friede, Publishers 1935)

Modzalevskii, B.L. *V.G. Ruban, istoriko-literaturnyi ocherk* (St Petersburg 1897)

Mordovtsev, D. *Russkie zhenshchiny novago vremeni. Biograficheskie ocherki iz russkoi istorii. Zhenshchiny vtoroi poloviny XVIII veka* (St Petersburg 1874)

Mueller, Ursula *Die Gestalt Lucifers in der Dichtung vom Barock bis zur Romantik*

Germanische Studien, Heft 229 (Berlin 1940; Nendeln/Liechtenstein 1969)
Muggeridge, Malcolm *The Chronicles of Wasted Time* vol 1 (London 1972)
Murat, Jean *Klopstock, Les Thèmes principaux de son œuvre* (Strasbourg: Faculté de Lettres de l'université de Strasbourg 1959)
Murav'ev, M.N. *Obitatel' predmestiia i Emilievy pis'ma* (St Petersburg 1815)
– *Polnoe sobranie sochinenii ...* parts 2 and 3 (St Petersburg 1819–20)
– *Sochineniia Murav'eva* vol 2 (St Petersburg 1847)
Mutschmann, H. *Further Studies concerning the Origins of Paradise Lost* (Folcroft PA: 1977)
– 'Milton in Russland' *Estländisch-Deutscher Kalender* (Dorpat 1925) 268–75
Nadezhdin, N.I. *Literaturnaia kritika estetika* ed Yurii Mann (Moscow 1972)
Naidich, E.E. 'Posledniia redaktsiia "Demona" ' in *Russkaia Literatura* 1 (1971)
Neustroev, A.N. *V.G.R[uban]* (St Petersburg 1896)
Nicolson, M.H. *The Breaking of the Circle: Studies on the Effect of the 'New Science' upon Seventeenth-Century Poetry* rev ed (New York 1960)
– *Mountain Gloom and the Mountain Glory: The Development of the Aesthetic of the Infinite* (Ithaca NY: 1959)
Novikov, N.I. *Opyt istoricheskago slovaria o rossiiskikh pisateliakh* (St Petersburg 1772)
Oakeshott, Walter 'A Tudor Explorer and His Map of Russia' *Times Literary Supplement* 22 June 1984:703–4
Obolensky, Dmitri *The Bogomils: A Study in Balkan Neo-Manichaeism* (Cambridge 1948)
Orlov, V. *Danilo' the Violist* trans Antonina W. Bouis (New York 1987)
Orlov, V.L. *Puti i sud'by* (Moscow and Leningrad 1963)
Paramonova, T.I. 'Dzhon Mil'ton v otsenke "Novoi Kritiki" ' *Vestnik Moskovskogo universiteta* 4(1972)
Parker, William Riley *Milton A Biography* 2 vols (Oxford: Clarendon Press 1968)
Parks, George B. 'The Occasion of Milton's *Moscovia*' *Studies in Philology* 40:3 (July 1943) 399–404
Petrov, V.P. *Oda na velikolepnyi karrusel', predstavlennyi v Sanktpeterburge 1766 goda, v chetvertoe leto mirnago vladeniia ... gosudaryni Ekaterin' Vtoryia ...* (Moscow 1766)
Pokrovskii, V. (ed) *Aleksandr Petrovich Sumarokov. Ego zhizn' i sochineniia – sbornik istoriko-literaturnykh statei* (Moscow 1911; Oxford: Willem A. Meeuws 1976)
Pope, Alexander *Opyt o cheloveke* trans N.N. Popovskii (Moscow 1757)
Praz, Mario 'Milton et Poussin' in Jacques Blondel (ed) *Le Paradis perdu 1667–1967* (Paris: Minard Lettres Modernes 1967)

Priima, F.Ia. *Russkaia literatura na zapade. Stati i razyskaniia* (Leningrad 1970)
Proffer, Carl K. (ed and trans) *Alexander Pushkin with Critical Essays by Four Russian Romantic Poets* (Bloomington and London: Indiana University Press 1969)
Proffer, Ellendea *Bulgakov, Life and Times* (Ann Arbor 1984)
Pushkin, A.S. *The Bronze Horseman: Selected Poems of Alexander Pushkin* trans D.M. Thomas (London: Secker and Warburg 1982)
- *Polnoe sobranie sochinenii v desiati tomakh* 10 vols (Moscow and Leningrad: Izdatel'stvo Akademii nauk SSSR 1950–1)
- *Polnoe sobranie sochinenii* ed D.D. Blagoi, V.D. Bonch-Bruevich, S.M. Bondi, M.A. Tsiavlovskii, D.P. Yakubovich et al, vol 12 (Leningrad 1937)
Pyman, Avril *The Life of Aleksandr Blok* (Oxford: University Press 1979)
Pypin, A.N. *Dlia liubitelei knizhnoi stariny. Bibliograficheskii spisok rukopisnykh romanov, skazok, poem i pr., v osobennosti iz pervoi poloviny XVIII veka* (Moscow 1888)
- *Russkoe masonstvo XVIII i pervaia chetvert' XIX v.* ed G.N. Vernadskii (Petrograd 1916)
Radishchev, A.N. *A Journey from St. Petersburg to Moscow* trans L. Wiener; ed with introduction and notes R.P. Thaler (Cambridge Mass: 1958)
- *Polnoe sobranie sochinenii* vols 1 and 2 (Moscow and Leningrad: Izdanie Akademii nauk SSSR 1938, 1941)
Raikov, B.E. *Ocherki po istoriigeliotsentricheskogo mirovozzreniia v Rossii-iz proshlogo russkogo estestvoznaniia* 2nd ed (Moscow and Leningrad: Ak Nauk 1947)
Rajan, Balachandra *Paradise Lost and the Seventeenth-Century Reader* (London: Chatto and Windus 1947)
Rashkov, N. 'Klopshtok' *Blagonamerennyi zhurnal slovesnosti i nravov* 11 (St Petersburg 1825) 47–62
Riasanovsky, N.B. *The Image of Peter the Great in Russian History and Thought* (New York and Oxford: Oxford University Press 1965)
Riazanovskii, F.Ya. *Demonologiia v drevne-russkoi literature* (Moscow 1915; Leipzig 1964)
Rodzevich, S.I. 'K voprosu o vliianii Bairona i A. de Vin'i na Lermontova (iunosheskie stikhotvoreniia Bairona i Lermontova: *Demon* i *Eloa*)' *Filologicheskie zapiski* 1st ed (Voronezh 1915) 49–62
Rosenthal, B.G. *Nietzsche in Russia* (Princeton: Princeton University Press 1986)
Rothe, Hans *N.M. Karamzin's europäische Reise: Der Beginn des russischen Romans* Philologische Untersuchungen (Berlin and Zürich: Verlag Gehlen 1968)
Rozanov, V. '*Demon* Lermontova i ego drevnie rodichi' *Russkii vestnik* 9 (1902)

Rudwin, M. *The Devil in Legend and Literature* (Chicago 1931, 1959)
Russell, J.B. *Mephistopheles: The Devil in the Modern World* (Ithaca and London: Cornell University Press 1986)
Sakulin, P.N. *Iz istorii russkogo idealizma Kniaz' V.F. Odoevskii. Myslitel'-pisatel'* vol 1 (Moscow 1913)
Samarin, R.M. 'Tvorchestvo Dzh. Mil'tona v otsenke V.G. Belinskogo' in N.L. Brodskii (ed) *Belinskii istorik i teoretik literatury sbornik statei* (Moscow and Leningrad: Akademiia nauk 1949)
– *Tvorchestvo Dzhona Mil'tona* (Moscow 1964)
– *Zarubezhnaia literatura* (Moscow 1978)
Saurat, Denis *Milton Man and Thinker* (London 1925; 1944)
Segel, H.B. *The Literature of Eighteenth-Century Russia* (New York: E.P. Dutton 1967)
Semeka, A.V. 'Russkoe masonstvo v XVIII v.' in S.P. Mel'gunov and N.P. Sidorov (eds) *Masonstvo v ego proshlom i nastoiashchem* vol 1 (Moscow 1914)
Semennikov, V.P. *Knigoizdatel'skaia deiatel'nost' N.I. Novikova v tipograficheskoi kompanii* (Petersburg 1921)
– *Radishchev ocherki i issledovaniia* (Moscow and Petrograd 1923)
Semenov, Leonid *M.Iu. Lermontov stat'i i zametki* vol 1 (Moscow 1915)
Serman, I.Z. (ed) *Poetry XVIII veka* vol 1 (Leningrad 1972)
Shavrov, M.V. *Iov i druz'ia ego. Po povodu proizvedeniia Glinki 'Iov.' Svobodnoe podrazhanie sviashchennoi knigi Iova* (Moscow 1872)
Shawcross, John T. *Milton – The Critical Heritage* (London: Routledge and Kegan Paul 1970)
Shchapov, Ya.M. *Opisanie rukopisei sobraniia Moskovskoi dukhovnoi akademii po vremennomu katalogu* (Moscow 1966)
Shevyrev, Stepan *Istoriia poezii* (Moscow 1835)
– *Lektsii o russkoi literature chitannye v Parizhe v 1862* (St Petersburg 1884)
– *Stikhotvoreniia* intro M. Aronson (Leningrad 1939)
– 'Teoriia poezii v istoricheskom razvitii u drevnikh i novykh narodov ... (Moscow 1836)
Shuvalov, S.V. 'Vliianie na tvorchestvo Lermontova russkoi i evropeiskoi poezii' in *Venok M.Yu. Lermontovu* (Moscow and Prague 1914)
Sichkarev, Luka (trans) *Zabavnyi filosof* ... (St Petersburg 1766)
– *Zritel' mira i deianii chelovecheskikh* (St Petersburg 1784)
Skabichevskii, A.M. *Ocherki istorii russkoi tsenzury, 1700–1863 g.* (St Petersburg 1892)
Smith, Logan Pearsall *Milton and His Modern Critics* (Oxford University Press 1940)
Solov'ev, Evgenii *Mil'ton ego zhizn' i literaturnaia deiatel'nost'* (St Petersburg 1894)

Solov'ev, V.S. *Sobranie sochinenii* vol 3 (St Petersburg 1901)
Solzhenitsyn Alexander (with Mikhail Agursky et al) *From under the Rubble* (New York: Bantam Books 1976)
Sopikov, V.S. *Opyt rossiiskoi bibliografii. Redaktsiia, primechaniia, dopolneniia i ukazetel'* V.N. Rozhina parts 1–5 (St Petersburg 1904–6)
Sorokin, Yu. 'Istoricheskii zhanr v proze 30-kh gg. XIX v.' *Doklady' soobshcheniia filologichoskogo fakul'teta* 2nd ed (Moscow 1947)
Spasevich, V.D. *Baironizm u Pushkina i Lermontova* (Vilna 1911)
Speranskii, M.N. *Rukopisnye sborniki XVIII veka. Materialy dlia istorii russkoi literatury XVIII veka* (Moscow: Izdanie Akademii nauk 1963)
Staehlin, J. *Original Anecdotes of Peter the Great Collected from the Conversations of Several Persons at Petersburgh and Moscow* (London 1788)
Sukhomlinov, M.I. *Istoriia rossiiskoi akademii* vol 1, 1st ed (St Petersburg 1874)
Sumarokov, A.P. *Izbrannye proizvedeniia* (Leningrad 1957)
– *Selected Tragedies of A.P. Sumarokov* trans Richard and Raymond Fortune, intro John Fizer (Evanston: Northwestern University Press 1970)
Suzdalev, P. '*Demon* Vrubelia' in *Panorama iskusstv* 78 (Moscow 1979) 101–38
– 'O miravozrenii Vrubélia' in *Iskusstvo* 11 (Moscow 1976) 50–64
– *Vrubel'; Lermontov* (Moscow 1980)
Svendsen, Kester *Milton and Science* (Cambridge Mass: Harvard University Press 1956)
Telleen, John Martin *Milton dans la littérature française* (Geneva: Slatkine Reprints 1971)
Thiergen, P. *Studien zu M.M. Cheraskovs Versepos 'Rossijada'* (Bonn 1970)
Tiander, K. 'Dzhon Mil'ton (k 300-letiiu dnia ego rozhdeniia' '*Sovremennyi mir* 1(Jan 1909) 13–26
Tillyard, E.M.W. *The English Epic and Its Background* (London 1954)
– *Milton* (London 1930)
Timkovsky, F. 'Poteriannyi rai, poema Ioanna Mil'tona. Novyi Perevod s angliiskogo podlinnika' *Vestnik evropy* 6:21 (1810)
Tisch, J.H. 'Irregular Genius: Some Aspects of Milton and Shakespeare on the Continent at the End of the Eighteenth Century' in Miklós J. Szenci and László Ferenczi (eds) *Studies in Eighteenth-Century Literature* (Budapest: Akadémiai Kiadó 1974)
Tynianov, Ia. *Pushkin i ego sovremenniki* (Moscow: Izdatel'stvo 'Nauka' 1959)
Tukalevskii, V.N. 'N.I. Novikov i I.G. Shwarts' in S.P. Mel'gunov and N.P. Sidarov (eds) *Masonstvo v ego proshlom i nastoiashchem* vol 1 (Moscow 1914)
Udodov, B.T. *M.Yu. Lermontov Khudozhestvennaia individual'nost i tvorcheskie protsessy* (Voronezh: Izdanie Voronezhskogo universiteta 1973)
Vasilevskii, Andrei 'Stalin (li)s nami? Fol'klor o vozhde narodov' *Literaturnaia gazeta* (Moscow) 18:5292 (2 May 1990)5

Vatsuro, E.E. 'K tsenzurnoi istorii *Demona*' in M.P. Alekseev (ed) *M.Yu. Lermontov – issledovaniia i materialy* (Leningrad: 'Nauka' 1979) 410–14
Vengerov, S.A. *Istochniki slovaria russkilch pisatelei* (Petrograd 1914)
– *Kritiko-biograficheskii slovar' russkikh pisatelei* (Petrograd 1915)
– *Russkaia poeziia* (St Petersburg 1893–1901)
Vigny, Alfred de *Œuvres complètes* (Paris: Editions de Seuil 1965)
– *Œuvres complètes* vol 1 (Paris: Editions Gallimard 1950)
Viskovatov, P.A. 'Vospominaniia A.Z. Zinov'eva v pereskaze P.A. Viskovatogo' in A. Vasil'ev (ed) *M.Yu. Lermontov v vospominaniiakh sovremennikov* (Penza: Penzenskoe knizhnoe izdatel'stvo 1960)
Vostokov, A. 'Bog v nravstvennom mire' in *Tsvetnik* 6:4 (Apr 1823) 1–17
Vrubel, Mikhail *Mikhail Vrubel* ed S.G. Kaplanov (Leningrad 1975)
– *Perepiska. Vospominaniia o khudozhnike* (Leningrad and Moscow 1963)
– *Perepiska. Vospominaniia o khudozhnike* Vtoroe izdanie (Leningrad and Moscow 1976)
Vvedenskii, A.A. *Dom Stroganovykh XVI–XVII vekakh* (Moscow 1962)
Walicki, Andrzej *Rosyjska Filozofia i Myśl Społeczna od Oświecenie do Marksizmu* (Warsawa: Wiedza Powszechna 1973)
Warner, Rex *John Milton* (New York: Chanticleer Press 1950)
Whittaker, Cynthia *The Origins of Modern Russian Education: An Intellectual Biography of Count Sergei Uvarov, 1786–1855* (De Kalb: Northern Illinois University Press 1984)
Wilson, Edmund *Letters on Literature and Politics 1912–1972* (New York 1977)
Wittreich, J.A., Jr *The Romantics on Milton: Formal Essays and Critical Asides* (Cleveland and London: Press of Case Western Reserve University 1970)
Woroszylski, Wiktor *The Life of Mayakovsky* trans Boleslav Taborski (New York: Orion Press 1976)
Young, R.F. *Comenius in England* (Oxford 1932)
Zaborov, P.R. *Russkaia literatura i Vol'ter XVIII-pervaia tret' XIX veka* (Leningrad: Nauka 1978)
Zhadovskaya, Elizaveta *Dve legendy* (Moscow 1860)
– *Pervoobraz smerti i bratoubiitsa* (Moscow 1857)
– *Pesni i stikhotvoreniia* (Moscow 1857)
– (trans) *Poteriannyi rai Poema Ioanna Mil'tona ... v stikhakh* (Moscow 1859)
Zhirmunskii, V.M. *Gëte v russkoi literature* (Leningrad 1937)
Zhukovskii, V.A. *Sobranie sochinenii v chetyrekh tomakh* (Moscow and Leningrad: Gosudarstvennoe izdatel'stvo 'Khudozhestvennaia literatura' 1959)
Zinov'ev, Z.Z. 'O vospitanii' in *Moskvitianin* 10 (1843) 371–84
– 'Ot perevodchika poem Mil'tona' in Mil'ton *Poteriannyi rai* (Moscow 1861)

Index

For entries on Milton's epics, see both the names of individual characters and subentries throughout this index.

Abbadon, Abbadona (Apollyon) 215, 222; Klopstock's penitent angel and Zhukovsky 90; Zhukovsky's poem *Abbadona* 113; and Lermontov 114

Adam: temptation of, Faustian legend among Slavs xix, 18; and lovemaking xxiv; ms genealogies of 199; Barsov ms of *PL* 27–9; Masonic ms ... 'Concerning Adam's Fall' 48–9; in Durand's 'Chute de l'homme' 54; Old Believer visual representations of 19; status as hero of *PL* affirmed 14; contested 89; Amvrosii's critical allusions to 33, 37–8; and Calvin 42; and Luka Sichkarev 31; Satan's jealousy of xxiv, 18, 104; temptation and transgression of 14; Christ's intercession for 29; Chateaubriand's view of 104; and Novikov 60; compared with Kheraskov's hero 61–2; Kheraskov's interpretation of 65–6; Karamzin's Miltonic Adam 75;
Shevyrev's 'dramatic piece' on the expulsion of Adam and Eve 83; Zhadovskaya's characterization of Milton's Adam and Eve 116; early Soviet Marxist view of 141; and Kievan Miltonists 152–3

Adams, Clement 171, 233

Addison, Joseph 4, 6, 88, 96, 185, 220; and Constantin de Magny 10

Aeschylus 85, 124, 140; and Prometheus 136

Alembert, Jean d' 212

Alexander I, Emperor 6, 61, 71

Alexander II, Emperor 90

Alexander III, Emperor 136, 226

Alexis Mikhailovich, Tsar 143

Alferoff 102, 106–8, 111, 158, 220, 229; school oration on Milton 174–7

Alfieri, Vittorio 107

Algarotti, Francesco 205

Amis, Kingsley 205

Ammonite (the nation of Palestine east of the Jordan) 22

Andreev, Leonid xxv
Angels 33, 38, 65, 176, 198, 218; cherubim and seraphim 22, 81, 190, 197; archangels – Gabriel 87; Michael xix, 29, 51, 52, 169, 175, 196; Raphael 218; Uriel 25, 26
Anikst, A.A. 49, 228
Antichrist 4, 133, 184, 189
Archangel (White Sea port, a source of ms copies of the Stroganov-Milton) 40
Areopagitica 78, 134
Aretino, Pietro 85
Ariosto, Ludovico 61
Aristotelians 56
Arndt, Ernst Moritz 60; *On True Christianity* 49
Arthur, King 233
Arzamassians 82
Augustans: attitude to Milton 96
Avvakum, archpriest 22
Azazel (one of the fallen angels) 237
Azazello (an angel in Bulgakov's *Master and Margarita*) 184
Azaziel (an angel in Byron's *Heaven and Earth*) 105

Baba Iaga: in Pushkin's 'Ruslan and Liudmila' 95
Bacon, Francis 84; and Baconian science 122
Bakunin, Michael 103
Balabanova, Angelica 164, 231
Balliol College, Oxford 44
Baring, Maurice 216, 218
Batiushkov, Konstantin N. 82
Batteux, Charles 89
Beelzebub (a prince of devils, one next in power to Satan) xxiii, 15, 21, 23; likened to Oliver Cromwell 135; in PL 172; and Mayakovsky 138

Beethoven 133
Beketov, Platon 47, 201
Belial (one of the fallen angels) 19, 23
Belinsky, V.G. xvii, 102, 103, 218, 222; on PL 124, 160
Bellini, Giovanni 130
Benckendorff, Count Alexander (head of Third Section) 120
Berge, E.G. von 6, 9
Beria, Lavrentii (head of NKVD): as a character in Korkia's play 163, 231
Bestuzhev (pseud Marlinsky), A.A. 214; Romanticism and Reformation compared 87, 160
Bible 8, 10, 33, 37, 44, 58, 60, 68, 159, 161, 175, 196, 216, 223, 230, 255; and eighteenth-century Russian transcriptions 19; attitude of Russian Masons to 60; and Kheraskov 62; and Klopstock's *Messias* 114; Mayakovsky's rejection of 137, 157; and Orthodox Decembrists 159; Russian public awareness of 160; exegesis on Soviet television 163
– Old Testament: and the Bogomils 18; and the Romantics 101; and Pushkin's and Byron's use of 102; and Milton 114, 150
– New Testament 8, 10, 18, 46, 54, 60, 114, 196
Blair, Hugh 215, 220; on PL 89; and Countess Dashkova 89; cited in Lermontov's school 107
Blake, William x, xxii, xxv, 59; approval of Satan 67, 140, 149, 153; on 'farting Klopstock' 113; and Belinsky 124; *Marriage of Heaven and Hell* 153
Blok, Alexander 131, 137, 226, 237; and Lucifer 138; *Retribution* 79, 119, 132, 225

Bobrov, S.S.: and Miltonic *Creation* by Radishchev 76
Boccaccio, Giovanni 107
Bodmer, Johann Jakob 187, 206; and *PL* 9, 66–7; feud with Gottsched 9; praise of Klopstock's *Messias* 57–8, 158; and *das Wunderbare* 66, 158; parallels with Kheraskov's *Universe* 66
Boehme, Jakob 206–8; and Novikov 59; and Schwarz 60; *Path to Christ* 49
Bogomils 183, 189
Boileau, Nicolas 36, 188, 212
Boismorand, Abbé Chélon de 4, 9, 44
Boris Godunov 87
Borrow, George 230
Bosch, Hieronymus 148
Botkin, V.P. 124
Bowra, Maurice 232
Breitinger, J.J. 59, 206
Brezhnev, L.I. xi, xiv, 163; and promotion of Milton's Satan xxvi, 133, 147
Brief History of Moscovia, A 143
Brik, Lili 226
Briusov, V.Y. 237
Brockes, Hermann 187
Brodsky, Joseph 155, 229; on the ambiguity of evil xviii; evil stripped of official status xx
'Bronze Horseman, The' 99, 100
Brothers Karamuzov, The 153, 158, 237
Buchner, G.: influence of *Stoff und Kraft* 124
Bulgakov, Mikhail x, xxv, 237; *Master and Margarita* xxv, 115, 139; and *PL* 230
Bunyan, John xiii, xxiv, 3, 155; *The Pilgrim's Progress* 59

Burns, Robert x, xxii, xxv, 109
Bush, Douglas 149
Buslaev, Pyotr 186; and Milton 10, 11
Byron, George Gordon, Lord x, xix, xxii, xxv, 67, 124, 159, 219; influence of, on Russian Romanticism 83–5; and Satanism 84; and the Decembrists 85; and Kiukhel'beker 86; and Nadezhdin 83–4; and Pushkin 102–3; and Lermontov 107–10, 112; and Lady Byron 103; poetic comments on Milton 109, 110; works – *Cain* 83, 103, 105, 108; *Childe Harold's Pilgrimage* 86; *Don Juan* 83, 110, 221; *Heaven and Earth* 105; 'The Prisoner of Chillon' 91
Byronism xix, 83–4, 220
Byzantine art 126; and demonic tradition 57

Cabbala, the 97
Caesar, Julius 78
Cain 83, 105, 112, 219, 221
Calderon de la Barca, Pedro 57, 156
Caligula 32
Callot, Jacques 42
Calvin, Jean 42
Camoëns 81, 90, 167
Carlyle, Thomas 135
Catherine II, the Great xxii, xxiii, 6, 12, 33, 47, 48, 50, 60, 61, 68, 89, 187, 211, 212, 226, 236; inspires Vladykin's odes 30; and 'pocket-poet' Petrov 31; relationship with Countess Dashkova 34; encouragement of Khrapovitskaya and other female translators 35; persecution of Novikov 41; hostility towards Masonic movement 49, 59; dislike of Klopstock 57; approval of by Der-

zhavin 71; arrest of Radishchev 73, 76; and the *Philosophes* 76; and the Legislative Commission 73
Catholicism, Roman 87, 96; Edmund Wilson on Milton's use of 162
Catiline 78
Caudwell, Christopher 207
Cawley, Robert R. 168, 170–3, 232, 233
Chaadaev, Peter 105, 120
Chaldeans 82
Chancellor, Richard 125, 233
Chaos: as represented in the Barsov ms of *PL* 25; as seen by Lucretius 42; as portrayed by Kheraskov 62, 65; as described by Milton 92, 170, 176, 208; in Zhukovsky's translation of *PL* 94
Charles I, King of England: defence of, by Salmasius 70; execution of, approved by Radishchev 77; and Oliver Cromwell 134; compared to Russian despots 136; as Satan 141
Chartists 136
Chateaubriand xv, xxii, xxiv, 201, 213, 215–17, 225, 236; translation of *PL* 9; criticism of *PR* 44; and Christianity 82; contrast with Mme de Staël and Viazemsky 82; read by Zhukovsky 88; on Dante and Milton 96; on Milton's Satan's envy of Adam 104
Chaucer, Geoffrey 82
Chekhov, Anton xxv; and Vrubel 128; and Evg Soloviev 135
Chernyshevsky, N.G. 115; and *The Contemporary* 123; and Dobroliubov 123; dispute with Sluchevsky 125; *What Is to Be Done?* 124
Cherubim 190; as depicted in the Barsov ms of *PL* 22; and Pushkin's parody of Milton and Camoëns 81
Chesterton, G.K. 144
Childe Harold's Pilgrimage 86
Chiumina, Ol'ga (translator of *PL*) 226
Chizhevskii, Dmitrii 186
Christianity: popular Russian association of with *PL* and *PR* 137; and Church Fathers 114; and the Devil 97, 162; and Goethe 96; and Vrubel and Nietzsche 133; and Paul Lafargue 140; and C.S. Lewis 144; and D.S. Mirsky 144; and Pushkin's blasphemy 160
Cicero 36
Coleridge, S.T. 57, 200; 'Kubla Khan' 169
Communism 157 and *passim*
Conegliano, Cima da 130
Copernicus 56
Cosmas Indikopleustes xxi, 19, 189
Cossacks 108
Cowper, William 142
Crashaw, Richard 189
Cromwell, Oliver, Lord Protector xxiii, 173, 183, 211, 226; and Milton's Satan 69, 127, 135–6, 142; correspondence with Tsar Alexis Mikhailovich 143; Catherine the Great's attitude to 77–8; Radishchev's qualified praise of 77–8; caricatured in Victor Hugo's drama 87; mentioned in Gray's 'Elegy in a Country Churchyard' 91; Evg Soloviev's biography 135–6; as interpreted in Lunacharsky's *Literary Encyclopedia* 142

Dante Alighieri 18, 156, 160, 219; compared to Milton by

Kiukhel'beker 85; by Byron 109; by Romantic Russian critics 114; by a Legal Marxist 136; by an early Soviet critic 142; and Beatrice 109; *Inferno* 114

Darwin, Charles: *The Origin of Species* 124

Dashkova, Princess, E.R. 33, 34, 36, 215; and Hugh Blair 89

Davydova, E.V. 204; owner of Russian ms of *PL* 178

Death: in *PL* and the Barsov ms 24–6; in *True Light* 52; in Handel's *Messiah* 76; Milton's allegorical treatment of Sin and Death praised by Kiukhel'beker 85; ridiculed by Voltaire 88; reassessed in Alferoff's school oration 175; Russian gender of, as problem for translators of *PL* 125–7; and Satan 125

Decembrists: rebellion of xxiii, 121, 214; Byron's influence on 85; Bestuzhev-Marlinsky 87, 120; Glinka 85, 159; Kiukhel'beker 85; Raevsky 101; and Zhukovsky 90; and Lunacharsky and Mirsky 157

Delille, Jacques xv

Demidov, Nikita Aleksandrovich 192; on Newton and Milton 32

Demon: Pushkin's 'Demon' – as 'evil genius' 97–8; as state of mind, in Pushkin's 'Scene from Faust' 98–9; the demonic as politics in 'The Bronze Horseman' 100; Pushkin's Miltonic demon 100; Lermontov's *Demon* – novelty of 103; plot of 104, 107; later drafts of 105; influence on of *PL* 106, 110; seduction of Tamara by 108; demonic incantation 111; as fugitive lover 113; Klopstock's 'cry-baby' demon 113–17, 159; Vrubel's representations of 128–33; meaning of *daimon* and classical demonology 131; as *Übermensch* 133; and Mayakovsky 138

Derzhavin, Gavrilo Romanovich xv, xxiii, 30, 112, 118, 208, 209, 212, 235; on Satan's politics 68–70; on the tyranny of the *narod* 70; on God and monarchy 70; response to French Revolution 70–3, 156; friendship with Kheraskov and Novikov 71; works – 'Felitsa' 71; 'Ode to God' 71; 'On the Perfidy of the French Turmoil' 71

Deutsch, Babette xvii

Devil x, xv, 163, 176, 183, 184, 189, 237; in early Russian mss xx–xxi; secularization of xxii–xxiii; as embodiment of an ideological conception of evil xxiii; in Bunyan 3; Peter the Great's attitude to 4; representation in secular literature before *PL* 4; legend of Adam's pact with 18; how legend reached Slavs 18; ms of 'The handwriting our First Parent Adam gave the Devil' 19; in popular lore 26, 95, 160; as bloody trickster in *True Light* 54, 58; French Revolution transforms feudal image of 57, 72, 157; and Pugachev 74 and figs 8 and 9; in Russian folklore and in Milton's England 95; Pushkin's and Dostoevsky's devils 95; and the satyrs of Poussin and Picasso 95; as portrayed in 'The Bronze Horseman' 100; in Klopstock 114; in Mayakovsky 138–9; in William Blake 153; global pres-

ence of 155; as intellectual 156; in *Brothers Karamazov*, and Gogol and Sologub 158; Milton's conception of 158 and *passim*; folkloric devil in the twentieth century 160; Aleksei Tolstoy's drawing of 160 and fig 34; and Mikhail Gorbachev and Snow White 161
Diderot, Denis 212
Dilthey, Wilhelm 206
D'Israeli, Isaac 185
Dmitriev, Ivan Ivanovich 30, 191
Dobroliubov, N.A. 223, 224; criticism by, of Zhadovskaya-Milton 115, 118; and Chernyshevsky 123; ignorance of Milton's politics 124
Dolgorukova, E.A. 34
Don Juan 110, 221; Byron's poem as *Odyssey* of the nineteenth century 83
Doré, Gustave 129
Dostoevsky, F.M. x, xiii; reading of *PL* xxv; biblical demonic tradition kept alive by 115; and Vrubel 128; on the limits of human freedom 153; attitude to revolutionary movement 158; the Grand Inquisitor and *PR* 144; biography by Evg Soloviev 135; 'Besy,' 'Demons,' 'Devils' or *The Possessed* 95, 101, 158; *The Brothers Karamazov* 153, 158, 237
Druzhinin, A.V. 124
Dryden, John 14, 83
Durand, David 53

Earth 26, 28, 92, 113, 114, 116, 171
Eden (the first home of Adam and Eve) 14, 27, 29, 38, 72, 83, 91, 104–6, 116, 152, 175, 194, 195
Eikhenbaum, B.M. xx, 111, 157, 183, 221

Eikonoklastes 168
Einstein, Albert 155
Eisenstein, Sergei 190; and shooting script of *PL* 21
Elagin, I.P. 49, 50, 204
Eliot, Ebenezer 142
Eliot, T.S. 144, 145, 150, 162
Elisabeth Petrovna, Empress of Russia 6, 11, 34, 39
Elizabethans 3, 117, 137
Ellwood, Thomas 44, 200
Eloa 11, 112
Elton, Oliver 217
Elysium (the abode of the blessed after this life) 31
Empson, Sir William xi, 151, 153, 228, 229; on Chinese reaction to Milton's Satan 150
Enlightenment x, xi, 159, 160, 184, 236; and secular Devil xx; and the St Petersburg Academy of Sciences xxi; and Peter the Great xxi, 99, 101; and the Devil's seditious politics 4; and publication of *PR* and *PL* 41; Milton's appeal in 48; and activity of Novikov, Schwarz, and Kheraskov 50; universal gravitation and the Great Chain of Being 56; Milton's cosmology and Newton's 56; Russian reaction to 60; and attitude to Milton's Satan 68, 155; response to, of Derzhavin, Kheraskov, and Radishchev 69; and Pushkin 89, 159; and Milton 96, 152; and decline of Hell 111; and French Revolution 120; and Satan 155
Erasmus, D. 36
Erebus (Hell) 25
Ermak: as subject of Radishchev's Miltonic epic 74, 104
Ermolaev, Boris 230

Esenin, Sergei 231
Etkind, E.G. 217
Euripides 82
Eve: public fascination with xx; Devil's complicity with xxi; Satan's attraction to 14, 27, 107, 110, 161; and *Tale of the Host of Igor* 18; Old Believer portrayals of 19; as depicted in Barsov ms of PL 27–9; considered immoral in Poland 39; Masonic attitude to 48–9; expelled from Eden 62; Kheraskov's evocation of her charms 65; beauty of 104; Byron on 107; Soviet Marxist criticism of 141, 152–3
Evgenii Onegin 82, 111, 212

Fanshawe, Sir Richard 232
Faust: legend of xxii; Goethe's, as the negating spirit 87, 159; and the Romantic period 96; influence of, on Pushkin xxiv, 96, 97, 98; Pushkin's 'Scene from Faust' 98–9; and the Enlightenment 113; and Vrubel 128
Fénelon, F.: *Télémaque* 7, 212
Fenton, Elijah (early biographer of Milton) 40, 42
Fet, A.A. 125
Firdausi 215
Fletcher, Giles 232; on Muscovy 168
Fonvizin, D.I. 105
Frederick William, Prince of Prussia 50
Freemasonry x, xiii, xxii; fresh view of good and evil 48; earliest connection with Milton ms 48; first Russian lodge 49; and English Masons 49; and Rosicrucianism 49; and Voltaireanism 49–50; and Elagin 49–50; and James Keith 49; and Kheraskov 50–1; and Novikov 49–51; and Schwarz 50–1; and *True Light* 51; and Russian literary devils 48

Gagarin, Grigorii 220; prince 50
Gagarin, Yurii (Soviet cosmonaut) xv
Galileo, Galilei 26
Gama, Vasco da 167
Gardiner, S.R. (historian of Puritan Revolution) 135
Gassendi, Pierre 42
Gay, Peter 32, 48
Gehenna (the valley of Hinnom, or the valley of lamentation, from the cries of the children thrown to Moloch) 22
Gellert, Christian Fürchgott 76
Gennadi, Archbishop of Novgorod 186, 200
Georgian England 31
Gessner, Salomon 75, 221
Gibbon, Edward 214, 216
Gillel'son, M. 212
Gillet, Jean 185, 200, 236
Gireev, D.A. 221
Glebova, T.N. 148
Glinka, Fedor Nikolaevich 85, 159, 214
Gnedich, Nikolai Ivanovich 116, 223
God: Satan as adversary of xi, 116, 125, 132, 139, and *passim*; displaced by Satan in Barsov ms of PL 15; role in narrative of PL 14, 33; Barsov version and PL compared 25–7; and Creation 14, 27, 62–3, 75; and Pushkin's 'Arselickers of the Almighty' 87, 89; in Goethe's theology 96; tyranny of 99; Goethe's and Milton's conceptions compared 97, 99, 111, 159; in Zhadovskaya-Milton 117; Russian Marxist views

of 49, 59, 60, 134, 140–1, 151–3; Vrubel's attitude to 133; Mark Twain on dubious procedures of 152; Empson on Milton's dislike of 150, 153; verdict of Gerard Manley Hopkins 153; in Alferoff's oration 107, 158, 174–7; in Derzhavin 70–1; in *Demon* 104, 119; in Kheraskov's *Universe* 62, 63, 64; in Kiukhel'beker 86; in Klopstock 113; caricatured by Mayakovsky 139; and Milton's *De Doctrina Christiana* 96; burlesqued in Pushkin parody of war in Heaven 87; and Einstein 155

Godfrey of Bouillon 20

Goethe, J.W.: and Aeschylus 124; and Bulgakov xxv, 237; and Byron 124; and Dante 160; and Milton xxiv, 95–7, 124; and Pushkin xxiv, 94–9; and Radishchev 76; and Tasso 160; and Turgenev 124; and Vrubel 128; and Zhukovsky 94, 96; earliest Russian translations of xxii, 97; *Faust* xxii, xxiv, 95, 97, 108, 113, 124, 237; and the Devil 94, 96, 99; Mephistopheles x, xiv, xxii, 90, 99, 101, 111, 156, 237; compared with Milton's Satan 96 and *passim*; 'Der Geist der stets verneint' 87, 159; theology of 97

Gogol, N.V. xvii, 103; and the Devil 3, 148, 158; on the piety of Russians 160; *Dead Souls* 128; *Evenings on a Farm near Dikanka* 114–15, 148

Good Old Cause, the (the English revolutionary tradition that survived the Restoration) 69

Gorbachev, Mikhail 147, 161

Gorky, Maksim xxv, 135, 140, 227; on *PL* 139; and Marxist edition of Milton 142

Gottsched, Johann Christoph: on translating Milton 9; as foe of Bodmer 58

Gourdon of Hull 173

Gradova, B.A. xiv

Gray, Thomas: Zhukovsky's translation of 'Elegy in a Country Churchyard' 91

Greshishchev, Ivan 200, 201; and translation of *PR* 41, 43–7

Griboedov, A.S. 105

Grierson, Sir Herbert J.C. 228; on Satan's rebellion 151

Grigoriev, Apollon Aleksandrovich 124

Gronicka, André von 184, 224, 235

Grotius, Hugo: literary devil of 57; Russian neglect of 156

Gruditsyn, Savva 184

Guber, Eduard 97, 217

Guizot, François Pierre Guillaume (statesman and historian of English revolution) 134, 135

Gukovsky, G.A. 60, 192

Gulag: and Stalin 162, 164

Haak, Theodor 9

Hakluyt, Richard: *The Principal Navigations* 233

Hamlet 187

Hampden, John 91

Handel, George Frederick: Karamzin's reaction to *The Messiah* in Westminster Abbey 76

Hanford, J.H. 168

Haydn, Franz Josef 76, 211

Heaven x, xxi, xxii, 83, 87, 110, 112,

132, 133, 160, 184, 190, 193, 197, 198, 204, 213, 214, 227, 229; in Barsov's adaptation of PL 15, 18, 22, 23, 26–8; in *True Light* 52, 54, 55–7, 58; in Kheraskov's *Universe* 62–4; and Zhukovsky 88, 92; Romantic depictions of 103–5; in Lermontov 105 *et seq*; in Zhadovskaya-Milton 116; Gustave Doré's illustrations to the expulsion from Heaven 129; in Mayakovsky 138; Soviet Marxist view of 141–2; expulsion from Heaven in first illustrated Russian edition of PL fig 27

Heine, Heinrich 160, 230

Hell xx, Christ's descent into 18; Satan's escape from 24–6; Satan in 33; Milton's depiction of 38; in *True Light* 51, 52, 54; in PL 38; compared to Heaven, by Satan 58; in Kheraskov's *Universe* 65; in Lermontov's *Demon* 108, 110–13; in Zhadovskaya-Milton 116, 117; in PL and Sluchevsky's translation 125–6; in Vrubel 129, 132; in Mayakovsky 138; in *lubki* 148; traditional torments in 143 and fig 32

Helvétius, Claude Adrien 212

Herzen, Alexander 103

Hill, Christopher 184, 201, 207, 214, 218, 226; on Pushkin and Milton xxv; on Milton and Enlightenment 96

Hinnom (valley of, southwest of Jerusalem) 22

Hitler, Adolf: and Satan 146

Holy Ghost 96

Holy Mother Russia 138

Holy Synod: and Stroganov-Milton 10; and Amvrosii's translation of PL 36; and proscription of PL 39–40, 121, 122; on proscription of *Demon* 121, 199, 224

Homer: and Amvrosii 37; and Gnedich 61; and Kheraskov 207; and Mareuil 43; and Milton 43, 82, 85; and Nadezhdin 85; and Stroganov 4, 10; and Count Uvarov 122; and Vrubel's 'Homerism' 130; *Odyssey* 91; likened to Byron's *Don Juan* 83

Hopkins, Gerard Manley: explanation of the fall compared to atheist reading of PL 153

Horace 4, 11

Horsley, Sir Jerome 5

Hugo, Victor xxii, xxiii; *Cromwell* 87, 135–6

Hume, David 192

Hunter, William B. xiv

Ianushevich, A.S. 215, 216

Iazykov, D. 220

Isdebsky-Pritchard, Aline 225

Jacobinism: and Oliver Cromwell 134; and Kheraskov's Satan 69; and 'Pugachevshchina' xxiii; and Radishchev 73

Jesuit critics of Milton xxiv

Jesus Christ 175, 176, 193, 201, 226, 235; and New Testament apocrypha xix, 18; temptation of, by the Devil xx; and Milton's epics xxi; Milton's unconventional portrayal of 6; antipathy to demons in Polish ms on 'Satan's Ejection from Heaven' 18–19; intercession on Adam and Eve's behalf 29; divinity diminished in PR 43, 74; and Dos-

toevsky's Grand Inquisitor 44;
Satan's temptation of 45; roles in
True Light and PR compared 51–4;
and John the Baptist 51; and Judas
53; humanized Masonic view of 60;
as depicted in Kheraskov's *Universe* 62–4; dialogues with God
judged weakest in *PL* 107, 158;
superimposed by Vrubel on Lermontov's *Demon* 129; demonic transformation of Vrubel's *Virgin and Child* 130; and Red Guard in Blok's *The Twelve* 137; likened to Lenin,
the new Messiah 138; the triumph
of, and revolution 141; and Milton's
intent to expose God's ways to man
152; and Soviet exegesis – left in the
lurch by God 153
Jesus College, Cambridge 148
Johnson, Dr. Samuel: and Lauder's
charge of Milton's plagiarism 11;
and T.S. Eliot 144; and Nadezhdin
83; and *Life* of Milton 32, 88, 109,
213
Jonson, Ben 187
Joseph II, Emperor of Austria 50
Jovius, Paulus 168
Judas Iscariot: in *True Light* 52, 53, 58;
Milton's and Russian characterizations compared 58
Juno (wife of Jove) 161

Kabbalah. *See* Cabbala
Kant, Immanuel 207; and Kheraskov
61; and Goethe 97; Vrubel 128
Kantemir, Antiokh 5, 10, 185, 188,
195, 205, 210, 215; first published
allusions to Milton 4, 11; and
Milton's cosmology 14; as satirist
50; proscription of satires 12; and
Voltaire 88

Kantemir, Mariia Dmitrievna: first
woman in St Petersburg to read
PL 10
Kanunova, F.E. xiii
Karamzin, N.M. 135, 192, 206, 208,
211; his Gallic style 8, 82, 91; horror of English bloodshed 32; on
hearing Haydn 76; and Milton 32,
75, 76; 'To Poetry' 75–6
Keats, John 84
Keith, James: and Russian Masons 49
Kepler, Johannes 56
Keynes, John Maynard 114
Kheraskov, M.M. xv, 34, 48–51,
59–72, 156–8, 189, 207, 208, 235;
and Bible 60; and Enlightenment
60; and golden age 60; and French
Revolution 67 *et seq*; and ideological
Devil 64, 74; and Masonic
movement 50, 53, 60, 66, 72, and
passim; and Moscow University
50–1, 61; and Klopstock 66; and
Milton 60–6, 67, and *passim*; and
Novikov 50–1; and Jean-Jacques
Rousseau 60; and *True Light* 53;
Pilgrims, or the Seekers after Happiness 60–1, 65; *Rossiade* 61;
Universe 59, 61–6
Kheraskova (née Princess Drutskaia-
Sokolinskaia) 61
Kholodkovsky, N.A. 113, 222, 237
Khrapovitskaya, Mariya Vasil'evna xv,
236; her family 34; as translator
of *PL* 34–5; comparison with
Petrov's translation 193–4, 195–6,
236
Khrushchev, N.S. xxvi, 147
Kiukhel'beker, V.K. xv, 85–7; and
Decembrists 85, 159, 160; and the
Devil 87, 160; and Klopstock's 'crybaby' demon 87; and Satan's apos-

tasy 85; and Byron 85; and Milton 85–7
Klimov, Evgenii Evgenievich xv
Klimov, N.P.: and *The Art of John Milton* 147, 148
Klopstock, Friedrich Gottlieb xx, xxiv, 12, 108, 205, 206, 211, 215, 222, 223, 236; Catherine the Great's verdict on 57; William Blake's 113; Coleridge's 57; Lessing's 113; Franz Mehring's 58–9; and Derzhavin 71; and Karamzin 75; and Kheraskov 62; and Marino 56; and Milton 57–60, 75; and Pushkin 81; and Tasso 156, 158; and Zhukovsky 81, 89, 90, 113; and Satan's portrayal in *Messias* 20, 58, 83, 85; Abbadona 85; Andremelech 83
Kniazhnin, Ya.B. 20
Kochetkova, N.D. 76
Kolakowski, Leszek 184
Koran, the 137
Korkia, Viktor: verse drama on Stalin and Beria 163–4, 231, 237
Kramskoi, I.: *Christ in the Wilderness* 129
Kropotkin, Peter 77
Kutuzov, Aleksei 206; translation of Klopstock's *Messias* 57–8, 113–14

Lafargue, Paul 140, 227
Lafayette, Marquis de 212
Lafontaine, Jean de 212
Lamartine, Alphonse de 219
Landsbergis, Vytautis (son of Lithuanian President) 161
La Rochefoucauld, François, duc de 212
Lasky, Harold 144
Lauder, William 11
Lavretskii, Alexander 227; and early Soviet view of Milton 140, 142

Lawrence, D.H. 144
Leavis, F.R. 148, 162
Leibniz, Gottfried Wilhelm 59
Lemke, Mikhail 224
Lenin, V.I. 110, 136, 159, 224, 226, 227, 231; and cultural revolution 139; and Legal Marxism 135; compared with Milton 44, 110; parallels with *PR* and *The Twelve* 138; and Paul Lafargue 140; and D.S. Mirsky 143; and Angelica Balabanova 164
Lermontov, M.Yu. x, xv, xxv, 67, 90, 102–14, 118–22, 128–31, 157–9, 220, 221; education 102, 106–8, 158, 174; Russian and English tutors 105–7; preoccupation with Satanic theme 106–8; first acquaintance with *PL* 107–8; *Demon* as a challenge to Orthodoxy 111; sexual congress with Christian deities 161; Tamara's seduction 105; Imperial family's interest in *Demon* 104; and Milton's Satan 103–13; and Alfieri 107; admiration for Byron 103, 106, 108–9; and Pugachev 108; and Pushkin's demonism 95; and Shevyrev 106; and Zhukovsky 89; and Zinoviev 105–6; and Ivanenko 107, 220; *Demon* xi, xv, xx, xxiv, 87, 110, 113, 130, 220, 222; genesis of 101, 103–5, 108, 110, 112, 114, 129, 162; Belinsky's praise of 103; Boris Eikhenbaum's criticism of 111; Lunacharsky's preference for Milton's Satan 110; parallels between *Demon* and *PL* 106, 110, 112, 113; parallels with Zhadovskaya-Milton 113; and Byron's *Cain* 103, 112; *Heaven and Earth* 105; *Don Juan* 110; and

Goethe's *Faust* 108; and Kheraskov's demons 157; and Klopstock's *Messias* 108; and Moore's *Lalla Rookh* 103, 105; *Loves of the Angels* 112; and Nietzsche's *Antichrist* 133; and Radishchev's *Ermak* 104; and Stroganov-Milton 109; and Tasso's *Gerusalemme Liberata* 107; and Alfred de Vigny's *Eloa* 103, 111; other works – *A Hero of Our Time* 108, 110, 111; *Vadim* and *PL* 108–9, 112; and Vrubel 132; Vrubel's *Demon Downcast* 128, 130, and fig 18; Vrubel's *Demon in Flight* 132 and fig 24; Vrubel's *Demon Seated* 131 and fig 21; Vrubel's 'Head of the Demon' 131 and fig. 18; Vrubel's *Tamara's Dance* 130 and fig 19; Vrubel's *Tamara and the Demon* 130 and fig 20; Vrubel's tetralogy – *The Demon, Tamara, The Death of Tamara, Christ at Tamara's Grave* 129

Lessing, Gottfried Ephraim 128
Levin, Yu.D. xiii, 184, 216, 217
Lewis, C.S. 185, 208, 227, 229; on the style of *PL* 6–8; on Saurat 144; on Satan's original condition 151; and Satan's 'world of lies and propaganda' 154
Lidley (or Liddell) 76
Liutsenko, Efim (translator of *PL* and Pushkin's tutor) 46, 105, 109, 200, 201, 219
Locke, John 61, 84, 207
Loginovskaia, Elena 105, 219
Lomonosov, M.V. 7, 30, 31, 36, 107, 188, 207, 211
Lotman, Yurii 155

Louis XVI, King of France 70
Lucian, Marcus Annaeus 36
Lucretius 42
Lunacharsky, A.V. xi, xx; and Marxist view of *PL* xx, 110, 111; interpretation of *PL* after October Revolution 127; defence of Milton's Satan 135; drama *Oliver Cromwell* 136–7; attack on, by left-wing Bolsheviks 136–7; first post-revolutionary treatment of *PL* 137, 139; on Prometheus and Milton's Satan 140; on Milton's 'great revolutionary heart' 153; the Romantic and Marxist interpretations compared 157; negative assessment of *Demon* and idealization of Satan 159
Luther, Martin xix, xxi, 148

Mably, Gabriel Bonnot de 76
Macaulay, Thomas Babington 134–5
McColley, G. 205
McConnell, Allan 210
Macpherson, James 75, 219
Magny, Constantin de 6, 10
Maikov, V.I. 30
Maiskii, F.F. 219, 220
Maistre, Joseph de 122
Makogonenko, G.P. xiii, 192, 204, 205, 208
Malyshev, I. 204
Mammon (one of the fallen angels) 23
Manicheanism: in *PL* 97; in Russian culture 155, 161
Mann, Dr Yurii xiii, 213, 214
Manning, Clarence 196, 199
Manzo, Giovanni Battista, of Naples 190
Manuilov, B. 224

Mareuil, Pierre de, Abbé: criticism by, of *PL* 41–2; on Milton's materialism 42; influence on Amvrosii's translation 42; translation of *Il Penseroso* 47; Beketov's and Ribouville's translations compared 201–3; and Ivan Greshishchev 43; Mareuil's and Greshishchev's translations of *PR* compared 45–6
Marino, Giovanni Battista 18, 156, 190; Kniazhnin's translation of *La Strage degl' Innocenti* 20
Marlowe, Christopher 18, 156; Faust 117
Marmontel, Jean-François 193, 212
Marx, Karl xx; Prometheanism of xxv; and Franz Mehring 58; and Russian followers 134–6; and Paul Lafargue 140; on Christianity and monotheism 140; and Lenin 140
Matuzova, N.M.: and Kievan Miltonists 148
Maude, Aylmer 225
Mavor, E. 192
Mayakovsky, V.M. xi, xx, 226; and Christian symbols 137; biblical influence on 138; Devil 138; on *PL* and *PR* 137, 157; notion of good and evil 139; caricature of Hell 148; *Mystery Bouffe* 137–8
Mehring, Franz xx; criticism of Klopstock's Satan 58; English and German middle-class compared 58; admiration of *PL* 111
Mephistopheles xxiv, 217, 235, 237; and Enlightenment 96; in Goethe's *Faust* 87, 113, 124, 159; compared with Milton's Satan 97, 124; and Pushkin 96, 98
Meredith, George 142

Merezhkovskii, D.S. 225
Michelangelo 133; *Last Judgement* 128
Milman, Henry 84
Milton, John
– critical response to, during Enlightenment: Addison 4, 6, 10, 88, 96, and *passim*; Charles Batteux 89; Dr Johnson 11, 32, 83, 88, 144; Constantin de Magny 6, 10; Pierre de Mareuil 41–2; V.G. Ruban 8, 38, 40; Voltaire 5, 85, 88, 89, 126; Thomas Warton 32
– in Romantic era: Alferoff Appendix Two and *passim*; Belinsky 160; Byron 109–10 and *passim*; Chateaubriand 44, 96, and *passim*; Coleridge 57; Kiukhel'beker 85–7; Macaulay 134–5; Nadezhdin 83; Pushkin xxv, 96, and *passim*; Shevyrev 83, 85; Alfred de Vigny 103–4
– later criticism of: Douglas Bush 149; T.S. Eliot 144, 145, 150, 162; William Empson xi, 150, 151; H.J.C. Grierson 151; Christopher Hill xxv, 96, 184; Kievan Miltonists 148 *et seq*; and C.S. Lewis 6–8, 144, 151, 154; Lunacharsky xx, 110, 111, 127, 135, 139, 140, 153, 157, 159; D.S. Mirsky 143–6; Middleton Murry 144; Denis Saurat 139, 140, 142, 144, 149; Mark Twain 152; V. Vasiutinskii 140–2; A.J.A. Waldock 149; Rex Warner 44, 200; Werblovsky 140; Edmund Wilson 162
– response to, in art: Gustave Doré 129; Vrubel 128–33 and *passim*;
– in poetry: Buslaev 10–11; Byron

106–10 and *passim*; Derzhavin 68–71, 76–8, and *passim*; Antiokh Kantemir 4, 5, 10, 11, 14; Karamzin 32, 74–6; Kheraskov 60–6, 67, and *passim*; Kiukhel'beker 85–6 and *passim*; Klopstock 57–60; Lermontov 107–13, 161, and *passim*; Mayakovsky 137, 157; Robert Montgomery 84; Thomas Moore 83, 91, 105, 107, 109, and *passim*; Pushkin xxii, xxv, 87, 93, 96, 102, and *passim*; Radishchev 69, 73, 76, 78, and *passim*; Sumarokov 11; Trediakovsky 4, 5; *True Light* 51–9; Alfred de Vigny 103–4; Ivan Vladykin 57; Henry Kirke White 84; Zhukovsky 88–94 and *passim*;
– translators of PL into Russian: Amvrosii (Serebrennikov) 33–42, 194–200, and *passim*; the Barsov translation-adaptation 14–17, 19–29, 188–91, and *passim*; Ol'ga Chiumina 226; Kholodkovsky 113, 222, 237; Efim Liutsenko 46, 105, 109, 200, 201, 219; Khrapovitskaya 34–5, 193–4, 195–6, 236; Pavel Petrov 116; Vasilii Petrov 30–5, 38, 57, 193–4; S.N. Protas'ev 142–4, 228; Luka Sichkarèv 47; Konstantin Sluchevsky 124–7; Baron Stroganov 3–13, 17–20, 37–9, and *passim*; M.P. Vronchenko 93–4, 113, 116; Elizaveta Zhadovskaya, translation-adaptation of PL and PR 115–18, 127; Zhukovsky 88–94 and *passim*; Z.Z. Zinoviev 105–6, 134, and *passim*
– into Italian: Paolo Rolli 6, 9, 188, 215
– into French: Chateaubriand 9, 44, 82, 88, 93, 96, 104; Chélon de Boismorand 4, 9, 44; Dupré de Saint-Maur 4, 6–9, 11, 21–3, 27, 35, 39, 47, 53, 56; Louis Racine 9, 11
– into German: E.G. von Berge 6, 9; Bodmer 9; Theodor Haak 9
– into Polish: Jacek Przybylski 39
– translators of PR, into Russian: Ivan Greshishchev 41, 43–7, 200, 201;
– into French: Pierre de Mareuil 41–7
– translators of *Il Penseroso*, into Russian: Platon Beketov 47, 201, 202;
– into French: Pierre de Mareuil 47; Ribouville 47
– biographies of: by Elijah Fenton 40, 42; by Evg Soloviev 135–6
– publishers and editors of: John Baskerville 11; Novikov 41; Thomas Newton 11, 88; Simmons 21; Tonson 11
– other works: *Areopagitica* 134; *Brief History of Moscovia* 143, 168–71, 173; *De Doctrina Christiana* 96; *Eikonoklastes* 168; *History of Britain* 168; *Samson Agonistes* 141, 178, 188

Mirabeau, Comte de 78, 212
Mirollo, J.V. 190
Mirsky, D.S. (Sviatopolk-) 157, 162, 167, 168, 208, 216, 226–9, 232; as editor of Marxist PL 143–6; as editor of Milton's *Brief History of Moscovia* 143; as critic of T.S. Eliot and British 'intellidzhentsia' 144; on Lenin and *Proletcult* 139; on Kheraskov 61; on Zhukovsky 81
Modzalevskii, V.G. 199
Moloch 22, 23, 190, 193
Montgomery, Robert 84, 213
Moore, Thomas x, 91, 220; and Ler-

montov 105, 109, 112; and Lermontov's school 107; and Byron's *Life*, read by Lermontov 109; Nadezhdin on 'ideal lyre of Byron and Moore' 83; *Lalla Rookh* 103, 130; *Loves of the Angels* 112
Moslems 137
Moussorgsky 183
Mozart: *The Magic Flute* 51
Mueller, Ursula 205
Muggeridge, Malcolm 227
Murav'ev, M.N. 82
Murry, Middleton 144
Muse (Heavenly: also called Urania) 15, 27, 32, 92, 94, 120, 194, 195
Mutschmann, Heinrich 232, 233; on Milton's Russian interests 167, 169, 171

Nabokov, Vladimir 44
Nadezhdin, N.I. xiii, 85; on the break with classicism 83; assault on Satanist school 84; on *PL* as a Romantic work 83; on Francis Bacon 84; on Dryden 84; on Locke 84; on Shakespeare 84; on Voltaire and Byron as polar opposites 83; 'De Origine, Natura et Fatis Poeseos Quae Romantica Audit' 83
Napoleon Bonaparte xxiii, 223; and Zhukovsky 89; and Satan's image in Napoleonic France 163
Napoleon III: and Brezhnev 147
Naturphilosophie 99
Nero 78
New Movement (school in Milton criticism) 140, 144
Newton, Isaac: and Milton as England's greatest 'adornments' 32; Antiokh Kantemir's interest in Newtonian cosmology 4, 205; Milton's supposed anticipation of universal attraction 56; in Kheraskov's *Pilgrims ...* 62; Pope's poetization of Bolingbroke-Newton 40; and science 68
Newton, Thomas, Bishop: editor of Milton's *Works* 11, 88; and Khrapovitskaya's translation of *PL* 34
Nicholas I, Emperor: reaction to Pushkin's *Gabrieliade* 87; commissions Pushkin's history of Peter the Great 99; and Uvarov 106; and censorship of *Demon* and *PL* 101, 118; disapproves of Lermontov 120; and the ideology of autocracy 121
Nicolson, Marjorie 62, 205, 208
Nietzsche, Friedrich 132, 133
Novikov, N.I. 184, 186, 190–2, 199, 200, 204, 205, 207, 208; as publisher of Marino 20; verdict on Petrov 31; as publisher of Milton 41; on Greshishchev 43; as Mason 49–50; as publisher of *True Light* 53; arrest of 59; friendship with Derzhavin 71; 'Library of Christian Readings' 74; circle of 75
Novosil'tsevs (Russian merchants): and family copy of Stroganov-Milton ms 8, 185, 200

Obolensky, Dmitri 183, 189
Odoevskii, V.F. 207
Old Believers xv, xxi; popularity of *PL* with 19; and demonic tradition 57
Orcus (the Latin name for the god of the lower world – in *PL* an attendant upon the throne of Chaos) 25
Orlov, Aleksei G.: and brother, Grigorii Grigor'evich 30–1

Orthodoxy: and confession 157; and Decembrists 85, 159; and Romantics 160; and *Demon* 96, 104; and Klopstock's *Messias* 114; and Stroganov-Milton 120; and Nicholas I 121; and Tolstoy 133; and Zhukovsky 96; and revival under *glasnost'* 153
Ossian. *See* Macpherson, James
Ovid 37, 186

Pan (the classical two-horned, goat-footed god of shepherds) 161, 162
Pandemonium (the capital of Satan) 18, 20, 22, 52, 145
Parker, W.R. 41, 168, 200, 232, 233
Parny, Evariste 216, 217; Pushkin's fondness for 96
Pavlenkov, I.I. 135
Peter the Great 4, 5; and Antichrist 4; on Martin Luther xxi; and Shikhmatov 82; and Pushkin 99, 101; *The Blackamoor of Peter the Great* 99
Peter III, Emperor 49
Petrarch 34, 201
Petrov, Pavel: and Milton's invocation to Light 116
Petrov, Vasilii xv, 1, 8, 9, 12, 20, 41, 71; and first published Russian translation of *PL* 30–5, 38, 116; compared with other translations 38, 57, 193–4; reluctance concerning Milton's politics 40; relationship with Catherine the Great 31; and Duchess of Kingston 32
Picasso, Pablo 95, 128
Pindar 82
Pisarev, D.I. 125, 135
Pisarev, Sergei (translator of *Messias* and *PL*) 114

Plekhanov, G.V. 135
Podolinsky, A.I. 159
Pogodin, M.P. 105, 214
Polevoi, N.A. 87, 214, 222
Polezhaev, A.I. 159
Pomona (the goddess of fruit and fruit trees) 156, 171, 172
Pope, Alexander 12, 32, 205; proscription of *Essay on Man* 39–40; and Kheraskov 65; *Rape of the Lock* 65
Pordage, John 59, 206, 207
Potemkin, P.S., Prince 30, 35, 36, 40, 208
Pound, Ezra 162
Poussin, Nicolas: and *PR* 45; and Pushkin's satyrs 95
Prakhov[a], Adrian and Emil'ia 129, 130
Proffer, Ellendea and Carl 184, 216, 217, 237
Proletcult 139, 227
Prometheus x, 124, 127; and Milton's Satan 139–40, 157–8, 162; and Radishchev's 'Angel of Darkness' 73; and Byron 107; and Soviet critics 95, 140; the Promethean transformation of Satan xxv, 157
Protas'ev. S.N. (Soviet translator of *PL*) 142–4, 228
Proudhon, Pierre Joseph 128
Przybylski, Jacek (Polish translator of *PL*) 39
Pugachev, Emel'ian x, xv, and Figs 8 and 9; and English Civil War 40; and French Revolution 67 and *passim*; and Kheraskov 59; and Derzhavin 68–9, 71, 77–8; and Radishchev 77–9; and rebellion xxii, xxiii, 40, 68–9, 71, 77–8; and Satan 79, 108, 157, 208, 210, 236
Purchas, Samuel 167

Purgatory: and Russian attitudes to good and evil 155
Puritanism: in England 3; alien to Goethe's Mephistopheles 87; and revolution 97; and Satan 162
Pushkin, A.S. x–xi, xvii, xx, xxii, 113, 115, 124, 135; admiration of, for Milton and Bunyan xxii; on English literature 111; as 'a very Miltonic poet' xxv, 102; and *PL* 93, 96; tutor's translation of Milton 46; defence of 'genuine Romanticism' 82; on *narod* and *narodnost'* 82, 95; attitude to the epic 81–2; on biblical matter in *PL* 87; and Old Testament 101–2; parody of war in Heaven 87; on 'Arselickers of the Almighty' 87; on Satan 87–8, 97, and *passim*; on 'besy,' demons, devils, and satyrs 87, 95–7; criticism of Chateaubriand's translation of *PL* 93; and Decembrists 101; and democratic radicals 124; and Bestuzhev-Marlinsky 160; and Byron 102–3 and Camoëns 81; and Dostoevsky 101; and Goethe 98–9; and Karamzin 78; and Kiukhel'beker 87; and Lermontov 101–3, 108, 113, 120, 164; and Mirsky 143; and M.N. Murav'ev's 'fugitive verse' 82; and Parny 96; on Peter the Great 99, 101; and Poussin 95; and Raevsky 101; and Shevyrev 83; and Voltaire 90, 99; and Zhukovksy 81, 90–1, 93, 97; works – 'Besy' 95; *The Blackamoor of Peter the Great* 99; *Boris Godunov* 87; 'Bova' 81, 87; 'The Bronze Horseman' 99, 100; *The Captain's Daughter* 108; 'Demon' 97–8; *Evgenii Onegin* 82; *Fountain of Bakhchisarai* 82; 'Gavriliada' 87, 97; 'On Milton and Chateaubriand's Translation of *PL*' 93; 'Ruslan and Liudmila' 61, 95; 'Scene from Faust' 96, 98
Pypin, A.N. 12, 178, 183, 188, 204

Quintilian 36

Rabba (the capital of the Ammonites) 22
Rabelais 42–3
Racine, Louis 9, 11
Radishchev, Alexander: education 76–7; and Freemasonry 49, 60; and Enlightenment 73; and French Revolution 68; and English Revolution 77, 134; attitude to political reform 60; Milton's influence on 78; and *Areopagitica* 78; censorship of 121; and *PL* 69, 73, 76, 78, and *passim*; and Satan 4, 69, 73, 74; and Bobrov 76; and Catherine II 76–7; on Oliver Cromwell 77, 134; and Derzhavin 68–9, 77; on Lafayette 212; and Karamzin 76–8; and Kheraskov 68–9, 157; on Robespierre 134; and Voltaire 76; and Zhadovskaya-Milton 118, 206, 209–12; works – 'Angel of Darkness' xxii, 69, 73–4, 118, 157; *The Creation* 76; *The Journey from St. Petersburg to Moscow* 77–8; 'Liberty' 77; 'The Life of F.V. Ushakov' 77
Raevsky, Alexander 101, 218
Raich, S.E. 105
Ranke, Leopold von 135
Razumovsky, K.G. 35
Redon, Odilon 130
Reformation 87
Remizov, A.M. 115, 148
Renaissance 3

Repnin, P.I. 31
Reshetnikov, A. 195
Restoration: in England 3, 141
Riasanovsky, Nicholas 217
Richards, I.A. 144
Robespierre 77, 134
Robinson, I.N.B. xiv
Rolli, Paolo 6, 9, 188, 215
Romanticism 220, 235; Romantic Satan xxiii, 158, Satan's secularization in Romantic period 74; Romantic spirit 83; and poetry 82–3; early Russian Romanticism and Zhukovsky 89; Russian Romantics and Goethe 94; and Pushkin's generation 95, 101; Russian Romantic verse 97; Russian Romantic literature 220; and Milton 83; and the sexuality of angels 104; social alienation and the exclusion from Heaven 112; Romantic rebellion 158
Ronsard, Pierre de 81
Rostovtsev, Dmitrii 19
Rousseau, Jean-Jacques 207, 212, 219; and Russian readers xxiii, 60; and Kheraskov 60; and Milton 60; and science 60; and Lermontov's school 107
Rozanov, M.: and proposed Soviet edition of Milton 143, 144, 227
Ruban, V.G. 8, 38, 40, 199
Rubinstein, Anton 129, 131
Rushdie, Salman 161
Russell, Bertrand 144, 183, 216, 217, 229
Ryleev, K.F. 159

Saint-Martin, Louis Claude de xxii, 60, 184
Saint-Maur, Dupré de 4; Mme de 4

St Paul 33
St Vladimir 61, 82
Salmasius (Saumaise), Claude 70, 168
Samson Agonistes 141, 178, 188
Satan xiv, xv, and *passim*; early sightings in Russia xix; evolution as literary character xxi–xxii; weaker rivals to Milton's creation xxiv–xxv; Milton's hero as revolutionary 3; role in *PL* 6, 14; expulsion from Heaven 18; Russian profile in Barsov adaptation of *PL* 15, 22–9; first formal steps as Russian literary character 17–18; as Prince of Darkness 26, 155; as Prince of Light 155; as atheist 118; earlier foreign devils 20; and Petrov's translation of *PL* 33; in *True Light* 51–8; in Klopstock 58–9, 113; in Kheraskov 59, 62–7, 69; on evil and good 64; in Derzhavin 71–4; in Radishchev 73–4; change of status in Romantic era 82, 84, 87–90, 94, 150; and Pushkin 87–8; and Goethe 95; as Christian Devil 97, 162; identified with freedom 70, 101, 118; human attachment of 104; Lermontov's obsession with 105, 107, 108, 110–13; on Heaven and Hell 110, 150; as a tearful tempter in Zhadovskaya's adaptation of *PL* 115–18; and the pagan-Christian rift in Vrubel 128–33; early Marxist praise of 135–7; in Mayakovsky and Blok 137–9; Promethean transformation of 139–40; and early Soviet assessments 141–2; as Great Sultan, Stalin, or *vozhd'* 142, 145–6, 231; as anti-imperialist under Brezhnev 147–54; under *glasnost'* 163–4

Satanism xi, xix–xxiii, 183, 237; Byronism and the Satanist school 84; as a literary and ideological phenomenon 122–3; revival of 128; Milton's association with 132; confusion of Milton's with Satan's character 132; attacks on it as corrupting and antisocial 159; Satanic argument in its most secular form 153–4

Saurat, Denis 139, 140, 142, 144, 149, 227

Schiller, F. 85, 216

Schlegel, August Wilhelm 82

Schwarz, Johann Georg: and Masonic movement in Russia 50, 51, 53, 58, 60

Scott, Walter xxii, 83; 'Eve of St. John' 91

Semennikov, V.P. 77, 205, 211

Shakespeare, William 187, 192, 212, 236; read by early Russian poets 11, 32, 75, 78; as remote as Voltaire 83; rediscovered as a Romantic 83; compared to Dryden and Milton 84; placed lower than Milton by Byron 119; higher, by Kiukhel'beker 119; and Lermontov 106, 109; and Nadezhdin 83; and Tolstoy 133; and Shevyrev 83–4; and Zhukovsky 91; *Julius Caesar* 75

Sharapov, P.N. xv

Shelley, Percy Bysshe x, xix, xxii, xxv, 67, 84, 124; influenced by Milton 142; Prometheus and Milton's Satan 140

Shevyrev, S.P. 213, 214; and reassessment of Milton 83, 85; and Lermontov's tutor 105; poem on Adam and Eve 106

Shostakovich, D. 183

Sichkarev, Luka 31, 192, 204; as translator of Milton 47

Simmons, Matthew 21

Sin (the being that sprang from the head of Satan) 24, 26, 52, 85, 88, 125, 126

Slavophiles 124, 160, 214

Sluchevsky, K.K.: as translator of *PL* 124–7; poetic rendition of Satan's encounter with Sin and Death 125–7; and Dostoevsky 125; and Willoughby 125

Snow White 161

Sologub, F.K. x, 3, 115, 158

Soloviev, E.A. 226; biographies of Milton and Oliver Cromwell 135; Milton's Satan as Prometheus 136; Charles I and 'Eastern despots' 136

Soloviev, Vladimir 131, 225

Solzhenitsyn, A.I. xviii, 231; and changing face of evil 164

Sophocles 82

Southey, Robert 83, 91, 213, 214

Spasovich, V.D. 105, 219, 222

Spenser, Edmund 81, 203

Staël, Mme de 82, 223

Stalin, J.V. 231; and restrictions on writers 139; as Satan and *vozhd'* 142–6, 164; return to semi-official favour 147; and most recent demonic portrayal in *Chernyi chelovek ili ia, bedny, Soso Djugashvili* 163

Stroganov, (Baron) Aleksandr Grigor'evich xxi, 32, 35, 36, 111, 156, 183, 185, 195, 196, 204, 219, 235; genesis of his translation of *PL* 3–4; what prompted it 5–7; Church-Slavonic and the problems of literary idiom 7–9; early Russian verse influenced

by the translation 10–11; the manuscript's fate 11–13; the Barsov translation-adaptation 14–17; the manuscript tradition 17–20; Satan's prominence 21–9; Amvrosii's and Stroganov's translations compared 37–9; published edition of 1820 109; and censorship 120
Stroganov, Aleksandr Sergeevich 40, 199
Stroganova, Mariia Iakovlevna (the translator's mother) 186
Sukhomlinov, M.M. 195, 199
Sumarokov, A.P. 34, 36, 75, 186, 187, 207; early allusion to Milton 11
Sushkov, N.V. 34
Sushkova, Mariia Vasil'evna 193
Suzdalev, P. 225
Svendsen, Kester 205
Swift, Jonathan 56

The Tale of the Host of Igor xix, 18
Talmud xix
Tartakov, I. 131
Tartar (a native of territory between Muscovy, China, and India) 169, 170, 201
Tartarus (Hell) 173
Tasso, Torquato 18, 107, 156; and Milton 20, 85, 136; and stereotyped devils 85, 156; *Gerusalemme Liberata* 20, 61
Thomson, James 75, 83, 211
Tiepolo, Giambattista 130
Tillyard, E.M.W. 200, 228, 232; and Kievan Miltonists 148–9, 153
Tintoretto 130
Titov, A.A. 178, 204
Tolstoy, A.N. xv, 160, 220
Tolstoy, Leo xiii, xxv, 225; and self-awareness 59; and Vrubel 128; and the people 133; and project for a people's library 135; and devil 160; *War and Peace* 59, 90
Tonson, Jacob 11
Tourneur, Cyril 156
Trediakovsky, V.K. 4, 5, 186; and Church-Slavonic 7, 36; and Buslaev 11; and Karamzin 75; and Lomonosov 7, and Sumarokov 75; *Tilemakhida* 12
Tree of Knowledge, the 19, 27
Trinity, the 36, 139
Trubetskoi, N.I. 61
Trubetskoi, P.N. 40, 199
True Light: and PL and PR 51–7, 58–9
Turgenev, I.S.: and Mephistopheles 124; *Fathers and Sons* 124; and Sluchevsky 124; and Evg Soloviev 135; and Vrubel 128
Twain, Mark 152
Tynianov, Yu.N. 85, 212, 214

Udodov, B.T. 105, 218–22
Uriel (the archangel) 25, 26
Ushakov, F.V. *See* Radishchev
Uvarov, Count S.S. 106, 121, 122, 224, 230

Vasiutinskii, V. 227; and early Soviet interpretations of Milton 140–2
Vatsuro, V.E. 120, 224
Vaugelas, Claude Favre, Seigneur de 36
Viazemsky, P.A. 82, 178, 212
Vigny, Alfred de xxii, xxiii, 218, 222; and Lermontov 103; and Milton 104; *Eloa* 103, 104
Virgil 186, 192, 232; and Stroganov 4, 10; and V. Petrov 30; *Aeneid* 30
Virgin Mary xxiv; and Satan 87; as portrayed by Vrubel 130

Vladykin, Ivan 30, 57, 236
Voltaire 198, 212, 215, 216; and French translations of *PL* 5; criticism of Sin and Death 85, 126; of Satan 88, 89; and Voltaireanism 48, 50; Russian reputation in Pushkin's time 83; and Byron 84; and Nadezhdin 84; and Peter the Great 99; and Radishchev 76, 78; *Micromégas* xxiii, 56
Vondel, Joost van den 18, 156, 219
Vronchenko, M.P. 216, 222; and Milton 93, 113, 116; translation of *PL* compared with Zhukovsky's 93–4; and Goethe's *Faust* 97; and Lermontov 113
Vrubel, Mikhail: and demonic tradition xv, xvii, xx, xxii, 95, 114; demonic obsession 128–33; androgynous sexuality of his demons xxiv; mental breakdown 116; and father 130; and Lermontov 95, 98, 114, 128, 130, 131; and Milton 128–33 and *passim*; and Pushkin's 'Demon' 98; and Antichrist 133; and Kramskoi's *Christ in the Wilderness* 129; and decadence 130; and problem of evil 161; and symbolism 130; and Goethe 128, 133, and *passim*; and Gogol 128; and Michelangelo 128; and Picasso 128; and Odilon Redon 130; and Mayakovsky 138; and Nietzsche 132–3; works – *The Demon, Tamara, Tamara's Death, Christ at Tamara's Grave* 129; *Demon Downcast* 128, 132, and fig 23; *Head of Demon* 131 and fig 22; *Demon Seated* 131 and fig 21; *Demon in Flight* 132 and fig 24; *Tamara and the Demon* 130 and fig 20; *Tamara's Dance* 130 and fig 19; *Virgin and Child* 130 and fig 17

Waldock, A.J.A. 149, 228
Walicki, Andrzej 200
War and Peace 59
Warner, Rex 44, 200
Warton, Thomas 32
Werblovsky, R.J. Zwi 140
White, Henry Kirke 88, 214
Wieland, Christoph Martin 61
Wilhelm II, Kaiser: compared with Satan 161 and fig 33
Willoughby, Sir Hugh (navigator and explorer) 125; and Milton's Satan 171–3
Wilson, Edmund 162, 230
Wittreich, Joseph Anthony, Jr 200, 221
Wolff, Christian 59
Women 207, 208; as translators in Catherinian era 33–4
Wordsworth 91

Young, Edward: and Mariia Khrapovitskaya 34; and Kheraskov 61; and Karamzin's Christian faith 75; Milton's influence on 142

Zachariä, Friedrich Wilhelm 187
Zeus 140
Zhadovskaya, Elizaveta xi, xv; translation-adaptation of *PL* and *PR* 115–18; compared with Sluchevsky's translation 127, 222–3; her Satan's atheism 133; Satan as tempter 116–18, 132, 159; Satan as freethinker 121–3; on Milton 115; and censorship 121–3

Zhadovskaya, Iuliia 115
Zhirmunsky, V.M. 184, 217, 235
Zhukovsky, V.A. x, xiii, xxii, xxiv, 216, 222, 236; affection for *PL* 88–91; translation of 91–4; compared with Vronchenko's 94; and demonic theme xxiv, 159; faith in epic 82, 89; and Pushkin 81; and Romanticism 82; and Klopstock's *Messias* 89–90, 113–14; translations – 'Abbadona' 89–90, 113; Gray's 'Elegy in a Country Churchyard' 91; Byron's 'The Prisoner of Chillon' 91; Scott's 'Eve of St. John' 91; Tom Moore's 'Death of the Peri' 91
Zinoviev, Zinovii Zinovievich xvii, 219, 220, 224, 226; interest in Milton 105–6; as Lermontov's tutor 106–7; translation of *PL* 134